EU Digital Markets Law

European Monographs Series Set

VOLUME 120

Editor

Prof. Andrea Biondi is Professor of European Law and Director of the Centre of European Law at King's College London

Introduction & Contents/Subjects

As the process of European integration assumes an increasingly complex character, the EU legal system continues to undergo sweeping changes. The European Monographs series offers a voice to thoughtful, knowledgeable, cutting edge legal commentary on the now unlimited field of European law. Its emphasis on focal and topical issues makes the series an invaluable tool for scholars, practitioners, and policymakers specializing or simply interested in EU law.

Objective

The aim is to publish innovative work appealing to academics and practitioners alike. The result is an original and ongoing library of detailed analyses, theories, commentaries, practical guides, and proposals, each of which furthers the cause of meaningful European integration. Cumulatively, the series may be regarded as a 'work in progress' engaged in building a sharply defined representation of law in Europe.

Readership

Academics and practitioners dealing with EU law.

The titles published in this series are listed at the end of this volume.

EU Digital Markets Law

Federico Ferretti
Allegra Canepa
Francesca Mattassoglio

Co-funded by
the European Union

Wolters Kluwer

Published by:
Kluwer Law International B.V.
PO Box 316
2400 AH Alphen aan den Rijn
The Netherlands
E-mail: lrs-sales@wolterskluwer.com
Website: www.wolterskluwer.com/en/solutions/kluwerlawinternational

Sold and distributed by:
Wolters Kluwer Legal & Regulatory U.S.
920 Links Avenue
Landisville, PA 17538
United States of America
E-mail: customer.service@wolterskluwer.com

ISBN 978-94-035-0888-7

e-Book: ISBN 978-94-035-0898-6
web-PDF: ISBN 978-94-035-0908-2

About the Authors

Prof. Ferretti Federico is Jean Monnet Chair of Digital Market Law (2022-2025), co-funded by the European Union (EU). Associate Professor in Economic and Financial Markets Law with habilitation as Full Professor, Department of Sociology and Economic Law, University of Bologna (Italy). Director of the Jean Monnet Centre of Excellence "Consumers and SMEs in the Digital Single Market" ('Digi-ConSME'), co-funded by the EU (2019-2023). Qualified Lawyer of the High Courts of Italy. Formerly, Senior Lecturer in Law at Brunel University London (UK). Member of the Consumer Advisory Group (CPAG) of the European Commission. Member of the Financial Services User Group (FSUG) of the European Commission (2010-2020). He advises in the preparation of legislation or policy initiatives which affect consumers and the users of financial services, providing insight, opinion and advice concerning the practical implementation of consumer policies. As a practitioner, he served as a lawyer for multinational companies internationally. He also advised national and European consumer interest groups. He held various visiting positions in several countries. From the academic year 2023, he is a visiting professor at the Royal University of Law and Economics (Phnom Penh, Cambodia), teaching the module 'Data Protection Law'.

Full list of publications available at: https://www.unibo.it/sitoweb/f.ferretti/publications.

Prof. Allegra Canepa is an Associate Professor of Economic Law with habilitation as Full Professor at the University of Milan since 2016 at the Department of International, Legal, Historical and Political Studies. She is the scientific unit coordinator (University of Milan) of a national research project (PRIN) funded by the Italian Ministry of Education and University, and she participated in other national research projects, such as PRIN and PNRR, and European Projects, such as J. Monnet and Erasmus 4EU+.

She is also the coordinator of two advanced courses: NFT and Crypto Art and Digital Finance and Crypto Football. Allegra has published over ninety papers and essays in national and international journals and Books. She is the author of two books on European Networks (2010) and Digital Platforms (2020) and editor of seven books. Her main research interests are currently related to the Platform Economy and EU Digital Markets, Artificial Intelligence, and the Digitalisation of Financial Markets.

Full list of publications available at https://www.unimi.it/en/ugov/person/allegra-canepa.

Prof. Francesca Mattassoglio is Associate Professor in Economic Law at the University of Milan-Bicocca. In 2023, she obtained the habilitation as Full Professor. She holds a PhD in Constitutional Law (University of Milan) and has received various merit-based scholarships. She participated in several nationally and internationally relevant research projects and intensively published and presented at banking and financial regulation conferences. Her research interest is now focused on Fintech, with particular attention to the regulation of DLT and artificial intelligence (AI) phenomenon. She is a member: of the Doctorate Committee in Business for Society, University of Milan-Bicocca; CryptoAssetLab (University of Milan-Bicocca and Digital Gold Institute); Association of Professors in Economic Law (ADDE).

Full list of publications available at https://en.unimib.it/francesca-mattassoglio.

Attributions

The authors certify the following attributions:

Federico Ferretti is the holder of the Jean Monnet Chair in Digital Market Law (E-DSM) E-DSM – 101047038 – GAP-101047038 co-funded by the EU of which this book is an integral part.
Federico Ferretti is the author of the Introduction, Chapter 1, Chapter 2, Chapter 3, Chapter 5, and Chapter 8. Allegra Canepa is the author of Chapter 4 and Chapter 7 (par. 7.6; 7.7 e 7.8). Francesca Mattassoglio is the author of Chapter 6 and Chapter 7 (par. 7.1; 7.2; 7.3; 7.4 e 7.5).

Table of Contents

About the Authors v

Attributions vii

List of Abbreviations xv

Acknowledgements xvii

Introduction 1

PART I
EU Data Law 11

CHAPTER 1
The Regulation of Personal Data 13
1.1 Data Protection: Concept, Origins and Evolution 13
1.2 The CoE's Activity in Data Protection and Its Continuing Relevance 18
1.2.1 Structure and Content of Convention 108 19
1.2.2 The Continuing Relevance of the CoE, Convention 108+ and Its Relationship with the GDPR 20
1.3 The Development of Data Protection Law in the EU: From the Data Protection Directive to the GDPR 23
1.4 Key Provisions of the GDPR 27
1.4.1 Key Definitions 27
1.4.2 Structure, Content, and Exclusions/Derogations of the GDPR 28
1.4.3 Principles and General Rules on Lawfulness 30
1.4.4 Rights of Data Subjects 36
1.4.4.1 Transparency 36
1.4.4.2 Information Notices 37

1.4.4.3 Right of Access 38
1.4.4.4 Rectification and Erasure 38
1.4.4.5 Right to Data Portability and Right to Object 40
1.4.4.6 Automated Decision-Making and Profiling 40
1.4.5 Data Governance Obligations 41
1.4.5.1 Data Protection by Design and by Default 41
1.4.5.2 Data Protection Impact Assessments 42
1.4.5.3 Data Protection Officer 42
1.4.6 Personal Data Breaches and Notification 43
1.4.7 Codes of Conduct and Certification 44
1.4.8 Transfer of Personal Data to Third Countries 46
1.4.8.1 Transfers Subject to Adequacy of the Third County 46
1.4.8.2 Transfers Subject to Appropriate Safeguards 46
1.4.8.3 Binding Corporate Rules 47
1.4.9 Supervisory Authorities and the European Data Protection Board 49
1.4.10 Remedies and Liabilities 50

CHAPTER 2
Data Markets and Data-Related Rights 53
2.1 The Emergence of Data Markets 53
2.2 The Nature and Value Chain of Data 56
2.3 Data-Related Rights 59
2.3.1 Personal Data Protection 60
2.3.2 Non-personal Data 61
2.3.3 Intellectual Property Laws 63
2.4 De Facto Control 67
2.5 The Limits of Competition Law Enforcement 69
2.5.1 EU Competition Law 69
2.5.2 Article 101 TFEU 71
2.5.3 Article 102 TFEU 72
2.5.4 The Unsuitability of the Essential Facility Doctrine under Article 102 TFEU 73
2.5.5 Data Portability under Article 20 GDPR 76
2.5.6 The Intersection Between Competition Law and Data Protection 78
2.5.7 The New EU Approach: *Ex ante* Regulation 81

CHAPTER 3
The Data Act 85
3.1 Regulating the Policy Objectives of the European Data Strategy 85
3.1.1 The Data Governance Act 86
3.1.2 The Data Act 87

3.2 Key Provisions of the Data Act 89
3.2.1 General Provisions 89
3.2.2 Rules on Data Sharing 91
3.2.3 Further Obligations of Data Holders 93
3.2.4 B2G Data Sharing 96
3.2.5 Switching Between Data Processing Services 97
3.2.6 Interoperability 98
3.3 The Relationship Between the Data Act and the GDPR 99
3.3.1 Legal Basis for Data Processing 100
3.3.2 Information Provision 101
3.3.3 The Distinction Between Personal and Non-personal Data 101
3.3.4 Data Portability 102
3.4 The Relationship Between the Data Act and Consumer Law 103
3.5 Risks of Legal Fragmentation 104

PART II
Regulating the EU Digital Strategy 107

CHAPTER 4
The Digital Markets Act 109
4.1 The Design of Ecosystems 109
4.2 Relationship Between Treaty Rules and the DMA 111
4.3 The DMA and the Recognition of the Gatekeeper 113
4.4 Self-Preferencing and Interoperability 115
4.5 Killer Acquisitions and Merger Control: An Open Problem? 118
4.6 The Link Between Competition and Consumer Choice 121
4.7 Compliance and Effectiveness of DMA 123

CHAPTER 5
The Digital Services Act 125
5.1 Regulating the Policy Objectives of the DSA 125
5.2 Background: Outline of the E-Commerce Directive 126
5.3 Key Provisions of the DSA 130
5.3.1 General Provisions 130
5.3.2 Liability of Providers of Intermediary Services 131
5.3.3 Due Diligence Obligations 133
5.4 The DSA, Regulatory Patchwork, and Consumer Protection 140

CHAPTER 6
The Artificial Intelligence Act 145
6.1 Introduction to AI 145
6.1.1 Benefits of AI 146
6.1.2 Risks of AI 147
6.2 The Artificial Intelligence Act 149

6.2.1 The History of the AI Act 149
6.2.2 The AI Act Structure 151
6.2.3 The Notion of AI Adopted by the AI Act 152
6.2.4 Objectives and Scope of the AI Act 153
6.2.5 Area of Application 154
6.3 Risk-Based Classification of AI Systems 155
6.3.1 Unacceptable AI Risk Systems: Banning Harmful Applications 156
6.3.2 Rationale Behind the Ban 157
6.3.3 Enforcement of the Ban 158
6.4 The High-Risk AI System 158
6.5 Transparency Requirements for Certain Kinds of AI Models 161
6.6 General-Purpose and Generative AI Models 162
6.7 Regulatory Sandboxes 163
6.8 The European Council for AI, the Forum, the Independent Scientific Panel, and AI Database 163
6.9 Post-Market Monitoring, Information Sharing, and Sanctions 165
6.10 Challenges and Criticisms 165

PART III
Digital Identities and Consumer Protection 167

CHAPTER 7
The European Digital Identity 169
7.1 From Personal to Digital (or Numerical) Identity 169
7.2 The Notion of the Digital Identity 170
7.3 From Digital Identification to Digital Wallet 172
7.4 The Main Benefits of the EDIWs 173
7.5 The eIDAS 2 Regulation 174
7.6 Virtual Words, Metaverse, and the Issue of Identity 176
7.7 Avatar, Digital Identity, Data Protection and Privacy 179
7.8 Deepfake and the Metaverse 182

CHAPTER 8
The Protection of Digital Consumers 185
8.1 Consumers in Digital Markets 185
8.2 The 'Average Consumer' 188
8.3 The 'Vulnerable Consumer' 192
8.4 New Markets, Old Law 194
8.5 The Latent, Dispositional, Systemic Vulnerability of Digital Consumers 197
8.6 Prospects for Consumer Protection in Digital Markets 199
8.6.1 A Paradigm Shift in Regulation? 199
8.6.2 The Re-evaluation of the Notion of 'Consumer' under EU Law 201
8.7 Adapting the Legal Benchmarks of an 'Average Consumer' 205

Bibliography 209

Table of Cases 227

Table of Legislation 231

Index 237

List of Abbreviations

3D	Three Dimensions
ACR	Automatic Content Recognition
AI	Artificial Intelligence
AI Act	Artificial Intelligence Act
AI HLEG	High-Level Expert Group on AI
B2B	Business-to-Business
B2C	Business-to-Consumers
B2G	Business-to-Government
CEN	European Committee for Standardisation
CENELEC	European Committee for Electrotechnical Standardisation
CJEU	Court of Justice of the EU
CoE	Council of Europe
CPS(s)	Core Platform Service(s)
CRD	Consumer Rights Directive
DGA	Data Governance Act
DMA	Digital Markets Act
DPIA	Data Protection Impact Assessments
DPO	Data Protection Officer
DSA	Digital Services Act
EAIB	European Artificial Intelligence Board
EC	European Community/ies
ECHR	The European Convention for the Protection of Human Rights and Fundamental Freedoms
ECN	European Competition Network
EDIW	European Digital Identity Wallet
EDPB	European Data Protection Board

EEA	European Economic Area
EEC	European Economic Community
eIDAS	Electronic Identification, Authentication and Trust Services
ENISA	European Union Agency for Cybersecurity
ETSI	European Telecommunications Standards Institute
EU	European Union
EUDI	European Digital Identity
FCO	Federal Cartel Office
FIDA	Financial Data Access
GAN	Generative Adversarial Networks
GDPR	General Data Protection Regulation
IoT	Internet of Things
IT	Information Technology
ITRE	Parliament's Committee on Industry, Research and Energy
LIBE	Parliament's Committee on Civil Liberties, Justice and Home Affairs Committee
Member State	Member State of the European Union
MLM	Machine Learning Models
OECD	Organisation for Economic Co-operation and Development
PSD2	Payment Services Directive 2
SGEI	Services of General Economic Interest
SMEs	Small and Medium Enterprises
TEC	Treaty Establishing the European Community
TEU	Treaty on European Union
TFEU	Treaty on the Functioning of the European Union
UCPD	Unfair Commercial Practices Directive
UCTD	Unfair Contract Terms Directive
UDHR	Universal Declaration of Human Rights
USA	United States of America
VLOPs	Very Large Online Platforms
VLOSEs	Very Large Search Engines
VR	Virtual Reality
Web 4.0	Fourth Generation of the World Wide Web
XR	Extended Reality

Acknowledgements

This research has been carried out within the Jean Monnet Chair in Digital Market Law (E-DSM) E-DSM - 101047038 - GAP-101047038 co-funded by the European Union. The European Union's support for the research does not constitute an endorsement of the contents, which reflect the views only of the author, and the Commission cannot be held responsible for any use which may be made of the information contained therein.

Jean Monnet Chair of Digital Market Law (E-DSM)

Co-funded by
the European Union

Introduction

The policy and legal themes posed by digitalisation are multiple. This book looks at the main regulatory initiatives taken by the European Union (EU) legislature on digital markets, with a particular eye on those which affect individual users, prominently consumers.

The digital revolution and technologies are transforming the economy and social relations across the world, posing unprecedented policy and regulatory challenges and undermining existing legal frameworks and principles.

New actors have emerged. The so-called platforms are companies that act as both traders and intermediaries. As intermediaries, they bring together distinct groups of market players: users who are attracted to the services offered and traders and advertisers who are interested in the channelling of the users. Traditional commercials are being replaced by online services designed to capture every nuance of people's reactions in order to use them and then sell that data to others. Emblematic is the figure of the broker who retrieves information online, aggregates, interprets and analyses it and then sells it on the market.

The COVID-19 pandemic has shown the importance of digital products and services. It has also given way to the acceleration of the digital economic model. Digital technologies have become essential for working, learning, entertaining, socialising, shopping and accessing all sorts of services. Simultaneously, the sudden outburst of the pandemic has exposed the vulnerabilities of the digital space, including its dependencies on large global technological providers (the so-called Big-Techs), notably companies from outside the EU. If it is true that the digital domain has changed the lives of people and - of more focus here - markets, it is also true that these large platforms have changed and shaped the digital sphere, turning into powerful gatekeepers that exercise a decisive influence over markets and societies.

Digitalisation presents opportunities and risks for the European economy and markets. At the same time, digital technologies and models place public policy and law-making at a crossroad.

Every economic actor is involved in this process, but consumers and Small and Medium Enterprises (SMEs) are particularly affected. Fundamental rights and other economic rights are involved. Examples are data protection, consumer protection, ownership and property, contracts and competition, and so on.

Within the process of digitalisation, the EU Digital Single Market attempts to remove regulatory barriers and move from national markets to a single EU market. Innovation and the Digital Single Market have become pivotal not only to the process of European integration but also for the global economic challenge and competitiveness vis-à-vis extra-EU countries, such as the United States, China and India, to name the ones at the vanguard of technological innovations.

The Digital Single Market has become the strategic goal of the EU to ensure access to and full participation in online activities for individuals and businesses under conditions of fair competition, consumer and data protection, and the removal of all market barriers. According to the European Commission, it "could contribute €415 billion to the European economy, boosting jobs, growth, competition, investment and innovation. It can expand markets, offering better and more cost-effective services, transform public services and create new jobs. It can create opportunities for new start-ups and allow companies to grow and innovate in a market of over 500 million people."[1]

Along these lines, the achievement of an EU Digital Single Market is a policy high on the agenda of the European Commission, especially under the Recovery Plan and the rebuilding of Europe for future generations. Regulation plays a pivotal role in the shaping of an EU Single Market fit for a sustainable digital economy, ensuring an optimal economic and social balance. Also, in principle, a properly regulated market may offer an unprecedented opportunity for a competitive model in the world economy.[2]

However, legitimate concerns may be cast against regulatory intervention, especially if pervasive and substantial. Arguments for caution may be of various natures but usually focus on regulation that may stifle innovation, that may be counterproductive in fast-changing environments, and that comes with costs, especially for emerging markets.

Notwithstanding the foregoing debate – though important – and accepting the reality of the current regulatory activities, the digital revolution undermines existing legal frameworks and principles. How it is decided what the rules are is one of the most important challenges facing policymakers today.

New technologies present new challenges, opportunities and risks for the markets and their actors. Disruptive technologies call for action, review and reflection – particularly from the point of view of the existing regulations. Innovation and

1. European Commission, 'A Europe Fit for the Digital Age', available from https://ec.europa.eu/commission/priorities/digital-single-market_en; European Parliament, 'Digital Transformation. Briefing EU Policies: Delivering for Citizens', available at https://www.europarl.europa.eu/RegData/etudes/BRIE/2019/633171/EPRS_BRI(2019)633171_EN.pdf.
2. European Commission, 'Recovery Plan for Europe', available at https://commission.europa.eu/strategy-and-policy/recovery-plan-europe_en. *See also* all the policy documents there enclosed; *see also* Consolidated text: Regulation (EU) 2021/241 of the European Parliament and of the Council of 12 February 2021 establishing the Recovery and Resilience Facility, OJ L 057, 18.2.2021, p. 17.

protection from risks (economic, social and individual) demand an appropriate balance.

In recent times, a number of new EU Directives, Regulations, legislative proposals or policy strategies have attempted to deal with some of the new challenges presented in the digital age. Yet, it remains to be seen to what extent EU law deals with the issues of new and emerging technologies adequately.

A rich body of law has been lately passed by the EU legislature, and other regulatory acts are currently being developed in response to the digital age.

Even before the COVID-19 pandemic, EU law affecting the digital and technological sphere was becoming an important area of EU law, with a growing number of Directives and Regulations. Examples are the General Data Protection Regulation (GDPR),[3] the Law Enforcement Directive,[4] the Open Data Directive,[5] the Regulation on the free flow of non-personal data,[6] and sectoral legislation such as the Payment Services Directive 2 (PSD2),[7] – just to name a few. Likewise, early decisions of the Court of Justice of the EU (CJEU) started to come through.[8]

These days, an important number of legislative acts have been enacted. The newly passed legislations within a short period of time of the Digital Markets Act (DMA),[9]

3. Regulation (EU) 2016/679 of the European Parliament and of the Council of 27 April 2016 on the protection of natural persons with regard to the processing of personal data and on the free movement of such data, and repealing Directive 95/46/EC, OJ L 119, 4.5.2016, p. 1-88.
4. Directive (EU) 2016/680 of the European Parliament and of the Council of 27 April 2016 on the protection of natural persons with regard to the processing of personal data by competent authorities for the purposes of the prevention, investigation, detection or prosecution of criminal offences or the execution of criminal penalties, and on the free movement of such data, and repealing Council Framework Decision 2008/977/JHA, OJ L 119, 4.5.2016, p. 89-131. The Law Enforcement Directive is EU legislation, parallel to the GDPR, which deals with the processing of personal data by data controllers precisely for law enforcement purposes, an area which falls outside of the scope of the GDPR.
5. Directive (EU) 2019/1024 of the European Parliament and of the Council of 20 June 2019 on open data and the re-use of public sector information (recast), OJ L 172, 26.6.2019, p. 56-83. The Open Data Directive and the re-use of public sector information provides common rules for a European market for government-held data.
6. Regulation (EU) 2018/1807 of the European Parliament and of the Council of 14 November 2018 on a framework for the free flow of non-personal data in the European Union, OJ L 303, 28.11.2018, p. 59-68. The Regulation on a framework for the free flow of non-personal data in the EU aims at removing obstacles to the free movement of non-personal data between different EU countries and IT systems in Europe.
7. Directive (EU) 2015/2366 of the European Parliament and of the Council of 25 November 2015 on payment services in the internal market, amending Directives 2002/65/EC, 2009/110/EC and 2013/36/EU and Regulation (EU) No. 1093/2010, and repealing Directive 2007/64/EC, OJ L 337, 23.12.2015, p. 35-127. The PSD2 supports innovation and competition in retail payments and enhances the security of payment transactions and the protection of consumer data.
8. E.g., *see* Case C-434/15, *Asociación Profesional Elite Taxi v. Uber Systems Spain*, ECLI:EU:C:2017:981; Case C-390/18, *Airbnb Irland UC*, ECLI:EU:C:2019:1112; Case C-311/18, *Data Protection Commissioner v. Facebook Ireland Limited and Maximillian Schrems*, EU:C:2020:559.
9. Regulation (EU) 2022/1925 of the European Parliament and of the Council of 14 September 2022 on contestable and fair markets in the digital sector and amending Directives (EU) 2019/1937 and (EU) 2020/1828 (Digital Markets Act), OJ L 265, 12.10.2022, p. 1-66; *see infra* in this Introduction and Chapter 4 of this book.

the Digital Services Act (DSA),[10] the Data Governance Act (DGA),[11] and the Artificial Intelligence Act (AI Act),[12] alongside the prospective creation of a European Data Space[13] through the Data Act,[14] the Cybersecurity Act,[15] and the European Digital Identity (EUDI) Regulation,[16] all introduce deep changes for the regulation of the digital environment.

Other regulatory instruments are in the legislative pipeline or under discussion. For example, the proposed e-Privacy Regulation,[17] the proposed Cyber Resilience

10. Regulation (EU) 2022/2065 of the European Parliament and of the Council of 19 October 2022 on a Single Market for Digital Services and amending Directive 2000/31/EC (Digital Services Act), OJ L 277, 27.10.2022, p. 1-102; *see infra* in this Introduction and Chapter 5 of this book.
11. Regulation (EU) 2022/868 of the European Parliament and of the Council of 30 May 2022 on European data governance and amending Regulation (EU) 2018/1724 (Data Governance Act), OJ L 152, 3.6.2022, p. 1-44; the Data Governance Act encourages safe, transparent, and cross-sector data sharing, with a particular focus on public-sector data and data altruism (i.e., voluntary sharing of data for the public good). While the DGA is not aimed specifically at educational institutions, it offers opportunities for the sector to benefit from enhanced data sharing, particularly through the reuse of public data and the implementation of data altruism initiatives.
12. Regulation (EU) 2024/1689 of the European Parliament and of the Council of 13 June 2024 laying down harmonised rules on artificial intelligence and amending Regulations (EC) No. 300/2008, (EU) No. 167/2013, (EU) No. 168/2013, (EU) 2018/858, (EU) 2018/1139 and (EU) 2019/2144 and Directives 2014/90/EU, (EU) 2016/797 and (EU) 2020/1828 (Artificial Intelligence Act), OJ L, 2024/1689, 12.7.2024; *see infra* in this Introduction and Chapter 6 of this book.
13. Communication from the Commission to the European Parliament, the Council, the European Economic and Social Committee and the Committee of the Regions, 'Towards a Common European Data Space', COM/2018/232 final; Commission Staff Working Document, Guidance on sharing private sector data in the European data economy Accompanying the document Communication from the Commission to the European Parliament, the Council, the European economic and social Committee and the Committee of the Regions "Towards a Common European Data Space," SWD(2018) 125 final; a data space brings together relevant data infrastructures and governance frameworks in order to facilitate data pooling and sharing within the EU.
14. Regulation (EU) 2023/2854 of the European Parliament and of the Council of 13 December 2023 on harmonised rules on fair access to and use of data and amending Regulation (EU) 2017/2394 and Directive (EU) 2020/1828 (Data Act), OJ L, 2023/2854, 22.12.2023; *see infra* in this Introduction and Chapter 3 of this book.
15. Regulation (EU) 2019/881 of the European Parliament and of the Council of 17 April 2019 on ENISA (the European Union Agency for Cybersecurity) and on information and communications technology cybersecurity certification and repealing Regulation (EU) No. 526/2013 (Cybersecurity Act), OJ L 151, 7.6.2019, p. 15-69; The Cybersecurity Act aims to strengthen cybersecurity across the EU and is focused on the creation of a robust cybersecurity framework supported by the ENISA. In the educational sector, the Act brings about changes by raising awareness of cybersecurity and promoting cyber literacy in educational institutions.
16. Regulation (EU) 2024/1183 of the European Parliament and of the Council of 11 April 2024 amending Regulation (EU) No. 910/2014 as regards establishing the European Digital Identity Framework, OJ L, 2024/1183, 30.4.2024.
17. Proposal for a Regulation of the European Parliament and of the Council concerning the respect for private life and the protection of personal data in electronic communications and repealing Directive 2002/58/EC (Regulation on Privacy and Electronic Communications), COM/2017/010 final; once passed, the e-Privacy Regulation is a legal instrument for privacy in the digital age, and more specifically, the confidentiality of communications and the rules regarding tracking and monitoring. While GDPR only applies to the processing of personal data, e-Privacy regulates electronic communication even if it concerns non-personal data.

Act,[18] the European Health Data Space,[19] and the EU Smart Cities Marketplace[20] are seen as essential to pursue digital policies that empower people and businesses to seize a human-centred, sustainable and more prosperous digital future for Europeans.[21]

Despite the copious regulatory efforts, the definition of the legal environment seems far from being over. The European Consumer Summits of the last few years on the next steps in the implementation of the EU New Consumer Agenda[22] – the policy document that presents a vision for EU consumer policy – continued to focus on the challenges for consumer protection posed by the green and digital transitions and the online enforcement of consumer rights.[23] The EU now has just announced a forthcoming Digital Fairness Act as a legislative follow-up.[24]

Even assuming a leading role as a tech regulatory superpower, the EU remains at a crossroad in its digital transformation, with geopolitical tensions and growing

18. Proposal for a Regulation of the European Parliament and of the Council on horizontal cybersecurity requirements for products with digital elements and amending Regulation (EU) 2019/1020, COM/2022/454 final; once passed, the Cyber Resilience Act aims to establish a robust cybersecurity framework aimed at enhancing the security of all products with digital elements, including products with AI components, within the EU, targeting particularly the IoT. The Act aims to ensure that manufacturers maintain cybersecurity through the lifecycle of products, and provide appropriate information to consumers.
19. European Commission, 'European Health Data Space', available at https://ec.europa.eu/health/ehealth/dataspace_en; Proposal for a Regulation of the European Parliament and of the Council on the European Health Data Space, COM/2022/197 final; once in place, the European Health Data Space is a health specific ecosystem comprised of rules, common standards and practices, infrastructures and a governance framework that aims at empowering individuals through increased digital access to and control of their electronic personal health data, fostering a single market for electronic health record systems, and providing a trustworthy and efficient set-up for the use of health data for research, innovation, policy-making and regulatory activities.
20. European Commission, Smart Cities, available at https://commission.europa.eu/eu-regional-and-urban-development/topics/cities-and-urban-development/city-initiatives/smart-cities_en; once in place, the EU Smart Cities Marketplace aims to engage through digitalisation urban living spaces of all sizes to deliver more sustainable urban environments and offers all the information needed to explore solutions, shape sustainable urban projects, and successfully close a deal for financing them.
21. Communication from the Commission to the European Parliament, the Council, the European Economic and Social Committee and the Committee of the Regions, '2030 Digital Compass: The European Way for the Digital Decade', COM(2021) 118 final.
22. Communication from the Commission to the European Parliament and the Council, 'New Consumer Agenda. Strengthening Consumer Resilience for Sustainable Recovery', COM/2020/696 final.
23. European Consumer Summit 2022 held on 10 February 2022 under the French Presidency in cooperation with the European Commission, available at https://european-consumer-summit-2022.b2match.io/; European Consumer Summit 2023 held on 28 March 2023 under the Swedish Presidency in cooperation with the European Commission, available at https://european-consumer-summit-2023.eu/home; European Consumer Summit 2024 held on 18 April 2024 under the Belgian Presidency in cooperation with the European Commission, available at https://consumer-summit-2024.b2match.io/.
24. Ursula Von der Leyen, *'Mission Letter' to Commissioner-Designate for Democracy, Justice, Rule of Law* (Brussels, 17 September 2024), available at https://commission.europa.eu/document/download/907fd6b6-0474-47d7-99da-47007ca30d02_en?filename=Mission%20letter%20-%20McGRATH.pdf; Commission Staff Working Document Fitness Check on EU consumer law on digital fairness, SWD(2024) 230 final. The Digital Fairness Act will have the aim to tackle unethical techniques and commercial practices related to dark patterns, marketing by social media influencers, the addictive design of digital products and online profiling especially when consumer vulnerabilities are exploited for commercial purposes.

dependence on foreign Big Tech giants highlighting the need for greater technological sovereignty. Surely, the EU will have to develop its own robust digital industry. Yet, first and foremost it has to make sure that the passed legislation will be followed by the digital gatekeepers and enforced by the competent EU authorities. Supervision and enforcement are ongoing struggles key for EU citizens, consumers, EU businesses, and genuine digital markets.

Conversely, from a different angle, it could be argued that more than extra legislative rules and better enforcement, the EU needs to look for other ways to reduce its dependence on large extra-EU platforms to provide it with essential digital infrastructures. The role of regulatory superpower that the EU is taking could precisely serve the purpose of rebalancing such a dependency through regulation and favour the development of a digital industry that the EU currently does not have, especially by limiting the Big-Techs and favouring SMEs, which are the bulk of the EU's economy and its infant digital industry.

From the perspective of the users of digital products and services, especially individuals, the digital economy is transforming, or even disrupting, traditional economic and social relationships and habits, as well as the ensuing traditional legal principles, concepts, and framework enshrined in established EU Law. The interaction between these instances challenges European integration at many levels, where information technology (IT), big data and artificial intelligence (AI) have disruptive or transformative effects on many aspects of the economic and social life of consumers, consumer rights, and fundamental rights of the person. Legal principles and protections are constantly tested. For example, new technologies, platforms, and business models already challenge the GDPR or established consumer protection legislation.

This begs for a redefinition of rights, wrongs or the suitability of existing juridical principles and frameworks. It is therefore necessary to question the profound significance of the new intense regulatory season and the impact it will have on the rights and freedoms of individuals.

Similarly, digital networked technologies open up new possibilities to access services and markets, which can only be achieved if the system of rights adapts to the technological change. Likewise, new business models brought by digitalisation, the shared economy, and the dominance of monopolistic technological giants and platforms challenge SMEs. Issues of competition outside and inside the platforms, creativity, innovation and proprietary rights depart from traditional schemes and test the economic life of SMEs or dictate changes.

As already mentioned, it remains undeniable that the bulk of present and future regulatory acts start building a comprehensive EU legislative framework, placing the EU at the forefront of the regulation of the digital sphere with the ambition to become a world leader vis-à-vis other jurisdictions.[25] At the same time, this regulatory hyperactivity poses questions of over-regulation, simplicity versus complexity, coexistence and coordination of overlapping rules, and coherence of the resulting legal framework.

25. *See also* Bart van der Sloot, *Editorial*, 3 European Data Protection Law Review, 351-357 (2021) https://doi.org/10.21552/edpl/2021/3/3.

Non-trivial questions of perimeter delimitation and non-conflicting interpretation already arise not only between the enacted regulations but also between these and the ones in the pipeline. For example, the necessary reference is to the regulation of personal data protection granted by the GDPR. If it is true that in most of the new acts, the legislator has been careful in maintaining intact and without prejudice to the rights and obligations relating to the processing of personal data under the GDPR, they actually provide much broader rules that apply to all data. Only at the time of their factual implementation, the GDPR will undergo a tangible stress test.

Legal overlaps and fragmentation, alongside problems of coordination, become particularly pressing in the occurrence of technological convergence, which blurs sectorally regulated boundaries. Likewise, the speed of technological developments and innovation may often outstrip regulation. As common sense suggests, the race between technologies and regulation is one that the legislator can never win.

These problems can make it difficult to determine the applicable law, and they may lead to inconsistencies or gaps. Ultimately, they may cause legal uncertainty – arguably the worst enemy of markets. Equally, compliance with multiple or diverging rules may be too burdensome for traders and expose users to poor protection.[26]

In a market that is mainly supply-driven and governed by the supply-side, there may be conduct of business risks. Aggressive business models may expand via digital development. Innovation and competition are welcome, but digital technologies are complex, and business models take new unconventional forms where data feed new scenarios and create new markets. This can result in an environment favourable for targeted individual marketing, exploitation of consumers' behavioural biases, mis-selling of products and services, economic and social sorting or discrimination. Freeriding wallows in legal uncertainty and may flourish.

The timely understanding by the legislator of the different technologies and business models is crucial to recognise how the market develops and the weaknesses or loopholes of the current legal framework. Most of the new digital laws have just entered into force and others still have to come. Their capability to regulate digital markets effectively and efficiently and become game changers has yet to be proven. This is especially the case afore the pervasiveness of online transactions and in consideration of the unprecedented pace of the technological developments that still lie ahead. Arguably, the EU needs rationalisation and simplification, bearing clearly in mind at all times which legal assets actually need protection. For example, jurists could start questioning whether the choice of not enacting and rationalising a single organic and all-encompassing 'corpus juris digitalis' (a body of digital law) was the most coherent and efficient one, instead of a plethora of complex overlapping diverse acts.

To examine the challenges of the regulation of EU digital markets, this book is organised in three parts.

26. Cristina Poncibò, *AI Platforms: Safeguarding Consumer Rights in the EU*, in *The Cambridge Handbook of AI and Consumer Law: Comparative Perspectives*, 236-251 (Larry Di Matteo, Cristina Poncibò and Geraint Howells eds, Cambridge University Press 2024).

Part I is dedicated to data law. Data have been branded as the "new oil,"[27] as they fuel all the data-driven technologies that not only are powering digital markets but are also considered the key drivers of innovation and economic growth. In the last few years, the EU has witnessed the evolution of data law from the need to protect personal data to regulate access to both personal and non-personal data – the whole through control over data, data sharing, and data analytics. Hence, it can be maintained that this area of law has been transformed from 'Data Protection Law' to 'Data Law' to express an evolutionary view of a significant regulatory expansion in the scope of data and data governance. It also shows how regulation has responded to the digital challenges and its reach to new activities, risks and actors.

Chapter 1 deals with the GDPR, the piece of legislation that sets the milestone and initial step in the journey of data governance. Its objective is to achieve consistent and effective legal implementation and application of the fundamental right to protection of personal data in all areas of the EU's activities, alongside the facilitation of free movement of such data while continuing to guarantee a high level of protection of individuals. In essence, it establishes rules on the mechanisms for processing data and their free movement in the EU, empowering individuals to control them and reflecting a rights-based approach to data governance.

Chapter 2 disentangles key legal aspects of datafication in their policy context that impact the envisaged European digital markets and the creation of a single European Data Space, conceived as a "genuine single market for data (...) where personal as well as non-personal data (...) are secure and businesses also have easy access to an almost infinite amount of high-quality data."[28] These aspects not only include data protection law but also issues over the economic value of data, the distinction between personal and non-personal data, proprietary data rights, and competition law. The digital expansion has placed data at the centre of major economic and social transformations. After all, to the extent that data are the lifeblood of innovation, they have become an essential resource for creating innovative products and services in the Single Market.

Chapter 3 explores the Data Act. To make the EU a leader in the data-driven economy and achieve a properly functioning European data space that could enable a fair distribution of the value of data, it aims to establish clear and fair rules for accessing and using data within the European data economy. It is a horizontal measure that introduces changes to how data is accessed, shared, and managed across various sectors, as well as obligations to improve data portability and protect intellectual property and outlines (emergency or crisis) conditions under which public sector bodies may access private sector data. Its primary objectives are to promote fair use of data, prevent imbalances in the market, and foster innovation. The Data Act also emphasises the importance of data literacy.

Part II of the book analyses the key mayor pieces of legislation of the EU's digital strategy and the resulting shaping of the EU's legal framework. These are, namely, the

27. Terminology introduced by the title of a speech delivered by British mathematician Clive Humby at the 2006 Association of National Advertisers conference.
28. European Commission, 'A European Strategy for Data' (Communication) COM(2020) 66 final.

DMA, the DSA, and the AI Act. Whilst at the macro-level and in the long term, the aim of DMA, DSA, and AI Act is to restore democratic control of societies vis-à-vis dominant large digital platforms, their immediate effects are the protection of companies - especially the European ones - against anti-competitive practices, the protection of consumers against unsafe products or services and illegal content, and the promotion of human-centred technologies.

Chapter 4 covers the Digital Markets (DMA) Act. It is a regulation which applies to very large tech companies (Big-Techs) - or 'gatekeepers' - that provide services to both businesses and end users in the EU. To date, seven of these have been identified by the European Commission: *Alphabet, Amazon, Apple, Booking, ByteDance, Meta,* and *Microsoft*. In essence, the DMA aims to ensure fair competition and foster transparency and innovation within the digital economy by regulating the gatekeepers with respect to their impacts in the EU. The DMA also emphasises data portability and interoperability from a pro-competition perspective.

Chapter 5 presents the provisions of the DSA. Its main aim is to improve the safety and accountability of digital services across the EU, whether these are EU-based or not, with a specific focus on content moderation and transparency. It applies to a broad range of online intermediaries, including internet access providers, cloud hosting services, social networks, online marketplaces, and app stores. It also imposes specific rules on very large online platforms (VLOPs) and very large online search engines (very large, meaning platforms having more than 45 million active users).

Chapter 6 examines the AI Act. It addresses potential risks to citizens' health, safety, and fundamental rights. Based on a general risk-based approach, the AI Act pays particular attention to AI systems that are classified as high-risk, i.e., those which can negatively affect safety or fundamental human rights. The AI Act distinguishes between a provider (an entity that develops an AI system and makes it available) and a deployer (any user of an AI system except for personal and non-professional activities) and defines requirements and obligations for each category.

Finally, Part III takes the angle of the users of digital services, especially individuals. At first, it considers the issue of digital identities and their protection. Next, it moves to the protection of individuals acting as consumers in the new environment of digital markets.

Chapter 7 studies the newly passed EUDI Regulation. It addresses the shortcomings of the preceding regulation on electronic identification and trust services for electronic transactions in the internal market (Electronic Identification, Authentication and Trust Services (eIDAS) Regulation)[29] by improving the effectiveness of the framework for digital identity and extending its benefits to the private sector. With EUDI, Member States have to offer citizens and businesses the so-called digital wallets, which are applications on an electronic device that can link their national digital identities with proof of other personal attributes like driving licences, diplomas, and bank accounts. The aim is to provide Europeans with full control over their data while

29. Regulation (EU) No. 910/2014 of the European Parliament and of the Council of 23 July 2014 on electronic identification and trust services for electronic transactions in the internal market and repealing Directive 1999/93/EC, OJ L 257, 28.8.2014, p. 73-114.

accessing digital services, allowing portability and eliminating unnecessary data sharing among providers. Service providers legally obliged to identify their customers unequivocally become obliged to accept digital wallets for authentication purposes.

Chapter 8 focuses on the protection of digital consumers. The EU has in place an existing consumer law acquis that needs adaptation and application in the new digital markets. The Chapters before presented the introduction of new and specific provisions for digital platforms, services, data governance, and AI. All these initiatives outlined from different angles the need to strengthen consumer protection in digital markets. At the same time, the new regulations are embedded in EU consumer law, which builds on various consumer law directives mostly enacted at the time of 'analogical' or 'offline' markets. Such EU directives are mainly the Unfair Contract Terms Directive (UCTD),[30] the Unfair Commercial Practices Directive (UCPD),[31] and the Consumer Rights Directive (CRD)[32] (all three directives modernised and amended by the Omnibus Directive).[33] These rules provide a broader framework that applies to all consumer dealings, including transactions in digital markets. The new Acts overlap with existing law. However, the coordination of laws and the application of the traditional EU consumer law acquis to emerging digital markets and new technologies require amendments, integration, reinterpretation, or adaptation. The Chapter puts forward its preferred view for a rethinking of the consumer protection regime to reconcile the needs of new markets and the protection of its consumer users. Accordingly, the existing consumer law acquis should be maintained by reinterpreting the fundamental notion of who is the 'consumer' addressed by the law.

30. Council Directive 93/13/EEC of 5 April 1993 on unfair terms in consumer contracts, OJ L 95, 21.4.1993, p. 29-34.
31. Directive 2005/29/EC of the European Parliament and of the Council of 11 May 2005 concerning unfair business-to-consumer commercial practices in the internal market and amending Council Directive 84/450/EEC, Directives 97/7/EC, 98/27/EC and 2002/65/EC of the European Parliament and of the Council and Regulation (EC) No. 2006/2004 of the European Parliament and of the Council ('Unfair Commercial Practices Directive'), OJ L 149, 11.6.2005, p. 22-39.
32. Directive 2011/83/EU of the European Parliament and of the Council of 25 October 2011 on consumer rights, amending Council Directive 93/13/EEC and Directive 1999/44/EC of the European Parliament and of the Council and repealing Council Directive 85/577/EEC and Directive 97/7/EC of the European Parliament and of the Council, OJ L 304, 22.11.2011, p. 64-88.
33. Directive (EU) 2019/2161 of the European Parliament and of the Council of 27 November 2019 amending Council Directive 93/13/EEC and Directives 98/6/EC, 2005/29/EC and 2011/83/EU of the European Parliament and of the Council as regards the better enforcement and modernisation of Union consumer protection rules, OJ L 328, 18.12.2019, p. 7-28.

PART I EU Data Law

Chapter 1
The Regulation of Personal Data

1.1 DATA PROTECTION: CONCEPT, ORIGINS AND EVOLUTION

Data protection is a complex and multifaceted concept both from a social and a legal point of view. Traditionally, it has been identified with the protection of personal privacy within the context of processing operations involving personal data. However, at least under EU law, the two are distinct, though complementary, fundamental legal rights. They derive their normative force from values that, although at times coincidental and interacting in a variety of ways, may be conceptualised independently.

Even though the recognition of the idea of privacy is deeply rooted in history,[1] as a concept it has been seen as always in transition.[2] It was first developed as an independent legal value when Brandeis and Warren identified it as a tort action, defining it as "the right to be left alone."[3] Since then, it has been largely accepted that in its most general form, privacy protection is a legal way of drawing a line at how far society or other individual subjects may intrude into a person's own affairs. It entails that persons should be able to conduct their personal legitimate affairs relatively free

1. There is recognition of privacy in the Qur'an [an-Noor 24:27-28 (Yusufali); al-Hujraat 49:11-12 (Yusufali)] and in the sayings of Mohammed [Volume 1, Book 10, Number 509 (Sahih Bukhari); Book 020, Number 4727 (Sahih Muslim); Book 31, Number 4003 (Sunan Abu Dawud)]. The Bible has numerous references to privacy: *see* Richard Hixson, *Privacy in a Public Society: Human Rights in Conflict* (Oxford University Press 1987); Barrington Moore, *Privacy: Studies in Social and Cultural History* (Routledge 1984). Jewish law has long recognised the concept of being free from being watched: *see* Jeffrey Rosen, *The Unwanted Gaze: The Destruction of Privacy in America* (Random House 2000). There were also protections in classical Greece and ancient China: *see* Robert Ellis Smith, *Ben Franklin's Web Site: Privacy and Curiosity from Plymouth Rock to the Internet* (Sheridan Books 2000).
2. Rosemary Jay and Angus Hamilton, *Data Protection: Law and Practice* (Thomson Sweet & Maxwell, 2003); Duncan MacDonald, *Myths in the Privacy Debate*, in *The Future of Financial Privacy*, 54-75 (CEI Staff ed., Competitive Enterprise Institute 2000).
3. Samuel Warren and Louis Brandeis, *The Right to Privacy*, 4 Harvard Law Review, 193-220 (1890) https://doi.org/10.2307/1321160.

from unwanted intrusions. As such, privacy is an expression of human dignity, development of human personality, and individual freedom.[4]

However, modern ideas of privacy have been first tested and then shaped by innovation and the fast development of information technologies and electronic data usage in the last few decades. Today the world cannot be imagined without information technologies. Yet, with the developments and opportunities they bring, the need emerged for new standards that allowed individuals to exercise control over their personal information while permitting innovation and a certain flow of information necessary to support international trade, business, enhanced security, and so on. In practice, there is an unprecedented scale of personal data stored on the internet and used for commercial purposes. Information processing and technologies have a clear

4. *See, e.g.*, Edward Bloustein, *Privacy as an Aspect of Human Dignity: An Answer to Dean Prosser*, 39 New York University Law Review, 962-1007 (1964) https://doi.org/10.1017/cbo9780511625138.007; Stig Stromholm, *Right of Privacy and Rights of the Personality* (Norstedt 1967); *Privacy* (Roland Pennock and John Chapman eds, NOMOS XIII 1971); *The Right of Privacy* (Ellen Frankel Paul, Fred Miller and Jeffrey Paul eds,Cambridge University Press 2000); James Rachels, *Why Privacy Is Important*, 4 Philosophy and Public Affairs, 323-333 (1975) https://doi.org/10.4324/9781315246024-2. Other narrower views of privacy *see* it as self-determination, intimacy, or a meaningful aspect of interpersonal relationships, personal expression, and choice. *See, e.g.*, William Parent, *Privacy, Morality and the Law*, 12 Philosophy and Public Affairs, 269-288 (1983); Robert Gerstein, *Intimacy and Privacy*, 89 Ethics, 76-81 (1978) https://doi.org/10.1086/292105; Alan Westin, *Privacy and Freedom* (Atheneum 1967); Julie Inness, *Privacy, Intimacy, and Isolation* (Oxford University Press 1992); Charles Fried, *An Anatomy of Values: Problems of Personal and Social Choice* (Harvard University Press 1970); Ruth Gavison, *Privacy and the Limits of the Law*, 89 Yale Law Journal, 421-471 (1980) https://doi.org/10.2307/795891; Adam Moore, *Intangible Property: Privacy, Power, and Information Control*, 35 American Philosophical Quarterly, 365-378 (1998) https://doi.org/10.1515/9780295803661-011; *Philosophical Dimensions of Privacy: An Anthology* (Ferdinand Schoeman ed., Cambridge University Press, 1984); Judith DeCew, *In Pursuit of Privacy: Law, Ethics, and the Rise of Technology* (Cornell University Press 1997). Such an individualistic approach to privacy has been criticised by scholarship arguing that greater recognition should be given to the broader social importance of privacy: other than a common value in which individuals enjoy some degree of it, privacy is seen as a public and collective value vis-à-vis technological developments and market forces, requiring minimal levels of privacy for all. Priscilla Regan, *Legislating Privacy: Technology, Social Values, and Public Policy* (University of North Carolina Press 1995). There exist also a number of works critical of privacy. The so-called "reductionist approach," for example, takes the view that the right to privacy is derivative, meaning that it can be explained in the context of other rights without meriting any separate attention. As such, it can be protected through other rights without any explicit protection on its own. Any privacy violation is better understood as the violation of other more basic rights: ultimately, the right to privacy is merely a cluster of rights, where these rights always overlap property rights or rights over the person such as bodily security. Judith Thomson, *The Right to Privacy*, 4 Philosophy and Public Affairs, 295-314 (1975) https://doi.org/10.1017/cbo9780511625138.012. For another strong criticism of privacy *see also* Robert Bork, *The Tempting of America: The Political Seduction of the Law* (Simon & Schuster 1990). These "reductionist approaches" have been criticised by a number of commentators: *see* Thomas Scanlon, *Thomson on Privacy*, 4 Philosophy and Public Affairs, 323-333 (1975); Jeffery Johnson, *Constitutional Privacy*, 13 Law and Philosophy, 161-193 (1994) https://doi.org/10.1007/bf01001201. Another well-known contribution to the "reductionist approach" is that of Richard Posner who made an economic, cost-benefit analysis of privacy. He argued that the types of interests protected under privacy are not distinctive. Most of all, the central proposition is that privacy protection is economically inefficient. Protection of individual privacy is difficult to defend because it does not maximise wealth. With this line of argument, Posner defends organisational or corporate privacy as more valuable than personal privacy, the reason being that the former is likely to improve economic efficiency. Richard Posner, *The Economics of Justice* (Harvard University Press 1981).

potential to influence people's lives dramatically, and this provides an exceptional power in the hands of those who use them. Thus, after the landmark definition by Warren and Brandeis, other definitions have followed, from the right to control how others use personal information[5] to the vindication of the boundaries protecting individuals' right not to be simplified, objectified or evaluated out of context.[6]

Despite the continuing terminological misuse, dominant views have started seeing data protection as the protection through regulation of personal information pertaining to an identified or identifiable individual (Data Subject). Individuals do not own information about themselves and those who process personal data (Data Controllers and Data Processors) have the right to process data pertaining to Data Subjects as long as such processing is lawful, i.e., it abides by procedural rules set by a law whose objective is to protect individual citizens not against data processing per se but against unjustified collection, storage, use, and dissemination of the data pertaining to them. According to this stance, data protection cannot be reduced to a late privacy spin-off echoing a privacy right with regard to personal data, but it formulates the conditions under which processing is legitimate. While privacy laws exist to protect the legitimate opacity of the individual through prohibitive measures, data protection forces the transparency of the processing of personal data, enabling its full control by individuals where the processing is not authorised by the law itself as necessary for societal reasons. In short, data protection law focuses on the activities of the processors and it enforces their accountability, thus regulating an accepted exercise of power.[7]

Personal data processing operations are performed predominantly in large volumes with information and communications technologies. Data are increasingly processed over international electronic communications networks and across national and geographic boundaries. Over time, these factors have encouraged the development of a harmonised European regulatory framework for data processing operations involving personal data, which has had an impact further afield. Until May 2018, within the European Economic Area (EEA), the most important legal instrument was the Directive of the European Parliament and Council of 24 October 1995 'on the protection of individuals with regard to the processing of personal data and on the free movement of such data' (the Data Protection Directive).[8] With the ratification of the Treaty of Lisbon, Article 16 of the Treaty on the Functioning of the European Union (TFEU) has upgraded the provision on data protection to a 'provision of general

5. E.g., *see* the landmark decision of the German Constitutional Court Bundersverfassungsgericht, Judgment of 15 December 1983, 1 BvR 209/83, BVerfGE 65 establishing the right of informational self-determination.
6. Rosen, *supra* n. 1.
7. Cfr Paul De Hert and Serge Gutwirth, *Data Protection in the Case Law of Strasbourg and Luxembourg: Constitutionalisation in Action*, in *Reinventing Data Protection?*, 3-44 (Serge Gutwirth et al. eds, Springer 2009); Orla Lynskey, *Deconstructing Data Protection: The 'Added-Value' of A Right to Data Protection in the EU Legal Order*, 63 International and Comparative Law Quarterly, 569-597 (2014) https://doi.org/10.1017/s0020589314000244.
8. Directive 95/46/EC of the European Parliament and of the Council of 24 October 1995 on the protection of individuals with regard to the processing of personal data and on the free movement of such data, OJ L 281, 23.11.1995, p. 31-50.

application' under Title II alongside other fundamental principles of the EU. It also imposes on the EU legislator to establish a certain and unequivocal legal framework for data protection beyond the areas covered by what was covered by Pillar I (essentially, the internal market). Equally, the Charter of Fundamental Rights of the EU has become binding, which in its Article 8 recognises the protection of personal data as an autonomous right from privacy.

Consequently, the European Commission has reviewed the former legal framework for data protection to modernise it vis-à-vis the new upgraded Treaty framework for data protection, as well as the challenges posed by technologies and globalisation. The Commission's proposal updated the principles enshrined in the 1995 Data Protection Directive to guarantee enhanced data protection rights in the future. They included a policy Communication setting out the Commission's objectives and two legislative proposals:

- a proposal for a regulation of the European Parliament and of the Council on the protection of individuals with regard to the processing of personal data and on the free movement of such data (GDPR), which sets out a general EU framework for data protection;[9] and
- a proposal for a directive on protecting personal data processed for the purposes of prevention, detection, investigation or prosecution of criminal offences and related judicial activities.[10]

The Commission's proposals have gone through lengthy negotiations between the European Parliament and the Council of Ministers for discussion and approval. The final texts were approved by the EU Parliament on 14 April 2016. The GDPR is directly enforceable from 25 May 2018 in all Member States.[11] It is set to lead to a uniform application and enforcement of data protection law across EU jurisdictions. In contrast to a 'Directive', the use of the legal form of a 'Regulation' means that it has a direct effect and does not need national implementation. This is designed to eliminate risks of national particularities and diversity of practices, which would frustrate the goal of using that precise EU legal instrument to achieve uniformity. Instead, Directive (EU) 2016/680 provides for the protection of natural persons with regard to the processing of personal data by competent authorities for the purposes of the prevention, investigation, detection or prosecution of criminal offences or the execution of criminal penalties, and on the free movement of such data.[12]

9. COM/2012/011 final.
10. COM/2012/010 final.
11. Article 99 GDPR.
12. Regulation (EU) 2016/679 of the European Parliament and of the Council of 27 April 2016 on the protection of natural persons with regard to the processing of personal data and on the free movement of such data, and repealing Directive 95/46/EC, OJ L 119, 4.5.2016, 1-88 and Directive (EU) 2016/680 of the European Parliament and of the Council of 27 April 2016 on the protection of natural persons with regard to the processing of personal data by competent authorities for the purposes of the prevention, investigation, detection or prosecution of criminal offences or the execution of criminal penalties, and on the free movement of such data, and repealing Council Framework Decision 2008/977/JHA, OJ L 119, 4.5.2016, 89-131.

To fully understand the nature, scope and provisions of current European data protection law, it is important to understand its normative origins and evolution, which occurred at national and international levels. Those who are involved in data protection operations - particularly Data Controllers, practitioners and students - require an understanding of European and international laws in the field: the GDPR was reactive to pre-existing European and international advances in the field, and domestic law is increasingly permeated by these external influences. Furthermore, Data Controllers can be subject to foreign regulation depending on how they structure their data processing operations.[13]

The first data protection regimes emerged as a political issue in post-war European countries in a time of important social and economic changes, later followed by a transition from an industrial to a post-industrial economy and ensuing social reforms.

Legal systems in Europe have a tradition of laws on privacy, tort, secrecy and confidentiality. Fascinating as this historical perspective may be, its study is beyond the scope of this work.[14] Narrowing this down to the roots of personal data processing, to understand in depth the fundamental nature of the right to data protection, it is necessary to recall how it was the experience of totalitarian regimes in the twentieth century that pushed European nations into attaching great importance to the right to privacy in its modern form. These experiences demonstrated how easily personal information could be accessed, used, manipulated and abused and revealed the extreme consequences of such violations. It is not surprising that the first data protection laws were enacted on a national basis, with the German State of Hesse adopting the first data protection statute of general application in 1970.[15] Following the horrors of recent history under the Nazi regime and looking eastward to controversial practices of the Communist regime in East Germany, such legal measures represented an attempt to stem the ability of public and private sector bodies to access and abuse personal data to eliminate or punish undesirable people. Likewise, developments in automated data processing techniques demanded the need to limit the power of governments in the exploitation of information for different purposes.[16]

Accordingly, the basic tenets of this law influenced the future development of data protection legislation in Europe for decades to come, even in countries with a completely different history and needs. The second example of data protection legislation is that of Sweden in 1973, which was not motivated by a history or dangers

13. *See also*, Marko Milanovic, *Human Rights Treaties and Foreign Surveillance: Privacy in the Digital Age*, 56 Harvard International Law Journal, 81 (2015).
14. *See, e.g.*, David Banisar and Simon Davies, *Global Trends in Privacy Protection: An International Survey of Privacy, Data Protection, and Surveillance Laws and Developments*, 18 John Marshall Journal of Computer & Information Law, 1-111 (1999); Gary Schober et al., *Transcript: Colloquium on Privacy & Security*, 50 Buffalo Law Review, 703-754 (2002).
15. Hessian Act of 7 October 1970. *See* Michael Kirby, *Transborder Data Flows and the 'Basic Rules' of Data Privacy*, 16 Stanford Journal of International Law, 27-66 (1980).
16. Spiros Simitis, *Privacy: An Endless Debate?*, 98 California Law Review,1995-2005 (2010); Herbert Burkert, *Privacy: Data Protection - A German/European Perspective*, in *Governance of Global Networks in the Light of Differing Local Values*, 43-70 (Herbert Burkert, Nomos Verlagsgesellschaft 2000); Frits Hondius, *Emerging Data Protection in Europe* (North-Holland Publishing Company 1975).

of totalitarianism, but a long tradition of freedom of information. Here, the need for open government suggested the adoption of a law extending some of the concepts of freedom of information into the private sector, at the same time offering protection from misuse or abuse.

Indeed, with the progressive developments in computers and information technologies, together with the dangers these could represent for individuals, other European countries followed the former examples: by the end of the 1970s, France, Germany, Denmark, Norway and Austria established their national data protection legal framework.[17]

With the flourishing of national legal regimes, concerns started to emerge that national laws, which applied rigid controls over the export of data, might have protectionist effects and businesses could delocalise in third countries to circumvent restrictions. International solutions became necessary to reconcile individual rights, national obligations, and commercial interests. Thus, a range of international organisations have become active in the field of privacy and data protection, with the Council of Europe (CoE) representing the most prominent actor.[18]

1.2 THE CoE's ACTIVITY IN DATA PROTECTION AND ITS CONTINUING RELEVANCE

European data protection law was preceded by the CoE Convention of 28 January 1981 for the protection of individuals with regard to automatic processing of personal data (Convention 108). The CoE, whose forty-six member states include the twenty-seven EU Member States, was established in 1949 and is the continent's oldest political organisation, most famous for its activity in the field of human rights. The European Convention for the Protection of Human Rights and Fundamental Freedoms (ECHR) and the European Court of Human Rights are both emanations of the Council.

The Statute of the CoE provides the legal foundation for the Council and for all its subsequent activities, including Convention 108. The ECHR is arguably the most well-known legal instrument of the CoE. Article 8 ECHR provides:

> 1. Everyone has the right to respect for his private and family life, his home and his correspondence.
> 2. There shall be no interference by a public authority with the exercise of this right except such as is in accordance with the law and is necessary in a democratic society in the interests of national security, public safety or the economic well-being of the country, for the prevention of disorder or crime, for the protection of health or morals, or for the protection of the rights and freedoms of others.

The ECHR has been incorporated into the domestic laws of the Member States, which require primary legislation and subordinate legislation to be read and given effect in a way which is compatible with the Convention rights, so far as it is possible

17. Lars Ilshammar, *When Computers Became Dangerous: The Swedish Computer Discourse of the 1960s*, 9 HUMAN IT, 7-37 (2007); Hondius, *supra* n. 16.
18. Ian Lloyd, *Information Technology Law* (Oxford University Press 2020), 27-38.

to do so, as well as making it unlawful for a public authority to act in a way that is incompatible with a Convention right.

However, the spur to CoE activity in the field of data protection was an emerging concern in the mid-late 1960s about the ability of the ECHR to adequately protect personal privacy within the context of increasing computerisation and other advances in technology. In particular, the Council was concerned that Article 8 ECHR dealt only with interferences by public authorities and not by private parties, that it was concerned with the protection of privacy in a limited sense, such as privacy in correspondence, and that the Convention did not permit the participation of non-European and non-member states.[19]

In response, the Council adopted two resolutions on data protection. The first, Resolution (73) 22, established principles of data protection for the private sector[20] and the second, Resolution (74) 29, did the same for the public sector.[21] These Resolutions paved the way towards the drafting of Convention 108.

The Preamble to Convention 108 affirms the aim of the CoE to achieve greater unity between its members on the respect for the rule of law and human rights; it extends the safeguards for everyone's rights, particularly the right to privacy in an increasing flow across frontiers of personal data undergoing automatic processing; it reaffirms the commitment to freedom of information regardless of frontiers; it recognises the need to reconcile the respect for privacy and the free flow of information between peoples.

These issues were also at the heart of the Data Protection Directive and, later, of the TFEU, the Charter of Fundamental Rights of the EU, and the GDPR.

1.2.1 Structure and Content of Convention 108

Convention 108 requires member states to apply its provisions to public sector and private sector automated processing only whilst recognising that they may extend their domestic rules to manual files. Its object and purpose, which it calls 'data protection', are contained in Article 1:

> The purpose of this convention is to secure in the territory of each Party for every individual, whatever his nationality or residence, respect for his rights and fundamental freedoms, and in particular his right to privacy, with regard to automatic processing of personal data relating to him ('data protection').

The main structure of the Convention early recognised the following.

Quality of data - Article 5 provides that personal data undergoing automated processing shall be: (a) obtained and processed fairly and lawfully; (b) stored for specified and legitimate purposes and not used in ways incompatible with those

19. Council of Europe, Explanatory Report to the Convention for the Protection of Individuals with regard to Automatic Processing of Personal Data (Strasbourg, 28 January 1981).
20. Council of Europe Committee of Ministers Resolution (73) 22 on the Protection of the Privacy of Individuals vis-à-vis Electronic Data Banks in the Private Sector (26 September 1973).
21. Council of Europe Committee of Ministers Resolution (74) 29 on the protection of the privacy of individuals vis-a-vis electronic data banks in the public sector (20 September 1974).

purposes; (c) adequate, relevant and not excessive in relation to the purposes for which they are stored; (d) accurate and, where necessary, kept up to date; and (e) preserved in a form that permits identification of the Data Subject for no longer than is required for the purposes for which the data are stored.

Special categories of data – Article 6 provides that special category data shall not be processed automatically in the absence of adequate safeguards in domestic law. Special category data is: (a) personal data revealing racial origins, political opinions or religious or other beliefs; (b) personal data concerning health or sexual life; and (c) personal data relating to criminal convictions.

Data security – Article 7 requires appropriate measures to be taken for the protection of personal data stored in automated data files. This is to guard against: (a) accidental or unauthorised destruction; (b) accidental loss; and (c) unauthorised access, alteration or dissemination.

Additional safeguards for Data Subjects – Article 8 provides Data Subjects with a series of personal rights. These enable the Data Subject to: (a) establish the existence of an automated personal data file, its main purposes, as well as the identity and habitual residence or principal place of business of the Controller of the file; (b) obtain at reasonable intervals and without excessive delay or expense confirmation of whether personal data relating to him are stored in the automated data file as well as communication to him of such data in an intelligible form; (c) obtain rectification or erasure of such data if they have been processed contrary to the provisions of domestic law giving effect to the basic principles set out in Articles 5 and 6; and (d) a remedy if a request for confirmation or communication, rectification or erasure is not complied with.

Exceptions and restrictions – Article 9 provides the member states with the power to make derogations from the requirements of Articles 5, 6 and 8, where the derogations are necessary to protect state and public interests or in the interests of the Data Subject or third parties, together with a power to limit the access rights in Article 8, where the processing is for statistics or scientific research.

Sanctions and remedies – Article 10 requires member states to provide for appropriate penalties and remedies for violation of domestic laws.

Transborder data flows – Article 12 provides, subject to derogations, that member states may not prohibit or restrict transborder data flows (transfers across national borders) or make them subject to authorisations on the ground of protection of privacy. Member states may derogate from this rule, except where the recipient country provides ‘equivalent protection’ to that provided by national legislation.

These principles early reflect the later normative provisions of EU law and its evolutions.

1.2.2 The Continuing Relevance of the CoE, Convention 108 + and Its Relationship with the GDPR

During the early stages of European activity in data protection, the EU (then European Economic Community (EEC)) was willing to allow the CoE to take the lead in the development of policy.

Six months after Convention 108 was opened for signature, the European Commission issued a Recommendation[22] that those Member States that had not already done so sign Convention 108 for the protection of individuals with regard to automatic processing of personal data and ratify it before the end of 1982. The Commission reserved the right to propose that the Council adopt an instrument on the basis of the EU (then EEC) Treaty in the event that all the Member States did not within a reasonable time sign and ratify the convention. The Commission eventually exercised this right with its proposal for a Data Protection Directive in 1990.

Despite an expansive EU, the emergence of the Data Protection Directive and the unwillingness of non-CoE States to sign up and ratify Convention 108, the CoE and Convention 108 have continued to enjoy great influence.[23]

Factors in the CoE's favour include the size of its membership (forty-six Member states), its function in the EU enlargement process (all EU Member States have first been CoE member states), its age and history (generally and in respect of data protection), its special focus on human rights and fundamental freedoms, its prestige work in related areas (e.g., the Cybercrime Convention), its ownership of the world-famous European Convention on Human Rights, and continuing uncertainty over the extent of EU competence in the area of human rights.

The CoE maintains prominence through the issue of Recommendations. These Recommendations approach data protection from a sectoral perspective, drawing attention to substantial matters of concern. These Recommendations carry influence within the EU. For example, the CoE Recommendation[24] on the protection of personal data collected and processed for insurance purposes was supported by the European Commission.[25]

A process of modernisation of Convention 108 was launched in 2011, which marked the beginning of a public consultation organised in this context.

On 18 May 2018, one week before the GDPR came into force, the modernisation of Convention 108 was completed by the CoE, with the parties to the existing Convention agreeing to a Protocol amending it ('Convention 108 + ').[26]

The need for global data protection standards and the adaptation to the GDPR prompted the adoption of Convention 108 + , which can be signed and ratified by any country around the world. Given the increasing data flows, having different degrees of

22. European Commission, Recommendation of 29 July 1981 relating to the Council of Europe Convention for the protection of individuals with regard to automatic processing of personal data (81/679/EEC).
23. *See, also*, Paul de Hert and Vagelis Papakostantinou, *The Council of Europe Data Protection Convention Reform: Analysis of the New Text and Critical Comment on Its Global Ambition*, 30 Computer Law & Security Review, 633-642 (2014) https://doi.org/10.1016/j.clsr.2014.09.002.
24. Recommendation Rec(2002)9 of the Committee of Ministers to Member States on the protection of personal data collected and processed for insurance purposes (18 September 2002).
25. Recommendation for a Council Decision on the vote to be taken by Member States within the competent bodies of the Council of Europe, on behalf of the EC, in favour of adopting the draft Recommendation on the protection of personal data collected and processed for insurance purposes, and of authorising the publication of its Explanatory Memorandum (SEC/2002/0280 final), 18 March 2002.
26. Protocol amending the Convention for the Protection of Individuals with regard to Automatic Processing of Personal Data (CETS No. 223) or Treaty 223.

data protection in different regions would represent a threat to those countries and regions that are advanced in their legislations (e.g., the EU). Harmonisation among countries around the world is also key to ensuring that enforcement is equally strong everywhere and companies do not engage in forum shopping processing data in jurisdictions with lower levels of protection.

Any individual is covered by its protection, independently of their nationality, as long as they are within the jurisdiction of one of the parties who have ratified the Convention.

All EU Member States ratified Convention 108 + . At present, fifty-five countries are parties, including all member states of the CoE (forty-six countries), Uruguay (the first non-CoE country to accede), Argentina, Mexico, Cape Verde, Burkina Faso, Morocco, Mauritius, Senegal, and Tunisia. The EU as a supranational body is also a party to the Convention 108 + .

The EU sees the protocol as a way of encouraging third countries to adopt the basic tenets of the GDPR. In fact, accession to Convention 108 + carries a positive effect on applications for 'adequacy' assessments to the EU under the GDPR. In legal terms, the European Commission should take account of obligations arising from the third country's participation in multilateral or regional systems.[27] In particular, the third country's accession to Convention 108 + should be taken into account. Nonetheless, the extent to which compliance with Convention 108 + will be sufficient for EU adequacy is still uncertain.

To conclude, the CoE and EU law share common origins and principles. EU law now aims to become the global data protection standard that, by means of its adequacy criterion, is exporting to third countries.

For its part, the CoE Convention constituted a binding text that came to be addressed predominantly to States that are also EU members committing to data protection law. For third countries, the option for ratification signals an attempt for the CoE to contribute to the achievement of a global standard. At international level, it represents the only mandatory text regulating the processing of law enforcement agencies. All personal data processing is to be governed by its provisions, including therefore both public and private sectors as well as that of law enforcement agencies.[28]

Its interconnectedness with the ECHR and the European Court of Human Rights provides an individual right to data protection as a spin-off of the human right to privacy.[29]

However, the relationship between the right to privacy and the right to data protection in the ECHR remains unclear. Instead, EU law has clearly distinguished the right to data protection from the right to privacy, giving them an independent, standalone status in the text of its Treaty. In this way, data protection has evolved into autonomous principles in the GDPR rather than remaining guidelines derived from the general right to privacy.

27. Recital 105 GDPR.
28. de Hert and Papakostantinou, *supra* n. 23.
29. de Hert and Gutwirth, *supra* n. 7.

Through this process, nowadays, the EU actively promotes its data protection legislation via its adequacy system.

Nonetheless, in a fragmented international environment and in the absence of a globally accepted data protection legislation standard, it is important to have a formal set of rules open to non-members of the EU, such as that of now Convention 108 + . Its adherence is increasingly becoming a positive element for the EU adequacy requirements, thus showing how international laws have not only shaped EU law but continue to have a prominent autonomous relevance.

1.3 THE DEVELOPMENT OF DATA PROTECTION LAW IN THE EU: FROM THE DATA PROTECTION DIRECTIVE TO THE GDPR

As seen, the horrors of recent European history and the international conventions that followed played an important role in the development of data protection laws across Europe and, ultimately, at the EU level in the adoption of the Data Protection Directive. Two other factors, however, proved decisive for the enactment of the latter piece of legislation under the remit of the EU: (i) the progressive development in computers and information technologies, i.e., ultimately in the information society, together with the dangers that this could represent for individuals, seen as an issue transcending national affairs; and (ii) the need for the free movement of personal data within the Community to solve trade disputes arising from separate national regimes, hence the harmonisation of data protection laws of the Member States.[30]

Whilst it endorsed Convention 108 and the work of the CoE, the European Commission expressly reserved the right to legislate under the Treaty Establishing the European Community (TEC),[31] a right which it exercised through the Data Protection Directive.[32]

In the end, the real aims and scope of the Data Protection Directive were: (i) the protection of fundamental rights and freedoms of Europeans and (ii) the achievement of the Internal Market. Both objectives were equally important, though in mere legal terms, the existence of the Directive and the jurisdiction of the EU, rather than the national ones, rested on Internal Market grounds, having its legal basis in then Article 100a TEC (now Article 114 TFEU). To achieve the objectives contained in the then Article 14 TEC (ex 7a), Article 95 TEC allowed the Council to 'adopt the measures for the approximation of the provisions laid down by law, regulation or administrative action in Member States which have as their object the establishment and functioning of the internal market'. The measure was taken for the completion of the internal

30. Recitals 1-11 Directive 95/46/EC.
31. Commission Recommendation of 29 July 1981 relating to the Council of Europe Convention for the protection of individuals with regard to automatic processing of personal data (81/679/EEC).
32. Commission Proposal of 27 July 1990 for a Council Directive concerning the protection of individuals in relation to the processing of personal data (COM(90) 314 final), OJ No. C277.

market, defined as 'an area without internal frontiers in which the free movement of goods, persons, services and capital is ensured'.[33]

The Directive was designed to apply to 'the processing of personal data wholly or partly by automatic means' and to the processing of personal data that 'form part of a filing system or are intended to form part of a filing system'.[34]

The central thesis at the heart of the Data Protection Directive was that for the Internal Market to flourish, it is necessary for there to be a high level of protection for data processing operations involving personal data; this prevents the erection of legal obstacles to the free flow of personal data around Europe and the distortion of competition.

It has been emphasised by many commentators how in the drafting of the law the EU institutions consistently took a rigorous 'fundamental human rights' approach.[35] This latter stance was particularly important because it meant that data protection automatically trumped other interests and could not be traded-off for economic benefits, as early confirmed by the CJEU in *Rundfunk*.[36]

At the same time, however, the right to the protection of personal data is not an absolute right but must be considered in relation to its function in society.[37]

With the passing of the Treaty of Lisbon, Article 16 TFEU elevates the provision on data protection to a 'provision of general application' under Title II, alongside other fundamental principles of the EU. It also imposes on the EU legislator to establish a certain and unequivocal legal framework for data protection. Equally, with the Treaty of Lisbon, the Charter of Fundamental Rights of the EU has become binding, and in its Article 8 it recognises the protection of personal data as an autonomous right (also distinguished from 'privacy').

Article 16 TFEU holds that:

> 1. Everyone has the right to the protection of personal data concerning them.
> 2. The European Parliament and the Council, acting in accordance with the ordinary legislative procedure, shall lay down the rules relating to the protection of individuals with regard to the processing of personal data by Union institutions, bodies, offices and agencies, and by the Member States when carrying out activities which fall within the scope of Union law, and the rules relating to the free movement of such data. Compliance with these rules shall be subject to the control of independent authorities.

---

33. Treaty Establishing the European Community, Article 14(2) now replaced by the TFEU, Article 26(2).
34. Article 3 Directive 95/46/EC.
35. Dorothee Heisenberg, *Negotiating Privacy* (Lynne Rienner, 2005), Chapters 1, 2, 3; Viktor Mayer-Schonberger, *Generational Development of Data Protection in Europe*, in *Technology and Privacy: The New Landscape*, 219-241 (Philip Agre and Marc Rotenberg eds, MIT Press 1997); Spiros Simitis, *From the Market to the Polis: The EU Directive on the Protection of Personal Data*, 80 Iowa Law Review, 445-469 (1995).
36. Joined Cases C-465/00, C-138/01 and C-139/01, *Rechnungshof v. Österreichischer Rundfunk and Others and Christa Neukomm and Joseph Lauermann v. Österreichischer Rundfunk*, ECLI:EU:C:2003:294.
37. Case C-112/00, *Eugen Schmidberger, Internationale Transporte und Planzüge v. Austria*, ECLI:EU:C:2003:333.

Article 8 of the Charter of Fundamental Rights of the EU reads:

1. Everyone has the right to the protection of personal data concerning him or her.
2. Such data must be processed fairly for specified purposes and on the basis of the consent of the person concerned or some other legitimate basis laid down by law. Everyone has the right of access to data which has been collected concerning him or her, and the right to have it rectified.
3. Compliance with these rules shall be subject to control by an independent authority.

The Charter of Fundamental Rights of the EU has the same legal value as the Treaties and it forms an integral part of the body of constitutional rules and principles by reference to which the CJEU can deliver a judgment.

The EU institutions must act consistently with the Charter, including in the making of EU law. However, the Charter's impact on national laws is more limited as it only applies to Member States when they implement EU law.

Based on its nature of an EU fundamental right, the CJEU invalidated the existing Data Retention Directive[38] in the case of *Digital Rights Ireland.*[39] The Court held that the obligation of telecommunication service providers and internet service providers to retain telecommunications metadata and make it available to European law enforcement authorities under given circumstances is disproportionate, constituting an interference with the right to data protection. Thus, it held that it is in violation of the EU fundamental rights law. The case illustrates the key role of the Charter in the area of data protection.

Data protection qualifies as a relative right, as confirmed by the late jurisprudence of the CJEU since it has started to recognise data protection as an autonomous right in the *Promusicae,*[40] *Rijkeboer,*[41] and *Volker*[42] cases, albeit not yet completely separated from the right to respect for private life.[43] The learned judges have stressed that the right to data protection is not absolute, but it must be considered in relation to its functions in society.

38. Directive 2006/24/EC of the European Parliament and of the Council of 15 March 2006 on the retention of data generated or processed in connection with the provision of publicly available electronic communications services or of public communications networks and amending Directive 2002/58/EC, OJ L 105, 13.4.2006, p. 54-63, no longer in force.
39. Joined Cases C-293/12 and C-594/12, *Digital Rights Ireland Ltd v. Minister for Communications, Marine and Natural Resources and Others and Kärntner Landesregierung and Others,* ECLI: EU:C:2014:238.
40. Case C-275/06, *Productores de Música de España (Promusicae) v. Telefónica de España SAU,* ECLI:EU:C:2008:54.
41. Case C-553/07, *College van burgemeester en wethouders van Rotterdam v. MEE Rijkeboer,* ECLI:EU:C:2009:293.
42. Joined Cases C-92/09 and C-93/09, *Volker und Markus Schecke GbR and Hartmut Eifert v. Land Hessen,* ECLI:EU:C:2010:662.
43. On data protection as an autonomous right in the jurisprudence of the CJEU *see* Juliane Kokott and Christoph Sobotta, *The Distinction Between Privacy and Data Protection in the Jurisprudence of the CJEU and the ECtHR,* 3 International Data Privacy Law, 222-228 (2013) https://doi.org/10.1093/idpl/ipt017.

The CJEU has provided precedents for such a balancing of rights. Limiting the analysis on the right to data protection, the latter was balanced with the freedom of expression back in *Lindqvist*,[44] later confirmed in *Satamedia*,[45] emphasising that it was the responsibility of national authorities and courts to ensure a fair balance between the two.

Lately, the balancing exercise was clear in the *Scarlet*[46] and *Netlog*[47] cases, where the CJEU evaluated the relationship between the right to data protection vis-à-vis copyright infringement, particularly as regards the disclosure of personal data in order to ensure effective protection of copyright in civil proceedings. The Court concluded that the systematic processing of personal data in the name of copyright enforcement is incompatible with the protection of EU fundamental rights.

As to the relationship between the Charter and the ECHR, where rights under the same Charter correspond to rights guaranteed by the ECHR, then their meaning and scope should be the same as those under the latter.[48] In any case, it should not restrict or adversely affect rights recognised by the ECHR.[49]

Thus, the case law of the ECHR is relevant when considering rights under the Charter, notably the ECHR cases on respect for private life and protection of personal data. For example, the ECHR has affirmed that 'the protection of personal data is of fundamental importance to a person's enjoyment of his or her right to respect for private and family life'.[50]

Taking stock of the aforementioned Article 16(2) TFEU, the EU has enacted the GDPR, which is enforceable from 25 May 2018. In addition to a uniform application of the law, it promotes uniformity of application and enforcement across the EU and it transforms its governance. The move from a decentralised to a centralised system of governance of the law ensures the uniform application and interpretation of its norms having direct effect from their EU origin through the use of the legal instrument of a 'Regulation'.

The key principles of data protection law set by Directive 95/46/EC still hold true. However, the GDPR brings many changes. In essence, the ethos of the GDPR is to move towards greater accountability for Data Controllers and Processors and a uniform application across the EU. It directs towards a new model for managing data protection, one that aspires to let people themselves be in control of their data.

44. Case C-101/01, *Criminal Proceedings Against Bodil Lindqvist*, ECLI:EU:C:2003:596.
45. Case C-73/07, *Tietosuojavaltuutettu v. Satakunnan Markkinaporssi Oy*, ECLI:EU:C:2008:727.
46. Case C-70/10, *Scarlet Extended SA v. Société belge des auteurs, compositeurs et éditeurs SCRL (SABAM)*, ECLI:EU:C:2011:771.
47. Case C-360/10, *Belgische Vereniging van Auteurs, Componisten en Uitgevers CVBA (SABAM) v. Netlog NV*, ECLI:EU:C:2012:85.
48. Article 52(3) Charter.
49. Article 53 Charter.
50. *S and Marper v. United Kingdom* (Applications 30562/04 and 30566/04) (2008) 48 EHRR 1169, [2009] Crim LR 355, [2008] All ER (D) 56 (Dec).

1.4 KEY PROVISIONS OF THE GDPR

1.4.1 Key Definitions

For the purposes of the GDPR, it is essential to familiarise with key definitions.

'Personal data' are any information relating to an identified or identifiable natural person ('Data Subject'); an identifiable individual is one who can be identified, directly or indirectly, in particular by reference to an identifier (e.g., a name, an identification number, location data, an online identifier or to one or more factors specific to the physical, physiological, genetic, mental, economic, cultural or social identity of that individual).[51]

'Processing' relates to any operation or set of operations performed on personal data or on sets of personal data. These operations are irrespective of the methods used, e.g., by automated means or else. They include collection, recording, organisation, structuring, storage, adaptation or alteration, retrieval, consultation, use, disclosure by transmission, dissemination or otherwise making available, alignment or combination, restriction, erasure or destruction of personal data.

'Pseudonymisation' is a new definition which refers to the technique of processing personal data in such a manner that they can no longer be attributed to a specific Data Subject without the use of additional information, which must be kept separately and be subject to technical and organisational measures to ensure non-attribution.

A 'Controller' is any natural or legal person, public authority, agency or other body which, alone or jointly with others, determines the purposes and means of the processing of personal data. Therefore, a Controller defines the scope and extent of activities involved in data processing to meet its objectives and derive benefits. Controllers are typically primary organisations and entities that have direct contact with consumers. Where two or more Controllers jointly determine the purposes and means of processing, they are considered 'Joint Controllers'. In this case, they have to determine in a transparent manner their respective responsibilities for compliance with the obligations under the GDPR, in particular as regards the obligations vis-à-vis Data Subjects.

A 'Processor' is a natural or legal person, public authority, agency or other body which processes personal data on behalf of the Controller. Processors are usually agents of Controllers. They typically include service providers and others such as software, servicers of information and records, etc.

A 'Recipient' of data is a natural or legal person, public authority, agency or another body to which the personal data are disclosed, whether a Third Party or not.

A 'Third Party' is a natural or legal person, public authority, agency or body other than the Data Subject, Controller, or Processor who, under the direct authority of the Controller or Processor, is authorised to process personal data (e.g., any third-party undertaking activities having an express or implied agreement with an organisation for commercial purposes).

51. Article 4(1) GDPR.

A 'Main Establishment' is either the place of the central administration in the EU of a Controller with establishments in more than one Member State (unless the decisions on the purposes and means of the processing of personal data are taken in another establishment of the Controller in the EU and the latter establishment has the power to have such decisions implemented, in which case the establishment having taken such decisions is to be considered to be the main establishment), or the place of the central administration of a Processor with establishments in more than one Member State in the EU or the establishment of the Processor in the EU – in case the Processor has no central administration in the Union – where the main processing activities take.

A 'Representative' is a natural or legal person established in the EU who is designated in writing by the Controller or Processor when they are not established in the EU. The Representative represents the Controller or Processor with regard to their respective obligations under the GDPR.

'Cross-border processing' is a processing which takes place in the context of the activities of establishments in more than one Member State where the Controller or Processor is established in more than one Member State. It also means a processing of personal data which takes place in the context of the activities of a single establishment of a Controller or Processor in the EU but which substantially affects or is likely to substantially affect Data Subjects in more than one Member State.[52]

1.4.2 Structure, Content, and Exclusions/Derogations of the GDPR

The GDPR consists of 173 recitals, 11 chapters and 99 articles. It is formulated as an EU Regulation. It provides for the protection of personal data. However, such a right is not an absolute one, but it must be considered in relation to its function in society and be balanced against other fundamental rights in accordance with the principle of proportionality, including the freedom to conduct a business.

As noted earlier, the objectives of the GDPR are to ensure an equivalent level of protection of natural persons and the free flow of personal data throughout the EU. Such goals would not be achievable by the Member States on their own. Instead, by reason of the scale or effects of the action, such objectives may be better achieved at EU level. Therefore, the EU adopts measures in accordance with the principle of subsidiarity as set out in Article 5 of the Treaty on European Union (TEU), according to which the EU does not take action (except in the areas that fall within its exclusive jurisdiction), unless it is more effective than action taken at the national, regional or local level.

The articles of the GDPR describe the Member States' obligations without leaving them the same room for manoeuvre as was the case under Directive 95/46/EC. In contrast to a 'Directive', the use of the legal form of a 'Regulation' means that it has a direct effect and does not need national implementation. This is designed to eliminate risks of national particularities and diversity of practices, which would frustrate the

52. Article 4 GDPR.

goal of using that precise EU legal instrument to achieve uniformity. Through the use of the legal instrument of a 'Regulation', the move from a decentralised to a centralised system of governance shall ensure the uniform application and interpretation of norms in the Member States having direct effect from their EU origin.

In distinction to the articles, the recitals are very detailed, explaining the theories and assumptions behind the law, its drivers and motivations. They provide tremendous assistance with interpretation, providing an important evidential record of huge historical significance showing what was in the mind of the lawmaker.

The GDPR lays down rules relating to the protection of natural persons with regard to the processing of personal data and rules relating to the free movement of personal data.[53] The right to the protection of personal data is accounted as a fundamental right and freedom of individuals.[54] At the same time, the free movement of personal data within the EU shall be neither restricted nor prohibited for reasons connected with the protection of natural persons with regard to the processing of personal data.[55] This means that the circulation of personal data in the EU is allowed as long as the rules laid down in the GDPR are respected.

The law applies to the processing of personal data wholly or partly by automated means and to the processing other than by automated means of personal data which form part of a filing system or are intended to form part of a filing system.[56]

By contrast, the GDPR does not apply to processing carried out by individuals purely for personal or household activity.[57] This exemption also covers social networking and online activities undertaken as long as these are for social or domestic purposes (as per the extension of the CJEU case of *Bodil Lindqvist*).[58]

Despite being a Regulation, Member States retain the ability to introduce national derogations. The GDPR does not apply to the processing of personal data by the Member States when carrying out activities in relation to the common foreign and security policy of the Union.[59] In addition, by the express disposition of Articles 2(2) and 23 GDPR, Member States retain the ability to introduce certain derogations where these are related to activities which fall outside the scope of EU law, such as activities concerning national security and the prevention and detection of crime (regulated by Directive 2016/680[60] and Directive 2016/681).[61] Likewise, Member States can introduce derogations as regards important public interests, in particular economic or financial interests (e.g., budgetary or taxation matters), the protection of judicial independence and proceedings, and the enforcement of civil law matters. To be acceptable, a derogating national measure must include specific provisions setting out:

53. Article 1(1) GDPR.
54. Article 1(2) GDPR.
55. Article 1(3) GDPR.
56. Article 2(1) GDPR.
57. Article 2(2)(c) GDPR.
58. Bodil Lindqvist, *supra* n. 44.
59. Recital 16 GDPR.
60. *Supra* n. 12.
61. Directive (EU) 2016/681 of the European Parliament and of the Council of 27 April 2016 on the use of passenger name record (PNR) data for the prevention, detection, investigation and prosecution of terrorist offences and serious crime, OJ L 119, 4.5.2016, p. 132-149.

the purposes of the processing or categories of processing; the categories of personal data; the scope of the restrictions introduced; the safeguards to prevent abuse or unlawful access or transfer; the specification of the Controller or categories of Controllers; the storage periods and the applicable safeguards taking into account the nature, scope and purposes of the processing or categories of processing; the risks to the rights and freedoms of Data Subjects; and the right of Data Subjects to be informed about the restriction, unless that may be prejudicial to the purpose of the restriction.[62]

The territorial scope of the GDPR has been extended to include the processing of personal data in the context of the activities of an establishment of a Controller or a Processor in the Union, regardless of whether the processing takes place in the Union or not.[63]

For Data Controllers or Processors outside the EEA, the GDPR applies to the processing of personal data of Data Subjects who are in the Union anytime the processing activities are related to the offering of goods or services, irrespective of whether a payment of the Data Subject is required, to such Data Subjects in the Union; likewise, the GDPR applies to any processing activity relating to the monitoring of the behaviour of Data Subjects, as far as their behaviour takes place within the Union.[64]

Where the Controllers or Processors are not established in the EU but are caught within the territorial scope of the GDPR above, such Controllers or Processors must designate in writing a Representative in the EU Member State where the Data Subjects, whose personal data are processed in relation to the offering of goods or services, or whose behaviour is monitored, are located, unless an exception applies. An exception is a processing which is occasional, does not include processing of special categories of data listed in Article 9(1) GDPR or processing of personal data relating to criminal convictions and offences on a large scale, and is unlikely to result in a risk to the rights and freedoms of natural persons. Such an assessment should consider the nature, context, scope and purposes of the processing. Another exception is data processed by public authorities and bodies.

1.4.3 Principles and General Rules on Lawfulness

Broadly, the general principles laid down by the GDPR are similar to those in the Data Protection Directive. However, the novel overarching principle introduced by the GDPR is that of 'accountability', according to which Controllers are responsible for and must be able to demonstrate compliance with the principles listed in Article 5 GDPR. These are:

- 'Lawfulness, fairness and transparency': personal data must be processed lawfully, fairly and in a transparent manner in relation to the Data Subject.
- 'Purpose limitation': personal data must be collected for specified, explicit and legitimate purposes and not further processed in a manner that is incompatible

62. Article 23(2) GDPR.
63. Article 3(1) GDPR.
64. Article 3(2) GDPR.

with those purposes; any further processing for archiving purposes in the public interest, scientific or historical research purposes or statistical purposes are not considered to be incompatible with the initial purposes.
- 'Data minimisation': personal data must be adequate, relevant and limited to what is necessary in relation to the purposes for which they are processed.
- 'Accuracy': data must be accurate and kept up to date; every reasonable step must be taken to ensure that personal data that are inaccurate are erased or rectified without delay.
- 'Storage limitation': data must be kept in a form which permits identification of Data Subjects for no longer than is necessary for the purposes for which they are processed; longer periods of storage are allowed for archiving purposes in the public interest, scientific or historical research purposes or statistical purposes, subject to implementation of the appropriate technical and organisational measures to safeguard the rights and freedoms of Data Subjects. The case of *Google Spain* under the Data Protection Directive has set an important precedent for EU data protection law with respect to the online world. The CJEU has granted the possibility to Data Subjects to request to search engines the delisting of links appearing in search results based on a person's name when the information is no longer relevant. Commentators have labelled the case as introducing the right to be forgotten.[65]
- 'Integrity and confidentiality': data must be processed in a manner that ensures appropriate security and protection against accidental loss, destruction or damage; Controllers must ensure that appropriate technical or organisational measures are in place.

In turn, Article 6(1) GDPR sets out the conditions that must be satisfied for the processing of personal data to be lawful. The precise conditions are determined by the application of at least one of the following circumstances, which broadly replicate those in the Data Protection Directive:

(a) Consent: the Data Subject has given consent to the processing of his or her personal data for one or more specific purposes. At first sight, the condition for obtaining consent has become stricter than those required under the Data Protection Directive. The legal regime of Directive 95/46/EC already provided for 'unambiguous consent' as a general ground for the lawfulness of the processing of personal data. This was the first of six different bases to legitimise data processing.[66] In the majority of Member States, consent was given primary status over other criteria. Even if consent was already a key requirement for the legitimacy of many forms of data processing (especially for marketing and online behavioural advertising), the conditions that needed to be met for consent to be legally valid had been far from clear. In legal terms,

65. Case C-131/12, *Google Spain SL and Google Inc v. Agencia Espanola de Protecciòn de Datos (AEPD) and Mario Costeja Gonzàlez*, ECLI:EU:C:2014:317.
66. Article 7 Directive 95/46/EC.

under Directive 95/46/EC, the problem was that consent had to be unambiguous, informed, specific, freely given, and revocable (as a unilateral act). However, uncertainty as to the meaning of consent accelerates in the digital world, where technology has given way to unclear methods for expressing this indication of wish. Each one of its features has had problematic interpretations and applications. Examples are opt-in, opt-out or pre-ticked boxes techniques as a way of obtaining consent; how much information is needed before consent is sufficiently informed; questions of specificity, purpose limitation, proportionality, or knowledge of what someone is consenting; free choice, proper understanding of complex matters, power imbalance between Data Controllers and Data Subjects, and non-negotiable terms and conditions; practical aspects of revocability; etc. Legal uncertainty as to the scope and meaning of consent in data processing has not only led to divergent approaches in the EU jurisdictions but has also created controversy as to which practices digital providers should follow to comply with EU data protection law. Consent is again a core tenet of the GDPR, which reinforces its concept of providing for new, stricter conditions. As before, it must be 'freely given, specific, informed and unambiguous'.[67] However, the law now mandates 'affirmative' consent, requiring the Data Subject to signal agreement by 'a statement or a clear affirmative action'.[68] At the same time, it continues to distinguish between 'explicit' consent if the data in question is sensitive (i.e., the data related to any of the categories listed as sensitive by Article 9(1) GDPR, such as physical or mental health data, racial or ethnic origin, and so on) and 'unambiguous' consent for data considered of non-sensitive nature, i.e., all the other personal data.[69] The issue of what standard of consent should apply under the GDPR was the subject matter of intense debates and negotiations at the lengthy proposal stage of the GDPR. The legislative history of the GDPR demonstrates that the final drafting was intentional in maintaining different qualifiers of consent and making the explicit distinction between 'unambiguous' and 'explicit' consent depending on the ordinary or sensitive nature of the data to be processed. To the extent that the GDPR makes clear that 'explicit' and 'unambiguous' consent is not the same, the boundaries of what is 'unambiguous' remain unclear, with the additional complication that the law now states that it must be given by an 'affirmative action'. For example, it is unclear to what extent implied consent remains possible. While the GDPR provides that 'silence, pre-ticked boxes or inactivity should not (...) constitute consent',[70] it also states that consent can be given through 'another statement or conduct which clearly indicates in this context the Data Subject's acceptance of the proposed processing of his or her personal data'.[71] The

67. Article 4(11) GDPR.
68. *Ibid.*
69. Combined disposition of Articles 4(11) and 6 GDPR.
70. Recital 32 GDPR.
71. *Ibid.*

conditions of consent under the express provision of the GDPR require that the Controller must be able to demonstrate that the Data Subject has consented to the processing. If the Data Subject's consent is given in the context of a written declaration which also concerns other matters, the request for consent shall be presented in a manner which is clearly distinguishable from the other matters, in an intelligible and easily accessible form, using clear and plain language. Any part of such a declaration which infringes said requirement is not binding. As a unilateral act, it remains firm that Data Subjects have the right to withdraw their consent at any time. Clearly, the withdrawal of consent does not affect the lawfulness of processing based on consent before its withdrawal. Prior notice by Controllers is necessary for obtaining consent. For Data Subjects, the withdrawal of consent must be as easy as the provision of consent. In the assessment of the freely given provision of consent, an utmost account will be taken of whether the performance of a contract or the provision of a service is conditional on consent to the processing of personal data that is not necessary for their performance.[72] What is clear, therefore, is that consent must rely on transparency and an 'affirmative action' (whether explicitly given or inferred through conduct), as well as a subsequent right of withdrawal (i.e., opt-out). Nevertheless, the distinction between 'explicit' and 'unambiguous' remains relevant in practice as long as different models of consent translate into very different engineered solutions within products and services, especially in the digital domain. In the 'explicit' consent model, an 'opt-in tick box' or declaratory consent statement will be clearly necessary. However, in the 'unambiguous' consent model that dominates commercial services, a prominent notice together with an 'affirmative action' may suffice to obtain an implied consent without the need for an opt-in box. This can make a substantial difference in terms of the interfaces presented to users and the way in which they interact with the products or services in question, including consenting to data sharing with third parties. Ultimately, this makes a difference as to the real knowledge and control that users may have on the processing of their personal data, including the sharing and the uses that can be made with the data.[73] In essence, the ethos of the new law is to move towards greater accountability for Data Controllers and Processors and a uniform application across the EU. It directs towards a new model for managing data protection, one that aspires to let people themselves be in control of their data. However, this can be easily frustrating if there are no consistent practices that permit individual control. Application and enforcement are therefore critical for public awareness and trust. To what extent the

72. Article 7 GDPR.
73. Maurizio Borghi, Federico Ferretti and Stavroula Karapapa, *Online Data Processing Consent under EU Law: A Theoretical Framework and Empirical Evidence from the UK*, 21 International Journal of Law and Information Technology, 109-153 (2013) https://doi.org/10.2139/ssrn.2358921.

public is sufficiently educated on data protection is an open question. Consent is valid only if obtained from Data Subjects older than 16 years. Whenever the personal data refers to a Data Subject below the age of 16, the processing is lawful only if and to the extent that consent is given or authorised by the holder of parental responsibility over the child. Member States may provide by law for a lower age as long as such lower age is not below 13 years.[74]

(b) Contractual necessity: processing is necessary for the performance of a contract to which the Data Subject is party or in order to take steps at the request of the Data Subject prior to entering into a contract.
(c) Legal compliance: processing is necessary for compliance with a legal obligation to which the Controller is subject. Member States may maintain or introduce more specific provisions to adapt the application of the rules of the GDPR with regard to processing for compliance with this point by determining more precisely specific requirements and measures for the processing. The basis for the processing must be laid down by union law or Member State law to which the Controller is subject.
(d) Vital interests: processing is necessary in order to protect the vital interests of the Data Subject or of another natural person.
(e) Public interest: processing is necessary for the performance of a task carried out in the public interest or in the exercise of official authority vested in the Controller. Member States may maintain or introduce more specific provisions to adapt the application of the rules of the GDPR with regard to processing for compliance with this point by determining more precisely specific requirements and measures for the processing. The basis for the processing must be laid down by union law or Member State law to which the Controller is subject.
(f) Legitimate interest of Data Controllers or third parties: processing is necessary for the purposes of the legitimate interests pursued by the Controller or by a Third Party, except where such interests are overridden by the interests or fundamental rights and freedoms of the Data Subject which require protection of personal data, in particular where the Data Subject is a child (this point does not apply to processing carried out by public authorities in the performance of their tasks). The CJEU had already clarified under the Data Protection Directive the meaning of 'processing that is done in the Data Controller's legitimate interests' as a ground for processing personal data in *ASNEF*, where it held that it must be interpreted as precluding national rules which, in the absence of the Data Subject's consent, and in order to allow such processing of that Data Subject's personal data as is necessary to pursue a legitimate interest of the Data Controller or of the Third Party or parties to whom those data are disclosed, require not only that the fundamental rights and freedoms of the Data Subject be respected but also that the data should appear in public

74. Article 8 GDPR.

> sources, thereby excluding, in a categorical and generalised way, any processing of data not appearing in such sources.[75]

Where the processing is not based on the Data Subject's consent or on a Union or Member State law which constitutes a necessary and proportionate measure, the Controller must take into account any link between the purposes for which the personal data have been collected and the purposes of the intended further processing, the context in which the personal data have been collected, the nature of the personal data, the possible consequences of the intended further processing for Data Subjects, and the existence of appropriate safeguards, which may include encryption or pseudonymisation.[76] In sum, the processing of personal data for purposes other than those for which the personal data were initially collected should be allowed only where the processing is compatible with the purposes for which the personal data were initially collected. In such a case, no legal basis separate from that which allowed the collection of personal data is required. Further processing for archiving purposes in the public interest, scientific or historical research purposes or statistical purposes should be considered to be compatible with lawful processing operations.[77]

Article 9 GDPR prohibits the processing of special categories of personal data. The special categories of personal data are personal data revealing racial or ethnic origin, origin, political opinions, religious or philosophical beliefs, trade-union membership, and the processing of data concerning health or sex life. The processing of these data is permitted only if the Data Subjects have given their 'explicit consent'.[78]

The other grounds for legitimately processing such data are where:

- the processing is necessary for the purposes of carrying out the obligations and exercising specific rights of the Controller or of the Data Subject in the field of employment and social security and social protection law in so far as it is authorised by EU or national law, or a collective agreement pursuant to national law providing for appropriate safeguards;
- the processing is necessary to protect the vital interests of the Data Subject or of another person where the Data Subject is physically or legally incapable of giving consent;
- the processing is carried out in the course of legitimate activities with appropriate safeguards by a foundation, association or any other not-for-profit body with a political, philosophical, religious or trade union aim. This is on condition that the processing relates solely to the members or to former members of the body or to persons who have regular contact with it in connection with its purposes and that the personal data are not disclosed outside that body without the (explicit) consent of the Data Subjects;

75. Joined Cases C-468/10 and C-469/10, *Asociación Nacional de Establecimientos Financieros de Crédito (ASNEF)* and *Federación de Comercio Electrónico y Marketing Directo (FECEMD) v. Administración del Estado*, ECLI:EU:C:2011:777.
76. Article 6(4) GDPR.
77. Recital 50 GDPR.
78. Article 9(2)(a) GDPR.

- the processing relates to personal data which are manifestly made public by the Data Subject;
- the processing is necessary for the establishment, exercise or defence of legal claims or whenever courts are acting in their judicial capacity;
- the processing is necessary for reasons of substantial public interest on the basis of EU or national law, which must be proportionate to the aim pursued;
- the processing is necessary for the purposes of preventive or occupational medicine, for the assessment of the working capacity of the employee, medical diagnosis, the provision of health or social care or treatment or the management of health or social care systems and services on the basis of EU or national law, or pursuant to contract with a health professional;
- the processing is necessary for reasons of public interest in the area of public health, such as protecting against serious cross-border threats to health or ensuring high standards of quality and safety of healthcare and of medicinal products or medical devices on the basis of EU or national law;
- the processing is necessary for archiving purposes in the public interest, scientific or historical research purposes or statistical purposes.[79]

Any processing of personal data relating to criminal convictions, offences, or related security measures must be carried out only under the control of official authority or when the processing is authorised by EU or national law. Any register of criminal convictions must be kept only under the control of official authority.[80]

1.4.4 Rights of Data Subjects

1.4.4.1 Transparency

Controllers must provide information to individuals about the processing of their data in a concise, transparent, intelligible and easily accessible form, using clear and plain language. The information must be provided in writing or by electronic means. When requested by the Data Subject, the information may be provided orally, provided that the identity of the Data Subject is proven by other means.[81] The Controller must act without undue delay and in any event within one month of receipt of the request. That period may be extended by two further months where necessary, considering the complexity and number of the requests. In such a case, the Controller must inform the Data Subject of the extension within one month of receipt of the request, together with the reasons for the delay.

The information notice to Data Subjects must be provided free of charge. Where requests from a Data Subject are manifestly unfounded or excessive, the Controller may charge a reasonable fee considering the administrative costs, or he/she may refuse

79. Article 9(2)(b)-(j) GDPR.
80. Article 10 GDPR.
81. Article 12(1) GDPR.

to act on the request. However, the Controller bears the burden of demonstrating the manifestly unfounded or excessive character of the request.

1.4.4.2 Information Notices

At the time when personal data are collected from the Data Subject, the Controller must provide the Data Subject with all of the following information, unless the individual already has this information:

- the identity and the contact details of the Controller and, in case, of its Representative;
- the contact details of the data protection officer (DPO) of the organisation;
- the purposes of the processing of the personal data and the legal basis for the processing;
- the legitimate interests pursued by the Controller or by a Third Party, if this is the ground for processing the data;
- the recipients or categories of recipients of the personal data, if any;
- whether or not the Controller intends to transfer personal data to a third country, together with the existence or absence of an adequacy decision by the Commission (*see* below) or reference to the appropriate or suitable safeguards employed (*see* below).[82]

In addition, the Controller must provide Data Subjects with the following further information necessary to ensure fair and transparent processing:

- the period for which the personal data will be stored, or if that is not possible, the criteria used to determine that period;
- the existence of the right to request access to and rectification or erasure of personal data or to object to processing. Equally, the existence of the right to data portability;
- the existence of the right to withdraw consent at any time, without affecting the lawfulness of processing based on consent before its withdrawal;
- the right to lodge a complaint with a supervisory authority;
- whether the provision of personal data is a statutory or contractual requirement, and if the Data Subject is obliged to provide the personal data as well as the possible consequences of failure to provide such data;
- where applicable, the existence of automated decision-making, including profiling and meaningful information about the logic involved, the significance, and the envisaged consequences of such processing.[83]

Any time the Controller intends to further process the personal data for a purpose other than that for which they have been originally collected, the Controller has the

82. Article 13(1) GDPR.
83. Article 13(2) GDPR.

obligation to inform the Data Subject of that other purpose and any other relevant information.[84]

Similar obligations exist for the Data Controller whenever the personal data have not been obtained directly from the Data Subject, unless the individual already has the information or the provision of said information involves a disproportionate effort. In this case, the Data Controller must act promptly, at least within one month after obtaining the personal data. If the personal data are to be used for communication with the Data Subject, the information notice must be given at the latest at the time of the first communication to that Data Subject or, if a disclosure to another recipient is envisaged, at the latest when the personal data are first disclosed.[85]

1.4.4.3 Right of Access

Data Subjects have the right to know whether or not their personal data are being processed. They have the right of access to their personal data and the following information:

- the purposes of the processing;
- the categories of personal data concerned;
- the recipients or categories of recipient to whom the personal data have been or will be disclosed;
- the envisaged period for which the personal data will be stored or the criteria used to determine that period;
- the existence of the right to request from the Controller rectification or erasure of personal data, or restriction of processing of personal data or to object to such processing;
- the right to lodge a complaint with a supervisory authority;
- where the personal data are not collected from the Data Subject, any available information as to their source;
- the existence of automated decision-making, including profiling, as well as meaningful information about the logic involved, significance and consequences of such processing.[86]

1.4.4.4 Rectification and Erasure

According to the GDPR, Data Subjects have the right to obtain from the Controller the rectification of inaccurate personal data without undue delay. Equally, in case of incomplete data and depending on the purposes of the processing, Data Subjects have the right to obtain completion.[87]

84. Article 13(3) GDPR.
85. Under Article 14 GDPR.
86. Article 15 GDPR.
87. Article 16 GDPR.

In turn, the law provides for what has sometimes inappropriately been referred to as the 'right to be forgotten'. This right comes from the earlier jurisprudence of the CJEU in *Google Spain*.[88] Under the codified provision, Data Subjects have the right to obtain from the Controller the erasure of personal data where one of the following grounds applies:

- the personal data are no longer necessary in relation to the purposes for which they were collected;
- the Data Subject withdraws consent and there is no other legal ground for the processing;
- Data Subjects object to the processing and there are no overriding legitimate grounds for the processing;
- the personal data have been unlawfully processed;
- the personal data have to be erased for compliance with a legal obligation to which the Controller is subject;
- the personal data have been collected in relation to the offer of information society services offered to a child.[89]

The right to erasure does not apply when the processing is necessary for exercising the right of freedom of expression and information, for compliance with a legal obligation, for the performance of a task carried out in the public interest or in the exercise of official authority of the Controller, for reasons of public health, for archiving or research purposes in the public interest, or for legal claims.[90]

Data Subjects also enjoy the right to obtain restriction of processing. This right occurs where the accuracy of the personal data is contested for a period enabling the Controller to verify the accuracy of the personal data. Similarly, processing can be restricted when it is unlawful and the Data Subject opposes the erasure of the personal data and requests the restriction of their use. Other obligations entailing the restriction of data processing occur when Controllers no longer need the personal data for the purposes of the processing, but they are required for legal claims, or Data Subjects have objected to the processing pending the verification whether the legitimate grounds of the Controller override those of the Data Subject.[91]

The Controller must communicate any rectification or erasure of personal data or restriction of processing to each recipient of said data, unless this proves impossible or involves a disproportionate effort. The Controller has to inform Data Subjects about those recipients at their request.[92]

88. Google Spain, *supra* n. 65.
89. Article 17 GDPR.
90. *Ibid.*
91. Article 18 GDPR.
92. Article 19 GDPR.

1.4.4.5 Right to Data Portability and Right to Object

Data Subjects have the right to receive their personal data in a structured, commonly used and machine-readable format. To this end, they have the right to transmit those data to another Controller where the processing is based on consent or on a contract. Equally, the right to data portability applies when the processing is carried out by automated means. Data Subjects have the right to have their personal data transmitted directly from one Controller to another, where technically feasible.[93]

As seen earlier, personal data may be lawfully processed when processing is necessary for the performance of a task carried out in the public interest or in the exercise of official authority vested in the controller, or on grounds of the legitimate interests of a Data Controller or a third party. In these cases, Article 21 GDPR provides that Data Subjects should, nevertheless, be entitled to object to the processing of any personal data relating to their particular situation. Here, the Controller should demonstrate that its compelling legitimate interest overrides the interests or the fundamental rights and freedoms of the Data Subjects.

Where personal data are processed for the purposes of direct marketing, under Article 21 GDPR Data Subjects have the right to object to such processing, including profiling to the extent that it is related to such direct marketing, no matters if it relates to initial or further processing, at any time and free of charge. Such a right should be explicitly brought to the attention of the Data Subjects and presented clearly and separately from any other information. Where Data Subjects object to processing for direct marketing purposes, the personal data in question can no longer be processed for such purposes.

1.4.4.6 Automated Decision-Making and Profiling

Profiling is considered by the GDPR as 'any form of automated processing of personal data consisting of the use of personal data to evaluate certain personal aspects relating to a natural person, in particular to analyse or predict aspects concerning that natural person's performance at work, economic situation, health, personal preferences, interests, reliability, behaviour, location or movements'.[94]

Data Subjects have the right not to be subject to a decision based solely on automated processing, including profiling, which may affect them significantly. Such significant automated processing can be used if it is:

- necessary for entering into, or performing, a contract between Data Subjects and a Controller;
- authorised by EU or national law; or
- based on the Data Subject's explicit consent.

93. Article 20 GDPR.
94. Article 4(4) GDPR.

In the case of automated decisions based on explicit consent or contractual fulfilment, Controllers must have in place suitable measures to safeguard Data Subjects. At a minimum, these must include a right for Data Subjects to obtain human intervention, express their point of view and contest decisions. In any event, automated decisions cannot be based on the sensitive data of Article 9(1) GDPR, unless there is explicit consent and there are suitable measures to safeguard Data Subjects.

Differently from the Data Protection Directive, the GDPR no longer states that the above Data Subjects' rights are not necessary if the effect of the decision is to grant the individual's request.

1.4.5 Data Governance Obligations

The GDPR places accountability obligations on Controllers and Processors to demonstrate compliance with the GDPR. Some elements that must be demonstrated are explicit but others are implied, e.g., the implementation of appropriate governance models so that data protection receives the due level of attention by Controllers.

Generally, considering the nature, scope, context, purposes and risks of processing, Controllers have the obligation to implement appropriate technical and organisational measures to be reviewed and kept up-to-date to demonstrate that processing complies with the GDPR. For example, these measures include the implementation of appropriate data protection policies or adherence to approved codes of conduct ex Article 40 GDPR or approved certification mechanisms ex Article 42 GDPR.

The GDPR also provides for specific obligations. The key ones follow.

1.4.5.1 Data Protection by Design and by Default

The Controller has to adopt internal policies and implement technical and organisational measures to ensure the respect of the GDPR principles by design or by default. These include:

- pseudonymisation, systems designed to implement data minimisation, the use of cryptographic procedures for the protection against unauthorised or unlawful external or internal processing;
- measures which provide that only personal data which is necessary for each specific purpose of the processing is processed (in particular in relation to the amount of data collected, the extent of its processing, the period of its storage and its accessibility);
- measures to prevent accessibility to more individuals than necessary for the purpose, using applications or processes which allow them to implement such controls and, where available, have been certified by a body accredited by a Supervisory Authority under Article 42 GDPR.[95]

95. Article 25 GDPR.

1.4.5.2 *Data Protection Impact Assessments*

A Data Protection Impact Assessments (DPIA) is an assessment to identify and minimise the risks of non-compliance formalised in Article 35 GDPR.

Controllers must undertake DPIA where there is a high-risk processing, in particular using new technologies.

The GDPR gives some examples of where a DPIA is required (e.g., in the event of a systematic monitoring of a publicly accessible area, in the context of profiling on which decisions affect individuals, or processing on a large scale of sensitive data). It also contemplates Supervisory Authorities publishing further guidance and examples of when a DPIA should be necessary or else.

The essential elements that a DPIA must contain are:

- a systematic description of the envisaged processing operations and the purposes of the processing, including the legitimate interest pursued by the Controller (if any);
- an assessment of the necessity and proportionality of the processing operations in relation to the purposes;
- an assessment of the risks for Data Subjects; and
- the measures envisaged to address the identified risks.

If a DPIA indicates that processing results in a high level of risk, in the absence of measures taken to mitigate the risk, Controllers must consult the Supervisory Authority prior to the processing.[96]

1.4.5.3 *Data Protection Officer*

Generally, Controllers and Processors are free to appoint a DPO. However, they are under the obligation to do so if they are either public authorities (except for courts acting in their judicial capacity) or organisations whose core activities require regular and systemic monitoring of Data Subjects on a large scale or a large-scale processing of sensitive data. National or local law may also demand a specific obligation to appoint a DPO.

If appointed, the DPO has to be designated on the basis of professional expertise in data protection law and practices. However, if a DPO is not mandatory or not appointed voluntarily, organisations may choose to delegate staff members or consultants to carry out similar tasks, with the foresight to avoid calling them DPOs in order to avoid confusion.[97]

Controller and Processors must ensure that DPOs do not receive any instructions regarding the exercise of their tasks.

96. Article 35 GDPR.
97. Article 37 GDPR.

By express disposition, DPOs have at least the following tasks:

- to inform and advise Controllers or Processors and their employees of their obligations;
- to monitor compliance with the GDPR and with the policies of the Controller or Processor in relation to the protection of personal data, including the assignment of responsibilities, awareness-raising and training of staff involved in processing operations, and the related audits;
- to provide advice on the DPIA and monitor its performance;
- to cooperate with Supervisory Authorities;
- to act as the contact point for Supervisory Authorities.[98]

In short, in practical terms, organisations should:

- consider whether or not they have to appoint a DPO and, if not, whether they still wish to do so;
- if they have more than one establishment, consider whether a single DPO would be easily accessible from each establishment and would therefore be able to perform his/her tasks or whether more than one DPO is required;
- ensure that the DPO reports to the highest management level and is involved in a timely manner in all issues which relate to the protection of personal data;
- if the DPO performs other tasks and duties, consider if the DPO does not become subject to a conflict of interest;
- consider how to support the DPO with the necessary human and budgetary resources;
- publish the contact details of the DPO and make sure that the Supervisory Authorities can access him or her.

1.4.6 Personal Data Breaches and Notification

A personal data breach is an incident defined as a breach of security leading to the accidental or unlawful destruction, loss, alteration, or unauthorised disclosure of, or access to, personal data transmitted, stored, or otherwise processed.[99]

All personal data breaches have to be reported.

The law prescribes that Processors must notify Controllers without undue delay after becoming aware of a personal data breach. In this respect, the GDPR does not provide for exemptions.

In turn, Controllers have to report, not later than seventy-two hours after having become aware of it, the personal data breach to the competent Supervisory Authority, unless the breach is unlikely to result in a risk to the rights and freedoms of individuals. In case the notification of a breach to the supervisory authority is not made within seventy-two hours, it has to be accompanied by reasons for the delay.

98. Article 39 GDPR.
99. Article 4(12) GDPR.

The notification to the competent Supervisory Authority must contain at least the following elements:

- a description of the nature of the personal data breach, as well as the categories and approximate number of Data Subjects concerned and the categories and approximate number of personal data records concerned;
- a communication of the name and contact details of the DPO or other contact point where more information can be obtained;
- a description of the likely consequences of the personal data breach;
- a description of the measures taken by the Controller to address the personal data breach, including measures to mitigate its possible adverse effects; if such measures have not been taken at the time of the notification, the Controller must indicate the proposed to be taken.[100]

If Controllers have not yet done so, they are under the obligation to communicate in clear and plain language the personal data breach to the Data Subjects involved. This must occur without undue delay.[101]

By contrast, the communication to Data Subjects is not required if:

- the concerned Controller had implemented the appropriate technical and organisational protection measures (in particular, those that render the personal data unintelligible, such as encryption);
- the concerned Controller has taken subsequent measures which ensure that risks are no longer likely to materialise;
- it would involve disproportionate efforts. In this event, the concerned Controller has to issue a public communication or similar measure informing Data Subjects in an equally effective manner.[102]

Finally, the GDPR imposes stringent documentation requirements on the affected Controllers: they must document all breaches, comprising the facts relating to the breach, its effects and the remedial action taken in order to enable Supervisory Authorities to verify compliance with their obligations above.

Failure to meet the above requirements exposes Controllers to an administrative fine of up to EUR 10,000,000, or in the case of an undertaking of up to 2% of the total worldwide annual turnover of the preceding financial year, whichever is higher.[103]

1.4.7 Codes of Conduct and Certification

The GDPR makes provision for the approval of codes of conduct by way of semi self-regulation, with the goal of adapting its legal tools to specific features of various sectors, as well as the needs of micro, small and medium-sized enterprises. Likewise,

100. Article 33 GDPR.
101. Article 34 GDPR.
102. *Ibid.*
103. Article 83(4) GDPR.

it provides for accreditation of certifications, seals and marks to help Controllers and Processors demonstrate compliance and best practices.

Associations and other bodies representing categories of Controllers or Processors are entitled to prepare, amend or extend codes of conduct for the purpose of specifying the application of the law, specifically as regards:

- fair and transparent processing;
- the legitimate interests pursued by Controllers in specific contexts;
- the collection of personal data;
- the pseudonymisation of personal data;
- the information provided to the public and to Data Subjects;
- the exercise of the rights of Data Subjects;
- the information provided to children and how the consent of the holders of parental responsibility over children is to be obtained;
- the technical and organisational measures and procedures regarding data protection by design and by default, as well as those to ensure security of processing;
- the notification of personal data breaches to supervisory authorities and the communication of data breaches to Data Subjects;
- the transfer of personal data to third countries;
- out-of-court proceedings and other dispute resolution procedures for resolving disputes with regard to processing.[104]

Codes of conduct need the approval of the relevant Supervisory Authority. Where the code of conduct concerned does not relate to processing activities in several Member States, the said Supervisory Authority will register and publish the code. By contrast, if a code of conduct relates to processing activities in several Member States, the competent Supervisory Authority will have to submit it to a Board composed of the supervisory authorities of the other Member States. This Board will then provide an opinion on whether the code of conduct complies with the GDPR and it will submit it to the European Commission. In turn, the Commission will decide whether the approved code of conduct has general validity within the EU or else.[105]

Monitoring of compliance with codes of conduct will be carried out only by bodies accredited by the competent Supervisory Authority.

Finally, the establishment of data protection certification mechanisms and data protection seals and marks are expressly encouraged. Certification remains voluntary but it is important for the purpose of demonstrating compliance with the law or the existence of appropriate safeguards by Controllers and Processors. In any event, obtaining a certification does not reduce the responsibility of the Controller or the Processor.[106]

104. Article 40 GDPR.
105. Article 41 GDPR.
106. Article 42 GDPR.

1.4.8 Transfer of Personal Data to Third Countries

1.4.8.1 Transfers Subject to Adequacy of the Third County

Transfers of personal data outside the EEA continue to be restricted. Articles 44-50 GDPR deal with this situation. These provisions apply also for onward transfers of personal data from a third country or an international organisation to another third country or to another international organisation. As before, transfers to third countries may take place only if the third country ensures an adequate level of protection for personal data. The 'adequacy' of a third country is a decision taken by the European Commission. When the third country in question is considered 'adequate', the transfer does not require any specific authorisation.

The criteria that the Commission follows for assessing the 'adequacy' of the level of protection provided by a third country are:

- the existence of the rule of law, respect for human rights and fundamental freedoms, relevant legislation, case law, and effective and enforceable Data Subject rights (including administrative and judicial redress);
- the existence and effective functioning of one or more independent supervisory authorities in the third country, with responsibility for ensuring and enforcing compliance with the data protection rules; and
- the international commitments the third country or international organisation concerned has entered into, or other obligations arising from legally binding relevant conventions or instruments, as well as from its participation in multilateral or regional systems.[107]

1.4.8.2 Transfers Subject to Appropriate Safeguards

In the absence of an 'adequacy' decision of the European Commission, Controllers or Processors may transfer personal data to a third country or an international organisation only if they have provided appropriate safeguards. In addition, there must exist enforceable Data Subject rights and effective legal remedies for Data Subjects.

The necessary, appropriate safeguards above may be provided, without requiring any specific authorisation from a Supervisory Authority, by:

- a legally binding and enforceable instrument between public authorities or bodies;
- binding corporate rules;
- standard data protection clauses adopted by the European Commission;
- standard data protection clauses adopted by a Supervisory Authority and approved by the European Commission;
- an approved code of conduct alongside binding and enforceable commitments of Controllers or Processors in the third country concerned; or

107. Articles 44-45 GDPR.

- an approved certification mechanism together with binding and enforceable commitments of Controllers or Processors in the third country concerned.

Provided a competent Supervisory Authority has given specific authorisation, appropriate safeguards can be contractual clauses between Controllers or Processors and Controllers or Processors in the third country concerned. Likewise, the GDPR considers appropriate safeguards provisions to be inserted into administrative arrangements between public authorities or bodies which include enforceable and effective Data Subject rights.[108]

1.4.8.3 Binding Corporate Rules

Binding corporate rules are personal data protection policies adhered to by a Controller or Processor established on the territory of a Member State. These policies are in place precisely for transfers of personal data to a Controller or Processor in one or more third countries within a group of undertakings or group of enterprises engaged in a joint economic activity. The use of binding corporate rules is another accepted appropriate safeguard which requires prior approval by the competent Supervisory Authority.

Such an approval is granted provided that they:

- are legally binding and apply to every member of the group of undertakings or group of enterprises engaged in a joint economic activity (including their employees);
- expressly confer enforceable rights on Data Subjects; and
- specify at least the following: the structure and contact details of the group of undertakings, or group of enterprises engaged in a joint economic activity and of each of its members; the data transfers, categories of personal data, type of processing and purposes, type of Data Subjects affected, and identification of the third country or countries concerned; their legally binding nature, both internally and externally; the application of the general data protection principles of the GDPR (purpose limitation, data minimisation, limited storage periods, data quality, data protection by design and by default, legal basis for processing, processing of special categories of personal data, measures to ensure data security, and the requirements in respect of onward transfers); the rights of Data Subjects and the means to exercise those rights (including the right not to be subject to decisions based solely on automated processing, profiling, the right to lodge a complaint with a competent supervisory authority and before the competent courts of the Member States, to obtain redress and compensation for a breach of the binding corporate rules); the acceptance by Controllers or Processors established on the territory of a Member State of liability for any breaches of the binding corporate rules by any member not established in the EU (in that case, Controllers or Processors are exempt from liability, in whole or in part, only if they prove that the member concerned is

108. Article 46 GDPR.

not responsible for the event giving rise to the damage); how the information on the binding corporate rules is provided to Data Subjects; the tasks of any designated DPO; the complaint procedures; the mechanisms within the group of undertakings, or group of enterprises engaged in a joint economic activity, for ensuring the verification of compliance with the binding corporate rules (e.g., data protection audits and methods for ensuring corrective actions to protect the rights of the Data Subject); the mechanisms for reporting and recording changes to the rules and reporting those changes to Supervisory Authorities; the cooperation mechanism with the Supervisory Authority to ensure compliance by any member of the group of undertakings, or group of enterprises engaged in a joint economic activity (in particular, by making available to the supervisory authority the results of verifications of the measures of compliance with the binding corporate rules); the mechanisms for reporting to the competent Supervisory Authority any legal requirements to which a member of the group of undertakings, or group of enterprises engaged in a joint economic activity is subject in a third country and which are likely to have a substantial adverse effect on the guarantees provided by the binding corporate rules; and the appropriate data protection training given to personnel.[109]

Finally, the GDPR makes it clear that it is not lawful to transfer personal data outside the EEA in response to a legal requirement from a third country, unless the requirement is based on an international agreement or one of the other grounds for transfer applies.[110]

In the absence of an adequacy decision by the European Commission or of appropriate safeguards (including binding corporate rules), data transfers to third countries can still occur provided that:

- the Data Subject has explicitly consented to the proposed transfer after having been properly informed of the absence of an adequacy decision and appropriate safeguards;
- the transfer is necessary for the performance of a contract;
- the transfer is necessary for the conclusion or performance of a contract concluded between a Controller and a Third Party in the interest of the concerned Data Subject;
- the transfer is necessary for important reasons of public interest recognised in the EU or in the national law to which the Controller is subject;
- the transfer is necessary for the establishment, exercise or defence of legal claims;
- the transfer is necessary in order to protect the vital interests of the Data Subject or of other persons in those occasions where the Data Subject is physically or legally incapable of giving proper consent;

109. Article 47 GDPR.
110. Article 48 GDPR.

- the transfer is made from a register which according to EU or national law is intended to provide information to the public and is open to consultation either by the public in general or by any person who can demonstrate a legitimate interest. This condition may apply only to the extent that the conditions laid down by EU or Member State law for consultation are fulfilled in the particular case.[111]

Moreover, if none of the above derogations apply, a transfer to a third country is still possible if the transfer is not repetitive, it concerns only a limited number of Data Subjects, it is necessary for the purposes of compelling legitimate interests pursued by the Controller, and the Controller has assessed all the circumstances surrounding the transfer putting in place suitable safeguards vis-à-vis the risks. In this circumstance, moreover, the Controller must inform the competent Supervisory Authority and the concerned Data Subjects of the transfer and the compelling legitimate interests pursued.[112]

1.4.9 Supervisory Authorities and the European Data Protection Board

Supervision and enforcement have been significantly improved by the GDPR. Directive 95/46/EC provided that each Member State had in place a National Authority responsible in their jurisdiction for monitoring and enforcing compliance with the law. However, Member States implemented in different ways the measures to ensure the full implementation of the Directive. National Authorities were empowered to conduct investigations, engage in legal proceedings, and intervene in the processing of personal data. This decentralised governance of data protection has led to divergent or competing claims regarding the interpretation, application and enforcement of the law. For example, only some Member States had opted for fines that could be imposed by the relevant National Authority, while others had left pecuniary measures exclusively to the private law sphere between Data Subjects and Controllers via the national courts. Such a decentralised governance structure led to regulatory arbitrage and jeopardised the objectives of the EU data protection regime, especially the effective protection of individual rights.

The GDPR changes it all. A 'Supervisory Authority concerned' is defined as the authority concerned with the processing of personal data for the following reasons:

- the Controller or Processor is established on the territory of the Member State of that Supervisory Authority;
- Data Subjects residing in the Member State of that Supervisory Authority are substantially affected or likely to be substantially affected by the processing; or
- a complaint has been lodged with that Supervisory Authority.[113]

111. Article 49 GDPR.
112. *Ibid.*
113. Article 4(22) GDPR.

Supervisory Authorities are still national bodies responsible for monitoring and enforcing compliance with the law in their Member State, but they have the same sanctioning powers and enforcement actions for any breach of the GDPR. The GDPR does not limit or reduce the liability of Data Controllers towards Data Subjects, but instead, it provides Supervisory Authorities with greater enforcement powers to incentivise compliance. For the first time, it grants them the power to impose standardised significant sanctions up to the same amounts, representing a major innovation in many jurisdictions either in terms of competence or size of the sum.[114] It sets out details on the types of breaches for which the higher and lower caps will be available, the higher cap being reserved for more serious areas of concern such as, for example, breaches in respect of consent.[115]

To make sure that the law will be applied uniformly in the EU, the GDPR provides that Supervisory Authorities will have to contribute to the consistent and uniform application throughout the EU and cooperate with each other and with the European Commission.[116] When the data processing occurs at a cross-border level or a Data Controller is established in more than one Member State, a Lead Supervisory Authority has to be designated to exercise not only its powers in the territory of its national jurisdiction but must also be competent for the supervision and enforcement of such a processing in all Member States.[117] Moreover, in case of disagreement between national Supervisory Authorities regarding certain practices, a newly established centralised official agency of the EU composed of the heads of all national Supervisory Authorities (the European Data Protection Board (EDPB), which replaces the Article 29 Working Party established by Directive 95/46/EC) will step in to activate a 'consistency mechanism' to ensure uniform application and consistent enforcement.[118] For this purpose, the European Commission may adopt specific additional regulations on the provisions of the GDPR to provide further clarity, detail, or interpretation of the rights or obligations it provides.[119]

In so establishing, the GDPR not only encourages cooperation between national Supervisory Authorities but also promotes uniformity of enforcement across the EU on practices or towards specific Data Controllers. Supervisory Authorities will have to strengthen the safety net for data protection, build capacity, and coordinate enforcement to achieve uniformity.

1.4.10 Remedies and Liabilities

Data Subjects have the right to lodge a complaint with a suitable Supervisory Authority. This may be a Supervisory Authority in the Member State of the Data Subject's habitual residence, place of work or place of the alleged infringement. The right in question is

114. Article 83 GDPR and Recitals 130, 148 and 150 GDPR.
115. Article 83(5) GDPR. Depending on the breach, such maximum fines can be up to 2% or 4% of an 'undertaking's' total worldwide annual turnover in the previous year ex Article 85(6) GDPR.
116. Article 51(2) GDPR.
117. Article 56 GDPR.
118. Articles 60, 63, and 68-76 GDPR.
119. Articles 92-93 GDPR.

to obtain an effective judicial remedy against a legally binding decision of such Supervisory Authority. The same applies in case the Supervisory Authority fails to handle a complaint or does not inform the Data Subject within three months of the progress or outcome of the complaint. This right of effective judicial remedy occurs without prejudice to any other administrative or judicial remedy at the disposal of Data Subjects.[120]

Equally, without prejudice to any available administrative or non-judicial remedy (including the right to lodge a complaint with a Supervisory Authority as above), Data Subjects have the right to an effective judicial remedy against Controllers or Processors before the courts of the Member State where the latter have an establishment. Alternatively, legal proceedings may be brought before the courts of the Member State where the Data Subject has the habitual residence, unless the Controllers or Processors taken to court are a public authority of a Member State acting in the exercise of its public powers.[121]

Whoever has suffered material or non-material damages as a result of an infringement of the GDPR has the right to receive compensation from the Controller or Processor concerned. However, Processors are liable for the damage caused only where they have not complied with the obligations of the GDPR specifically directed to them. Likewise, they are responsible if they have acted outside or contrary to lawful instructions given by Controllers. In all other cases, Controllers remain liable for the processing carried out by Processors. By contrast, Controllers or Processors remain exempt from liability if they prove that they are not in any way responsible for the event giving rise to the damage.[122]

In those cases where more than one Controller or Processor is involved in the same processing and they are responsible for damages, each one of them is liable for the entire damage. Thus, in the situation where a Controller or Processor has paid full compensation to Data Subjects, that Controller or Processor is entitled to claim back the part of the compensation corresponding to their part of responsibility from the other Controllers or Processors.[123]

As noted, the GDPR applies to Data Subjects – natural persons – in order to protect the fundamental right to the protection of personal data. In the first instance, therefore, the beneficiaries of the guarantees provided for by the GDPR are natural persons and not a company's competitors. Whereas the breach of the GDPR has been so far only considered a matter of data protection or privacy that could lead to substantial fines or the award of damages to Data Subjects, but had no direct effect in the market, it has now become a crucial element for the competitiveness and survival of companies in the market. A company can now sue its competitors claiming that the latter are able to gain unfair business advantages by not fulfilling their GDPR

120. Article 77 GDPR.
121. Article 79 GDPR.
122. Article 82 GDPR.
123. *Ibid.*

obligations. This multiple wrongfulness character of GDPR violations has been recognised by the CJEU decision in *Lindenapotheke*.[124]

The ruling establishes that obtaining economic advantages by violating the GDPR is an act of unfair competition. The GDPR in fact does not preclude the possibility of taking legal action against a competitor for its violations. On the contrary, the CJEU explains that this undoubtedly contributes to strengthening the rights of Data Subjects and guaranteeing them a high level of protection.

The striking novelty of the case is the paradigm shift that this ruling represents and the additional dimension of liability for companies that process personal data. With this ruling, in fact, a data protection breach can lead to very serious consequences, such as damages in a civil lawsuit paid to competitors or even exit from the market for unfair commercial practice. These are in addition to damages to Data Subjects and/or the aforesaid administrative sanctions.

124. Case C-21/23 *ND v. DR* (Lindenapotheke) [2025] ECLI:EU:C:2024:846.

CHAPTER 2

Data Markets and Data-Related Rights

2.1 THE EMERGENCE OF DATA MARKETS

The data economy usually refers to the accumulated value of wealth generated by all forms of data exploitation. The EU strives to attain a leading role in the data economy by exploiting an expanding amount of data to create innovative products and services in the Single Market. It views digitalisation as a tool for relaunching economic growth and social welfare.

As part of the Digital Single Market Strategy,[1] the European Commission's latest policy goal is to foster the creation of a secure single market for personal and non-personal data and eventually create a single European Data Space, conceived as a "genuine single market for data (...) where personal as well as non-personal data (...) are secure and businesses also have easy access to an almost infinite amount of high-quality data,"[2] alongside the creation of multiple common sector-specific data spaces to ensure that the EU's global competitiveness and data sovereignty.

The digital expansion has placed data at the centre of major economic and social transformations. To the extent that data are the lifeblood of innovation, they have become an essential resource in economic terms. Data are no longer seen as mere outputs generated by the use of technology. Instead, they are increasingly regarded as inputs for the creation or improvement of products and services such as information services, processes, or decision-making tools.[3] Thus, the full value of data for society and the economy needs to be unlocked and a framework for the free flow and access

1. European Commission, A Digital Single Market Strategy for Europe, (Communication) COM(2015) 0192 final.
2. European Commission, A European Strategy for Data, (Communication) COM(2020) 66 final.
3. Ikujiro Nonaka, *A Dynamic Theory of Organizational Knowledge Creation*, 5 Organization Science, 14-37 (1994) https://doi.org/10.1287/orsc.5.1.14; Francesco Mezzanotte, *Access to Data: The Role of Consent and the Licensing Scheme*, in *Trading Data in the Digital Economy: Legal Concepts and Tools*, 159-187 (Sebastian Lohsse, Reiner Schulze and Dirk Staudenmayer eds, Nomos 2017).

to such data by private and public entities needs to be established. Data accessibility has the potential to stimulate innovation and increase efficiency.

To achieve its policy objectives, the EU has committed to combining fit-for-purpose cross-sectoral (horizontal) legislation and governance to ensure the free flow, access and sharing of data within the Union.[4] This legislation integrates existing data laws such as the GDPR[5] and a few others[6] to support the viability and sustainability of an alternative model for the data economy that is at once open yet fair, transparent, and accountable.[7] In addition to furnishing a legislative framework for the governance of a common data space and the reuse of public sector data, data sharing among market players has a pre-eminent role to be achieved by means of a Data Act (*see* Chapter 3).[8]

Two major problems for the achievement of policy goals are the intense concentration of data in the hands of limited large online platforms (also known as 'Big-Techs') and market imbalances in the access and (re)use of data.[9] Big-Techs raise a number of different problems, some of which have already been addressed in other legislation.[10] Of concern here is that they are large multinational corporations that dominate the digital business. Within such a vast industry, Big-Techs dominate their respective niche market, using the data to expand subsequently into other markets. Big-Techs may have very different business models, levels of maturity and financialisation, or corporate governance. They share the capacity to act as intermediary infrastructure and become gatekeepers of the indispensable facility represented by the data. They also become market gatekeepers in this way.[11] Their models build on creating, maximising, and monetising network effects and economies of scale to

4. A European Strategy for Data, *supra* n. 2.
5. Regulation (EU) 2016/679 of the European Parliament and of the Council of 27 April 2016 on the protection of natural persons with regard to the processing of personal data and on the free movement of such data, and repealing Directive 95/46/EC (General Data Protection Regulation), OJ L 119, 4.5.2016, p. 1-88.
6. *See* Regulation (EU) 2018/1807 of the European Parliament and of the Council of 14 November 2018 on a framework for the free flow of non-personal data in the European Union, OJ L 303, 28.11.2018, p. 59-68; Regulation (EU) 2019/881 of the European Parliament and of the Council of 17 April 2019 on ENISA (the European Union Agency for Cybersecurity) and on information and communications technology cybersecurity certification and repealing Regulation (EU) No. 526/2013 (Cybersecurity Act), OJ L 151, 7.6.2019, p. 15-69; Directive (EU) 2019/1024 of the European Parliament and of the Council of 20 June 2019 on open data and the re-use of public sector information (recast), OJ L 172, 26.6.2019, p. 56-83.
7. European Data Protection Supervisor, Opinion 3/2020 on the European strategy for data (16 June 2020).
8. A European Strategy for Data, *supra* n. 2.
9. *Ibid.*
10. Regulation (EU) 2022/1925 of the European Parliament and of the Council of 14 September 2022 on contestable and fair markets in the digital sector and amending Directives (EU) 2019/1937 and (EU) 2020/1828 (Digital Markets Act), OJ L 265, 12.10.2022, p. 1-66, which proposes new *ex ante* rules for gatekeeper platforms as well as a new supervisory framework at EU level to address conduct and competition harm risks.
11. The European Commission defines a gatekeepers as "a provider of core platform services," where CPSs are any online intermediation services, online search engines, online social networking services; video-sharing platform services; number-independent interpersonal communication services; operating systems; cloud computing services; advertising services, including any advertising networks, advertising exchanges and any other advertising intermediation services, provided by a provider of any of the CPSs. *See* Article 2 Digital Markets Act.

dominate the market, reduce competition and consumer welfare, and stifle innovation driven by others. Due to their distinctive features, Big-Techs have given rise to the so-called platform economy which, overall, enjoys largely unchecked power in a regulatory vacuum.[12]

The key legal aspects of datafication in the policy and market context discussed above that impact the envisaged European Data Space and data-access regime under the Data Act need to be disentangled. These aspects include proprietary data rights, data protection, and competition law. Particular attention needs to be granted to the market imbalances in the platform economy created by Big-Techs and the extent to which such organisations should be allowed to monetise data acting as gatekeepers.

The strategy for creating a single European Data Space presupposes maximum data availability. These are considered an essential component - or raw material -for the development of a competitive digital market, especially in terms of data access and (re)usability. The policy vision and debate centre around the creation of a "single market for data" and the rebalancing of market power in relation to data access and sharing.[13]

In principle, the data market makes reference to the exchange of data as products or services, starting from the extraction and further development of data.

Inevitably, however, the idea of a 'data market' prompts questions about its nature and reintroduces the long-debated issue of data ownership or titles to data, i.e., the extent of exclusive right to use, exploit, and disclose data, subject only to the rights of persons with a superior interest or legal or contractual restrictions.

One fundamental reservation is the extent to which recognition of a title in rem to data, and therefore the resultant market type, can be justified. Claims to proprietary rights are linked to commercial exploitation and the delineation of the market. Simply put, the allocation of a title in rem to data, in whatever form this may be recognised, would give rise to important consequences. These lead in turn to the question of how to strike a balance between the rights, obligations, and limits of those claiming title and a general interest in access to - and reuse of - data for the innovation and development of the digital market.

Moreover, if rights in rem are recognised and allocated, they must have limits and exceptions that serve the public interest.[14]

Therefore, defining the nature of data is key to informing public policy and establishing the legal basis for claims of title, including the very existence of a 'data market'.[15] It is also instrumental in defining the boundaries of the public interest in access to and (re)usability of data as an essential resource.[16]

12. Rodrigo Fernandez et al., *The Financialisation of Big Tech* (SOMO 2020); Anne Helmond, *The Platformization of the Web: Making Web Data Platform Ready*, 1 Social Media + Society, no page (2015).
13. *Ibid.*
14. Also argued by Teresa Scassa, *Data Ownership*, CIGI Papers No. 187 (2018).
15. *See also* Vincenzo Zeno-Zencovich, *Do 'Data Markets' Exist?*, 2 Media Laws, 22-38 (2019).
16. Josef Drexl, *Data Access and Control in the Era of Connected Devices* (Study on Behalf of the European Consumer Organisation BEUC, December 2018), available at https://www.beuc.eu/publications/beuc-x-2018-121_data_access_and_control_in_the_area_of_connected_devices.pdf.

As previous scholarship suggests, delineating the concept of data and their economic properties is a challenging exercise.[17] Yet it is a necessary one if data are to be treated as a commodity in the market.

2.2 THE NATURE AND VALUE CHAIN OF DATA

The first difficulty is one of terminology and derives from the misleading interchangeability, in everyday jargon, of terms like 'data' and 'information'. However, the distinction between the two matters for policy and legal discourse. In information science, data is conceptualised in two ways: as signals, i.e., unprocessed reinterpretable digital representations, and as measurable and discrete observations of facts or acts in a formalised manner (such that there is a clear separation between the different possible values). However they are conceptualised, data must be suitable for communication, interpretation or processing.[18] The definition of data is often supplemented with the requirement that signals be readable, generated or observable by a machine.[19] Data are often viewed as a by-product of other activities.[20] Yet they are also a resource in their own right when converted into information, that is, the number of discernible signals or data points necessary to transmit a message.[21]

Other characterisations distinguish between a syntactic level (signs and their relationship with each other) and a semantic level (the meaning of data), which leads to a distinction between the content and code layers.[22] Information is instead a broader concept than data that depends on context and usage to convey meaning.

In the end, data are most appropriately defined in relation to the other parameters in their lifecycle, which can be illustrated in sequential order: data (any representation

17. For all, *see, e.g.*, Nestor Duch-Brown, Bertin Martens and Frank Mueller-Langer, *The Economics of Ownership, Access and Trade in Digital Data*, JRC Digital Economy Working Paper 2017-01 (2017).
18. Russel Ackoff, *From Data to Wisdom*, in *Ackoff's Best*, 170-172 (Russel Ackoff ed., John Wiely and Sons 1999) defines data as "symbols that represent the properties of objects and events. Information consists of processed data, the processing directed at increasing its usefulness." Chaim Zins, *Conceptual Approaches for Defining Data, Information, and Knowledge*, 58 Journal of the Association for Information Science and Technology, 479-493 (2007) https://doi.org/10.1002/asi.20508. *See also* European Commission, Towards a Thriving Data-Driven Economy, COM(2014) 442 final. *See also* the definition of Article 2(1) Regulation (EU) 2022/868 of the European Parliament and of the Council of 30 May 2022 on European data governance and amending Regulation (EU) 2018/1724 (Data Governance Act), OJ L 152, 3.6.2022, p. 1-44.
19. Herbert Zech, *Data as a Tradable Commodity* in *European Contract Law and the Digital Single Market*, 51-80 (Alberto De Franceschi ed., Intersentia 2017).
20. Wolfgang Kerber, *A New (Intellectual) Property Right for Non-Personal Data? An Economic Analysis*, 11 Gewerblicher Rechtsschutz und Urheberrecht, Internationaler Teil (GRUR Int), 989-999 (2016).
21. Max Boisot and Agustì Canals, *Data, Information and Knowledge: Have We Got It Right?*, 14 Journal of Evolutionary Economics, 43-67 (2004) https://doi.org/10.1007/s00191-003-0181-9; Ronaldo Vigo, *Complexity over Uncertainty in Generalized Representational Information Theory (GRIT): A Structure-Sensitive General Theory of Information*, 4 Information, 1-30 (2013) https://doi.org/10.3390/info4010001; Robert Losee, *A Discipline Independent Definition of Information*, 48 American Society for Information Science, 254-269 (1997) https://doi.org/10.1002/(sici)1097-4571(199703)48:3 < 254::aid-asi6 > 3.0.co;2-w.
22. Zech, *supra* n. 19.

of something in digital form) are the raw material for information, information (structured data with a discernible meaning) is the raw material for knowledge, and knowledge (information whose validity has been established through tests of proof or intellectual virtue) is the raw material for wisdom (the ability to use knowledge to achieve and establish desired goals).[23]

This multichotomy implies a linear flow and hierarchy that do not remain on a purely theoretical level but have important economic and legal consequences.

From an economic perspective, data represent a primary material. A sequential process of transformation adds value to the data, especially when combined with the resourcefulness, capability and experience of the agents who utilise the outcomes at each stage.[24] This is the value extraction process. The extensive availability of large volumes of diverse datasets from various unrelated sources (big data) is decisive in extracting maximum value.[25] The value of data grows progressively through the information, knowledge and wisdom conveyed by the data on the semantic level.[26]

In practical terms, the value chain distinguishes between data production, processing, collection, organisation and analysis and the achievement of set goals, including innovations based on the insights gained in the previous steps. As a raw material, data are an infinite resource generated at an insignificant cost. Moreover, they are immaterial and non-consumable (non-rival), which means usage does not exhaust the supply and they may be used simultaneously by more than one agent. These features are a novelty in economic theory, which considers limited or restricted resources, as well as production costs.[27]

Consequently, the economic value of data in their essential form is trivial and irrelevant.[28]

The paradox of the debate over titles to data is precisely that where there is no value, one would conclude that ownership or other rights of economic exploitation are

23. Paul Bierly, Eric Kessler and Edward Christensen, *Organisational Learning, Knowledge and Wisdom*, 13 Journal of Organisational Change Management, 595-618 (2000) https://doi.org/10.1108/09534810010378605; Yochai Benkler, *From Consumers to Users: Shifting the Deeper Structures of Regulation Toward Sustainable Commons and User Access*, 52 Federal Communications Law Journal, 561-579 (2000). According to Rob Kitchin, *The Data Revolution: Big Data, Open Data, Data Infrastructure and Their Consequences*, 1 (Sage 2014), data are not neutral. They reflect choices about which data to collect or exclude and cannot exist independently of the ideas, instruments, practices, contexts and knowledges used to generate, process and analyse them.
24. Antti Aine, Tom Bjorkroth and Aki Koponen, *Horizontal Information Exchange and Innovation in the Platform Economy: A Need to Rethink?*, 15 European Competition Journal, 347-371 (2019) https://doi.org/10.1080/17441056.2019.1687187.
25. Kitchin, *supra* n. 23.
26. Zech, *supra* n. 19; Drexl, *supra* n. 16.
27. Jean-Sylvestre Bergé, Stephane Grumbach and Vincenzo Zeno-Zenchovic, *The 'Datasphere', Data Flows Beyond Control, and the Challenges for Law and Governance*, 5 European Journal of Comparative Law, 144-178 (2018) https://doi.org/10.1163/22134514-00502001.
28. *See* Case AT.39740 *Google Search (Shopping)*, Commission Decision relating to proceedings under Article 102 of the Treaty on the Functioning of the European Union and Article 54 of the Agreement on the European Economic Area, C(2017) 4444 final; *See also* Edouard Bruc, *Data as an Essential Facility in European Law: How to Define the 'Target' Market and Divert the Data Pipeline?*, 15 European Competition Journal, 177-224 (2019) https://doi.org/10.1080/17441056.2019.1644576.

not an issue. This deduction is reinforced by the unique nature of data as limitless and non-rivalrous, which fits uneasily with the legal concept of a title in rem. As in the case of ideas, these features are the foundations for the classification of data as public goods.[29]

If property rights are difficult to extend to data, this, in turn, creates challenges in establishing usage rights.[30] Instead, the issue arises as soon as value is provided, i.e., at the later stage when data provide information, knowledge and wisdom.

Another complication that surfaces is the contribution of multiple actors to the datafication process and the relationship between them. Different persons (natural and/or legal) may contribute to generating data through human activities or technologies (e.g., data created or observed by a sensor, search engine, or website) or may add value during the processing, observation, aggregation, storage, selection, verification and analysis stages. Data can be directly generated by the person or by that person's use of services.[31] Value may also reside in the immediacy and instant availability of data.[32]

From this perspective, the distinction between personal and non-personal data – which has thus far remained indistinct – assumes relevance. Data may be non-personal or personal in nature, where the latter are broadly defined in relation to an identified or identifiable natural person.[33]

Natural persons would intuitively assert that they own data about themselves, as these comprise personal attributes. However, individuals do not own information about themselves. Personal data do not pre-exist prior to their expression or disclosure. They are always to some extent constructed or created by more than one agent.[34] They pertain to a person yet do not belong in a proprietary sense to him/her. Those who process personal data (data controllers) have the right to process data pertaining to

29. Harold Demsetz, *Toward a Theory of Property Rights*, 57 The American Economic Review, 347-359 (1967) https://doi.org/10.1057/9780230523210_9; Priscilla Regan, *Privacy as a Common Good in the Digital World*, 5 Information, Communication and Society, 382-405 (2010) https://doi.org/10.1080/13691180210159328. *See also* Drexl, *supra* n. 16, who makes also reference to constitutional principles of freedom of information and the EU Charter of Fundamental Rights [Article 11(1)].
30. Some scholarship, forcing the established economic and legal notion of property, debates whether its concept should be flexible enough to extend to new immaterial goods and eventually allow the commodification of data. *See* Nadezhda Purtova, *The Illusion of Personal Data as No One's Property*, 7 Law, Innovation and Technology, 83-111 (2015) https://doi.org/10.1080/17579961.2015.1052646; Alberto De Franceschi and Michael Lehmann, *Data as Tradable Commodity and New Measures for Their Protection*, 1 Italian Law Journal, 51-72 (2015).
31. Inge Graef, *Market Definition and Market Power in Data: the Case of Online Platforms*, 38 World Competition, 473-505 (2015) https://doi.org/10.54648/woco2015040; Josef Drexl, *Legal Challenges of the Changing Role of Personal and Non-Personal Data in the Data Economy*, Max Planck Institute for Innovation & Competition Research Paper No. 18-23 (2018), available at https://ssrn.com/abstract=3274519.
32. Duch-Brown et al., *supra* n. 17.
33. Descriptive definition based on Article 4(1) GDPR; *see also* the earlier Article 29 Working Party, Opinion 4/2007 on the concept of personal data, (20 June 2007).
34. In Federico Ferretti, *Competition, the Consumer Interest, and Data Protection* (Springer 2014). *See also* Annette Rouvroy and Yves Poullet, *The Right to Informational Self-Determination and the Value of Self-Development: Reassessing the Importance of Privacy for Democracy*, in *Reinventing Data Protection?*, 45-76 (Serge Gutwirth et al. eds, Springer 2009).

data subjects as long as such processing is lawful, i.e., they abide by procedural rules established by law (in the EU, the GDPR – *infra*) with the objective of protecting individual citizens not against data processing per se but against unjustified collection, storage, use and dissemination of the data pertaining to them.[35] Moreover, personal data may be turned into anonymous data, but they are still data (of a non-personal nature) that remain in existence without allocation to data subjects.[36]

In the end, the value chain and the role of different stakeholders are crucial from the legal perspective. Each transformation, creation of value, and interaction of different subjects at different levels epitomises a separate legal construction and allocation of rights. For this reason, it is crucial to determine whether and at what stage data may become a commodity giving rise to transferable rights and whether legal protections should intervene.[37]

2.3 DATA-RELATED RIGHTS

The value chain determines when legal rights should be allocated, who is entitled to claim a title over the data, and how to exercise such rights.

The fluid nature of data and their unsuitability to be defined and regulated in the same way as other tangible or intangible goods has generated debates about the potential creation of a new right in rem specific to data.[38] Under existing laws, however, no data property right can exist. Nor do there seem to be legal grounds for recognising rights of economic exploitation over data per se.[39] Likewise, no EU jurisprudence satisfactorily deals with the matter.[40]

35. E.g., individuals do not own their criminal records or credit history. In Ferretti, *supra* n. 34. *See also* the discussions about individuals not owning information about themselves in Jerry Kang and Benedikt Bunter, *Privacy in Atlantis*, 18 Harvard Journal of Law and Technology, 229-267 (2004); Rouvroy and Poullet, *supra* n. 34.
36. Gintare Surblyte, *Data Mobility at the Intersection of Data, Trade Secret Protection and the Mobility of Employees in the Digital Economy*, 12 GRUR International, 1121-1129 (2016) https://doi.org/10.2139/ssrn.2752989.
37. Viktor Mayer-Schonberger and Kenneth Cukier, *Big Data: A Revolution That Will Transform How We Live, Work and Think* (John Murray 2013); Barbara Evans, *Much Ado About Data Ownership*, 25 Harvard Journal of Law and Technology, 70-130 (2011).
38. For all, *see* Zech, *supra* n. 19.
39. Zech, *supra* n. 19; Mezzanotte, *supra* n. 3; Francesco Banterle, *Data Ownership in the Data Economy: A European Dilemma*, in *EU Internet Law in the Digital Era*, 199-225 (Tatiana-Eleni Synodinou et al. eds., Springer 2020); Sjef van Erp, *Ownership of Digital Assets and the Numerus Clausus of Legal Objects*, Maastricht European Private Law Institute Working Paper No. 2017/ (2017), available at https://papers.ssrn.com/sol3/papers.cfm?abstract_id = 3046402.
40. *See* Ivan Stepanov, *Introducing a Property Right over Data in the EU: The Data Producer's Right – An Evaluation*, 34 International Review of Law, Computers & Technology, 65-86 (2020) https://doi.org/10.1080/13600869.2019.1631621. According to the author, however, although no property rights as such over data exist, when faced with gaps, some national Courts seem to adapt and in certain aspects treat data as property offering points of divergence. German Courts ruled on the proprietary aspects of data on matters of mishandling by company employees, albeit in criminal and labour law cases. The Courts concluded that for the purposes of those fields of law, data can be owned, thus exhibiting traits associated with property. In the Netherlands, the Supreme Court stated that from the perspective of criminal law data could be

Instead, rights over data usability and allocation can be constructed as a bundle of other rights. These originate from a patchwork of existing laws protecting other goods or values that affect interested parties in data use without allocating property rights. Not surprisingly, these rights shift from a sales or transfer paradigm to a licence model based on access.[41]

Access requires a subject to hold the data, which presupposes control. In the debate over data accessibility, the point is to define the precise extent of control rights and entitlements, as well as the legal mechanisms to deal with access restrictions in a framework that does not presuppose a comprehensive data regime.

The assortment of laws that assign rights and obligations over data are discussed below.

2.3.1 Personal Data Protection

Personal data protection legislation has already been extensively discussed in Chapter 1.

What needs to be reiterated here is that data protection law dictates important rights and obligations in data usability and allocation relating to an identified or identifiable natural person.

As seen, the GDPR details the conditions under which data processing is legitimate. It forces processing to be transparent, enabling data subjects to control it where the processing is not authorised by the law itself as necessary for social reasons. In short, data protection law focuses on the activities of processors and enforces their accountability, thus regulating an accepted exercise of power.[42] The law is rooted in the idea that democratic societies should not be turned into societies based on control, surveillance, actual or predictive profiling, classification, social sorting, and discrimination. It is not only a question of individual liberty, privacy, integrity and dignity but also a wider personal right aimed at fostering the social identity of individuals as citizens and consumers alike. Accordingly, the data protection regime provides legal protection to pursue the common goal of a free and democratic society where citizens develop their personalities freely and autonomously through individual, reflexive self-determination. It provides for collective deliberative decision-making about the

---

the object of theft. Finally, Luxembourgian law gives the right to reclaim ownership in data from the cloud in bankruptcy proceedings if the circumstances provide for such an opportunity (p. 73-74).

41. Aaron Perzanowski and Jason Schultz, *The End of Ownership. Personal Property in the Digital Economy* (MIT Press 2016).

42. Paul De Hert and Serge Gutwirth, *Data Protection in the Case Law of Strasbourg and Luxembourg: Constitutionalization in Action*, in *Reinventing Data Protection?*, 3-44 (Serge Gutwirth et al. eds., Springer 2009). On a critical view that data protection acts are seldom privacy laws but rather information laws, protecting data before people, *see* Simon Davis, *Re-engineering the Right to Privacy: How Privacy Has Been Transformed from a Right to a Commodity*, in *Technology and Privacy – The New Landscape*, 143-165 (Philip Agre and Marc Rotenberg eds, MIT Press 1997).

rules of social cooperation.[43] Granting individuals control over their personal data is more than a mere tool allowing them to control the persona they project in society, free from unreasonable or unjustified associations, manipulations, distortions, misrepresentations, alterations or constraints on their true identity. It is the fundamental value of humans developing their personality in a way that allows them full participation in society without having to make thoughts, beliefs, behaviours, or preferences conform to those of the majority or those dictated from above by commercial interests.[44]

The conceptual principles outlined above are reflected in the provisions of the GDPR, the scope of which is to ensure those who determine the purposes and methods of personal data processing (the 'data controllers') engage in good data management practices. The GDPR incorporates a series of general rules on the lawfulness of personal data processing.[45] Data subjects must be informed of the processing, which has to be performed for legitimate, explicit and precise purposes. Processing is limited to the necessary time frame (principles of purpose specification and data minimisation).[46] Finally, data subjects are granted the right to access their data[47] and non-absolute data portability rights.[48]

A data controller can claim a valid basis for processing only if it meets one of the exhaustive criteria established by the law. If the data controller's processing does not satisfy one of them, it is unlawful.[49]

As noted above in section 2.2, it is important to stress again that individuals do not own information about themselves. Personal data do not pre-exist prior to their expression or disclosure and they are to some extent constructed or created by more than one agent. They pertain to a person yet do not belong in a proprietary sense to him/her. In fact, it may already be clear that data controllers have the right to process data pertaining to data subjects as long as such processing is lawful, i.e., they abide by procedural rules established by the GDPR (cfr. Chapter 1).

2.3.2 Non-personal Data

From a legal point of view, in the EU, data are divided into two categories, namely personal data and non-personal data. Although the regulation of data has been traditionally associated with the protection of fundamental rights, to unleash the potential of the data economy, the EU has launched from the incipit an initiative to establish a common, single framework to support a general principle of free data movement within the EU market.

43. Federico Ferretti, *Data Protection and the Legitimate Interest of Data Controllers: Much ado About Nothing or the Winter of Rights?* 51 Common Market Law Review, 843-868 (2014) https://doi.org/10.54648/cola2014063, and the literature there cited; Rouvroy and Poullet, *supra* n. 34.
44. *Ibid.*
45. Articles 13 and 14 GDPR.
46. Article 5 GDPR.
47. Article 15 GDPR.
48. Article 20 GDPR.
49. Article 6 GDPR.

As seen, Directive 95/46/EC first, and the GDPR next, whilst protecting personal data and individuals' freedom, explicitly endorsed the free movement of such data within the EU, subject to the obligations therein contained. As far as it concerns the data that are excluded from the scope of the GDPR, i.e., non-personal data, the EU Regulation 2018/1807 provides for the free movement of such data.[50] Together, the GDPR and Regulation 2018/1807 secure a free movement principle for all types of data. In principle, in case of mixed datasets, the provisions of the GDPR guaranteeing free flow of personal data apply to the personal data part of the set, and the provisions of Regulation 2018/1807 apply to the non-personal set of data.[51]

Before the passing of Regulation 2018/1807, the circulation of non-personal data was left to contractual arrangements and sectoral or national rules. Thus, Regulation 2018/1807 recognises that the effective and efficient functioning of data processing, as well as the development of the data economy, are hindered by two types of obstacles to data mobility and to the internal market: first, data localisation requirements put in place by the Member States, and second vendor lock-in practices in the private sector.[52] To overcome these obstacles and avoid market fragmentation, it provides for a concise legal instrument with a narrow target covering few specific services, allowing for the processing of non-personal data anywhere in the EU without unjustified restrictions and prohibiting localisation requirements, unless justified on grounds of public security in compliance with the principle of proportionality.[53] Also, without specific requirements, it encourages and facilitates the development of self-regulatory codes of conduct at the Union level to improve the conditions under which professional users may switch data storage or processing providers or port data back to their IT systems.[54]

To assess data accessibility for the creation of a data market, it becomes crucial to assess what non-personal data are.

Under Article 2(1) and Article 3(1) of Regulation 2018/1807, non-personal data are defined in the negative as data other than personal data, as defined in Article 4(1) of the GDPR. In turn, under Article 4(1) GDPR, personal data are defined as "any information relating to an identified or identifiable natural person ('data subject')"[55] where an identifiable natural person is "one who can be identified, directly or indirectly, in particular by reference to an identifier such as a name, an identification number, location data, an online identifier or to one or more factors specific to the physical, physiological, genetic, mental, economic, cultural or social identity of that natural person."[56]

At the same time, the GDPR itself provides for anonymised data, which are "information which does not relate to an identified or identifiable natural person or to

50. Regulation (EU) 2018/1807, *supra* n. 6.
51. Article 2(2) Regulation 2018/1807. *See also* European Commission, Explanatory Memorandum to COM(2019) 250 – Guidance on the Regulation on a framework for the free flow of non-personal data in the EU, COM(2019) 250.
52. Recital 2, Regulation 2018/1807.
53. Article 4 Regulation 2018/1807.
54. Article 6 Regulation 2018/1807.
55. Article 4 GDPR.
56. *Ibid.*

personal data rendered anonymous in such a manner that the data subject is not or no longer identifiable."[57]

Thus, the definition of personal data in the GDPR seems to assume a complete characterisation and concept of 'personal data' and the two categories of personal and non-personal data appear to be mutually exhaustive.

However, this binary distinction between personal and non-personal data has attracted criticism as the scope of personal data has proven contingent and context-specific, making it difficult to be applied in practice and leaving doubts regarding the applicability of Regulation 2018/1807.[58] The boundaries between personal and non-personal data become unclear in dynamic contexts such as the technological realm, where the status of data may change in an instant. Indeed, to determine whether it "relates to" an individual, information has to be considered to relate to someone either in content, purpose or result, making it difficult to distinguish between data that are not likely to impact somehow on people.[59] Thus, given the indeterminate and dynamic nature of the notions of personal and non-personal data, which are dependent on all the circumstances of the case, even data remotely connected to an individual can be increasingly used in various and continuously changing circumstances to gain insights into that person, especially in the era of expanding technological capacities and big data processing.[60]

In any event, notwithstanding that in the digital domain, the scope of personal data seems to increase exponentially vis-à-vis the rare circumstances where datasets are or can be untied to personal data, Regulation 2018/1807 is limited to the aim of stimulating cross-border data processing without providing any hint regarding claims of title, access or control rights of non-personal data, leaving the issue to market forces.

2.3.3 Intellectual Property Laws

Intellectual property is the traditional form of protection of intangible assets. Its normative frameworks, including related rights, are often used to provide some form of protection for rights over data.

- Copyright Law

Copyright protects the original expression of ideas or facts, but there is no protection for ideas or facts in the abstract. What is protected is originality in the form, not in the

57. Recital 26 GDPR.
58. Inge Graef, Raphael Gellert, Nadezhda Purtova and Martin Husovec, *Feedback to the Commission's Proposal on a Framework for the Free Flow of Non-personal Data*, SRN Electronic Journal (January 2018), available at https://papers.ssrn.com/sol3/papers.cfm?abstract_id=3106791.
59. Article 29 Working Party, *supra* n. 33; Case C-434/16, *Peter Nowak v. Data Protection Commissioner*, ECLI:EU:C:2017:994; Case C-582/14, *Patrick Breyer v. Bundesrepublik Deutschland*, ECLI:EU:C:2016:779.
60. Bart van der Sloot, *Regulating Non-personal Data in the Age of Big Data*, in *Health Data Privacy under the GDPR*, 85-105 (Maria Tzanou ed., 2020).

contents.[61] To enjoy protection, data must therefore result from creative choices, not merely technical ones, and cannot be the straightforward result of investments. Accordingly, raw data aggregations or compilations do not satisfy the requirement of originality.[62] Human authorship is moreover essential. This element excludes generations, aggregations or compilations of data performed by software or automated processes (the latter, by contrast, are protected as intellectual property).[63]

Considering that the utilitarian value of data in the big data context does not derive from creativity or originality, copyright protection offers very limited rights, if any, over data control and access restrictions.

– Trade Secrets and Confidentiality

In a business setting, anything may be confidential or secret in nature. Typically, the values protected by law are confidentiality and secrecy rather than the good itself. For example, ideas that cannot be protected under copyright law may find protection when shared under the private law setting of a confidentiality agreement. Likewise, information about customers and suppliers, business plans, market research and strategies can be used as business competitiveness or research innovation management tools.[64]

Thus, data may constitute the subject matter of confidential information or a trade secret, whether collected automatically or not and without any requirement of originality or creativity.

The Trade Secrets Directive sets forth a liability regime in tort against the unlawful acquisition, use and disclosure of trade secrets.[65] A trade secret is defined as information at the semantic level (i.e., it is different from data).[66] To enjoy protection, the information must be secret, i.e., it is not generally known among or readily accessible to persons within the circles that normally deal with the kind of information in question.[67] Its commercial value derives from secrecy and should be subject to adequate security measures to keep it secret.[68] Trivial information is excluded.[69] Here, the right holder controls the secret rather than the data that turns into information.[70]

As the scope of such protection is confidentiality and secrecy, both contracts and trade secrecy law confer rights in personam, applying only to the contractual parties or

61. Towards a Thriving Data-Driven Economy, *supra* n. 18; A Digital Single Market Strategy for Europe, *supra* n. 1.
62. Case C-145/10, *Eva-Maria Painer v. Standard VerlagsGmbH and Others* ECLI:EU:C:2011:798; Joined Cases C-403/08 to C-429/08, *Football Association Premier League Ltd and Others v. QC Leisure and Others* and *Karen Murphy v. Media Protection Services Ltd, ECLI:* EU:C:2011:631; Case C-604/10, *Football Dataco Ltd and Others v. Yahoo! UK Ltd and Others* ECLI:EU:C:2012:115.
63. Football Dataco, *supra* n. 62.
64. *See* Recital 2 of Directive (EU) 2016/943 of the European Parliament and of the Council of 8 June 2016 on the protection of undisclosed know-how and business information (trade secrets) against their unlawful acquisition, use and disclosure, OJ L 157, 15.6.2016, p. 1-18.
65. *Ibid.*
66. Zech, *supra* n. 19.
67. Article 1 Trade Secrets Directive.
68. Article 2(1) Trade Secrets Directive.
69. Recital 14 Trade Secrets Directive.
70. Article 2(2) Trade Secrets Directive.

persons who have unlawfully acquired, used or disclosed a trade secret.[71] Third parties are not bound by access restrictions and further dissemination. Equally, the law offers remedies only if parties knew or should have known of their secret nature.

Moreover, contracts or secrets presuppose a party holding the data. Questions remain regarding the legal title of control over data. This can be a de facto situation when data are generated internally by one agent only, with no other agent claiming rights over them.[72] This is already a substantial limit on value in the data economy.

As regards commercial value, the doubtful or trivial value of raw data has already been noted above. This is especially the case for data generated by multiple agents and/or interconnected machines.[73] The causal link between the secrecy of individual data and the commercial value of information or knowledge can be challenged too.[74] Some scholars use this point to argue that in a big data environment, trivial information may also have economic value when compiled in sufficient quantities, showing false premises in the law.[75] Nevertheless, whether their prospective value derives from their secrecy remains uncertain. Allocating value in a network environment may be unattainable.[76] By contrast, it is the secrecy of algorithms that holds value.

In light of the above considerations, some authors conclude that trade secrets legislation can nonetheless be better suited to serving the purposes of the data economy by focusing on the specific way someone has unlawfully gained access to the data, allowing a more flexible regime than *erga omnes* rights over the data.[77]

Overall, it appears clear that trade secrecy law grants relative protection over data control.

- Database Rights

At first sight, the legal protection of databases may appear to be the simplest model for data rights. The growing importance of data over time has given rise to support for and protection of investments in databases, without which early EU policymakers believed the database industry could not emerge.[78]

71. Article 2(3) Trade Secrets Directive.
72. E.g., *see* Andreas Wiebe, *Protection of Industrial Data: A New Property Right for the Digital Economy?*, 12 Journal of Intellectual Property Law & Practice, 62-71 (2017) https://doi.org/10.1093/jiplp/jpw175.
73. E.g., in the IoT that describes the network of physical objects owned by one or more parties that are embedded with sensors, software, and other technologies for the purpose of connecting and exchanging data with other devices and systems over the Internet.
74. Drexl, *supra* n. 16; Banterle, *supra* n. 39.
75. Zech, *supra* n. 19.
76. Wiebe, *supra* n. 72; Stepanov, *supra* n. 40.
77. Banterle, *supra* n. 39.
78. It can be questioned whether any backing law was needed and the scope of its success, especially if the experience of other non-EU jurisdictions is compared. *See* Bernt Hugenholtz, *Something Completely Different: Europe's Sui Generis Database Right Book*, in *The Internet and the Emerging Importance of New Forms of Intellectual Property*, 205-222 (Susy Frankel and Daniel Gervais eds, Wolters Kluwer 2016); Scassa, *supra* n. 14, comparing EU law with the experience of the US and Canada that have no specific database protection law.

With the creation in the Database Directive[79] of a sui generis right akin to copyright, the EU legislature has provided a right for database creators to demonstrate that "there has been qualitatively and/or quantitatively a substantial investment in either the obtaining, verification or presentation of the contents to prevent extraction and/or re-utilization of the whole or of a substantial part, evaluated qualitatively and/or quantitatively, of the contents of that database."[80] No originality obligation is required.[81]

The subject of the right is the substantial investment in the creation of a database, not the data themselves.[82] Under established jurisprudence, the investment should be in data that have been obtained, verified or presented. By contrast, investment in data created or generated by the person is excluded.[83] This is a limit of protection in the context of big data and AI.

In addition, the protection is circumscribed to extraction and/or reutilisation of the 'whole' or a 'substantial part' of the contents of a database, not individual datasets. Unauthorised insubstantial extractions or reutilisations do not qualify as infringement.

Another difficulty that emerges is that big data, given their volume and diversity, are incongruent with traditional databases as conceived by the law. The Directive defines databases as collections of "data or other materials which are systematically or methodically arranged and can be individually accessed."[84] With big data, new technologies produce non-relational databases; that is, software associated with databases provides a mechanism for data storage and retrieval that is modelled using different means than the tabular schemas of relational databases. The 'systemic or methodical arrangement' elements are lacking and data are not compiled in a way that preserves the semantic value of data. These circumstances have induced scholars to conclude that protection does not apply.[85]

Although it pertains to the field of data protection law, the recent *Schrems*[86] case confirms in a novel way that the data in a database, regardless of their substantiality, do not automatically belong to the database owner. Invalidating the agreement between the EU and the US on the international transfer of personal data, the CJEU

79. Directive 96/9/EC of the European Parliament and of the Council of 11 March 1996 on the legal protection of databases, OJ L 77, 27.3.1996, p. 20-28.
80. Article 7 Database Directive.
81. Bernt Hugenholtz, *Implementing the European Database Directive*, in *Intellectual Property and Information Law: Essays in Honour of Herman Cohen Jehoram*, 183-199 (Jan Kabel and Gerard Mom eds, Kluwer law International 1998).
82. European Commission, Building a European Data Economy, (Communication) COM(2017) 9 final. *See also* Case C-46/02, *Fixtures Marketing Ltd v. Oy Veikkaus Ab.*, ECLI:EU:C:2004:694; Case C-338/02, *Fixtures Marketing Ltd v. Svenska Spel AB.*, ECLI:EU:C:2004:696; Case C-444/02, *Fixtures Marketing Ltd v. Organismos prognostikon agonon podosfairou AE (OPAP)*, ECLI:EU: C:2004:697.
83. Case C-203/02, *The British Horseracing Board Ltd and Others v. William Hill Organization Ltd.*, ECLI:EU:C:2004:695.
84. Recitals 17 Database Directive.
85. Daniel Gervais, *Exploring the Interfaces Between Big data and Intellectual Property Law*, 10 Journal of Intellectual Property, Information Technology and E-Commerce Law, 3-19 (2019) https://doi.org/10.2139/ssrn.3360344.
86. Case C-311/18, *Data Protection Commissioner v. Facebook Ireland Limited and Maximillian Schrems*, ECLI:EU:C:2020:559.

prevented the database owner from moving the data to a different jurisdiction that did not offer adequate protection under EU standards. The case imposed new limits on the proprietary rights to databases composed of personal data.

As the above analysis suggests, database protection legislation prevents the simple extension of real rights or legal control over individual or raw data.

2.4 DE FACTO CONTROL

What emerges from the previous Sections is that the existing EU legal framework is not resolutive in allocating data rights.

Intellectual property protections or related regimes are unsuitable for granting legal recognition of exclusive powers of control over datasets.[87]

When data are personal, the law grants stronger control. Even here, however, legal control is not absolute but relative. The speciality is that the debate on data control and allocation is enriched with respect to fundamental rights. Nonetheless, data protection does not provide economic rights.

It can be argued that proprietary rights should be granted in case of market failures. However, the raise and predominance of big data make it difficult to conceive of a market failure concerning the generation, collection, and processing of data.[88] On the contrary, the exponential quantity and quality of data, alongside their ubiquitous processing, indicate the opposite incentives for data collection and processing.[89]

After the passing of the GDPR, the EU had envisioned the creation of a data producer right in machine-generated non-personal data, thus creating proprietary rights in such data, enhancing their tradability as an economic good and establishing a right in rem that would allow for assignments of exclusivity to use data.[90] However, as hinted above, such a measure lacked the identification of a specific market failure, it could lead to more inefficiencies than those that it aimed to cure, and the potential effects on intellectual property legal frameworks were not assessed.[91]

If there are no legal rights in rem or title transfer of data, in principle the latter should be freely available and access to them unrestricted. The 'data market' should

87. This conclusion is in line with those of Zech, *supra* n. 19; Wiebe, *supra* n. 72; Gervais, *supra* n. 85.
88. Joseph Drexl et al., *Data Ownership and Access to Data: Position Statement of the Max Planck Institute for Innovation and Competition of 16 August 2016 on the Current European Debate*, Max Planck Institute for Innovation & Competition Research Paper No. 16-10 (2016), available at https://papers.ssrn.com/sol3/papers.cfm?abstract_id=2833165; Wolfgang Kerber, *Governance of Data: Exclusive Property vs. Access*, 47 IIC – International Review of Intellectual Property and Competition Law, 759-762 (2016) https://doi.org/10.1007/s40319-016-0517-2.
89. Florent Thouvenin and Aurelia Tamò-Larrieux, *Data Ownership and Data Access Rights*, in *Big Data and Global Trade Law*, 316-339 (Mira Burri ed., Cambridge University Press 2021).
90. Commission Staff Working Document on the free flow of data and emerging issues of the European data economy Accompanying the document Communication Building a European data economy, SWD/2017/02 final.
91. *Ibid.*

not exist. The conception of data as a collective good is not an unfamiliar one (*res communis*),[92] with the caveat of the control conferred by the GDPR.

Yet, this scenario does not reflect reality. Data are regarded as a valuable economic asset, characterised by data gatekeeping, access restrictions, entry barriers, and lock-ins. The question of how such powers materialise conclusively leads to de facto control. In practice, the above-analysed legal vacuum means that data remains with the person who happens to have possession of them. This control allocates economic exploitation and allows sole use or access contracts. It transforms data from a non-rival good into a rival one. De facto control – which can also be termed 'possession' – is typically ensured by technical means and the ability of platforms to mine data from users. Simply put, de facto controllers are incentivised to invest in data collection because they appropriate the gains.

This finding could lead EU lawyers toward a nest of wasps regarding the law of possession in the absence of a legal title. Sharp divergences persist between civil and common law. Countries and doctrinal debates differ over the existence or nature of possessors' titles and the extent of protection.[93] These fascinating discussions would deviate from this study. Here, it is sufficient to acknowledge that the law of possession would lead to weak non-resolutive protection.[94] In any event, it would not fall within the competence of EU law but follow an impassable path for EU intervention that would frustrate from the outset any idea of harmonisation and a Single Digital Market.

Rather than a market for data, factual control defines a market for access to data holding. Due to regulatory gaps, the gatekeepers are dominant technological companies.

Big data and decentralised data processing are a game-changer. They have been exploited by new technologies for the collection, storage, mining, synthesis, pattern recognition, and analysis of large volumes of wide-scoped, varied, and accurate data almost in real-time.[95] The value lies in the cumulative features of the four Vs: volume, velocity, variety, and veracity.[96] The maximum value of data is created by mining and analytical tools of AI and machine-learning technologies. Competitiveness is a function

92. Demsetz, *supra* n. 29; Yoram Barzel, *Economic Analysis of Property Rights* (Cambridge University Press 1997). Collective goods (technically, things that are common to humankind) are not appropriable, but the public may acquire certain usufructuary rights (a limited real right of *usus*), directly and without altering them, and their fruits (*fructus*, the right to derive profit from them). They should be kept separate from no one's good (*res nullius*), in that the latter derives from private Roman law whereby they are considered ownerless property appropriable by means of occupation or possession if not regulated otherwise (e.g., wild animals). *See* Paul Du Plessis, *Borkowski's Textbook on Roman Law* (Oxford University Press 2020).
93. For a comprehensive account of comparative doctrines on the law of possession, *see* James Gordley and Ugo Mattei, *Protecting Possession*, 44 The American Journal of Comparative Law, 293-334 (1996) https://doi.org/10.2307/840711.
94. *Ibid.*
95. Mark Lycett, *Datafication: Making Sense of (Big) Data in a Complex World*, 22 European Journal of Information Systems, 381-386 (2013) https://doi.org/10.1057/ejis.2013.10.
96. *Ibid.*; *See also* Daniel Rubinfeld and Michal Gal, *Access Barriers to Big Data*, 59 Arizona Law Review, 339-381 (2017) https://doi.org/10.2139/ssrn.2830586; Maurice Stucke and Allen Grunes, *Big Data and Competition Policy* (Oxford University Press 2016).

of the sophistication of technologies and analyses they can perform. Arguably, data analysis is the real commodity rather than the data themselves.

As discussed above, 'data markets' should have no reason to exist, at least in conventional economic and legal terms. Rather, data are an essential, non-rivalrous, and infinite component of novel product or service markets best represented as 'data-driven markets', with different markets employing different types of big data as inputs for different outcomes.

As things stand, it seems that 'data markets' exist as the de facto result of unsuitable regulation over a fluid res that is collective in nature.[97]

To the extent that this conclusion is plausible, de facto control negatively impacts the ensuing data-driven markets. Hence, it is not only conceivable but also desirable that data access should become unrestricted.

In principle, the enforcement of competition law should overcome abuses of market power and anti-competitive practices such as barriers to the access of essential facilities and market development.

2.5 THE LIMITS OF COMPETITION LAW ENFORCEMENT

2.5.1 EU Competition Law

In digital markets, data are the central resources of the business models of tech companies and a vital source of market entry and power. Not surprisingly, for more than a decade, the EU has applied traditional competition enforcement in emerging digital markets.

The digital transformation has been characterised by the emergence of dominant companies in the form of large digital platforms. The activities of these online platforms are multi-sided, allowing them to act as gatekeepers for multiple business users and a very large base of consumers. At the same time, they offer services in their own right. In this scenario, it becomes evident that the control of data poses issues of competition as the other digital users are dependent on data availability, thus calling into play competition law.[98]

Under the teachings of the influential Chicago School, the main function of competition law is considered to be the safeguard and promotion of the competitive process of undertakings, encouraging an optimum allocation of resources and efficient and innovative financial services, and ultimately enhancing consumer welfare.[99]

Yet, under EU competition law, another objective is the achievement of EU market integration, which does not necessarily coincide with efficiencies in the

97. *Contra, see* Inge Graef, *EU Competition Law, Data Protection and Online Platforms: Data as Essential Facility* (Kluwer 2016) according to whom competition authorities and courts should define and analyse a potential market for data in addition to relevant product markets.
98. European Commission, Platform-to-Business Trading Practices, available at https://digital-strategy.ec.europa.eu/en/policies/platform-business-trading-practices.
99. *See, e.g.*, Richard Whish and David Bailey, *Competition Law* (Oxford University Press 2021), Giorgio Monti, *EC Competition Law* (Cambridge University Press 2012).

organisation of production and distribution.[100] From its inception, the European Community (EC) Treaty has mandated interaction between competition policy objectives and other goals which can be eventually re-conducted to market integration. After all, the fundamental underlying purpose of the EU is the creation of a single market and the elimination of barriers to integration. Moreover, even accepting that competition policy should aim at allocative efficiency and consumer welfare rather than forcing integration per se, the two goals may not necessarily be incompatible as competition plays a key role in keeping markets open.

The Lisbon Treaty no longer includes in its Article 3 Treaty on European Union (TEU) competition policy as a Union goal in itself, but it nevertheless remains part of the internal market, which is a central objective of the provision. Actually, Protocol 27 of the TFEU declares that the internal market includes a system in which competition is not distorted. At the same time, Article 7 TFEU explicitly affirms that the EU must ensure consistency between its policies and activities, taking all of its objectives into account, which makes it clear that normatively, other goals should be taken into account in addition to allocative efficiency.

Competition policy and law apply in all the areas arising from Treaty rules.[101] Broadly, it aims to control the following:

- Cartels, collusions, or any other anti-competitive practices having a distortive effect on the EU market (Article 101 TFEU).
- Market power, by means of abuses of a dominant position or via proposed mergers or acquisitions having an effect on the EU market (Article 102 TFEU).
- Direct or indirect aid given by the Member States to undertakings (Article 107 TFEU).

Thus, competition policy is governed by both primary and secondary EU law, traditionally characterised by *ex post* enforcement, where the European Commission and the CJEU intervene in individual cases after an infringement is contested.

In digital markets, there is a large consensus that the efficacy and efficiency of such traditional competition law enforcement have been challenged, exemplified by the major cases investigated by the European Commission.[102] For example, the *Google Shopping*[103] and *Google Adsense*[104] cases have exposed little effect of the Commission's decisions and the fines imposed on the gatekeepers' conducts, coupled with the

100. Roger Van den Bergh and Peter Camesasca, *European Competition Law and Economics: A Comparative Perspective* (London, Thomson Sweet and Maxwell 2006).
101. Case 172/80, *Zuchner v. Bayerisce Vereinsbamk AG*, ECLI:EU:C:1981:178.
102. Michell Cini and Patryk Czulno, *Digital Single Market and the EU Competition Regime: An Explanation of Policy Change*, 44 Journal of European Integration, 41-57 (2022) https://doi.org/10.1080/07036337.2021.2011260.
103. Google Search (Shopping), *supra* n. 28; followed by Case T-612/17, *Google LLC, formerly Google Inc. and Alphabet, Inc. v. European Commission*, ECLI:EU:T:2021:763.
104. Case AT.40411, *Google Search (AdSense)*, Commission Decision relating to a proceeding under Article 102 of the Treaty on the Functioning of the European Union (the Treaty) and Article 54 of the EEA Agreement, C(2019) 2173 final.

considerations that the latter are not necessarily dominant players in the traditional sense, the length of time necessary for the investigations in highly sophisticated technologies is excessive, and the multitude of business models involved make it difficult to tackle the differences in practices.[105] All in all, until now, a market for personal and non-personal data has not yet been defined, which makes traditional EU competition law enforcement difficult. What to date the authorities have defined are the markets of products or services which are fuelled by personal and/or non-personal data, and they have treated them accordingly. But a market for the personal and/or personal data themselves - specifying the buyers, the sellers, the role of consumers as those to whom the data pertain, monopoly or concentration tests, etc. - has not been defined or addressed.

2.5.2 Article 101 TFEU

Article 101(1)(2) TFEU prohibits and voids all agreements between undertakings, decisions by associations of undertakings and concerted practices which may affect, actually or potentially, trade between Member States and which have as their object or effect the prevention, restriction or distortion of competition within the internal market. This is a complex determination depending largely on the facts. Where it is clear that an agreement has as its object the restriction of competition, there is no need to demonstrate the anti-competitive effects.[106] Finally, Article 101(3) TFEU exempts anti-competitive agreements, decisions or concerted practices which contribute to improving the production or distribution of goods/services, at the same time allowing consumers a fair share of such benefit - the so-called consumer interest.

Under Article 101 TFEU, whilst the locutions 'agreement' and 'decision' pose little interpretative challenges, the meaning of what constitutes a 'concerted practice' may be more problematic. The CJEU has held that a concerted practice is:

> a form of coordination between undertakings which, without having reached the stage where an agreement properly so-called has been concluded, knowingly substitutes practical cooperation between them for the risks of competition.
>
> By its very nature, then, a concerted practice does not have all the elements of a contract but may inter alia arise out of coordination which becomes apparent from the behaviour of the participants.
>
> Conduct is such as to enable those concerned to attempt (...) to consolidate established positions to the detriment of effective freedom of movement of the products in the common market and of the freedom of consumers to choose their suppliers.[107]

Established case law specifies that for an Article 101 TFEU infringement to occur, it is sufficient for the existence of the wilful element (the "knowingly" above) even in

105. Cini and Czulno, *supra* n. 102.
106. Antonio Capobianco, *Information Exchange under EC Competition Law*, 41 Common Market Law Review, 1247-1276 (2004) https://doi.org/10.54648/cola2004047.
107. Case 48-69, *Imperial Chemical Industries Ltd v. Commission of the European Communities*, ECLI:EU:C:1972:70.

the absence of actual anti-competitive effects on the market, so that it is not necessary that the conduct in fact produces the specific effect of restricting, preventing or distorting competition.[108]

2.5.3 Article 102 TFEU

Article 102 TFEU prohibits any abuse by one or more undertakings of a dominant position within the internal market in so far as it may affect trade between Member States. According to the letter of the Article:

> Any abuse by one or more undertakings of a dominant position within the internal market or in a substantial part of it shall be prohibited as incompatible with the internal market in so far as it may affect trade between Member States. Such abuse may, in particular, consist in:
>
> (a) directly or indirectly imposing unfair purchase or selling prices or other unfair trading conditions;
> (b) limiting production, markets or technical development to the prejudice of consumers;
> (c) applying dissimilar conditions to equivalent transactions with other trading parties, thereby placing them at a competitive disadvantage;
> (d) making the conclusion of contracts subject to acceptance by the other parties of supplementary obligations which, by their nature or according to commercial usage, have no connection with the subject of such contracts.

The essence of this provision is to control market power once one or more undertakings have acquired a dominant position in relation to a particular market, i.e., a clearly identified geographical area where a product or service is marketed and the conditions of competition are sufficiently homogeneous.[109]

However, Article 102 TFEU does not prohibit dominance per se, but the abuse of such a dominant position is required, albeit no causal link between the two is required.[110] Thus, it is commonly represented that for a violation of Article 102 TFEU to occur, the four cumulative four conditions need to be met:

- A dominant position in the relevant market by one or more undertakings.
- Such a position must be held in the internal market or a substantial part of it.
- There has to be an abuse of such a dominant position.
- There are actual or potential effects on trade between Member States.[111]

108. Case C-199/92 P, *Hüls AG v. Commission of the European Communities*, ECLI:EU:C:1999:358.
109. Andrea Lista, *EU Competition Law and the Financial Services Sector* (Informa Law 2013); Robert O'Donoghue and Jorge Padilla, *The Law and Economics of Article 102 TFEU* (Hart Publishing 2013).
110. Case 6-72, *Europemballage Corporation and Continental Can Company v. Commission*, ECLI: EU:C:1973:22.
111. Whish and Bailey, *supra* n. 99; Cosmo Graham, *EU and UK Competition Law* (Pearson Education 2013).

The requisite of 'abuse' may be a challenging one to assess. There are several aspects to the concept of abuse, each one discussed for a long time in the literature.[112] All that can be succinctly said here is that to be abusive, a dominant undertaking needs to engage in an activity that negatively affects market structure and consumer welfare. This is a difficult analysis to undertake that requires the assessment of many variables and the specificities of each reference market. The assessment of Article 102 TFEU infringements remains a detailed analysis to be carried out with all the elements and complexities of the relevant markets. What needs to be pointed out here is that to the extent that abusive exclusionary conducts are used by dominant undertakings to protect or extend their dominant position, it becomes important to assess both exclusion from the same market and exclusion from a vertically integrated market, where the hardest issue is to distinguish between anti-competitive and procompetitive foreclosure. The competition authorities will intervene under Article 102 TFEU if there are coherent explanations of how the allegedly abusive conduct results in consumer harm or the fragmentation of the EU single market.

2.5.4 The Unsuitability of the Essential Facility Doctrine under Article 102 TFEU

In principle, the importance ascribed to data as an indispensable input for the Digital Single Market could trigger the application of competition law. In its traditional application to dominant firms,[113] the question is the extent to which the de facto control of gatekeeping platforms over data qualifies as anti-competitive conduct harming the competitive process, innovation and entrepreneurship. A market where a data-dominant firm may restrict or impose unfair conditions on access can create a bottleneck. Provided there is abuse, the natural suggestion would be to use competition law as a tool for creating a level playing field of unrestricted data access through a duty to share.

As seen, competition law provides two legal grounds to remedy gatekeeping: the prohibition of anti-competitive agreements under Article 101 TFEU if the gatekeeper's refusal is based on an agreement with other firms, or in the absence of such an agreement, the prohibition of the abuse of dominant position under Article 102 TFEU.

To the extent that data constitute the essential input in the hands of monopolists, the most appropriate enforcement instrument might be offered by the 'essential facility doctrine' under Article 102 TFEU. This doctrine may require a dominant firm to share its assets with others if those assets are indispensable to competing in the market and refusing access would eliminate effective competition. Market failure arising because control of data infrastructure and network effects (direct or indirect) force competing firms to depend on platforms, which become indispensable in the same fashion as physical infrastructures like railroads or ports.

---

112. *Ibid.*
113. Giorgio Monti, *Abuse of Dominant Position: A Post-Intel Calm?*, 3 CPI Antitrust Chronicle (2019), available at https://www.competitionpolicyinternational.com/abuse-of-a-dominant-position-a-post-intel-calm/.

The imposition of dealing with a dominant undertaking interferes with fundamental principles of freedom of contract and party autonomy. This is a controversial point that demands a limited application of the doctrine.[114] Moreover, it should be borne in mind that this is a measure meant to stimulate competition in the market and not for the market.[115] In the context of data and the European strategy, it may emerge as an important factor since competition in the market and for the market each lead to a different form of innovation: sustaining innovation that improves existing products/services in the former case and disruptive innovation that discontinues products or services in the latter. The scholarly literature highlights how competition authorities need to balance the two in determining whether or not to intervene.[116] In this scenario, competition law enforcement may be only partially useful to the goals of the European Data Strategy.

Given this caveat, there is no general approach to applying the essential facility doctrine. It is a test based on the analysis of the specific circumstances of each case: the specific characteristics of the relevant facility, the conduct under scrutiny, and its economic context. To apply the essential facility doctrine, the facility (data) must be defined as a distinct relevant market from derivative markets. However, there is no market for (big) data as such. Moreover, platforms act as gatekeepers in different service markets. Therefore, one would need to examine the competitive reality of the markets in which each platform operates and to which the data content relates.[117] Next, robust evidence of likely anti-competitive effects should be provided.

The application of the doctrine is notoriously narrow and cumbersome.

The first step in establishing dominance is to define the relevant market. However, a digital market per se cannot be identified. Instead, platforms are heterogeneous with different business models. Relevant markets must be defined anew each time. Moreover, the potential harm to competition posed by platforms' dominance may not always be recognised if measured in terms of price and output.[118] Instead, the economic feature of platforms is their multi-sidedness; they interconnect and operate in two or more markets with network economy effects and economies of scale, where the basis for deriving income may be very diverse. In so operating, the benefits that one

114. Inge Graef, *Rethinking the Essential Facilities Doctrine for the EU Digital Economy*, 53 Revue Juridique Thémis de l'Université de Montréal, 33-72 (2019) https://doi.org/10.2139/ssrn.3371457; Jaques Crémer, Yves-Alexandre de Montjoye and Heike Schweitzer, *Competition Policy for the Digital Era: Final Report* (European Commission 2019). *See also* Case T-41/96, *Bayer AG v. Commission of the European Communities*, ECLI:EU:T:2000:242; Opinion of Mr Advocate General Jacobs in Case C-7/97, *Oscar Bronner GmbH & Co. KG v. Mediaprint Zeitungs- und Zeitschriftenverlag GmbH & Co. KG, Mediaprint Zeitungsvertriebsgesellschaft mbH & Co. KG and Mediaprint Anzeigengesellschaft mbH & Co. KG.*, ECLI:EU:C:1998:264.

115. *Ibid. See also* Drexl, *supra* n. 16.

116. *Ibid.*

117. Joined Cases 6 and 7/73, *Istituto Chemioterapico Italiano S.p.A. and Commercial Solvents Corporation v. Commission of the European Communities*, ECLI:EU:C:1974:18.

118. Lina Khan, *Amazon's Antitrust Paradox*, 126 The Yale Law Journal, 710-805 (2017); Inge Graef and Francisco Costa-Cabral, *To Regulate or Not to Regulate Big Tech*, 1 Concurrences, 24-29 (2020). *See also* Google Search (Shopping), *supra* n. 28, according to which even if users do not pay a monetary consideration for the use of search services on the internet, they contribute by providing data with each query.

market (one side) derives from the platform depend on the participants of one or more other markets (other sides).[119] Data obtained in one market offer a competitive advantage in the other(s). Therefore, the definition of the relevant market depends not only on diverse data-driven markets to which undertakings may require access but also on the markets for the several types of information that can be extracted from the data.[120] In the big data age, defining relevant markets for the essentiality of data may prove highly complex, if not impossible.[121]

Second, the degree of dependence needs to be established. A successful claim must demonstrate the indispensability of the facility to business activity and that there are no other actual or potential substitutes for the facility. Moreover, there should be technical, legal, or economic obstacles that make it impossible, or unreasonably difficult, for competitors to obtain the facility.[122] Accordingly, exclusivity does not necessarily imply either essentiality or monopolistic power. Resources are not essential as such but relative to something or in comparison with other available inputs. With big data, it is impossible to recognise a certain set of data that could identify a product/service market. In principle, all data may be useful and they can be replaceable or interchangeable in connection with the purpose for which they are needed.[123] The very notion of big data suggests that they are an extremely heterogeneous resource whose applications cannot be known in advance. However, to be essential, a facility should serve a defined product/service in a cause-and-effect relationship.[124] Therefore, data should be divided into different categories and access granted only to the truly indispensable ones. From this perspective, the solution offered by the application of the doctrine appears far removed from the reality of big data and the goals of the European data policy.

Third, the refusal to provide access to the facility should exclude all effective competition on the market.[125] *Mutatis mutandis*, the features of platform business models and those of the facility (data) could impede the realisation of such a condition.

119. For example, a search engine provider offers its services to users for free, at the same time providing advertising services or tools to other companies for profit. Likewise, a retailer may offer its intermediation services to buyers for free, at the same time operating as retailer in competition with other retailers but with the advantage of having more complete profiles of users. On the two or multi-sidedness of platforms *see* Crémer et al., *supra* n. 114; Geoffrey Parker, Marshall van Alstyne and Sangeet Choudary, *Platform Revolution* (Norton 2017); Graef, *supra* n. 114.
120. Giuseppe Colangelo and Maria Teresa Maggiolino, *Big Data as Misleading Facilities*, 13 European Competition Journal, 249-281 (2017) https://doi.org/10.1080/17441056.2017.1382262; Mark Patterson, *Antitrust Law in the New Economy* (Harvard University Press, 2017).
121. Patterson, *supra* n. 120.
122. *Oscar Bronner*, *supra* n. 114; Case C-418/01, *IMS Health GmbH & Co. OHG v. NDC Health GmbH & Co. KG.*, ECLI:EU:C:2004:257; Case T-201/04, *Microsoft Corp. v. Commission of the European Communities*, ECLI:EU:T:2007:289.
123. Colangelo and Maggiolino, *supra* n. 120; Niels-Peter Schepp and Achim Wambach, *On Big Data and Its Relevance for Market Power Assessment*, 7 Journal of European Competition Law and Practice, 120-124 (2016) https://doi.org/10.1093/jeclap/lpv091.
124. *Ibid.*
125. *Microsoft Corp.*, *supra* n. 122.

Finally, the refusal to provide access should not be justified by objective reasons.[126] When data are personal, data protection rules may be used as a defence against data-access requests based on competition law.

All the above illustrates that the already cumbersome enforcement of the essential facility doctrine finds additional obstacles when platforms and data are involved, making competition law enforcement an inadequate tool for the goals of unrestricted data access and innovation.

2.5.5 Data Portability under Article 20 GDPR

When data are personal, Article 20 of the GDPR recognises the right of data portability. Data subjects have the right to have their data transmitted to another controller in a structured, commonly used and machine-readable format as long as the processing is based on consent or a contract.

Consent and contract necessity are only two of the grounds for lawful data processing as per Article 6 GDPR. The processing grounds of compliance with a legal obligation, protection of vital interests, the performance of a task carried out in the public interest, and the pursuit of legitimate interests of data controllers or third parties are therefore excluded from the data portability right.

Under the circumscribed range of situations in which the right is applicable, data subjects continue to have their data processed by the original controller after a data portability operation, since this operation does not trigger the erasure of the data from the former controller but simply a transfer to another controller for the provisions of services from the latter.[127] The decision of consumers to switch service providers becomes consent to pass their data to another provider, but the possibility of erasing their data from the former provider remains subject to a separate request and conditions as per Article 17 GDPR.

The absence of a general right to data portability in the GDPR already portrays a narrow scope. This is further restricted to data that data subjects have provided themselves to the data controller - so-called volunteered data. The scope of the provision includes observation of the data but excludes derived or inferred data or anything resulting from the analysis of the data.[128]

The norm also reduces the reach of the right by adding that controllers may transfer data where it is "technically feasible"[129] without providing any indication about its meaning. This vagueness allows significant leeway to data controllers unwilling to make a transfer.[130]

126. *Ibid.*
127. Article 29 Working Party, Guidelines on the right to data portability (Adopted on 13 December 2016, last Revised and adopted on 5 April 2017).
128. *Ibid. See also* Recital 68 GDPR.
129. Article 20(2) GDPR.
130. Aysem Vanberg and Mehmet Unver, *The Right to Data Portability in the GDPR and EU Competition Law: Odd Couple or Dynamic Duo?*, 8 European Journal of Law and Technology, 1-22 (2017).

Data protection rights of third parties provide an additional constraint when the request involves data of other individuals. This situation is not infrequent in social media, where individuals share activities and intertwine their data.[131]

Last but not least, true individual control over personal data – hence effective portability – has proven difficult to achieve due to the disproportionate costs or efforts borne by data subjects, especially with the advent of technologies utilising big data and the ability to turn anything into personal data without individuals' knowledge or communication.[132]

Keeping the above limitations in mind, legal scholars have already analysed the control mechanism of horizontal application of the right and its relationship with competition law.[133] The right is analogous to the control approach of data protection and its limited application (*see* above, section 2.3.2). The GDPR addresses the issue from the perspective of data subjects' rights. The main policy objective is to ensure that individuals are in control of their data and trust the digital domain. However, the perspective of competition remains outside the remit of the GDPR, which must be complemented by the limited applicability of competition law (above).[134] The primary aim of data portability is data subjects' control, not competition concerns. It enables access and transferability to or via individuals without creating an access system at the disposal of competitors for product development. Thus, even if data portability impacts competition for the prevention of service lock-ins alongside the equally limited Regulation 2018/1807 on the free flow of non-personal data,[135] its applicability is

131. Barbara Engels, *Data Portability Amongst Online Platforms*, 5 Internet Policy Review, 1-17 (2016) https://doi.org/10.14763/2016.2.408.
132. Nadezhda Purtova, *Do Property Rights in Personal Data Make Sense after the Big Data Turn: Individual Control and Transparency*, 10 Journal of Law and Economic Regulation, 64-78 (2017).
133. Inge Graef, Martin Husovec and Nadezhda Purtova, *Data Portability and Data Control: Lessons for an Emerging Concept in EU Law*, 19 German Law Journal, 1359-1398 (2018) https://doi.org/10.1017/s2071832200023075; Peter Swire and Yianni Lagos, *Why the Right to Data Portability Likely Reduces Consumer Welfare: Antitrust and Privacy Critique*, 72 Maryland Law Review, 335-380 (2013) https://doi.org/10.2139/ssrn.2159157; Inge Graef, *The Opportunities and Limits of Data Portability for Stimulating Competition and Innovation*, 2 Competition Policy International – Antitrust Chronicle, 1-8 (2020).
134. Ira Rubinstein, *Big Data: The End of Privacy or a New Beginning?*, 3 International Data Privacy Law, 74-87 (2013) https://doi.org/10.1093/idpl/ips036; Paul De Hert et al., *The Right to Data Portability in the GDPR: Towards User-Centric Interoperability of Digital Services*, 34 Computer Law and Security Review, 193-203 (2018) https://doi.org/10.1016/j.clsr.2017.10.003.
135. Regulation (EU) 2018/1807, *supra* n. 6. The Regulation operates on two specific obstacles to data mobility, i.e., data localisation requirements imposed by Member States and contractual vendor lock-in practices in the private sector (situations where customers are dependent on a single provider and cannot easily switch to a different vendor without substantial costs, legal constraints or technical incompatibilities). On the latter aspect, it facilitates and encourages EU companies to develop self-regulatory codes of conduct to improve the competitive data economy based on the principles of transparency, interoperability and open standards. Companies that provide data processing services should introduce some self-regulatory codes of conduct to ensure the provision of clear and transparent information and thereby avoiding vendor lock-ins. In the case of a dataset composed of both personal and non-personal data, the Regulation applies to the non-personal data part of the dataset.

narrow. The measure is very far from providing an appropriate data-access regime to satisfy the sharing obligation of European policy goals.[136]

2.5.6 The Intersection Between Competition Law and Data Protection

As seen in the digital economy, personal data have become an economic asset increasingly valued by firms, which have made them the core of their service or which may need them to continue or set-up their business models. Inevitably, from the regulatory perspective, their central role in the competitive dynamics of digital markets has led to the progressive intersection - or convergence - of data protection law and competition law.

Until very recently, competition authorities had not handled cases in which personal data were used to breach competition law. After all, most competition lawyers and economists have long taken the resilient stance that its rules are designed to protect economic interests and that other non-economic interests, as important as they may be, should be left to the protection of other means or laws in this instance data protection.[137]

Equally, until now, the judiciary has taken the same position, deferring to data protection law any assessment and carrying on a pure economic analysis.[138]

Traditionally, personal data and their legal assessment had been treated as the exclusive competence and target of data protection legislation. But to the extent that policymakers have shown awareness of the growth in the commercial value of personal data and the expansion of their reference markets, then competition law may no longer be exempted from application. Indeed, for some time, suggestions have been put forward that data protection should be considered a non-price dimension in the competition analysis and review of cases. For example, in the past, isolated voices took the stance that the European Commission should have focused on the protection of the data of customers in the review of the *Google/DoubleClick*[139] merger for the creation of a massive amount of data on consumer behaviour. If the European Commission failed to look at data protection in that case, it later corrected the position in the review of the *TomTom/TeleAtlas*[140] case, where data protection became part of the competitive analysis.

Under these precursory stances, data protection is compared to a form of product degradation that could induce consumers to not deal with companies that cannot

136. *See also* the European Commission's recognition that "as a result of its design to enable switching of service providers rather than enabling data reuse in digital ecosystems the right [to data portability] has practical limitations." A European Strategy for Data, *supra* n. 2, 10.
137. Maureen Ohlhausen and Alexander Okuliar, *Competition, Consumer Protection, and the Right (Approach) to Privacy*, 80 Antitrust Law Journal, 121-156 (2015).
138. For all, *see* Case C-238/05, *Asnef-Equifax, Servicios de Información sobre Solvencia y Crédito, SL v. Asociación de Usuarios de Servicios Bancarios (Ausbanc)*, ECLI:EU:C:2006:734.
139. Case No. COMP/M.4731, *Google/DoubleClick*, Commission decision declaring a concentration to be compatible with the common market and the functioning of the EEA Agreement (11 March 2008).
140. Case No. COMP/M.4854, *TomTom/TeleAtlas*, Commission decision declaring a concentration to be compatible with the common market and the EEA Agreement (14 May 2008).

guarantee the respect of their confidential information and switch to more respectful competitors. It is clear that, willingly or unwillingly, personal information has become a tradable or alienable commodity, which raises the issue of to what extent there may be a market for fundamental rights. Under human rights theory, these rights are usually inalienable and none is tradable, but someone may freely choose to exercise his/her specific right or not. Therefore, if it is becoming beyond doubt that there exists a reference market for personal data, the question arises as to how this would be compatible with the concept and values behind data protection that is felt so key for European societies to elevate its protection at the highest levels of EU legislation and as a fundamental right.

Already a long time ago, it had been pointed out how legal scholarship was divided over the real meaning of fundamental rights and what it truly encapsulates. As it has been stressed, the understanding of the meaning of 'fundamentality' differs from country to country. However, among the many differences, a basic common feature of the understanding of what accounts for fundamental rights is the expression of a legal principle recognised as 'constitutional' which concerns human dignity and personal freedom.[141]

In theory, thus, the idea of tradable or alienable fundamental rights may look like an oxymoron.

Generally, not many such other market examples exist. Some may think of the right to water of other natural resources as possible illustrations of other human rights containing a tradable element. Indeed, these are usually regulated markets also classified as Services of General Economic Interest (SGEI), which the public authorities classify as being of general interest and subject to specific public service obligations and regulated by a specific legislative framework. But personal data are not classified or treated as a SGEI.

True, it would be a violation that breaches a fundamental right; therefore, before engaging in any evaluation, one should give proof of such an occurrence. Trading in data that are lawfully processed cannot be accounted as a violation of a fundamental right. But regardless of any compliance analysis, the uncontested issue is that when consumers deal with businesses, especially if these are financial institutions and the contract at stake is the provision of personal finance, there is a significant imbalance between the parties that leaves consumers with little or no alternative to give away their data and further dissemination if they want to have a chance. The difficulty is that, like it or not, personal data in themselves have become a commodity. They make the market product. It is what is done later with the data that may be at odds with fundamental rights, especially in the age of big data.

In essence, as some legal doctrine has advanced, competition law should include data protection concerns by integrating them into a broader consumer interest

141. Chantal Mak, *Fundamental Rights in European Contract Law: A Comparison of the Impact of Fundamental Rights on Contractual Relationships in Germany, the Netherlands, Italy and England* (Kluwer Law International 2008).

non-economic parameters or welfare standard.[142] However, until now, these considerations have remained on a pure theoretical and doctrinal level.

The recent cases of *META*[143] and *Lindenapotheke*[144] seem to represent a turning point vis-à-vis this traditional approach regarding the boundaries between competition law and the GDPR, albeit still maintaining the perspective of the economic stance dear to competition law.

In *META*, the German Competition Law Authority (the Federal Cartel Office (FCO)) found that Meta abused its dominant market position through its general terms, as the processing of data was not compliant with the applicable requirements of the GDPR and, in particular, could not be justified in the light of the legal bases for processing of Article 6(1) and Article 9(2) of the GDPR [consent - *see supra*, section 1.4.3]. META appealed, questioning the authority of the national competition authority to enforce data protection rules under competition law. The German Court of Appeal thus requested a preliminary ruling of the CJEU under Article 267 TFEU. The CJEU ruled that competition authorities of a Member State have the authority to investigate and sanction an infringement of the GDPR under competition law, if the undertakings exploit their dominant market position. At the same time, in case of breaches of data protection law, the competition authorities need to consult with the competent data protection supervisory authority. Significantly, the CJEU stressed that:

> in view of the different objectives pursued by the rules established in competition matters, in particular Article 102 TFEU, on the one hand, and those laid down in relation to the protection of personal data under the GDPR, on the other, it must be held that, where a national competition authority identifies an infringement of that regulation in the context of the finding of an abuse of a dominant position, it does not replace the supervisory authorities. In particular, that national competition authority neither monitors nor enforces the application of that regulation [...] in order to protect the fundamental rights and freedoms of natural persons [...] or to facilitate the free flow of personal data within the European Union. Furthermore, by merely noting the non-compliance of a data processing operation with the GDPR for the sole purpose of establishing an abuse of a dominant position and by imposing measures to put an end to that abuse on a legal basis derived from competition law, that authority does not carry out any of the tasks set out in Article 57 of that regulation [i.e. the tasks reserved to the National Supervisory Authorities], nor does it make use of the powers reserved to the supervisory authority under Article 58 of that regulation.[145]

Hence, the CJEU justified the ability of national competition authorities to integrate the GDPR in their assessment of dominance and the fact that data processing has become a significant parameter of competition between undertakings in the digital economy. Conversely, the exclusion of the GDPR from the legal framework to be taken

142. Ferretti, *supra* n. 34; Christopher Kuner et al., *When Two Worlds Collide: The Interface Between Competition Law and Data Protection*, 4 International Data Privacy Law, 247-248 (2014) https://doi.org/10.1093/idpl/ipu025; Francisco Costa-Cabral and Orla Lynskey, *Family Ties: The Intersection Between Data Protection and Competition in EU Law*, 54 Common Market Law Review, 11-50 (2017) https://doi.org/10.54648/cola2017002.
143. Case C-252/21, *Meta Platforms Inc and Others v. Bundeskartellamt*, ECLI:EU:C:2023:537.
144. Case C-21/23, *Lindenapotheke – ND v. DR*, ECLI:EU:C:2024:846.
145. *Meta, supra* n. 143, para. 49.

into consideration by the competition authorities when examining an abuse of a dominant position would disregard the reality of digital markets and undermine the effectiveness of competition law in the EU.[146]

Lately, in *Lindenapotheke*, the CJEU ruled that the provisions of the GDPR do not preclude national legislations which confer on competitors of an undertaking allegedly infringing the GDPR the right to bring an action against that undertaking for such GDPR infringement on the basis of unfair commercial practices. The ruling centres around a German case involving two pharmacists, one of whom sold medicines using an online platform. The selling methods were challenged by the other competing pharmacist, who filed a lawsuit asking for an order against the competitor to stop selling online. The request was based on the fact that the first pharmacist, without asking for the consent of the persons concerned under Article 6(1) GDPR, collected and processed data of persons who filled in the online purchase order, entering their name, delivery address and purchased product. In essence, the online pharmacist, in breach of the duty to obtain consent, had many business contacts, but all of them were allegedly unlawful.[147] According to the judgment, therefore, the violation of data protection becomes recognised as an act of unfair competition. A firm can sue a competitor, claiming that the latter, by not fulfilling its obligations under the GDPR, is able to gain unfair business advantages.

Although significant in opening new ventures as regards the interrelation between two areas of law traditionally separate, these late judgments do not offer hints concerning data access or exchange. If anything, on the contrary, they point to an increasing demand for clear rules governing digital markets and a market for data, if any.

2.5.7 The New EU Approach: *Ex ante* Regulation

As seen in digital markets, many business models are built on monetising data and acting as gatekeepers. Because data are so important for the digital economy, it is rational to assess the extent to which 'data markets' exist or take shape. No matter how tempting it may be, in legal terms, data per se can hardly be qualified as tradable goods. The Sections above aimed to demonstrate the shortcomings of property, competition, and data protection law enforcement to offer a regulatory framework hospitable to a data access and sharing regime for the establishment of data markets and the creation of a European Data Space, and more broadly, the regulation of digital markets. The fluid nature of data finds no parallel with existing concepts and traditional legal doctrines deriving from property and contracts. Likewise, competition principles cannot be directly applied.

Instead, digital markets can be considered markets for data-driven products and services, where competition and innovation lie in the ability to exploit the data, e.g.,

146. *Ibid.*, para. 51.
147. *Lindenapotheke, supra* n. 144.

through the use of software algorithms, digital infrastructures, or product/service engineering and design. This distinction matters as it hardly justifies gatekeeping practices, where data are controlled de facto without proper legal title except in those established circumscribed situations where intellectual property rights or data protection law intervene. However, the controls granted by intellectual property escape individual data. Likewise, when data are personal, data protection law addresses data subjects' control as a relative right that does not necessarily exclude the possibility of others accessing or using the data. Moreover, third parties may well access personal data upon data subjects' consent. De facto control and gatekeeping negatively impact data-driven markets. Yet competition law enforcement is limited in application and does not offer a regulatory framework capable of challenging them. Not only data are amorphous and challenging to traditional legal constructs but also digital markets move too fast and are too varied and complex to be supervised *ex post* by the competent authorities. Moreover, competition law does not provide a general approach for applying the essential facility doctrine to dominant platforms; enforcement would depend on the specific circumstances of each case in terms of the specific conduct in question and its economic context. This does not mean that competition law is generally unfit to preserve the contestability of markets or other structural aspects not covered in this contribution.[148] Competition law may continue to serve the purpose of limiting anti-competitive practices but appears unsuitable to tackle data concentration and bottlenecking.

In this scenario, legal intervention could give regulators the power to require or prohibit behaviours to reach desired economic and social outcomes without having to engage in proving unfit competition rules on a case-by-case basis.

Unsurprisingly, *ex ante* regulation of the platform economy has recently gained popularity in EU policy circles. In preventing a level playing field and obstructing innovation, the bottlenecks created by data are a difficult issue that could be better addressed by the regulatory realm.[149]

On the one hand, regulation ensures higher technical specialisation and can be more effective in addressing the structural problems of markets like the digital ones that cannot be tackled under EU competition rules. On the other hand, it is also capable of more effectively addressing the unfair allocation of resources, welfare, and social harms.[150]

Indeed, as the European Commission has started to recognise:

> competition alone cannot address all the systemic problems that may arise in the platform economy. Based on the single market logic, additional rules may be needed to ensure contestability, fairness and innovation, and the possibility of

148. Nicolas Petit, *Big Tech and the Digital Economy: The Moligopoly Scenario* (Oxford University Press 2020).
149. A European Strategy for Data, *supra* n. 2, esp. 8 and 14.
150. Jean Tirole, *Economics for the Common Good* (Princeton University Press 2017); Niamh Dunne, *Competition Law and Economic Regulation, Making and Managing Markets* (Cambridge University Press 2015); Crémer et al., *supra* n. 114.

> market entry, as well as public interests that go beyond competition or economic considerations.[151]

As will be seen in Chapter 4, this shift in approach was the basis for the enactment of the DMA, which introduced a form of *ex ante* regulation to supplement the European Commission's and CJEU's *ex post* competition enforcement activities. Equally, this is the approach taken by the Data Act (Chapter 3), the new EU regulation put in place to achieve data sharing among market players, which attempts to eliminate the limits or uncertainties of competition law enforcement. The question remains of how it can achieve the expected results established in the policy goals.

151. European Commission, "Shaping Europe's Digital Future" (2021), available at https://ec.europa.eu/info/strategy/priorities-2019-2024/europe-fit-digital-age/shaping-europe-digital-future_en.

CHAPTER 3
The Data Act

3.1 REGULATING THE POLICY OBJECTIVES OF THE EUROPEAN DATA STRATEGY

As seen in the previous Chapter 2, data is an essential resource for economic growth, competitiveness, and innovation. The policy on the European Strategy for Data aimed at creating a single market for data to ensure that the EU remains globally competitive and maintains the authority and right to govern and control the data generated within its borders (data sovereignty). This policy is aimed at the creation of Common European Data Spaces, which could ensure that more data become available for use in the economy and society while keeping the legal or natural persons who generate the data in control. In particular, such an EU market needs to create spaces where data can flow within the EU and across sectors; European rules such as data protection and competition law are fully respected; the rules for access and use of data are fair, practical and clear European data are pooled in key sectors with common and interoperable data spaces; users have rights, tools and skills to stay in full control of their data.[1] This way, the EU intends to establish a legal framework around its core values that comprise of a competitive and functioning single market, fairness, proportionality, accountability, and transparency.

To achieve its strategic results, the legislature includes as many players as possible, building around three main types of interactions: Business-to-Consumers (B2C), Business-to-Business (B2B), and Business-to-Government (B2G).

Chapter 2 has discussed the difficulties of establishing a legal basis for claims of title over the data. Innovatively, the EU has abandoned a property-based approach, avoiding creating the extension of existing intellectual property rights or creating new ones. Instead, the legal technique chosen by the EU to achieve what has been termed

1. European Commission, 'A European Strategy for Data' (Communication) COM(2020) 66 final.

as the European single market for data has been that of introducing a set of access and portability rules combined with provisions regulating B2B and B2G data exchanges in a mixed public-private regulatory space. This legal technique, to some extent analogous to the GDPR, resolves around the adoption of a 'data governance' rather than a 'data property' approach.[2]

The two key pieces of legislation that have been enacted to achieve the objectives of the European Data Strategy are the DGA[3] and the Data Act.[4]

3.1.1 The Data Governance Act

The DGA has been designed to provide a framework to enhance trust in data sharing for the benefit of businesses and citizens. It aims to facilitate the reuse of certain categories of data held by public sector bodies for a fee derived from the costs involved[5] by regulating new entities known as data intermediaries and promoting data sharing for altruistic reasons.[6] Accordingly, important knowledge may be extracted from such data without compromising their protected nature. The DGA provides for rules and safeguards to facilitate their reuse for different purposes. As an act of a voluntary nature, it does not create any obligation on public sector bodies to allow the reuse of data, nor does it release public sector bodies from their confidentiality obligations under the applicable law.[7] To achieve its goals, it prohibits "agreements or other practices pertaining to the re-use of data held by public sector bodies [...] which grant exclusive rights or which have as their objective or effect to grant such exclusive rights or to restrict the availability of data for re-use by entities other than the parties to such agreements or other practices."[8] However, as an exception, it allows the granting of an exclusive right for no longer than one year to reuse such data if necessary in the general interest.[9] The data involved are those held by public sector bodies that are protected on grounds of commercial confidentiality, statistical confidentiality, the protection of intellectual property rights of third parties, or the protection of personal data.[10] Both personal and non-personal data are in the scope of the DGA, and wherever personal

2. Thomas Margoni, Charlotte Ducuing and Luca Schirru, *Data Property, Data Governance and Common European Data Spaces*, Computerrecht: Tijdschrift voor Informatica, Telecommunicatie en Recht, no pages (2023), available at https://ssrn.com/abstract=4428364 and http://dx.doi.org/10.2139/ssrn.4428364.
3. Regulation (EU) 2022/868 of the European Parliament and of the Council of 30 May 2022 on European data governance and amending Regulation (EU) 2018/1724 (Data Governance Act), OJ L 152, 3.6.2022, p. 1-44.
4. Regulation (EU) 2023/2854 of the European Parliament and of the Council of 13 December 2023 on harmonised rules on fair access to and use of data and amending Regulation (EU) 2017/2394 and Directive (EU) 2020/1828 (Data Act), OJ L, 2023/2854, 22.12.2023.
5. Article 1(1) DGA and Article 6 DGA.
6. Articles 10 to 25 DGA.
7. Article 1(2) DGA.
8. Article 4(1) DGA.
9. Articles 4(2) and 4(4) DGA.
10. Article 3 DGA.

data are involved, the GDPR applies.[11] Likewise, it is without prejudice to the application of competition law.[12]

3.1.2 The Data Act

The other piece of legislation that formalises the EU strategy on data is the Data Act, which entered into force on 11 January 2024 and becomes applicable from September 2025. It complements the DGA.

The overarching goal of the Data Act is to establish a single data market and make the EU competitive in the data economy by harnessing the potential of the ever-increasing amount of data, especially the industrial ones. Its aim is to provide legal clarity regarding the access to and use of data. Indeed, with the evolution of digitalisation and digital markets, the volume of data generated by humans and machines has been increasing exponentially and there has been a rapid growth in the availability of products on the market connected to the internet, as well as related services (i.e., anything that would make a connected product behave in a specific manner).

At the same time, the data represent the digitisation of user actions and events and should accordingly be accessible to the user. However, most data are unused, or their value is concentrated in the hands of a few large companies. In this context, the Data Act endeavours to empower the users of connected products to gain value from the data that they generate using the products themselves. It is an act addressed to businesses or individuals who own, lease, or rent connected products seeking to maintain incentives for those who invest in data technologies.[13]

Thus, in the intentions of the EU legislator, the Data Act should make more data available for the benefit of companies, citizens and public administrations. The designed measures are meant to create legal certainty for companies and consumers engaged in data generation by establishing clear rules on the permissible use of data and the associated conditions while sustaining incentives for Data Holders to continue investing in high-quality data generation. A clear framework should facilitate the transfer of data between Data Holders and data users while upholding their confidentiality. This is a measure to encourage more players to participate in the data economy, especially SMEs.[14] Likewise, to facilitate market participants in the negotiations and making of fair data-transfer contracts, the European Commission commits to developing model contract clauses. Another way to facilitate market participation and innovation is to mitigate the abuse of contractual imbalances that impede equitable data sharing. This entails safeguarding enterprises from unjust contractual terms imposed by a party wielding a considerably stronger market position. Equally, new rules should enable public sector bodies to access and use data held by the private sector for specific public interest purposes. For instance, in situations akin to the COVID-19 pandemic, public sector bodies should be able to request data necessary to respond to a public

11. Article 1(3) DGA.
12. Article 1(4) DGA.
13. Recitals 1-6, 14, 15 Data Act.
14. Recital 36 Data Act.

emergency with minimal burden on businesses. Another benefit that the Data Act attempts to achieve is to facilitate customers to effectively switch between different providers of data-processing services to unlock the EU cloud market and gain efficient data interoperability.[15]

To give effect to its many goals, the Data Act is a lengthy piece of legislation in the legal form of an EU Regulation. The legal basis for this proposal is Article 114 TFEU, whose objective is the establishment and functioning of the internal market by enhancing measures for the approximation of national rules.

To address the complex and heterogeneous set of issues of the data economy, the Data Act is structured into nine chapters. Each chapter aims to fulfil definite objectives (*see* section 3.2.1. below). The European Commission in its Explanatory Memorandum illustrates the chapters and corresponding objectives as follows:

- Chapter I establishes the general provisions which set out the scope of the regulation and defines key terms.
- Chapter II on B2B and B2C data sharing in the context of Internet of Things (IoT) provides for users of IoT objects to access, use and port data that they co-generate through their use of a connected product.
- Chapter III on B2B data sharing clarifies the data-sharing conditions wherever a business is obliged by law, including through the Data Act, to share data with another business.
- Chapter IV on unfair contractual terms aims to protect all businesses, in particular SMEs, against unfair contractual terms imposed on them.
- Chapter V on B2G data sharing seeks to enable public sector bodies to make more evidence-based decisions in certain situations of exceptional need through measures to access certain data held by the private sector.
- Chapter VI on switching between data processing services establishes the minimum requirements for providers of cloud and edge computing services to facilitate interoperability and enable switching between services.
- Chapter VII on unlawful third-country government access to data protects non-personal data stored in the EU against unlawful foreign government access requests.
- Chapter VIII on interoperability sets the criteria that participants in data spaces must fulfil to allow data to flow within and between such data spaces.
- Chapter IX on enforcement establishes the obligation for Member States to designate one or more competent authority(ies) to monitor and enforce the Data Act and, in case more than one authority is designated, provides for the appointment of a data coordinator to act as the single point of contact at the national level.[16]

The following Sections deal in more detail with the key provisions of the Data Act.

15. European Commission, Data Act Explained, available at https://digital-strategy.ec.europa.eu/en/factpages/data-act-explained.
16. *Ibid.*

3.2 KEY PROVISIONS OF THE DATA ACT

3.2.1 General Provisions

As anticipated, the Data Act covers personal and non-personal data, aiming to achieve mainly the five objectives of (subject matter and scope of the act):

(a) facilitating data sharing, i.e., access to and the use of data by consumers and businesses, while preserving incentives to invest in ways of generating value through data. This objective is implemented in Chapters II to IV of the Data Act;
(b) providing for the use by public sector bodies and EU institutions of data held by businesses in certain situations where there is an exceptional need for data in the public interest. This objective is implemented in Chapter V of the Data Act;
(c) facilitating switching between digital services processing data. This objective is implemented in Chapter VI of the Data Act;
(d) introducing safeguards against unlawful data transfer without notification by service providers. This objective is implemented in Chapter VII;
(e) providing for the development of interoperability standards for data to be reused among sectors and the removal of barriers to data sharing across data spaces. This objective is implemented in Chapter VIII.[17]

To achieve such objectives, Article 1 of the Data Act lays down harmonised rules on making data generated by the use of a connected product or related service available to the user of that product or service, on the making data available by Data Holders to Data Recipients, and on the making data available by Data Holders to public sector bodies or Union institutions, agencies or bodies for the performance of tasks in the public interest.[18]

To understand the scope of the provision and the actors involved, it is necessary to become familiar with the terminology used and key definitions offered by the Data Act itself.

Article 1 introduces three subjects who are the addressees of the norm. A data 'User' is a natural or legal person that owns, rents or leases a product or receives a service; a data 'Holder' is a legal or natural person who has the right or obligation by law (or in the case of non-personal data and through control of the technical design of the product and related services) to use and make available data which it has reused or generated during the provision of a related service; a data 'recipient', sometimes referred to as a third party, is a legal or natural person acting for business (but different from the User of a product or related service) to whom the Data Holder makes the data available.[19]

17. Article 1 Data Act.
18. *Ibid.*
19. Article 2 Data Act.

Under Article 2 of the Data Act, the definition of 'data' is taken from the DGA as "any digital representation of acts, facts or information and any compilation of such acts, facts or information, including in the form of sound, visual or audio-visual recording," distinguishing between personal data as defined by Article 4(1) GDPR and non-personal data as data other than personal data. In so doing, the provision thus recreates the difficulties of drawing a line between these two types of data, as stressed before in section 2.3.2.

In turn, data generation is the result of the actions of at least two actors, i.e., the designer or manufacturer of products, who may in many cases also be a provider of related services, and the User of such products or related services. These connected digital products and related services compose a network, often referred to as the IoT, which increases exponentially the volume of data available for reuse. Examples of connected products can be found in all aspects of the economy and society, including in private, civil or commercial infrastructure, vehicles, health and lifestyle equipment, ships, aircraft, home equipment and consumer goods, medical and health devices or agricultural and industrial machinery, and anything that is able of communicating those data via electronic communications such as telephone networks, television cable networks, satellite-based networks and near-field communication networks. The same can be said for cloud products and services, i.e., application and infrastructure resources that exist on the Internet, where third-party providers contract with subscribers for these services, allowing customers to leverage computing resources without having to purchase or maintain hardware and software.[20] In essence, the connected products targeted by the Data Act are items that obtain, generate or collect data concerning their use or environment and that are able to communicate product data via an electronic communications service,[21] with the exception of devices that have mere accessory functions (e.g., personal computers, servers, tablets and smartphones, cameras, webcams, sound recording systems and scanners).[22] Arguably, the exclusion of such devices known to generate large amounts of data substantially reduces the scope of the Data Act.

---

20. European Commission, Explanatory Memorandum, Proposal for a Regulation of the European Parliament and of the Council on harmonised rules on fair access to and use of data (Data Act), COM(2022) 68 final; European Commission, Impact Assessment Report and Support Studies Accompanying the Proposal for a Data Act, available from https://digital-strategy.ec.europa.eu/en/library/impact-assessment-report-and-support-studies-accompanying-proposal-data-act. Article 2 Data Act defines a 'connected product' as "an item that obtains, generates or collects data concerning its use or environment and that is able to communicate product data via an electronic communications service, physical connection or on-device access, and whose primary function is not the storing, processing or transmission of data on behalf of any party other than the user." In turn, a 'related service' is defined as "a digital service, other than an electronic communications service, including software, which is connected with the product at the time of the purchase, rent or lease in such a way that its absence would prevent the connected product from performing one or more of its functions, or which is subsequently connected to the product by the manufacturer or a third party to add to, update or adapt the functions of the connected product."
21. Article 2(5) Data Act.
22. Recital 15 Data Act.

Finally, like the DGA, the Data Act contains provisions concerning the relationship with other regulations that may overlap, clarifying from the outset that it complements and is without prejudice to their application. In so providing, the Data Act explicitly affirms the primacy of the GDPR, of norms that foster cooperation in criminal matters via data usage, of EU intellectual property rights, of EU competition law, and of Member States' prerogatives in specified areas.[23]

3.2.2 Rules on Data Sharing

The Data Act is a horizontal legal framework which envisages basic rules for all sectors as regards the rights to use data. At the same time, the rights and obligations on data access and use have also been already regulated to varying degrees at sectoral level. For example, in the payments sector, the PSD2[24] opens some types of payment information, thereby enabling the so-called Open Banking, a market model that shifts from the money business to the data business and vice versa where data are shared with new market players of the fintech industry. The Data Act does not change such existing legislation, but it envisages that legislation that will follow in these areas should in principle be aligned with its horizontal principles. Likewise, legislation in new areas will have to conform to the Data Act. For example, in the financial services sector, the new proposal for Financial Data Access (FIDA)[25] is aligned with the Data Act to introduce new legal obligations on financial institutions acting as Data Holders to share defined categories of data. In essence, this means that the Data Act leaves room for vertical legislation to set more detailed rules for the achievement of sector-specific regulatory objectives.[26]

In B2C and B2B dealings, to create fairness in the data economy and empower users to reap value from the data that they generate, the Data Act introduces an obligation to make data generated by the use of connected products and related services accessible to the Users.[27] According to Article 3(1), products and services must be designed, manufactured, or provided so that data generated by their use are directly accessible to the Users by default, easily, securely, free of charge, in a comprehensive, structured, commonly used and machine-readable format.

At first sight, the provision – applying to B2B and B2C use of connected products and related services and having horizontal character covering the whole IoT and cloud sector – seems to have a very broad scope of application. At the same time, however, it needs to be considered that it does not cover inferred or derived data, i.e., data based

23. Article 1(5) to (10) Data Act.
24. Directive (EU) 2015/2366 of the European Parliament and of the Council of 25 November 2015 on payment services in the internal market, amending Directives 2002/65/EC, 2009/110/EC and 2013/36/EU and Regulation (EU) No. 1093/2010, and repealing Directive 2007/64/EC, OJ L 337, 35-127.
25. Proposal for a Regulation of the European Parliament and of the Council on a framework for Financial Data Access and amending Regulations (EU) No. 1093/2010, (EU) No. 1094/2010, (EU) No. 1095/2010 and (EU) 2022/2554, COM/2023/360 final.
26. Explanatory Memorandum, *supra* n. 20.
27. *Ibid.*

on analysis of volunteered or observed data, data developed around the Users without their express input, such as those systematically generated based on search histories, content consumption, purchases, and social media activity, or new data created by combining and processing existing raw data.

Moreover, the data sharing obligation is limited to uses which do not compete with the products or services from which the data originate.

These inconsistencies have led some scholars to doubt the capability of the Data Act to tackle situations of abuse, be it of dominant market position under competition law or market imbalances under consumer law.[28]

In addition to the data sharing obligation, the Data Holder must provide Users with a minimum of relevant information concerning the data as provided in Article 3(2)(a-i) of the Data Act. For instance, it obliges Data Holders to inform Users about the nature and volume of data generated by the products or services and how to access, retrieve, or erase such data. In so doing, the EU legislator reproduces in the Data Act the information obligation paradigm that permeates EU consumer law and the GDPR to protect the users as the weaker party of the relationship by correcting information asymmetries and rebalancing market power relationships.

Where data access cannot be granted to Users directly or by default, Article 4 introduces a set of rights and obligations to make data available on request and free of charge.[29] Users are entitled to authorise the Data Holder to give access to the data on the basis of contractual agreement to third-party service providers, such as providers of aftermarket services. In turn, third parties receiving data at the request of the User have the obligation to process data only for the purposes and under the conditions agreed with the Users.[30]

Importantly, the sui generis right of the Database Directive[31] (*see supra* section 2.3.3.) does not apply when data is obtained from or generated by a connected product or related service.[32] As seen, investment in databases in the EU are protected under EU Law.[33] One of the most contentious elements of the Database Directive has been the distinction between investments in creating data vis-à-vis obtaining data. The former is generally excluded from the sui generis protection due to their potential anti-competitive effects in information markets. However, it may not always be straight-forward to distinguish and separate between the two types of investments as they may coexist.[34] In order to eliminate the risk that Holders of data in databases claim

28. E.g., *see* Matthias Leistner and Lucie Antonie, *Attention, Here Comes the EU Data Act! A Critical in-Depth Analysis of the Commission's 2022 Proposal*, 3 Journal of Intellectual Property, Information Technology and Electronic Commerce Law, 339-349 (2022); Onntje Hinrichs, *Consumer Law and the Regulation of the Free Flow of Data: Upsetting the Balance of the European Data Protection Framework*, 13 Journal of European Consumer and Market Law, 78-86 (2024).
29. Article 4 Data Act.
30. Article 5 Data Act.
31. Directive 96/9/EC of the European Parliament and of the Council of 11 March 1996 on the legal protection of databases [1996] OJ L 77/20.
32. Article 43 Data Act.
33. Database Directive, *supra* n. 31.
34. Case C-203/02, *The British Horseracing Board Ltd and Others v. William Hill Organization Ltd.*, ECLI:EU:C:2004:695; Case C-338/02, *Fixtures Marketing Ltd v. Svenska Spel AB.*, ECLI:EU:C: 2004:696.

protection, instead of reviewing the Database Directive, the Data Act clarifies that the sui generis right for the protection of databases does not apply to databases containing data obtained from or generated by a connected product or related service falling within its scope, in particular in relation to Articles 4 and 5 Data Act (*see supra*).[35] This means that machine-generated data should not pass the test for protection. All in all, the decision of the EU legislator to exclude databases containing data obtained from or generated by a connected product or related service from the application of the Database Directive may be considered consistent with the policy objectives of endowing enforceable access and portability rights to the Users.

Then, third parties - which cannot make the data they receive available to other third parties - must erase the data when these are no longer necessary for the agreed purpose, unless otherwise agreed with the User in relation to non-personal data. Likewise, such third parties must not prevent the Users who are consumers from making the data they receive available to other parties.[36]

Importantly, to favour innovation, competition, and the development of an EU digital industry, the EU legislator restricts data sharing with gatekeepers and it exempts SMEs from the obligations of Articles 2 to 6 of the Data Act, provided that they do not have partnerships or subcontracting obligations with companies that do not qualify as SMEs.[37]

In particular, SMEs are likely to struggle to obtain access to relevant data. Therefore, the Data Act aims to facilitate access to data for SMEs but not to gatekeepers, who shall not be included as beneficiaries of the data access right. This means that gatekeepers cannot request or be granted access to users' data generated by the use of a connected product or related service. Furthermore, third parties to whom data are made available at the request of the User may not make the data available to a gatekeeper, for example, by subcontracting the provision of services to gatekeepers. Having established such a norm does not mean that third parties cannot use data processing services offered by gatekeepers, nor does it prevent gatekeepers from obtaining and using the same data through other lawful means. Accordingly, as voluntary agreements between gatekeepers and Data Holders remain unaffected, the limitations on granting access to gatekeepers cannot exclude the former from the market or prevent them from offering their services.[38]

3.2.3 Further Obligations of Data Holders

Data Holders' obligations are further elaborated in Chapter III (Articles 8 to 12 Data Act) and Chapter IV (Article 13 Data Act) for B2B transactions under Article 5 Data Act

35. Article 43 Data Act and Recital 112 Data Act. For B2G, *see* Recital 71 Data Act according to which "where the sui generis database rights under Directive 96/9/EC *(...)* apply in relation to the requested datasets, data Holders should exercise their rights in such a way that does not prevent the public sector body, the Commission, the European Central Bank or Union body from obtaining the data, or from sharing it, in accordance with this Regulation."
36. Article 6 Data Act.
37. Article 7 Data Act.
38. Recital 40 Data Act.

(above) and where one party has a legal obligation under other EU or national law to make data available to another business party. In such dealings, Data Holders have to agree with Data Recipients on the arrangements for making the data available according to the principles of fairness, reasonableness, non-discrimination, and transparency.[39] These are already fundamental principles of EU Law in dealings with natural persons, now extended by the Data Act in B2B operations to the general framework of data sharing also covered by other legislation.

To give effect to the above and derogating the core principle of contractual freedom, the Data Act postulates that a contractual term concerning data sharing, or liability and remedies for the breach or termination of data-related obligations, is not deemed to be binding if it constitutes an unfair contractual term, i.e., it is severed from the contract.[40] Interestingly, the regulation introduces the concept of unfairness of contractual terms in B2B agreements. Under EU law, this is a normative concept and provision typical of B2C transactions to rebalance asymmetries and negotiating power in markets.

Like in the case of consumer contracts, unfair contractual terms in B2B data-sharing agreements are those unilaterally imposed on another enterprise. Thus, reproducing consumer law, the legislator intervenes in situations where one of the businesses is in a stronger bargaining position for its market size and imposes non-negotiable terms related to data access and use on the other. Either the other party accepts the unilaterally imposed terms, or it cannot conclude the contract and leaves. For example, this is often the case of SMEs which in the intention of the legislator will no longer find themselves in such situation and may be placed in the situation to develop and market products and services and innovate.[41]

The non-exhaustive list of terms in data sharing that are always considered to be unfair is explicated in Article 13(4) Data Act:

> (a) terms that exclude or limit the liability of the party that unilaterally imposed the term for intentional acts or gross negligence;
> (b) terms that exclude the remedies available to the party upon whom the term has been unilaterally imposed in the case of non-performance of contractual obligations or the liability of the party that unilaterally imposed the term in the case of a breach of those obligations;
> (c) terms that give the party that unilaterally imposed the term the exclusive right to determine whether the data supplied are in conformity with the contract or to interpret any contractual term.[42]

Alongside the above terms that are always considered unfair, there are terms that the legislator presumes to be unfair, thus allowing the party that imposed the terms to

39. Article 8(1) Data Act.
40. Article 8(2) Data Act.
41. Article 13(1) and (3) Data Act.
42. Article 13(4) Data Act.

demonstrate that they are not unfair, i.e., they remain valid and enforceable for the effects of the contract. These terms are those whose "object or effect" is to:

(a) inappropriately limit remedies in the case of non-performance of contractual obligations or liability in the case of a breach of those obligations or extend the liability of the enterprise upon whom the term has been unilaterally imposed;
(b) allow the party that unilaterally imposed the term to access and use the data of the other contracting party in a manner that is significantly detrimental to the legitimate interests of the other contracting party, in particular when such data contain commercially sensitive data or are protected by trade secrets or by intellectual property rights;
(c) prevent the party upon whom the term has been unilaterally imposed from using the data provided or generated by that party during the period of the contract or to limit the use of such data to the extent that that party is not entitled to use, capture, access or control such data or exploit the value of such data in an adequate manner;
(d) prevent the party upon whom the term has been unilaterally imposed from terminating the agreement within a reasonable period;
(e) prevent the party upon whom the term has been unilaterally imposed from obtaining a copy of the data provided or generated by that party during the period of the contract or within a reasonable period after the termination thereof;
(f) enable the party that unilaterally imposed the term to terminate the contract at unreasonably short notice, taking into consideration any reasonable possibility of the other contracting party switching to an alternative and comparable service and the financial detriment caused by such termination, except where there are serious grounds for so doing;
(g) enable the party that unilaterally imposed the term to substantially change the price specified in the contract or any other substantive condition related to the nature, format, quality or quantity of the data to be shared, where no valid reason and no right of the other party to terminate the contract in the case of such a change is specified in the contract."[43] However, this presumption may not affect terms by which the party that unilaterally imposed them reserves the right to unilaterally change the terms of a contract of an indeterminate duration, provided that the contract:
   - specified a valid reason for such unilateral changes;
   - that the party that unilaterally imposed the term is required to provide the other contracting party with reasonable notice of any such intended change; and
   - that the other contracting party is free to terminate the contract at no cost in the case of a change.[44]

---

43. Article 13(5) Data Act.
44. *Ibid.*

Data Holders are prevented from making the data available to Data Recipients without a request by the Users.[45] When allowed to make the data available, Data Holders cannot discriminate between comparable categories of Data Recipients, even when the latter are partners or otherwise linked with the Data Holders. In case a Data Recipient considers that the conditions under which data has been made available to it are discriminatory, the Data Holder has the obligation to provide the Data Recipient with information showing that there has been no discrimination.[46] As an incentive to data sharing, Data Holders that are obliged to share data may request reasonable and non-discriminatory compensation from the Data Recipients. This compensation may include the costs incurred for making the data available, as well as technical costs related to dissemination and storage. However, SMEs and non-profit research organisations cannot be charged more than the costs incurred for making the data available.[47] In case of disagreement on the compensation or conditions to come to an agreement, dispute settlement bodies certified by the Member States may assist parties.[48]

Finally, in order to protect Data Holders, the Data Act includes a non-exhaustive list of measures to remedy situations where third parties or Users have unlawfully accessed data. For example, a Data Holder could require that an infringing party stops producing a product or erases the data unlawfully obtained. Likewise, Data Holders may seek compensation for infringements.[49]

3.2.4 B2G Data Sharing

The Data Act introduces a harmonised framework for the use by public sector bodies and EU institutions of data held by private parties under exceptional needs for the data requested. The framework is based on an obligation on Data Holders who are legal persons to make data available and it applies only in the case of public emergencies or in situations where public sector bodies have an exceptional need to use certain data in the public interest, but such data cannot be obtained on the market.[50]

Exceptional circumstances may be justified in case of a public emergency, defined as an exceptional situation negatively affecting the population of the EU or a Member State, with a risk of serious and lasting repercussions for living conditions or economic stability, financial stability, or the substantial and immediate degradation of economic assets in the EU or a Member State.[51] In such exceptional circumstances (e.g., a health emergency such as the one which occurred with the COVID-19 crisis) or major natural or human-induced disasters, data would be made available for free. In other cases of exceptional need, including situations where it is necessary to prevent or

45. Article 8(4) Data Act.
46. Article 8(3) Data Act.
47. Article 9 Data Act.
48. Article 10 Data Act.
49. Article 11 Data Act.
50. Article 14 Data Act.
51. Article 2(29) Data Act.

assist the recovery from a public emergency, Data Holders are entitled to the compensation of the costs for making the data available in addition to a reasonable margin.[52]

Data access by the public sector may also be needed when the lack of availability of data prevents the relevant body from fulfilling a specific task in the public interest that has been explicitly provided by law (e.g., weather forecast or climate monitoring to prevent disasters).[53] The obligation to demonstrate that the public sector body was unable to obtain non-personal data by purchasing them on the market does not apply where the specific task carried out in the public interest is the production of official statistics and where the purchase of such data is not allowed by national law.[54]

To ensure that the right to request data is not abused and that the public sector remains accountable for the use of the data, the requests for data need to be specific and proportionate; it should clearly indicate the purpose to be achieved, and it needs to respect the interests of the Data Holders making the data available.[55] Competent authorities will have to ensure the transparency and public availability of all requests, and they will have to handle complaints.[56]

Crucially, public sector bodies are entitled to share the data that they have accessed under the above provisions with individuals or organisations carrying out scientific research or analytics or with statistical institutes for the production of official statistics.[57]

Finally, specific provisions are in place to promote and enhance mutual assistance and cross-border cooperation among public sector bodies regarding data sharing.[58]

3.2.5 Switching Between Data Processing Services

A major problem in digital markets is that users are likely to face a number of barriers to switch from one provider to another, covering the same type of products or services. For example, this is usually due to high charges associated with data egress, lengthy procedures, and absence of interoperability between providers that can result in a loss of data and/or functionality of applications. Therefore, to ensure a competitive market in the EU and overcome the imbalance of power between providers and customers of data processing services, the latter should be able to switch easily and seamlessly between products and services provided by a different provider. The Data Act introduces minimum regulatory requirements of contractual, commercial and technical nature imposed on providers of data processing services (e.g., digital services enabling ubiquitous and on-demand network access, providers of cloud, edge and other data processing services) to enable switching between such services. All providers are required to remove obstacles that their customers may face when they want to

52. Article 20 Data Act.
53. Article 15(1)(b) Data Act.
54. Article 15(3) Data Act.
55. Article 17 Data Act.
56. Article 37 Data Act.
57. Article 21 Data Act.
58. Article 22 Data Act.

switch to another provider or use several services from various providers at the same time.[59]

In particular, under Article 23 Data Act, providers of data processing services are not entitled to impose precommercial, commercial, technical, contractual and organisational obstacles which inhibit customers from terminating the relevant contract, concluding new contracts with a different provider, porting the exportable data and digital asset to a different provider, achieving functional equivalence in the use of the new data processing service, or unbundling data processing services from other data processing services provided by the provider of data processing services. There is an exception for technical unfeasibility, but the burden of proof remains on the service provider. Likewise, specific technical standards or interfaces are not mandated. However, there is the requirement for services to be compatible with EU standards or with open interoperability technical specifications where these exist (*see infra*, section 3.2.6.).[60]

The rights of the customer and the obligations of the providers must be clearly set out in a written contract. The Data Act details the rules regarding the minimum requirements of the contract between the parties.[61] For example, the contract must include at least the following clauses allowing the customer to switch or to port all exportable data and digital assets to a different provider without undue delay, at the same time guaranteeing the provision of reasonable assistance to the customer and third parties and maintaining functionality and security.[62]

The provider of data processing services is also under the obligation to provide customers with all relevant information on available procedures, methods, standards, and specifications for switching and porting to the data processing service.[63]

From 12 January 2027, providers are no longer allowed to impose any switching charges on the customer for the switching process. This means that there will be no charges for the operations that are necessary to facilitate switching or for data egress. However, as a transitional measure during the first three years after the Data Act's entry into force, providers may still charge their customers for the costs incurred in relation to switching and data egress.[64]

3.2.6 Interoperability

As seen above, standards and interoperability are essential for competition in digital markets and switching purposes. Standards and interoperability essentially mean that technical solutions should be able to communicate and exchange data among the various systems. They should make it possible to achieve data exchanges for the same service type, enhance portability of digital assets between different services, facilitate

59. Data Act Explained, *supra* n. 15.
60. Articles 23, 30, and 31 Data Act.
61. Article 25 Data Act.
62. *Ibid.*
63. Article 26 Data Act.
64. Article 29 Data Act.

functional equivalence between different services, not have an adverse impact on the security and integrity of data processing services and data, and be designed in such a way to allow for technical advances and the inclusion of new functions and innovation in data processing services.[65] This latter aspect is key to ensure that data from different sources can be used within and between operators to develop new products or services and foster innovation.

To these ends, rather than introducing general interoperability and standardisation obligations, the Data Act sets essential requirements to be complied with regarding interoperability of data and sharing mechanisms only for participants of data spaces and data processing service providers.

To achieve compliance, the dataset content, use restrictions, licences, data collection methodologies, data quality and uncertainty have to be sufficiently described in a machine-readable format. Such an obligation has been designed to allow Data Recipients to find, access and use the data.[66]

Equally, the data structures, data formats, vocabularies, classification schemes, taxonomies and code lists need to be described in a publicly available and consistent manner. The technical means to access the data, such as application programming interfaces and their terms of use and quality of service, should also be described to enable automatic access and transmission of data between parties.[67]

The European Commission will assess barriers to interoperability standardisation, and it may ask European standardisation organisations to draft harmonised standards that comply with the required requirements. Whenever necessary, the European Commission may adopt common specifications and guidelines.[68]

3.3 THE RELATIONSHIP BETWEEN THE DATA ACT AND THE GDPR

Data Holders under the Data Act are also Data Controllers under the GDPR. A data subject under the GDPR may be the User under the Data Act or another natural person. By express provision, the Data Act complements and is without prejudice to the GDPR.[69] In other words, data sharing obligations under the Data Act do not exempt data controllers from having to comply with the obligations of the GDPR (*supra*, Chapter 1) when applying the Data Act and sharing personal data. In principle, no provision of the Data Act should be applied or interpreted in such a way as to diminish or limit the right to the protection of personal data. Whilst this principle seems clear in theory, it is likely to become challenging to operationalise in practice. This is also because the Data Act provides only a few indications as to how the two regulatory regimes can be aligned.

65. Article 35 Data Act.
66. Article 33(1)(a) Data Act.
67. Article 33(1)(b)(c) Data Act.
68. Article 33(2-11) Data Act.
69. Article 1(5) Data Act and Recital 7 GDPR.

3.3.1 Legal Basis for Data Processing

Any processing of personal data pursuant to the Data Act should comply with the requirement of a valid legal basis for processing under Article 6 GDPR and Article 9 GDPR in case of sensitive data. The Data Act itself, however, does not constitute a legal basis for data processing. As Articles 6 and 9 GDPR need to be complied with, the first difficulty is that it may not be straightforward to identify the correct legal basis for processing under data sharing arrangements. Moreover, when consent is needed, this should be obtained in each case, which, in practice, in a number of cases that cannot be predetermined may reduce the efficiency of the data access and sharing rights of the Data Act. This may especially be the case also in consideration of the difficulties inherent to the concept of expressing a valid consent under the GDPR (*see supra* Chapter 1). Equally, the legal basis of the legitimate interest under Article 6(1)(f) GDPR, which is already a difficult legal basis to apply with an appropriate degree of certainty, may turn to create a number of uncertainties regarding its appropriate and proportionate use (*see supra* Chapter 1). Moreover, in order to use the legal basis of the legitimate interests, Users must weigh their legitimate interests against the interests of the data subjects. However, the Data Act does not specify any admissible case groups for this task of weighing the interests and rights at stake, which depends heavily on individual cases.

In the difficult search for the appropriate legal basis for processing, especially when big data are involved, it may also be challenging to distinguish sensitive data from non-sensitive data. The processing of non-personal data in vast amounts and aggregation from a variety of unrelated sources may easily reveal aspects of racial or ethnic origin, political opinions, religious or philosophical beliefs, trade union membership, health, sex life, or sexual orientation of a person. In the processing of sensitive data, however, Article 9(2) GDPR does not recognise the contractual necessity as an exception to the general prohibition to process special categories of data ex Article 9(1) GDPR. Instead, 'explicit consent' applies. For example, in the context of financial or payment data - which per se do not qualify as sensitive data - this observation challenges the legal basis that should be used to process payment account data. Depending upon the circumstances, such a processing may be considered either non-sensitive or sensitive. In certain situations, data can be processed on contractual grounds with no consent, in others on the 'explicit consent' by the data subject.

Then, there is the difficulty relating to the processing of personal data of third parties that are connected or even tied with the data of the User data subject. Take, for example, payment account data inevitably containing personal data of other third-party individuals - i.e., the so-called silent parties whose data are in a payment account for being the payee, the beneficiary of a payment, or a joint account Holder. Hence, the reservation whether the processing of third-party data is legitimate when consent for processing under Article 6 GDPR or explicit consent under Article 9 GDPR has been given by the User data subject or in cases when other grounds for processing are accepted. For example, it is doubtful that the contractual necessity of the User data subject under Article 6 GDPR permits the processing of third parties to the contract. It is objectionable that alien contractual relationships could constitute a legal obligation serving as a legal basis for the data processing of third parties. If this were the case, data protection law would be generally frustrated altogether, allowing for an indiscriminate processing of an undetermined number of data subjects only to satisfy private interests of contracts alien to data subjects. Hypothetically, the 'legitimate interest' pursued by the controller or a third party under Article 6(1)(f) GDPR may cover more appropriately the situation at hand and provide the legal basis for the processing. However, the legitimate interest of the controller is limited and determined by the reasonable expectations of data subjects, in this case, the third parties.[70]

3.3.2 Information Provision

As noted in Chapter 1, a key feature of the GDPR is that of providing extensive information to data subjects regarding data processing (Articles 12, 13 and 14 GDPR). The Data Act introduces a similar information obligation. Users of connected products or related digital services shall receive information about the data processing associated with such connected product or digital service before signing a purchase, rent or lease contract (Article 3 Data Act). Like the GDPR, this obligation aims to provide transparency over the data generated and to facilitate access to, and sharing of, such data. At the same time, the Data Act states that the obligation to provide information does not interfere with the obligation of the controller to provide information to the data subject pursuant to the GDPR.[71] This means that these obligations remain in parallel with one another. However, there are differences in the content of the information provided to data subjects under the GDPR and Users under the Data Act. Under the Data Act, it is sufficient that information is provided in a "clear and comprehensible manner"[72] whereas the GDPR sets a higher and more detailed requirement stating that information has to be provided in a "concise, transparent, intelligible and easily accessible form, using clear and plain language."[73] These considerations lead to the conclusion that businesses need to be careful in making such a distinction and need to engage in elaborated administrative burdens for legal compliance. From the side of the consumer data subject and User, by contrast, this contributes to addition information overload in a context of already controversial and failed use of information as the tool for consumer empowerment and the rebalancing of commercial power.

3.3.3 The Distinction Between Personal and Non-personal Data

Another practical difficulty appears to be that Data Holders may find it difficult to separate personal data from non-personal data, which are key in determining both the obligations that apply and the steps that must be taken to ensure lawful data sharing. The Data Act seems to take into consideration that Data Holders may comply with data sharing requests by anonymising personal data or, where the readily available data

70. Recital 47 GDPR.
71. Recital 24 GDPR.
72. Article 3 Data Act and Recital 24 Data Act.
73. Article 12 GDPR.

contain personal data of several data subjects, transmitting only personal data relating to the User. Anonymised data are data that were originally classified as personal data but that a process of technical operations removes elements of identification or identifiability. In this distinction between personal and non-personal (or even anonymised) data, however, the difficulty and ensuing criticism that may be perpetrated on the Data Act is that it reflects and exacerbates the same kind of problems experienced with the Regulation 2018/1807 on the free flow of non-personal data.[74] As put forward by legal scholarship for some time, personal and non-personal data in combined or large datasets are not clearly distinguishable. The concept itself of big data challenges such a distinction. A vast amount of data processed in digital markets relates at some point to an identified or identifiable natural person (*see supra*, section 2.3.2.).[75]

3.3.4 Data Portability

As noted in Chapter 1, the right to personal data portability was introduced by Article 20 GDPR. It is meant to foster competition, enhance data subjects' control over their data and potentially change the landscape of digital markets.

The GDPR right to data portability is enhanced and expanded by the Data Act. The data portability right of the GDPR is limited to personal data and requires certain conditions to be met (e.g., processing of personal data was carried out on the basis of consent or contractual relationship). It only applies to data subjects (natural persons) and to personal data provided by the concerned data subject. At the same time, the transmission from one controller to another has to be technically feasible.[76]

The Data Act aims to broaden the scope of the limited data portability right of the GDPR. Its obligations on data portability apply to both personal and non-personal data and to both individuals (natural persons) and businesses (legal persons), provided that they qualify as Users. Moreover, the legal basis for portability is no longer limited to consent or contractual necessity, but it applies to data processing grounded on any legal basis of the GDPR, including the legitimate interest clause.[77]

Moreover, the Data Act grants Users the right to access and make available to third parties data irrespective of the distinction between actively provided or passively observed data. Unlike Article 20 GDPR, it also mandates and ensures the technical feasibility of third-party access for all types of data falling within its scope, thus ensuring that technical feasibility is no longer an obstacle to data access and sharing.

74. Regulation (EU) 2018/1807 of the European Parliament and of the Council of 14 November 2018 on a framework for the free flow of non-personal data in the European Union, OJ L 303, 28.11.2018, p. 59-68.
75. E.g., *see* Inge Graef, Raphael Gellert, Nadezhda Purtova and Martin Husovec, *Feedback to the Commission's Proposal on a Framework for the Free Flow of Non-personal Data*, SRN Electronic Journal (January 2018) https://doi.org/10.2139/ssrn.3106791, available at https://papers.ssrn.com/sol3/papers.cfm?abstract_id=3106791; Bart van der Sloot, *Regulating Non-personal Data in the Age of Big Data*, in *Health Data Privacy under the GDPR*, 85-105 (Maria Tzanou ed., 2020); Leistner and Antonie, *supra* n. 28.
76. Article 20 GDPR.
77. Article 4 Data Act.

In short, the rights provided by the GDPR and the Data Act differ in scope, with the Data Act being without prejudice to the GDPR. It seems unclear the extent to which the Data Act may build new layers to the right under the GDPR. On the one hand, consumer Users potentially have more control over the data pertaining to them. These data are not only personal but also non-personal, raising the question of what sort of control individuals may or should have over the latter kind of data.

The positive side would be that of breaking data monopolies and boosting the EU data markets. However, as the rights in the GDPR and in the Data Act have different scopes and varying concepts, doubts remain on how individuals (especially in their capacity as consumers) may be able to effectively exercise the new right to data portability in practice in a way that is beneficial to them and the market.[78]

3.4 THE RELATIONSHIP BETWEEN THE DATA ACT AND CONSUMER LAW

The norms of the Data Act are not directly addressed to consumers but to Users, which may be natural or legal persons. At the same time, consumers feature explicitly in the B2C data sharing obligations of Chapter II Data Act. Moreover, the Data Act is particularly important for consumer Users as, in tandem with the GDPR, it attempts to empower them further with regard to their personal data.

For the avoidance of doubts, in conformity with EU consumer law a 'consumer' is defined as "any natural person who is acting for purposes which are outside that person's trade, business, craft or profession."[79]

The Data Act is clear in specifying that it does not affect national contract law and it complements and is without prejudice to the EU consumer law acquis, in particular the UCTD,[80] the UCPD[81] and the CRD.[82] Therefore, in contracts between a Data Holder and a consumer as User, EU consumer law applies.[83]

On the one hand, therefore, at first sight, the Data Act seems to complement the EU consumer law acquis.

78. Barbara Lazarotto, *The Right to Data Portability: A Holistic Analysis of GDPR, DMA and the Data Act*, 15 European Journal of Law and Technology, no pages (2024).
79. Article 2(23) Data Act.
80. Council Directive 93/13/EEC of 5 April 1993 on unfair terms in consumer contracts, OJ L 95, 21.4.1993, p. 29-34.
81. Directive 2005/29/EC of the European Parliament and of the Council of 11 May 2005 concerning unfair business-to-consumer commercial practices in the internal market and amending Council Directive 84/450/EEC, Directives 97/7/EC, 98/27/EC and 2002/65/EC of the European Parliament and of the Council and Regulation (EC) No. 2006/2004 of the European Parliament and of the Council ('Unfair Commercial Practices Directive'), OJ L 149, 11.6.2005, p. 22-39.
82. Directive 2011/83/EU of the European Parliament and of the Council of 25 October 2011 on consumer rights, amending Council Directive 93/13/EEC and Directive 1999/44/EC of the European Parliament and of the Council and repealing Council Directive 85/577/EEC and Directive 97/7/EC of the European Parliament and of the Council, OJ L 304, 22.11.2011, p. 64-88.
83. Recitals 9, 28 and 102 Data Act.

On the other hand, however, the references of being without prejudice to national contract law and EU consumer law directives may complicate – if not frustrate – the goal of a uniform application of the scope of the Data Act.

The contract law of the Member States, although for a number of respects it is influenced by the harmonisation process brought by the Directives in the field of consumer law, is largely governed by national law with different legal traditions. This means that in those occasions where consumer law or national law provisions impact data access and data sharing, there may be problems of different applications or interpretations. Thus, the Data Act may find a heterogeneous application in terms of levels of consumer protection or contract law. Likewise, national courts may create diverging national solutions.

Contrary to its intentions, therefore, the Data Act may create legal fragmentation any time contract law becomes applicable. A greater degree of harmonisation, further reducing differences in consumer laws and contract law at Member State level, may be needed.

Finally, it could not be underestimated that, by making reference to the EU consumer law acquis, the Data Act does not adapt old concepts to the new digital reality, but it expressly delegates and exacerbates the problems inherent to consumer protection typical of analogical markets. For example, the Data Act creates an additional layer of information overload for consumers. Under Article 3(2) Data Act, consumer Users are meant to receive additional pre-contractual information as to how they may access, retrieve or, where relevant, erase the data and other relevant terms. This additional layer of information is given to consumers who may not easily understand them. Insufficient weight is given to the question of 'who is the average consumer in digital markets?'. Consumer contracting parties are likely to bear a rational ignorance (*see* Chapter 8 *infra*).

Again, problems of legal fragmentation may also have the undesirable effect of creating market failures.

3.5 RISKS OF LEGAL FRAGMENTATION

It remains to be seen how data spaces will operate in practical terms. At present, the Data Act seems a highly technical and complex regulation which interplays with several equally intricate EU legislative acts that are structuring and framing the emerging digital markets. In addition to the legal instruments outlined above in this Section of the Chapter, several other pieces of EU law coexist.[84] The interaction of the

---

84. E.g., *see* the Open Data Directive, Directive (EU) 2019/1024 of the European Parliament and of the Council of 20 June 2019 on open data and the re-use of public sector information (recast), OJ L 172, 26.6.2019, p. 56-83; the Free Flow of Non-Personal Data Regulation, *supra* n. 74; the Platform-to-Business Regulation, Regulation (EU) 2019/1150 of the European Parliament and of the Council of 20 June 2019 on promoting fairness and transparency for business users of online intermediation services, OJ L 186, 11.7.2019, p. 57-79; the Payments Services Directive 2, Directive (EU) 2015/2366 of the European Parliament and of the Council of 25 November 2015 on payment services in the internal market, amending Directives 2002/65/EC, 2009/110/EC and 2013/36/EU and Regulation (EU) No. 1093/2010, and repealing Directive 2007/64/EC, OJ L 337,

Data Act with other relevant EU legal instruments is essentially based on the provision of a "without prejudice" clause or an explicit derogation.

Although the "without prejudice" clause or express derogations are present in the Data Act, the intersection between different pieces of legislation is often prone to cause misunderstandings, especially - but not limited to - of operational nature. These misunderstandings are likely to surface and will probably be solved on a case-by-case basis at the risk of engulfing Courts for the particularities and technicalities of the subject at stake.

As a general remark, it could be agreed with that scholarship that has begun to study the subject, according to which the relationship with other EU legislation needs to be further clarified and consolidated. As it stands, the legal framework for Data Law package appears fragmented and capable of reducing its potential effectiveness. In the absence of such endeavours, intricate overlaps and balancing issues remain unsolved or unclear, thus risking to be a major cause of legal uncertainty as well as fertile ground for opportunistic behaviour or free riding in digital markets.[85] Such an observation is topped off by a highly distinctive legislative technique that is overly complex, especially for markets characterised by ever-evolving technological innovation and technical mechanisms.

The Data Act is meant to be a crucial part of the Data Law framework, constituting a piece of the legal puzzle which is shaping the EU digital markets. Finding and maintaining coordination and coherence in such a technical and highly sophisticated domain within the broader Data Law framework seems to be the challenge that will accompany interpreters and operators for the years to come, with the ensuing risks created by legal uncertainty, not last the adequate protection of users (especially consumer users). Digital markets are markets characterised by particularly complex transactions, especially when it comes to data processing in the era of big data. Legal complexity, coordination and coherence may turn into a frustrating exercise when faced with the context of ever-changing technologies and innovation in a globally competitive environment that sees the EU already lagging behind vis-à-vis its eastern and western competitors alike.

23.12.2015, p. 35-127; the Digital Markets Act, Regulation (EU) 2022/1925 of the European Parliament and of the Council of 14 September 2022 on contestable and fair markets in the digital sector and amending Directives (EU) 2019/1937 and (EU) 2020/1828 (Digital Markets Act), OJ L 265, 12.10.2022, p. 1-66; the Digital Services Act, Regulation (EU) 2022/2065 of the European Parliament and of the Council of 19 October 2022 on a Single Market for Digital Services and amending Directive 2000/31/EC (Digital Services Act), OJ L 277, 27.10.2022, p. 1-102; the Artificial Intelligence Act, Regulation (EU) 2024/1689 of the European Parliament and of the Council of 13 June 2024 laying down harmonised rules on artificial intelligence and amending Regulations (EC) No. 300/2008, (EU) No. 167/2013, (EU) No. 168/2013, (EU) 2018/858, (EU) 2018/1139 and (EU) 2019/2144 and Directives 2014/90/EU, (EU) 2016/797 and (EU) 2020/1828 (Artificial Intelligence Act), OJ L, 2024/1689, 12.7.2024, etc.

85. Federico Casolari, Carlotta Buttaboni and Luciano Floridi, *The EU Data Act in Context: A Legal Assessment*, 31 International Journal of Law and Information Technology, 399-412 (2023) https://doi.org/10.1093/ijlit/eaae005; Leistner and Antonie, *supra* n. 28.

Equally, the Data Act intersects with consumer dealings and the bulk of both the EU consumer law acquis and national contract law. Different national legal traditions are likely to interfere substantially with data access and sharing provisions as far as the protection and rights of Users are concerned, especially when they are consumers.

Part II Regulating the EU Digital Strategy

CHAPTER 4

The Digital Markets Act

4.1 THE DESIGN OF ECOSYSTEMS

Technological innovation and the rise of the platform economy have significantly transformed traditional markets' structure, requiring a reassessment of new market dynamics and relevant regulations. The question of a legal definition of these operators is only a preliminary aspect of understanding their capacity for action. Market conditioning needs to be accompanied by an analysis of their structure.

Indeed, there have been substantial changes in the configuration of market operators, the ability of consumers to choose, and the design of economic relationships. Some platforms have acquired considerable market power through their business models, which are based on three key elements: (1) multifaceted operation, (2) the ability to ensure the exchange and management of information, and (3) the ability to create value through interaction with users and other operators. The relationship with operators is not merely a collaboration but a contractual agreement capable of generating an economic dependence.

The exchange of information, understood as the acquisition and processing of data through algorithms, is at the heart of the platform's activity and contact with the user. By managing large volumes of data, the platform can strengthen its position in a particular market segment and expand into new areas. These factors create new competitive dynamics, influence business strategies, and impact consumer choices through service personalisation and anticipation of purchasing preferences.

As highlighted in Regulation 2022/1925, the DMA, which was approved in September 2022,[1] these platforms have "an ability to connect many commercial users with many end users through their services, which, in turn, enables them to leverage

1. *See* Regulation (EU) 2022/1925 of the European Parliament and of the Council of 14 September 2022 on contestable and fair markets in the digital sector and amending Directives (EU) 2019/1937 and (EU) 2020/1828 (Digital Markets Act), OJ L 265, 12.10.2022, p. 1-66 and Commission implementing Regulation (EU) 2023/814 of 14 April 2023 on detailed arrangements

their advantages, such as their access to large amounts of data, from one area of activity to another" (Recital 3 DMA).

Gathering data from the interaction between the consumer and the platform is not just a routine but a crucial step. It enables later use through algorithms that can analyse and segment users based on their personalities, interests, and habits, thereby shedding light on their behaviour and preferences.

This aspect and its functioning are fundamental to understanding. Thanks to their modular structure that allows easy integration of new features and services, these platforms aim to attract other commercial users (complementors)[2] into a network of participatory relationships and contractual agreements. This structure creates a multi-actor or multi-product system to provide goods and services in multiple market segments, creating value.

These factors create new competitive dynamics, influence business strategies, and affect consumer choices through service personalisation and anticipation of purchasing preferences.

If we examine the details, the conclusion of agreements, or what will later be seen as acquisitions, affects the number of competitors in the competitive market that are considered 'external' to the platform. At the same time, there are problems of potential unfair competition within the 'internal' market or marketplace.[3]

Furthermore, the companies with which the platform may have an interest in concluding agreements and the sectors of interest are not always easily predictable *ex ante*. This marks a significant difference between traditional companies in the possibility of predicting development intentions, the sectors of activity, and the possible impact of these choices on the market. For traditional companies, any expansions into new sectors, especially if they are very different from the usual activity, were difficult to achieve quickly because they were complex and expensive.

Finally, it seems complicated to define this type of relationship as "the collaborative arrangements through which firms combine their offerings into a coherent, customer-facing solution."[4]

Consumer behaviour and the ability to anticipate their desires also play a key role in shaping market dynamics. The satisfaction generated by a personalised offer often leads consumers to conclude purchases mainly or exclusively with these platforms without even evaluating the offers of other operators.

---

for the conduct of certain proceedings by the Commission pursuant to Regulation (EU) 2022/1925 of the European Parliament and of the Council, OJ L 102, 17.4.2023, p. 6-19.

2. For this definition, *see* Michael Jacobides, Carmelo Cennamo and Annabelle Gawer, *Towards a Theory of Ecosystems*, 39 Strategic Management Journal, 2255-2276 (2018) https://doi.org/10.1002/smj.2904; Michael Jacobides and Ioannis Lianos, *Ecosystems and Competition Law in Theory and Practice*, 30 Industrial and Corporate Change, 1199-1229 (2021) https://doi.org/10.1093/icc/dtab061.
3. *See* Jacques Crémer, Yves-Alexandre De Montjoye and Heike Schweitzer, *Competition Policy in the Digital Era*, European Commission, Directorate-General for Competition Final Report, Publications Office (2019), available at https://op.europa.eu/en/publication-detail/-/publication/21dc175c-7b76-11e9-9f05-01aa75ed71a1/language-en.
4. Ron Adner, *Match Your Innovation Strategy to Your Innovation Ecosystem*, 84 Harvard Business Review, 98-107 (2006).

This dynamic determines the direction of purchases and generates critical competitive implications.[5] The ecosystem's appeal for market operators is underlined by the difficulty of being competitive outside of it. For this reason, many operators become part of the ecosystem, subject to the platform's rules, which significantly shape their actions and decisions.

These rules profoundly impact their decision-making, including contractual obligations and conditions for sustaining their presence within the ecosystem, such as maintaining satisfaction ratings and engaging in product and seller recommendation systems.

Regulation 1925/2022 (DMA) highlights that "the market processes are often incapable of ensuring fair economic outcomes with regard to core platform services."[6] This also highlights the limitation of market mechanisms in ensuring equitable economic results for core platform services CPSs. Indeed, Articles 101 and 102 of the TFEU deal with abusing dominant positions and agreements; however, they permit intervention only *ex post* and after lengthy and complex investigations.

For this reason, the objective pursued by the Regulation, as indicated in Recital 11 DMA, is to "ensure that the markets in which gatekeepers are present are and remain fair and containable" *ex ante*. This approach balances market fairness and consumer mobility. It applies to the platforms that provide basic platform services as defined in Article 2 DMA, namely: (a) online intermediation services, (b) online search engines, (c) online social network services, (d) video-sharing platform services, (e) number-independent interpersonal communication services, (f) operating systems, (g) web browsers, (h) virtual assistants, (i) cloud computing services, (j) online advertising services, including advertising networks, advertising exchanges, and any other advertising intermediation services. Among the platforms providing these services, those with identifying characteristics that make them gatekeepers capable of controlling access to the market will be subject to the regulation's obligations.

The European Commission document on the Digital Service Package defines these platforms as exhibiting significant network effects, boasting many loyal users, and possessing a considerable ability to leverage data for controlling market entry.[7]

4.2 RELATIONSHIP BETWEEN TREATY RULES AND THE DMA

As the European Commission recalls, gatekeepers offer benefits to consumers and advantages in product and service innovation, generating profound competitive imbalances and problems of user protection. Indeed, "a small number of large online

5. *See* OECD, *Handbook on Competition Policy in the Digital Age* (2022), available at www.oecd.org/daf/competition-policy-in-the-digital-age.
6. Recital 5 Regulation 2022/1925. *See also* DMA: rules for digital gatekeepers to ensure open markets start to apply, https://digital-markets-act.ec.europa.eu/dma-rules-digital-gatekeepers-ensure-open-markets-start-apply-2023-05-02_en.
7. *See* European Commission, Inception Impact Assessment, Digital Services Act package: *ex ante* regulatory instrument for large online platforms with significant network effects acting as gatekeepers in the European Union's internal market Ares(2020)2877647 (June 2020).

platforms increasingly determines the parameters for future innovations, consumer choice and competition."[8]

These platforms control key bottlenecks, making it difficult for operators and consumers to avoid engaging.

Competition law, particularly Article 102 TFEU, can only partially address these issues for two main reasons: first, the speed of action of the platforms often outpaces the legislative response time, and second, any intervention can only occur after problems have already emerged (*ex post*). The DMA was also approved to respond to similar difficulties by establishing pre-defined obligations accompanied by applicable sanctions, and it applies only to markets where gatekeepers are present.

Regarding the relationship between Treaty rules and DMA, Competition Commissioner Ms Vestager specified that "the DMA is not a competition law instrument. It doesn't affect how the competition rules apply in digital markets. Nor does it change our powers – or the powers of Europe's national competition authorities – to enforce those rules in the digital world."[9]

As the European Commissioner recalled, the purpose of the DMA is to create a filter installed a little way upstream to remove some of that debris before it reaches us. It would not change competition powers, but its presence does mean that we will not have the same problems to deal with in the future. It means some kinds of behaviour will not come because the Act will ensure those things do not happen.

In this perspective, the European Commission has also updated its communication on enforcement priorities related to (then) Article 82 of the EC Treaty regarding abusive exclusionary conduct by the dominant undertakings.[10]

Indeed, for example, "anti-competitive foreclosure" is used to describe a situation where the conduct of the dominant undertaking adversely impacts an effective competitive structure, thus allowing the dominant undertaking to negatively influence, to its advantage and the detriment of consumers, the various parameters of competition, such as price, production, innovation, variety or quality of goods or services.

Unlike the revision implemented by Regulation 1/2003 on decentralisation of control,[11] the DMA gives the European Commission a leading role, starting with the designation of gatekeeper. Article 1(7) DMA adds, "National authorities shall not take decisions which conflict with a decision taken by the European Commission under this Regulation." At the same time, it adds that "The Commission and the Member States

8. *Ibid.*
9. Speech by EVP Margrethe Vestager, *Competition in the Digital Age*, (European Internet Forum, 17 March 2021), available at https://ec.europa.eu/newsroom/comp/items/705929.
10. European Commission, Communication from the Commission Amendments to the Communication from the Commission – Guidance on the Commission's enforcement priorities in applying Article 82 of the EC Treaty to abusive exclusionary conduct by dominant undertakings (Text with EEA relevance) 2023/C 116/01, OJ C 116, 31.3.2023, p. 1-5.
11. Council Regulation (EC) No. 1/2003 of 16 December 2002 on the implementation of the rules on competition laid down in Articles 81 and 82 of the Treaty, OJ L 1, 4.1.2003, p. 1-25, came into force on 1 May 2004. *See also* Communication from the Commission to the European Parliament and the Council, Report on the functioning of Regulation 1/2003 (COM(2009) 206 final, 29.4.2009.

shall work closely together and coordinate their enforcement actions" through the European Competition Network (ECN).[12]

4.3 THE DMA AND THE RECOGNITION OF THE GATEKEEPER

The DMA establishes that gatekeeper status exists in the presence of three conditions. These conditions concerned the business's size (based on turnover), the number of commercial and end users of the platform, and a consolidated presence on the market. Specifically, they are defined as follows: an undertaking has a significant impact on the internal market, provides a CPS that is an essential gateway for business users to reach end users, and enjoys an entrenched and durable position in its operations, or it is foreseeable that it will enjoy such a position shortly.

Contestability of services in the digital sector may also be limited if there is more than one gatekeeper for a basic platform service.

Being an operator with the requirements set out in the regulation will imply immediate subjection to some obligations relating to the acquisition and management of data, interoperability,[13] the relationship with commercial and end users, and the protection of end users (Articles 5 DMA et seq.) through an *ex ante* action mechanism.

The significant market impact is evaluated on several key criteria. These include a turnover equal to or greater than EUR 7.5 billion in the last three financial years, an average market capitalisation, or an equivalent market value of at least EUR 75 billion in the previous financial year. When met, these thresholds signify a substantial presence in the market. Furthermore, providing the basic platform service in at least three Member States further underscores the company's market influence.

The second requirement concerns the number of users established or located in the Union, which in the last financial year was 45 million monthly active end users and at least 10,000 annual active business users established in the Union.

Lastly, the third parameter, which corresponds to the achievement of end users reached in each of the last three financial years, completes the set of criteria for evaluating market impact. The DMA relies on firms making a notification to trigger the proceedings.

It is useful to note that being identified as a gatekeeper may occur even if not all parameters are satisfied simultaneously. Specifically, the thresholds indicated take into account the size (turnover and capitalisation), the activity and position of the company, the number of commercial users, network effects, and scale effects, and the ability to give rise to lock-in effects of commercial and end users, and the company

12. *See also* Articles 37 and 38 DMA.
The ECN was established as a forum for discussion and cooperation for European competition authorities in cases where Articles 101 and 102 of the Treaty of the Functioning of the European Union (TFEU) are applied. *See* European Commission, Commission Notice on Cooperation within the Network of Competition Authorities (April 2004), OJ C 101, 27.4.2004, p. 43-53.
13. On the interoperability, *see* Neha Mishra, *Regulatory Interoperability in the Digital Economy* (April 2024), available at https://papers.ssrn.com/sol3/papers.cfm?abstract_id=4990518. Also, on this topic *see* Articles 33, 34, and 35 Data Act and Chapter 3 *supra*.

structure (a vertical integration, for example, favours the possibility of cross-subsidisation).

It is for the gatekeeper to contest designation. Article 3 DMA specifies that the undertaking providing Basic Platform Services may submit sufficiently substantiated arguments to demonstrate that, exceptionally. However, it reaches all the thresholds indicated; it does not meet these requirements due to the circumstances relating to the operation of the relevant service.

The European Commission evaluated the criteria and concluded that the online social networking service qualifies as a critical gateway under the DMA. According to the Regulation, it met the DMA's requirements by identifying the service as an essential gateway. *ByteDance* contends that the criteria outlined in Article 3(5) DMA were not sufficiently demonstrated and argues for a challenge to this classification.

Specifically, the Court determined that Article 3 DMA should be interpreted as permitting the involved company to present arguments and evidence - even if not quantified - to counter the presumptions established in Article 3 DMA, as long as these arguments relate directly to one or more of those presumptions.[14] "Accordingly, the standard of proof required to call into question the presumptions laid down in Article 3(2) DMA has been determined by the EU legislature itself, by requiring the undertaking concerned - on which the burden of proof lies - to submit sufficiently substantiated arguments, manifestly calling into question those presumptions"[15] During the proceedings, *ByteDance* argued that the European Commission failed to consider specific qualitative arguments and evidence, claiming that it misinterpreted Recital 23 DMA.[16] *ByteDance* maintained that the European Commission set an unreasonably high standard of proof by requiring additional evidence. Ultimately, the CJEU upheld the European Commission's decision, confirming its authority to designate *ByteDance* as a gatekeeper.

A preliminary list of platforms identified as gatekeepers was created in September 2023, followed by two additional designations in April and May 2024. Seven gatekeepers were responsible for twenty-four CPSs.[17]

14. Case T-1077/23, *Bytedance v. European Commission*, ECLI:EU:T:2024:478, esp. point 51.
15. *Ibid.*, point 61.
16. "An undertaking providing core platform services should be able, in exceptional circumstances, to rebut the presumption that the undertaking has a significant impact on the internal market by demonstrating that, although it meets the quantitative thresholds set out in this Regulation, it does not fulfill the requirements for designation as a gatekeeper. The burden of adducing evidence that the presumption deriving from the fulfillment of the quantitative thresholds should not apply should be borne by that undertaking. In its assessment of the evidence and arguments produced, the Commission should take into account only those elements that directly relate to the quantitative criteria, namely the impact of the undertaking providing core platform services on the internal market beyond revenue or market cap, such as its size in absolute terms, and the number of Member States in which it is present; by how much the actual business user and end user numbers exceed the thresholds and the importance of the undertaking's core platform service considering the overall scale of activities of the respective core platform service; and the number of years for which the thresholds have been met" (Recital 23 DMA).
17. The DMA defines a CPS as online intermediation services (e.g., marketplaces, app stores etc.), online search engines, online social networking services, video-sharing platform services, number-independent interpersonal communications services, operating systems, web browsers, virtual assistants, cloud computing services, and online advertising services provided by an

Once identified, gatekeepers are subject to a series of obligations (Articles 5, 6, and 7 DMA). They are responsible for ensuring compliance and bear the burden of proof. Their obligations cover various areas, including fair access to data, interoperability, and the prevention of practices that disadvantage competitors.

4.4 SELF-PREFERENCING AND INTEROPERABILITY

Self-preference refers to the behaviour of a dominant platform that leverages its market power to favour its products. The DMA and some decisions by the European Commission, such as the *Google Shopping*[18] ruling, do not specifically use the term 'self-preference' but instead refer to 'more favorable treatment'. While the DMA and certain European Commission decisions, such as the *Google Shopping* ruling, do not explicitly use the term 'self-preference', they do refer to 'more favorable treatment'. To understand this better, we can examine the rulings of the CJEU regarding the *Google Shopping* case. This 'more favorable treatment' is linked to exclusionary practices and implicit refusals to supply.[19] We have used the term 'self-preference' here to synthesise these two aspects.

A key aspect of self-preferencing behaviour involves using platform services to collect data from direct sources and third parties. This strategy allows the platform to leverage its strong position in one market to gain advantages over competitors in a related downstream market. By accumulating information and performing algorithmic analysis, the platform can create obstacles for potential competitors, effectively establishing barriers to entry. Consequently, a gatekeeper can attract more third-party operators than other companies, resulting in a self-reinforcing system. As more participants join the ecosystem, the volume of usable data increases, making it increasingly difficult for outsiders to compete. This challenge is not limited to external competitors; it also impacts operators within the ecosystem. These operators contribute to the data pool through their sales, which the gatekeeper can exploit without reciprocation.

---

undertaking that provides any of the other CPSs. On 6 September 2023 the European Commission designated for the first time six gatekeepers – *Alphabet, Amazon, Apple, ByteDance, Meta, Microsoft* – under the DMA. On 29 April 2024, the European Commission designated *Apple* for its *iPadOS*, its operating system for tablets, as a gatekeeper under the DMA. On 13 May 2024, the European Commission also designated under the DMA *Booking* as a gatekeeper for its online intermediation service *Booking.com*. In total, twenty-four CPSs provided by those gatekeepers have been designated. *See* https://digital-markets-act.ec.europa.eu/gatekeepers_en.

18. Case AT39740 *Google Search Shopping*, European Commission, Decision C (2017) 4444 of 27 June 2017, available at https://competition-cases.ec.europa.eu/cases/AT.39740. The European Commission has imposed a record fine of EUR 2.42 billion on Google for favouring its own price comparison service. On this decision *see also* Judgment of the General Court, Case T-612/17 *Google LLC, formerly Google Inc. and Alphabet, Inc. v. European Commission*, ECLI:EU:T:2021:763; Case C-48/22 P, *Google and Alphabet v. Commission (Google Shopping)*, ECLI:EU:C:2024:726.
19. *See* point 232 and 233 case T-612/17, *supra* n. 18.

In some cases, the gatekeeper may use the data collected from these operators to compete against them, as seen in *Amazon*'s practices with its products.[20] *Amazon* serves a dual purpose as a platform. First, it operates as a marketplace that enables independent sellers to sell their products directly to consumers. Second, *Amazon* also acts as a retailer, selling its products within the same marketplace and competing with these independent sellers. As a provider of marketplace services, *Amazon* has access to confidential business data from third-party sellers. This includes information such as the number of units ordered and shipped, sellers' revenues on the platform, the number of visits to sellers' listings, details related to shipping, past performance metrics for sellers, and consumer feedback on products, including claims made under activated guarantees.[21]

Article 5 DMA outlines some obligations for gatekeepers. Specifically, the gatekeepers shall not do any of the following:

(a) process to provide online advertising services, personal data of end users using services of third parties that make use of CPSs of the gatekeeper;
(b) combine personal data from the relevant CPS with personal data from any further CPSs or from any other services provided by the gatekeeper or with personal data from third-party services;
(c) cross-use personal data from the relevant CPS in other services provided separately by the gatekeeper, including other CPSs, and vice versa; and
(d) sign in end users to other services of the gatekeeper to combine personal data.

Article 6(2) DMA states that "the gatekeeper shall not use, in competition with business users, any data that is not publicly available that is generated or provided by those business users in the context of their use of the relevant core platform services or of the services provided together with, or in support of, the relevant core platform services, including data generated or provided by the customers of those business users."

This ban is in line with issues highlighted in cases opened by the European Commission in recent years, including the investigation of Amazon into the use of private data from sellers on its marketplace. Indeed, Amazon has a dual role as a platform and a retailer. It provides a marketplace where independent sellers can sell their products directly to consumers. At the same time, it sells products on its platform as a retailer, competing with independent sellers. Thanks to this dual role, Amazon can

20. *See also* Lina Khan, *Amazon's Antitrust Paradox*, 126 The Yale Law Journal, 564-907 (2017), esp. 713.
21. *See* Case AT.40462, *Amazon Marketplace*, European Commission Decision of 17 July 2019, available at https://competition-cases.ec.europa.eu/cases/AT.40462.
    In addition, the Commission opened a second antitrust investigation into *Amazon*'s business practices that might artificially favour its own retail offers and offers of marketplace sellers that use *Amazon*'s logistics and delivery services (the so-called fulfilment by *Amazon* or FBA sellers), Case AT.40703, *Amazon Buy Box*, European Commission Decision C(2022)9442 of 20th December 2022, available at https://ec.europa.eu/competition/antitrust/cases1/202310/AT_40703_8990760_1533_5.pdf.

access large data sets on the activities of independent sellers on its platform, including non-public business data.

The European Commission identified that significant non-public data from Amazon sellers were directly integrated into the platform's algorithm. Therefore, Amazon could calibrate its offers and make strategic business decisions, such as offering its sellers' best-selling products and adjusting its offers based on non-public data from competing sellers.

The European Commission opened an investigation into this behaviour in July 2019, followed in November 2020 by a statement of objections. A second investigation was then linked to it concerning the mechanism for inserting offers from external sellers into the buy box, which concluded with voluntary commitments.

Article 6(5) DMA adds that gatekeepers must not misuse the data collected from end users by third parties who either complement the platform or enhance its value for advertising services. The rationale behind this provision, together with those of the subsequent paragraphs of this Article, is to prevent the platform from adopting self-preferential behaviours, that is, behaviours aimed at strengthening its position of strength and preventing commercial users present and connected to the platform from competing with it on specific services or types of goods. Precisely on self-preference, paragraph 5 establishes that "the gatekeeper does not guarantee more favorable treatment, in terms of positioning and related indexing and crawling, to the services and products offered by the gatekeeper itself compared to similar services or products of third parties. The gatekeeper applies transparent, fair, and non-discriminatory conditions to such positioning."

To complete these measures, Article 6(9) DMA recognises the right to data portability for end users by establishing that "the gatekeeper shall provide, upon request and free of charge, to end-users and third parties authorized by an end-user the effective portability of data provided by the end-user or generated through the activity of the end-user in the context of the use of the relevant core platform service, including by providing free of charge tools to facilitate the effective exercise of such data portability, as well as by providing continuous and real-time access to such data."

This last measure would seem to be very useful to limit the exploitation of data that generates critical issues both from the point of view of the user's exercise of choice and from the point of view of the ability of operators external to the ecosystem to offer competitive services. This measure helps limit the exploitation of data that leads to critical issues, both in terms of the user's ability to make informed choices and the capacity of external operators to provide competitive services. However, its effectiveness may be limited because it is not guaranteed that end users will choose to exercise this right when presented with personalised services. Additionally, potential receiving platforms may not be able to utilise the data as effectively as the original platform.

One aspect to which attention should also be paid is interoperability.[22] Interoperability means the ability to exchange information and mutually use the information

---

22. Some years ago, Palfrey and Gasser stated "We have not yet developed a normative theory identifying what we want out of all this interconnectivity (...) And we have not yet refined a sense of which tools will get us to optimal levels of interoperability." John Palfrey and Urs

exchanged through interfaces or other solutions so that all elements of hardware or software work with other hardware and software and with users in all the ways in which they are intended to function.[23] Recital 57 DMA underlines, "The gatekeepers should, therefore, be required to ensure, free of charge, effective interoperability with, and access for the purposes of interoperability to, the same operating system, hardware or software features that are available or used in the provision of its own complementary and supporting services and hardware." The lack of interoperability allows gatekeepers that provide number-independent interpersonal communications services to benefit from strong network effects, which contributes to the weakening of contestability.[24]

For this reason, the DMA outlines specific obligations for gatekeepers. According to the DMA, gatekeepers must allow service providers and hardware manufacturers free and effective access to the same hardware and software features available or controlled through the operating system or virtual assistant. Additionally, gatekeepers must provide business users and alternative service providers who work alongside or support CPSs with free and effective interoperability access to the same operating system, hardware, or software features.[25]

Finally, the European Commission ensures compliance with the measures established by the Regulation, which can initiate a procedure to verify adherence to these obligations. This investigation may include inspections and the collection of documentation to determine non-compliance. If violations are confirmed, the European Commission can impose fines (as outlined in Article 30 DMA).

4.5 KILLER ACQUISITIONS AND MERGER CONTROL: AN OPEN PROBLEM?

The competition issues generated by gatekeepers require addressing not just through monitoring their presence on the market through *ex post* interventions such as the DMA but also by observing how these platforms consolidate their market power and limit the

Gasser, *Interop: The Promise and Perils of Interconnected Systems*, (Basic Books, 2012), esp. 3, available at https://cyber.harvard.edu/publications/2012/interop.

23. *See* definition 29 of Article 2 DMA.
24. *See* Recital 64 DMA.
25. *See* Article 6(7) DMA. The European Commission opened proceedings on 19 September 2024 to specify measures that Apple must implement to comply with its interoperability obligations under the DMA. the procedure focuses on interoperability between *iOS* and connected devices, such as smartwatches, headphones, and VR headsets. The European Commission's case reference is Case DMA.100203, *Apple – Operating systems – iOS – Article 6(7) – SP – Features for Connected Physical Devices*, European Commission Decision of 19 September 2024, available at https://digital-markets-act-cases.ec.europa.eu/cases/DMA.100203.

    In this case, the European Commission opened a consultation with third parties on the proposed measures *Apple* will implement to ensure effective interoperability between IOS and connected devices as required by Article 6(7) DMA. *See* Consultation DMA No. 100203 of 18 December 2024, available at https://digital-markets-act.ec.europa.eu/dma100203-consultation-proposed-measures-interoperability-between-apples-ios-operating-system-and_en.

    In the case of *Apple*, *see* Manuel Wörsdörfer, *Apple's Antitrust Paradox*, 20 European Competition Journal, 113-146 (2024) https://doi.org/10.1080/17441056.2023.2262870.

growth of potential competitors in different market segments. This involves cases in which the conduct of the dominant undertaking can lead to the total exclusion of competition and those in which it can weaken competition.[26]

One of the aspects of particular attention is acquisitions, specifically the purchase of other operators as start-ups capable of becoming potential competitors in some market segments. By acquiring these companies, gatekeepers achieve a dual objective: eliminate a potential competitor and gain access to innovative ideas developed by the acquired entity. Moreover, similar acquisitions greatly interest ecosystems because they attract new users. The novelties resulting from acquisitions determine greater satisfaction and loyalty among those subjects who have already used the platform.

An article published by the weekly newspaper *The Economist* on 26 October 2018, titled "American Tech Giants are Making Life Tough for Startups," highlighted that *Google* from 2011 to 2018 acquired a company each month.[27] *Google* was not the only platform that was particularly active in acquiring start-ups. In 2017 alone, *Alphabet, Apple, Amazon, Facebook*, and *Microsoft* spent 31.6 billion on startup acquisitions.

As the European Commission highlighted, such acquisitions can bypass merger control due to their turnover and envisaged thresholds. An acquisition is subject to regulatory control only when the parties involved reach certain turnover thresholds because it is considered capable of producing significant effects only in those cases.

Due to the advantages inherent in this type of acquisition and the risks associated with failing to evaluate them under merger legislation, these transactions have been labelled as 'killer acquisitions'.[28]

The European Commission has pointed out that the significance of these developments is vital in the digital economy, where companies often launch services to build a substantial user base and gather commercially valuable data before attempting to monetise their business. Similarly, in areas like pharmaceuticals, where innovation is a critical aspect of competition, there have been transactions involving innovative companies conducting research and development projects with strong competitive

26. *See* European Commission, Commission Communication, Amendments to the Communication from the Commission – Guidance on the Commission's enforcement priorities in applying Article 82 of the EC Treaty to abusive exclusionary conduct by dominant undertakings, 2023/C 116/01, OJ C116/1, 31 March 2023.
27. For more details on the history of Google's acquisitions, *see* Ioannis Lianos, *Competition Law for the Digital Era: A Complex Systems' Perspective* (30 August 2019), available at SSRN https://ssrn.com/abstract=3492730 or http://dx.doi.org/10.2139/ssrn3492730.
28. Cunningham and other authors have adopted this expression regarding the information technology sector and other fields, such as the pharmaceutical one. *See* Colleen Cunningham, Florian Ederer and Song Ma, *Killer Acquisitions*, 129 Journal of Political Economy, 649-702 (2019) https://doi.org/10.1086/712506; Marc Bourreau and Alexandre de Streel, Alexandre, *Dgital Conglomerates and EU Competition Policy* (11 March 2019), available at SSRN https://ssrn.com/abstract=3350512 or http://dx.doi.org/10.2139/ssrn.3350512. Also available at https://cerre.eu/news/digital-conglomerates-and-eu-competition-policy/; Kristen Limarzi and Harry Phillips, *"Killer Acquisitions," Big Tech and Section Solution in Search of a Problem*, Antitrust Chronicle, (26 May 2020), available at www.competitionpolicyinternational.com; OECD, *Start-ups, Killer Acquisitions and Merger Control' Background Note*, DAF/COMP(2020)5, (May 2020), available at https://www.oecd.org/en/publications/start-ups-killer-acquisitions-and-merger-control_dac52a99-en.html.

potential. The European Commission has examined the effectiveness of the turnover-based jurisdictional thresholds of the EU Merger Regulation[29] in these scenarios. It has concluded that the referral mechanisms outlined in the Merger Regulation have generally been effective in identifying transactions with a significant impact on competition.[30] However, several cross-border transactions that could potentially have an impact on competition were not immediately perceived at the time of assessment.

An example of this was *Apple*'s acquisition of *Shazam*, a developer of music recognition applications. This merger offered a double advantage for *Apple* because, thanks to *Shazam*, the platform increased its information assets by providing access to the preferences and behaviours of customers that, until then, were the exclusive property of its competitors. In this case, the European Commission considered that integrating the *Shazam* and *Apple* datasets on user data did not give "a unique advantage to the merged entity in the markets on which it operates."[31]

The European Commission considered that the integration of the *Shazam* and *Apple* user data sets did not confer "a unique advantage to the merged entity in the markets in which it operates" because, according to the European Commission, *Shazam*'s market position was overstated. It only holds a limited market share of approximately 5% to 10% worldwide in the automatic content recognition (ACR) software solutions market.

To address the start-up merger, the European Commission considered that reassessing the application of Article 22 of the EU Merger Regulation could be beneficial. In the EU Merger Regulation, the control over mergers between undertakings is based on the principle of notification of such transactions before their implementation.[32] In certain circumstances, it may be helpful to encourage Member States, under Article 22 of the EU Merger Regulation, to require the examination of mergers even below thresholds if they are likely to affect trade between Member States and competition significantly. This change in approach could help ensure that the European Commission examines additional transactions deserving review under the EU

29. Council Regulation (EC) No. 139/2004 of 20 January 2004 on the control of concentrations between undertakings (the EC Merger Regulation), OJ L 24, 29.1.2004, p. 1-22.
30. *See* European Commission, Communication from the Commission Guidance on the application of the referral mechanism set out in Article 22 of the Merger Regulation to certain categories of cases 2021/C 113/01, OJ C 113, 31.3.2021, Recital 11.
31. Case M.8788, *Apple – Shazam*, COM(2018) 5784, European Commission Merger Procedure Decision of 6th September 2018, available at https://ec.europa.eu/competition/mergers/cases/decisions/m8788_1279_3.pdf.
32. Article 22 and Recital 1 EU Merger Regulation establish that one or more Member States may request to the European Commission to examine any concentration as defined in Article 3 EU Merger Regulation that does not have a Community dimension within the meaning of Article 1 EU Merger Regulation but Affects trade between Member States and threatens to significantly affect competition within the territory of the Member State or States making the request. Such a request shall be made at most within fifteen working days of the concentration's notification, or if no notification is required, otherwise made known to the Member State concerned. *See* Regulation No. 139/2004 of 20 January 2004 on the control of concentrations between undertakings, OJ L 24, 29.1.2004 and also implementing Council Regulation (EC) No. 139/2004 on the control of concentrations between undertakings and repealing Commission Regulation (EC) No. 802/2004, OJ L 119, 5.5.2023.

Merger Regulation without imposing a notification obligation on transactions that would not justify such a review.

Furthermore, in a recent ruling regarding the regulation of mergers, the CJEU highlighted another aspect applicable to ecosystems. Specifically, at point 20 of the decision, it underlined how it is appropriate to treat single-merger operations that are closely linked to each other with a conditional constraint or are structured as a series of transactions on securities concluded in a relatively short time frame.[33]

The CJEU added that the EU Merger Regulation must be interpreted to mean that even a merger between undertakings without a European dimension and below the mandatory control thresholds established by national law, not referred to the European Commission under Article 22 of the EU Merger Regulation, may still constitute an abuse of a dominant position prohibited by Article 102 TFEU when considering the structure of competition in a national market.

It can also be helpful to remember that the ratio of defining these thresholds was not to evaluate the market position but to determine jurisdictional authority as indicated in the European Commission consolidated Jurisdictional Notice under Council Regulation (EC) No. 139/2004.[34]

Regarding concentrations and the challenges of assessment in ecosystems, the DMA establishes that "A gatekeeper shall inform the Commission of any intended concentration within the meaning of Article 3 of Regulation (EC) No. 139/2004, where the merging entities or the target of concentration provide core platform services or any other services in the digital sector or enable the collection of data, irrespective of whether it is notifiable to the Commission under that Regulation or to a competent national competition authority under national merger rules. A gatekeeper shall inform the Commission of such a concentration before its implementation and following the conclusion of the agreement, the announcement of the public bid, or the acquisition of a controlling interest."[35]

4.6 THE LINK BETWEEN COMPETITION AND CONSUMER CHOICE

In these ecosystems, two key elements deserve attention: (1) the ability to attract an increasingly large number of market operators and (2) consumer data to provide personalised services that anticipate consumer desires. These two interconnected aspects create a double lock-in effect for consumers and operators. Personalising services and anticipating needs enhance user loyalty and decrease their inclination to explore alternative options.

There is a strong correlation between the ability to anticipate consumer desires and a reduction in their interest in seeking other offers. The satisfaction derived from

33. Case C-449/21, *Towercast SASU v. Autoritè de la cuncurrence, Ministre chargè de l'economie*, ECLI:EU:C:2023:207.
34. European Commission Consolidated Jurisdictional Notice under Council Regulation (EC) No. 139/2004 on the control of concentrations between undertakings, 2008/C 95/01, OJ C 95, 16th April 2008, point 127; Council Regulation (EC) No. 139/2004 of 20 January 2004 on the control of concentrations between undertakings (the EC Merger Regulation), OJ L 24, 29.1.2004, p. 1-22.
35. Article 14(1) DMA.

a personalised offer often leads consumers to purchase primarily or exclusively with the platform that can guarantee similar support, often without considering other operators' offers.

The transformation, as correctly highlighted by the CoE, occurs in many cases without an exact perception by the individual of what is happening and of the role played by tools such as, name a few, recommendations, quick purchase paths, sending of products deemed desired in light of the profiling process. As underlined in the 2019 declaration, "contemporary machine learning tools have the growing capacity not only to predict choices but also to influence emotions and thoughts and alter an anticipated course of action, sometimes subliminally."[36]

Additionally, the platform utilises payment services to reinforce consumer lock-in and strengthen the ecosystem. These services and credit access facilitate quick and efficient purchases, further developing an ecosystem that already benefits from an influx of new data that complements existing information.

Furthermore, the user may be interested in delegating a growing part of his autonomy to minimise decision-making times and reduce potential dissatisfaction with his choice. The algorithm guarantees the user a filter between quantitative and qualitative offers and directs the subject's choice based on the study on his needs and preferences. A similar process influences the user's behaviour but simultaneously and inevitably also affects that of the operators, reducing their visibility and purchasing their products. Only if the operator is among those displayed in the search results or recommended by the platform or if he operates in the external market and maintains spaces of visibility can he hope to become a counterpart of the consumer.

This dynamic results in a merger of purchases within the platform, which has significant implications for competition. It diminishes the visibility of external operators, pushing them to become 'complementors' as they struggle to remain 'external' and competitive. Once integrated into the ecosystem, operators are bound by the platform's rules regarding permanence and operations, significantly influencing their actions and decisions when they enter the marketplace. This entry includes adherence to contractual conditions and compliance with permanence requirements, such as maintaining satisfaction ratings and participating in product and seller recommendation systems.

The dominant platform adversely impacts a compelling competitive landscape, allowing it to negatively influence various competition parameters, such as price, production, innovation, variety, or quality of goods or services, to its advantage and the detriment of consumers.[37] The DMA also aims to positively impact the position of end users of consumers thanks to specific actions towards gatekeepers and the protection of competition.

---

36. Council of Europe, *Declaration by Committee of Ministers on the Manipulative Capabilities of Algorithmic Processes*, Meeting of the Ministers' Deputies, February 2019, p. 8, available at www.coe.int.
37. *See* Case C-680/20, *Unilever Italia Mkt. Operations Srl/Autorità Garante della Concorrenza e del Mercato*, ECLI:EU:C:2023:33, esp. para. 36. *See also* Case T-604/18, *Google and Alphabet v. Commission (Google Android)*, ECLI:EU:T:2022:541, esp. para. 281.

4.7 COMPLIANCE AND EFFECTIVENESS OF DMA

The measures adopted also deserve some reflection on their effectiveness, combined with the competition regulations already in force concerning the objectives set. The importance of combining the two regulations has been highlighted since 2021 by the Competition Commissioner, Ms Vestager, who underlined how "the competition rules and the Digital Markets Act will work together in harmony, helping to make our digital markets work better for everyone. And that's the way it should be."[38] This synergy is essential for implementing a more effective intervention in gatekeepers' behaviour.

As highlighted in Recital 10 DMA, the DMA regulates "unilateral conduct based on the individualized assessment of the market position and behavior, including its actual or probable effects [...]." Its design emphasises an *ex ante* approach, which may enhance the ability to intervene against gatekeepers. Timelessness is an important variable that can affect the market. Furthermore, once the case is concluded before the European Commission, intervention could also be made by the CJEU.

The European Commission ensures compliance with the measures adopted by the DMA. Having ascertained non-compliance with the obligations imposed, the European Commission may determine the application of fines (Article 30 DMA). The sanction applied may not exceed 10% of the total worldwide turnover achieved during the previous financial year unless the platform committed an identical infringement in the last eight years. The parameters to quantify the infringement will be severity, duration, and frequency.

The approved regulation is also helpful because it allows targeted intervention on some of the critical issues that ecosystem platforms create for both end users and commercial users and the overall functioning of the market. At the same time, detailed rules that arise from the observed behaviours are quite compelling. However, some risks are associated with the frequent changes in these platforms' operational methods, which could require future amendments to the approved legislation.

38. Speech by EVP Margrethe Vestager, *supra* n. 9.

CHAPTER 5

The Digital Services Act

5.1 REGULATING THE POLICY OBJECTIVES OF THE DSA

As seen earlier in Chapter 4, the DMA and the DSA have been instituted by the EU as a response to the new challenges posed by the digital markets. These two legislative acts fall under the EU digital strategy, and they share the common goal of regulating digital markets where the fundamental rights of users are protected and a level playing field to foster innovation, growth, and competitiveness is established.

At the same time, however, the DMA and the DSA differ in scope and intended impact.

In general terms, as seen in the Chapter before, the DMA aims to prevent large digital companies from adopting practices that are considered restrictive of competition or unfair competition. By contrast, the DSA focuses mainly on regulating online content and protecting users.

Thus, the DMA - focusing on competition and targeting gatekeeper online platforms - aims to create a stable and competitive digital market by regulating the conduct of digital service providers, especially VLOPs and search engines.[1] As will be seen, some of these services are also covered in the DSA, but for different reasons and with different types of provisions.

Instead, the DSA is primarily aimed at ensuring a transparent, safe, predictable, and trustworthy digital environment. It places more emphasis on consumer protection and due diligence, and it focuses on the accountability of digital service providers.[2] It also aims to modernise and extend the 'E-Commerce Directive 200/31/EC', adopted by

1. Regulation (EU) 2022/1925 of the European Parliament and of the Council of 14 September 2022 on contestable and fair markets in the digital sector and amending Directives (EU) 2019/1937 and (EU) 2020/1828 (Digital Markets Act), OJ L 265, 12.10.2022, p. 1-66.
2. Regulation (EU) 2022/2065 of the European Parliament and of the Council of 19 October 2022 on a Single Market for Digital Services and amending Directive 2000/31/EC (Digital Services Act), OJ L 277, 27.10.2022, p. 1-102.

the EU back in the year 2000, whose main objective was to regulate various aspects of information society services in the EU internal market, facilitating cross-border e-commerce and ensuring a high level of consumer protection.[3] While the E-Commerce Directive provided the basis for online commerce and established basic rules for the liability of intermediaries, the DSA introduces more detailed and specific measures to address content moderation, transparency of platforms and protection of users' rights.

The DSA applies to a wide range of providers of digital services if these services are offered to users, whether natural or legal persons, established or located in the EU. It also targets VLOPs, intermediaries and search engines, which have to abide by stricter obligations set by the act.

The digital services covered by the DSA include a large category of information society and intermediary services, from websites to internet infrastructure services, online platforms and marketplaces, content-sharing platforms, app stores, and social networks. Digital service providers may control important ecosystems in the digital economy, whose rules sometimes result in unfair conditions for businesses and consumers using these platforms. Equally, there may be trade and exchange of illegal goods, services and content online. Digital services may be misused by manipulative algorithmic systems or digital architectures to amplify the spread of disinformation or other harmful purposes.

In conclusion, therefore, the overall objective of the DSA is to establish a modern legal framework that ensures the safety of digital users, governance with the protection of fundamental rights and consumer protection, and a fair and open digital environment.

The DSA is structured in five Chapters: Chapter I establishes its general provisions, including its subject matter and scope; Chapter II contains provisions on the liability of providers of intermediary services, building on earlier standards of the E-Commerce Directive; Chapter III covers the due diligence obligations for a transparent and safe online environment, distinguishing in separate Sections between obligations applicable to all online platforms and VLOPs; Chapter IV contains the provisions concerning its implementation and enforcement, as well as national and supranational cooperation; finally, Chapter V contains the final provisions of this Regulation, in particular containing the references to the abrogation of norms of the E-Commerce Directive.

5.2 BACKGROUND: OUTLINE OF THE E-COMMERCE DIRECTIVE

Back at the beginning of this century, the E-Commerce Directive[4] was intended to contribute to the approximation of national rules on information society services. The

3. Directive 2000/31/EC of the European Parliament and of the Council of 8 June 2000 on certain legal aspects of information society services, in particular electronic commerce, in the Internal Market ('Directive on electronic commerce'), OJ L 178, 17.7.2000, p. 1-16.
4. On the E-Commerce Directive in the literature, e.g., *see* generally Arno Lodder, *European Union E-Commerce Directive: Article by Article Comments* (2017). *Guide to European Union Law on E-Commerce, Update from 2016 (published 2017) of the 2001 (published 2002) version, published in EU Regulation of E-Commerce. A Commentary Elgar Commentaries series*, 15-58 (2017),

advent of the new economy, e-commerce B2B and B2C, and the coexistence in certain respects with the old economy resulted in a consumer legislation whose features were not clearly delineated.

The core objective of the E-Commerce Directive was the proper functioning of the EU internal market by guaranteeing and enabling freedom of information and the development of information society services. However, in parallel with this intention, there was a growing need for protection of the users from the risks associated with online activities. Specifically, subjects in a weak position were vulnerable due to a number of information limitations, especially consumers.

Hence, the Directive aimed to provide a harmonised legal framework by overcoming legal barriers to the free movement of services. It covered the most debated issues among practitioners at the time, namely the establishment of service providers, commercial communications, electronic contracts, liability of intermediaries transmitting or recording data, and out-of-court settlement of disputes.[5]

The scope of the E-Commerce Directive is broad-ranging. In the Directive, the concept of 'electronic commerce' gives way to the concept of 'information society services', defined as those services provided for remuneration at a distance by electronic means, using electronic equipment for the processing (including digital compression) and storage of data, and at the individual request of a recipient of services.[6] This definition, however, falls short of clarifying the distinction between online and offline services in those cases where online platforms combine an online interface with the provision of offline services. These are the cases, for example, of taxi or accommodation services. The CJEU, therefore, has examined whether the intermediation service should form an integral part of an overall service whose main component is a service coming under another legal classification, e.g., taxi or accommodation services that are not classifiable as online services. It has concluded that an 'information society service' remains in essence a factual issue, depending on whether the intermediation service is indispensable for the provision of the subsequent service to which it relates. Such a benchmark has led to diverging decision, where intermediation services could be regarded as merely ancillary to an overall service coming under a different legal classification[7] or, on the contrary, one service could not be offered without the other.[8]

Information society services include a wide range of activities performed online and do not include the delivery of goods or the provision of services offline. It includes

available at SSRN: https://ssrn.com/abstract=1009945. More recently, *see* Arno Lodder and Andrew Murray, *EU Regulation of E-Commerce: A Commentary* (Edward Elgar 2022), particularly Chapter 1.

5. Article 1 E-Commerce Directive.
6. Article 2(a) E-Commerce Directive, referring to Article 1(2) of Directive 98/34/EC as amended by Directive 98/48/EC laying down a procedure for the provision of information in the field of technical standards and regulations, OJ L 217, 5.8.1998, p. 18-26, no longer in force, repealed by Directive (EU) 2015/1535 of the European Parliament and of the Council of 9 September 2015 laying down a procedure for the provision of information in the field of technical regulations and of rules on Information Society services (codification), OJ L 241, 17.9.2015, p. 1-15.
7. Case C-390/18, *Airbnb Irland UC*, ECLI:EU:C:2019:1112.
8. Case C-434/15, *Asociación Profesional Elite Taxi v. Uber Systems Spain*, ECLI:EU:C:2017:981.

services that do not always lead to the conclusion of online contracts and also services that are not remunerated by their recipient insofar as they constitute an economic activity, such as the offering of online commercial communications or information or the provision of tools for searching, accessing and retrieving data.[9]

In particular, the Directive provides for the so-called internal market clause, also known as the 'country of origin' or 'single control' clause, according to which each Member State is obliged to verify, on the basis of its national provisions in the regulated area, the lawfulness of information society services provided by providers established in its territory, and may not restrict the free movement of information society services from other Member States.[10] The fundamental underlying idea is, therefore, that there should be a single control on the lawfulness of services only by the country of establishment of the service provider. This principle is not, however, of full and unconditional application. There are certain sectors, listed in the annex to the Directive, for which its application has to be excluded.[11] Also, there is a complex procedure by means of which Member States are allowed, under certain conditions, to adopt measures derogating from the aforementioned principle.[12]

The Directive establishes the principle of the exclusion of prior authorisation, according to which Member States have to ensure that the pursuit of the activities of information society service providers may not be made subject to prior authorisation or any other requirement having equivalent effect.[13] At the same time, they have also to ensure that the service providers render easily, directly and permanently accessible information to the recipients of the service. Such information includes the name of the service provider, its geographic address, contact details, trade registration details, etc.[14]

Following in section 2 of Chapter II, the Directive concentrates the commercial communications constituting an information society service. These are intended as all forms of communication which promote, directly or indirectly, the goods, services or image of the entities or persons engaged in a commercial, industrial, craft or liberal profession.[15] The Directive requires Member States to ensure that commercial communications constituting or forming an integral part of an information society service comply with minimal conditions. In particular, in commercial communications, the natural or legal person on whose behalf the commercial communication is made, promotional offers, promotional competitions or games must be clearly identifiable as such.[16] The application of these obligations must, however, be without prejudice to

9. Recital 18 E-Commerce Directive. *See also* the copious jurisprudence of the CJEU concerning the interpretation of the notion of 'information society services', e.g., Case C-108/09, *Ker-Optika bt v. ÀNTSZ Dél-dunántúli Regionális Intézete*, ECLI:EU:C:2010:725; Case C-291/13, *Sotiris Papasavvas v. O Fileleftheros Dimosia Etaireia Ltd and Others*, ECLI:EU:C:2014:2209; Case C-484/14, *Tobias Mc Fadden v. Sony Music Entertainment Germany GmbH*, ECLI:EU:C:2016:689; *Asociación Profesional Élite Taxi*, *supra* n. 8; *Airbnb Ireland UC*, *supra* n. 7.
10. Article 3 E-Commerce Directive.
11. Article 3(3) E-Commerce Directive.
12. Article 3(4)-(6) E-Commerce Directive.
13. Article 4 E-Commerce Directive.
14. Article 5(1) E-Commerce Directive.
15. Article 2(f) E-Commerce Directive.
16. Article 6 E-Commerce Directive.

other information obligations under EU Law.[17] Therefore, the E-Commerce Directive is intended to supplement the information obligations already laid down by other EU legislation in force for consumer protection in contractual matters, which continue to apply to information society services.

The Directive also adds another layer of obligations when commercial communications are unsolicited. This is the so-called spamming, which refers to sending unsolicited electronic communications to a large number of recipients. The content of the electronic messages in question can be varied. They mostly have an advertising character, but they may also have, for instance, political propaganda or religious proselytising purposes. When commercial communications are unsolicited, in addition to the other obligations under EU Law mentioned above, Member States have to ensure that such communications, transmitted by a service provider established on their territory, are identifiable as such, clearly and unambiguously, as soon as they are received by the recipient. Member States must also take the necessary measures to ensure that providers who send unsolicited commercial communications regularly consult and respect the negative registers in which natural persons who do not wish to receive such communications may register themselves (opt-out).[18]

Whilst Member States also have to ensure that the legal requirements applicable to the contractual process neither create obstacles for the use of electronic contracts nor result in such contracts being deprived of legal effectiveness and validity,[19] they also have to make sure that – in addition to all other information requirements established by EU Law – additional information is given by service providers about the conclusion of contracts and placing of orders.[20]

Articles 12 to 15 of the E-Commerce Directive concern exemptions from liability for 'mere conduit', 'catching', and 'hosting' services.

'Mere conduit' services are services that give users access to the internet and offer the possibility to send and receive data without the service storing these themselves. For example, a mere conduit is Internet Service Providers or online platforms that facilitate the transmission of information between different parties and are only responsible for ensuring that the content is transmitted correctly.

'Catching' services are services that help to reduce the amount of bandwidth required for content delivery. They are used to improve the speed and efficiency of online content delivery when users request digital content, e.g., a webpage or video. Digital contents are often stored in caches on the users' device or on a server closer to the users' location, which allows the content to be delivered more quickly and efficiently as the users do not have to wait for the contents to be downloaded from their original location.

'Hosting' services are services that provide a reliable and secure way to store and deliver online content. For example, websites, videos, and other types of digital content are stored on servers operated by hosting service providers, which are responsible for

17. Article 6 and Recital 11 E-Commerce Directive.
18. Article 7 E-Commerce Directive.
19. Article 9 E-Commerce Directive.
20. Articles 10 and 11 E-Commerce Directive.

ensuring that the content is available to users when requested. Hosting services can also provide additional features such as website builders, e-commerce platforms, and a variety of security tools.[21]

Importantly, Articles 12 to 15 of the E-Commerce Directive on exemptions for such services have now been deleted by the DSA. References to such Articles have to be construed as references to Articles 4, 5, 6 and 8 DSA, respectively.[22] Therefore, they will be covered in the next Section of this Chapter.

5.3 KEY PROVISIONS OF THE DSA

5.3.1 General Provisions

As anticipated, the DSA reforms the existing EU e-commerce legal framework while maintaining the core principles of its liability regime, the prohibition of general monitoring and the internal market clause. Building on the key principles of the E-Commerce Directive, it intends to adapt to the modern technological realm and provide measures which have consumer protection at their core.[23] It aims to ensure the conditions for the provision of innovative digital services in the internal market, contribute to online safety and the protection of fundamental rights, and set a governance structure for the supervision of providers of intermediary services.[24]

To achieve its goal, the DSA lays down harmonised rules on the provision of intermediary services in the internal market, establishing a framework for the conditional exemption from liability of providers of intermediary services, rules on specific due diligence obligations tailored to certain specific categories of providers of intermediary services, rules on its implementation and enforcement.[25]

The DSA applies to intermediary service providers that offer services to recipients established or resident in the EU, regardless of the place of residence of the providers of such services.[26]

Recipients of services may be "any natural or legal person who uses an intermediary service, in particular for the purposes of seeking information or making it accessible."[27]

---

21. On online intermediaries predominantly performing passive activities offering access or hosting services, e.g., *see* Mariarosaria Taddeo and Luciano Floridi (eds), *The Responsibilities of Online Service Providers* (Springer 2017). On providers becoming more active by offering services to share information which is indexed and organised over the Internet, e.g., *see* Giovanni Sartor, *Providers Liability: From the eCommerce Directive to the Future – In-Depth Analysis for the IMCO Committee*, (2017), available at https://www.europarl.europa.eu/RegData/etudes/IDAN/2017/614179/IPOL_IDA(2017)614179_EN.pdf.
22. Article 89 DSA.
23. European Commission, Explanatory Memorandum, Proposal for a Regulation of the European Parliament and of the Council on a Single Market for Digital Services (Digital Services Act) and amending Directive 2000/31/EC, COM(2020) 825 final.
24. Article 1(1) DSA.
25. Article 1(2) DSA.
26. Article 2 DSA.
27. Article 3(b) DSA.

In practice, the DSA applies to:

(a) intermediary service providers that offer network infrastructure as Internet access providers and domain name registration centres;
(b) cloud service providers (e.g., famous services such as Google Cloud and Amazon Web Service), web hosting (e.g., WordPress) and video hosting (e.g., YouTube, Vimeo);
(c) online platforms that bring together sellers and consumers as an online marketplace, app stores, and social media;
(d) very large online platforms (Very Large Online Platforms, VLOPs) or very large search engines (Very Large Search Engines, VLOSEs), i.e., platforms with more than 10% of the recipients' services established or located in the EU (which have a number of average monthly active recipients of the service in the Union equal to or higher than 45 million).[28]

The European Commission keeps a list of the designated VLOPs and VLOSEs that it updates regularly. For example, as of December 2024, the list of VLOPs included *Alibaba AliExpress, Amazon Store, Apple AppStore, Booking.com, Facebook, Google Play, Google Maps, Google Shopping, Instagram, LinkedIn, Pinterest, Pornhub, Snapchat, Stripchat, TikTok, Twitter* (under the old trade name, now called *X*), *Wikipedia, XVideos, YouTube, Zalando;*[29] the list of VLOSEs included *Bing* and *Google Search.*[30]

The concept of 'offering' services under the DSA is broad. Providers are covered by the regulation if they allow EU users to use their service and have a 'substantial connection' with the EU,[31] e.g., by directing their activities to a Member State.[32]

5.3.2 Liability of Providers of Intermediary Services

As in the E-Commerce Directive, intermediation services are classified into the three categories of 'mere conduit' services (i.e., transmission of information by a recipient through a communication network or access to a communication network), 'caching' services (i.e., automatic, intermediate and temporary storage of information provided by a recipient of services through a communication network to make further transmission more efficient), and 'hosting' services (i.e., storage of information provided by and at the request of a recipient of the service).

---

28. Recital 76 and Article 33 DSA.
29. *See* the formal List of the Designated VLOPs of the European Commission at https://digital-strategy.ec.europa.eu/en/policies/list-designated-vlops-and-vloses accessed on 26 November 2024.
30. *See* the formal List of the Designated VLOSEs of the European Commission at https://digital-strategy.ec.europa.eu/en/policies/list-designated-vlops-and-vloses accessed on 26 November 2024.
31. Article 3(d) DSA.
32. Article 3(e) DSA.

The rules of the DSA are graduated, with lower-level obligations applied to providers of network infrastructure and hosting services, while online platforms such as marketplaces and app stores are subject to stricter regulations. Such rules abrogate Articles 12 to 15 of the E-Commerce Directive on the liability of intermediary service providers[33] and substitute them, taking into account the bulk of the jurisprudence developed by the CJEU over the years.[34]

For 'mere conduit' services, the service provider is not liable for the information transmitted or accessed (including the automatic, intermediate and transient storage of the information transmitted if it takes place for the sole purpose of carrying out the transmission in the communication network, and provided that the information is not stored for a period longer than necessary), on condition that the provider does not initiate the transmission, does not select the receiver of the transmission, and does not select or modify the information contained in the transmission.[35]

For 'catching' services, the service provider is not liable for the automatic, intermediate and temporary storage of information on condition that the provider does not modify the information, complies with conditions on access to the information, complies with rules regarding the updating of the information in manners recognised by the industry, does not interfere with the lawful use of technology to obtain data on the use of the information, and acts promptly to remove or to disable access to the information it has stored as soon as the information at the initial source of the transmission has been removed from the network.[36]

Finally, for 'hosting' services, the service provider is not liable for the information stored at the request of a recipient of the service, on condition that the provider does not have knowledge of illegal activity or illegal content and regarding damages is not aware of facts or circumstances from which the illegal activity or illegal content is apparent, or upon obtaining such knowledge or awareness, acts promptly to remove or disable access to the illegal content.[37]

The discernment between one type of the above services or the other depends solely on the technical functionalities of the service. These must be assessed on a case-by-case basis as they may change over time. In general, providers are allowed to conduct voluntary investigations but are not obliged to monitor the information and

33. Article 89 DSA.
34. *See*, in particular, Joined Cases C-236/08 to C-238/08, *Google France SARL and Google Inc. v. Louis Vuitton Malletier SA, Google France SARL v. Viaticum SA and Luteciel SARL, and Google France SARL v. Centre national de recherche en relations humaines (CNRRH) SARL and Others*, ECLI:EU:C:2010:159; Case C–324/09, *L'Oréal SA and Others v. eBay International AG and Others*, ECLI:EU:C:2011:474; Case C-70/10, *Scarlet Extended SA v. Société belge des auteurs, compositeurs et éditeurs SCRL (SABAM), ECLI:EU:C:2011:771*; Case C-360/10, *Belgische Vereniging van Auteurs, Componisten en Uitgevers CVBA (SABAM) v. Netlog NV, ECLI:EU:C:2012:85*; Case C-314/12, *UPC Telekabel Wien GmbH v. Constantin Film Verleih GmbH and Wega Filmproduktionsgesellschaft mbH*, EU:C:2014:192; Case C-484/14, *Tobias Mc Fadden v. Sony Music Entertainment Germany GmbH*, ECLI:EU:C:2016:689; Case C–18/18, *Eva Glawischnig-Piesczek v. Facebook Ireland Limited*, ECLI:EU:C:2019:821.
35. Article 4 DSA.
36. Article 5 DSA.
37. Article 6 DSA.

content that they transmit or store, nor are they obliged to ascertain facts or circumstances indicating the presence of illegal activities.[38]

Furthermore, if providers carry out voluntary investigations aimed at detecting and removing illegal content, the above exemptions from liability of the DSA are not affected.[39]

At the same time, upon the receipt of an order issued by the competent national authorities to act against one or more specific items of illegal content, providers of intermediary services have to inform that authority of any effect given to the order, specifying if and when effect was given to the order.[40]

Equally, upon receipt of an order issued by the relevant authority to provide specific information about one or more specific individual recipients of the service, providers of intermediary services must inform the authority of its receipt and of the effect given to the order, specifying if and when effect was given to the order.[41]

5.3.3 Due Diligence Obligations

In the intention of the legislator, due diligence obligations are set for a transparent and safe online environment. The Chapter on the obligations of providers divides the rules according to operators. Thus, the following are prescribed:

(a) obligations applicable to all providers;[42]
(b) additional obligations applicable to hosting service providers (including online platforms);[43]
(c) additional obligations and powers for online platform providers;[44]
(d) additional obligations for online platform providers that enable consumers to conclude distance contracts with traders;[45]
(e) additional obligations for VLOPs and VLOSEs.[46]

(a) The Obligations Applicable to All Providers

The first provisions, set out in section I of Chapter III, apply indiscriminately to all providers. These consist of the duty to establish contact points for the relevant authorities of the Member States, the Commission and the Committee[47] and a contact point for recipients of the services.[48]

38. Article 8 DSA.
39. Article 7 DSA.
40. Article 9 DSA.
41. Article 10 DSA.
42. Articles 11-15 DSA.
43. Articles 16-18 DSA.
44. Articles 19-28 DSA.
45. Articles 29-32 DSA.
46. Articles 33-43 DSA.
47. Article 11 DSA.
48. Article 12 DSA.

In their general terms and conditions, the providers are required to specify in a concise, intelligible and accessible manner information regarding the restrictions they impose on the use of their services, including the policies, procedures, measures and tools used for content moderation, including algorithmic decision-making and human verification, as well as the procedural rules of their internal complaint handling system. Providers must act diligently, objectively and proportionately, taking into account the rights and interests of all parties involved, including freedom of expression, media pluralism and other rights and freedoms enshrined in the Charter of Fundamental Rights of the EU.[49] Providers are obliged to publish - on an annual basis - clear and intelligible reports on their content moderation activities. These must focus on elements including the number of orders received, number of reports submitted, use of automated tools, and number of complaints received.[50]

(b) The Additional Obligations Applicable to Hosting Service Providers

A mechanism for reporting illegal content electronically is imposed on hosting service providers. Decisions to follow up on alerts must be timely, taken diligently, and in a non-arbitrary and objective manner. If automated tools are used, adequate information on their use must be included.[51]

If restrictive measures are taken, they must be accompanied by adequate justification. There is an exception, however, if the information relates to widely disseminated misleading commercial content. Concrete cases could be the inauthentic use of the service, such as the use of bots or false accounts or other misleading uses.[52]

The statement of reasons and circumstances accompanying the restrictive measure must contain a range of information. This includes an indication of the subject matter (i.e., whether the decision involves the removal of information, disabling access, limiting visibility or other measures); the facts and circumstances on which it is based; information on the automated tools used for the decision; reference to the legal basis invoked; and the available remedies. This provision on the statement of reasons and circumstances, however, does not apply in the case of the adoption of a removal order by an authority.[53] In the event of suspicion that a criminal offence has been committed, the provider has to immediately inform the judicial authorities of the concerned Member State.[54]

The types of restrictions that service providers may adopt are not typical and, therefore, they are not mentioned by the legislator, but among them, there could be the restriction of visibility (which may consist in the downgrading of positioning or recommendation systems), as well as the restriction of accessibility by one or more recipients of the service, or the exclusion of the user from an online community without the latter being aware of it ('shadow banning'). Another conceivable restriction concerns the monetisation – through advertising revenue – of the information provided

49. Article 14 DSA.
50. Article 15 DSA.
51. Article 16 DSA.
52. Recital 55 DSA.
53. Article 17 DSA.
54. Article 18 DSA.

by the recipient of the service, which may be restricted by suspending or suppressing the payment of money or revenue related to such information.[55]

(c) The Additional Obligations and Powers of Online Platform Providers

Online platforms may be considered a subcategory with respect to hosting (storage) service providers. By 'online platforms', the legislator means social networks or those platforms that enable consumers to conclude distance contracts with traders (i.e., all those platforms that operate in e-commerce). They are defined as information hosting service providers that not only store information provided by the recipients of the service at their request but also disseminate it publicly at the recipients' request.[56]

A large number of obligations apply to these platforms. These, however, do not apply to those providers that qualify as micro or small enterprises (SMEs).[57] SMEs, in fact, make the most of the EU's digital industry and they are seen as a tool of innovation that needs to compete in digital markets dominated by large extra-EU firms.

The additional obligations for online platforms include:

- the establishment of an internal system for the handling of complaints against a decision made by the provider upon receipt of a complaint or against a series of decisions made by the provider. No automated tools may be used exclusively for decisions on complaints;[58]
- the provision of an option to settle disputes out of court. Recipients of the service must be informed of this possibility and it must be accessible on the online interface. The dispute resolution body may not adopt decisions that are binding on the parties;[59]
- the adoption of technical and organisational measures for the operation of the figure of 'trusted flaggers', designated by the national Digital Services Coordinators (the competent authority designated by each Member State responsible for all matters relating to supervision and enforcement of the DSA in that Member State). They are independent experts at detecting certain types of illegal content online, such as hate speech or terrorist content, and notifying it to the online platforms.[60]

In addition to the information on content moderation reporting seen earlier for all providers (under Articles 16 and 20 DSA), online platform providers must also indicate the number of disputes submitted to dispute resolution bodies, the results of those disputes, the average time for their resolution, and the number of suspensions applied.[61]

55. Recital 55 DSA.
56. Article 3(i) DSA.
57. Article 19 DSA.
58. Article 20 DSA.
59. Article 21 DSA.
60. Article 22 DSA.
61. Article 23 DSA.

Every six months, providers have to publish for each online platform and for each search engine information on the average monthly number of active recipients of the service in the EU.[62]

Also, online platform providers must design, organise and manage interfaces in such a way that the recipients of the services offered are not deceived or manipulated or so that their ability to make free and informed decisions is materially distorted or impaired. This prohibition does not apply to practices covered by the UCPD or the GDPR.[63]

In case of presenting advertisements on their interfaces, providers are obliged to ensure that recipients are able to identify clearly, concisely, unambiguously and in real-time: (i) that the information is an advertisement; (ii) the person on whose behalf it is presented; (iii) the person financing the advertisement if different from the previous letter; (iv) indications of parameters used to determine the recipient to whom it is presented and how these parameters can be changed. Providers must make a function available to recipients that allows them to declare whether the content they (the recipients) provide is or contains commercial communications. Finally, they may not submit advertisements on the basis of profiling as referred to in the GDPR on the basis of the use of special categories of personal data (the sensitive data of Article 9 GDPR).[64]

Those who make use of 'recommender systems' - i.e., AI or AI algorithms, usually associated with machine learning that use big data to suggest or recommend additional products to consumers - are required to specify in their contractual terms and conditions the main parameters used in the systems, as well as any options available to the recipients to change or influence these parameters. Where several parameter options exist, the recipient must be allowed to choose the preferred option.[65]

Finally, in the case of platforms accessible to minors, appropriate and proportionate measures must be taken to ensure high levels of privacy, security and protection. If an online platform is or becomes aware that the recipient is a minor, profiling-based advertising is not permitted.[66]

The DSA - although including them in the scope of obligations - also provides for certain powers for providers. It is stipulated that they may, after a warning, suspend their services - limited to a reasonable period of time - for certain recipients who repeatedly provide illegal content. They may also suspend the service of internal complaints to those repetitively submitting manifestly unfounded complaints or reports. Providers must determine their policy on such abuses, including by means of examples, in their general terms and conditions for using the service.[67]

62. Article 24 DSA.
63. Article 25 DSA.
64. Article 26 DSA.
65. Article 27 DSA.
66. Article 28 DSA.
67. Article 23 DSA.

(d) The Additional Obligations for Online Platform Providers That Enable Consumers to Conclude Distance Contracts with Traders

The additional obligations for providers that engage in e-commerce do not apply to those that qualify as SMEs. Again, this is a measure taken by the legislator to foster innovation and enhance the EU digital industry, which is composed mainly of SMEs.

Providers may only allow traders to use their platforms if the latter have provided certain information. This includes identification data, company registration or other register details. It is always up to the provider to diligently verify the veracity of this information.[68] The online interfaces have to be designed and organised in ways that enable traders to comply with their obligations regarding pre-contractual information, compliance and product safety information.[69]

Then, if the provider becomes aware of an offer of an illegal product or service from an operator, it is obliged to inform the consumers who purchased the product or service immediately (for purchases within the preceding six months).[70]

(e) The Additional Obligations for VLOPs and VLOSEs

As anticipated, the European Commission is in charge of determining which online platforms or search engines have to be considered 'very large'. This happens when the latter have an average monthly number of active service recipients in the EU of 45 million or more. This quality ceases, and the decision of the European Commission is revoked, if, for an uninterrupted period of at least one year, the aforementioned average monthly number has not been produced. An official list is produced.[71]

The additional obligations that follow below, therefore, only apply to the VLOPs and VLOSEs designated by the European Commission.

To begin with, VLOPs and VLOSEs are required to report annually to identify, analyse and evaluate any systemic risks arising from the design or operation of their service and systems, including algorithms or the use of their services. The systemic risks to be considered are:

- The dissemination of illegal content.
- The possible foreseeable negative effects on the exercise of fundamental rights.
- Any foreseeable negative effects on civic debate, electoral processes and public safety.
- Any foreseeable negative effects related to gender-based violence, public health and child protection.

In this evaluation, account must be taken of:

- The design of the recommender systems and any other relevant algorithmic systems.

68. Article 30 DSA.
69. Article 31 DSA.
70. Article 32 DSA.
71. Article 33 DSA.

- Their content moderation systems.
- The general conditions applicable.
- The advertising selection and presentation systems.
- The provider's data practices.[72]

With the aforementioned assessments, it is analysed how the risks are "are influenced by intentional manipulation of their service, including by inauthentic use or automated exploitation of the service, as well as the amplification and potentially rapid and wide dissemination of illegal content and of information that is incompatible with their terms and conditions."[73]

These risks may arise, therefore, from inauthentic use of the service, such as the creation of false accounts, the use of bots or other misleading uses of a service, and from other automated or partially automated behaviour that may lead to the rapid and wide dissemination to the public of information that constitutes illegal content or is incompatible with the general conditions of the online platform or online search engine.[74]

VLOPs and VLOSEs are required to take measures to mitigate identified systemic risks. Measures may include adaptation of:

- the design, characteristics or operation of services;
- the general terms and conditions;
- content moderation procedures;
- algorithmic systems, including recommendation systems;
- advertising systems and the adoption of measures to limit or adapt the presentation of advertising associated with the service provided; or
- the strengthening of internal processes, in particular for the detection of systemic risks;
- initiating or adapting cooperation with reputable reporters and implementing the decisions of dispute resolution bodies;
- initiating or adapting cooperation with other providers on codes of conduct and crisis protocols;
- adoption of awareness-raising measures and adaptation of the online interface to provide more information to recipients;
- adoption of targeted measures to safeguard the rights of minors;
- the use of a visible marker to ensure that an element of information (image, audio, generated or manipulated video) that resembles a person, object, place or otherwise, and that appears falsely authentic to a person, is distinguishable when presented on their online interfaces. A feature must be provided that allows the recipients of the service to point to this information (this is what is known as a 'deep fake').[75]

72. Article 34 DSA.
73. *Ibid.*
74. Recital 84 DSA.
75. Article 35 DSA.

In the event of exceptional circumstances that may lead to a serious threat to public safety or public health leading to a 'crisis', the European Commission may adopt a decision requiring one or more suppliers to take one or more actions for a period not exceeding three months, extendable once. Such actions include the following:

- an assessment of whether and how the operation and use of their services contribute to the crisis;
- the identification and application of specific, effective and proportionate measures to prevent, eliminate or limit such contribution;
- a report to the Commission on these assessments and the measures taken.[76]

VLOPs and VLOSEs, at least once a year, have to submit to independent audits on their own initiative in order to assess their compliance with their obligations above, their obligations under codes of conduct, and crisis protocols.[77]

In the case of use of recommender systems (*see* above), providers must ensure at least one option that does not involve profiling as defined in Article 4 GDPR,[78] i.e., "any form of automated processing of personal data consisting of the use of personal data to evaluate certain personal aspects relating to a natural person, in particular to analyse or predict aspects concerning that natural person's performance at work, economic situation, health, personal preferences, interests, reliability, behaviour, location or movements."

For online advertising, VLOPs and VLOSEs are required to make available to the public a register containing certain information including: (a) the content of the advertisement with the name of the product or service; (b) the person on whose behalf it is presented and who paid for it; (d) the period during which it was presented; (e) indications as to whether the advertisement was intended for a specific target group and the parameters used for this purpose; (f) the commercial communications published on the platforms; (g) the number of recipients reached and aggregate data broken down by Member State relating to the target groups for which the advertisement was intended.[79]

VLOPs and VLOSEs must also grant the Digital Service Coordinator access to data to assess compliance with the DSA,[80] and they are required to establish a compliance function independent of their operational functions composed of one or more compliance officers.[81]

Finally, for the purpose of the annual reports of Article 15 DSA [*see* above section 5.3.3.(a)], these providers are required to specify additional information, which includes the human resources dedicated to the service offered in the EU, the

76. Article 36 DSA.
77. Article 37 DSA.
78. Article 38 DSA.
79. Article 39 DSA.
80. Article 40 DSA.
81. Article 41 DSA.

qualifications and language skills of the persons performing the aforementioned activities, and accuracy indicators.[82]

Each Member State has to designate one or more competent authorities to be responsible for the supervision and enforcement of the DSA, including a Digital Service Coordinator, also for ensuring coordination at national level.[83]

The maximum fines that may be imposed for a failure to comply with an obligation of the DSA amounts to 6% of the annual worldwide turnover of the provider of intermediary services concerned in the preceding financial year. Instead, for the supply of incorrect, incomplete or misleading information, failure to reply or rectify incorrect, incomplete or misleading information and failure to submit to an inspection, the maximum fine that may be imposed amounts to 1% of the annual income or worldwide turnover of the provider of intermediary services concerned in the preceding financial year. Finally, Member States need to ensure that the maximum amount of a periodic penalty payment is 5% of the average daily worldwide turnover or income of the provider of intermediary services concerned in the preceding financial year per day, calculated from the date specified in the decision concerned.[84] In addition, recipients of the service remain entitled to seek compensation from providers of intermediary services in respect of any damage or loss suffered due to an infringement under the DSA.[85]

5.4 THE DSA, REGULATORY PATCHWORK, AND CONSUMER PROTECTION

The DSA represents just another piece of the complex regulatory mosaic that has been in the making in European institutions in recent years.

The EU has an evident competitive disadvantage in digital and technology markets compared to other jurisdictions such as the United States, China, and India. From this angle, it can be argued that, as a reaction, it has become a regulatory superpower and it has started a process of over-regulation of digital markets, including the governance of their dominant actors, in an alleged attempt to contain such a technological deficit.[86]

In this regulatory hyperactivity, the number of passed and proposed legislative acts to regulate digital markets (the main ones covered in this book and others mentioned), coupled with the various directives and regulations on cybersecurity, add to an existing bulk of other relevant legislation, including the still valid consumer law acquis.

Indeed, as seen, one of the main aims of the DSA is to create a safe, predictable, transparent, and reliable online environment adding to consumer protection. The

82. Article 42 DSA.
83. Articles 49-51 DSA.
84. Article 52 DSA.
85. Article 54 DSA.
86. E.g., *see* Bart van der Sloot, *Editorial*, 3 European Data Protection Law Review, 351-357 (2021) https://doi.org/10.21552/edpl/2021/3/3.

intention is to make certain technological tools already widely used today, such as recommender and other automated algorithmic systems, more transparent.

Pursuing such objectives is not a new policy goal. The other preceding legislation of the digital sphere, starting with the GDPR, aimed at the same goals. As far as the regulation of digital service providers is concerned, the E-Commerce Directive already established obligations to disclose information to information. In the same way, the acquis of EU consumer law employs the same legislative technique. For example, the CRD already required the disclosure by traders to consumers of a vast range of information.[87] Likewise, the Omnibus Directive contains information duties to be given to consumers by platforms for dealings with third-party traders operating on those platforms.[88]

Consumer law already employs an important amount of information and disclosure duties between traders and consumers. The DSA adds complimentarily to previous obligations by requiring platforms to retrieve information from the traders and verify it. Arguably, this creates an information overload for consumers and excessive administrative burdens to traders and platforms. Indeed, doubts have been cast about the cohesiveness of such a regulatory approach.

From the perspective of consumers, they will receive an important number of information from and about traders, as well as from and about platforms, which add to the data protection notices provided by data controllers for the purposes of the GDPR. However, consumers are already overwhelmed by information notices that they hardly read or understand, given the complexities behind technologies and digitalisation.[89]

From the perspective of digital businesses, who may find themselves in various positions as traders, intermediary services or both, there is an increasing number of compliance obligations and coordination of the various duties coming from different pieces of legislation that are not always consistent or coordinated. For example, the liability of online platforms under the UCPD and the DSA needs better clarification vis-à-vis the variety of business models employed. It needs to be absolutely clear when and to what extent liability exemptions under the DSA leave room to hold online platforms liable under consumer law legislation or to what extent it stands in the way of extending the platforms' liability.[90]

87. Directive 2011/83/EU of the European Parliament and of the Council of 25 October 2011 on consumer rights, amending Council Directive 93/13/EEC and Directive 1999/44/EC of the European Parliament and of the Council and repealing Council Directive 85/577/EEC and Directive 97/7/EC of the European Parliament and of the Council, OJ L 304, 22.11.2011, p. 64-88.
88. Directive (EU) 2019/2161 of the European Parliament and of the Council of 27 November 2019 amending Council Directive 93/13/EEC and Directives 98/6/EC, 2005/29/EC and 2011/83/EU of the European Parliament and of the Council as regards the better enforcement and modernisation of Union consumer protection rules, OJ L 328, 18.12.2019, p. 7-28.
89. Caroline Cauffman and Catalina Goanta, *A New Order: The Digital Services Act and Consumer Protection*, 12 European Journal of Risk Regulation, 758-774 (2021) https://doi.org/10.1017/err.2021.8.
90. Bram Duivenvoorde, *The Liability of Online Marketplaces under the Unfair Commercial Practices Directive, the E-commerce Directive and the Digital Services Act*, 2 Journal of European Consumer and Market Law, 43-52 (2022).

The DSA adds another layer of regulation. Adding to their information disclosures, they have duties to investigate, verify and share information with the competent authorities. The question is how all such duties will fare together.[91]

Arguably, the requirement on platforms to verify the identity of professional users of their online services could improve the quality of services for users, especially consumers. All in all, however, the addition and – under certain circumstances – the overlap of the DSA with the other pieces of the new digital rulebook and the consumer law acquis give rise to concerns about the effectiveness of the legal technique employed and uncertainty stemming out of an uncoordinated regulatory patchwork.[92] Moreover, the provision of effective remedies or tools for consumers for misleading information or unsafe products is to many extent weak.[93]

Other inconsistencies arising from the coordination of the DSA with other regulatory aspects emerge.

For example, the DSA does not put order to the issue of what accounts as an 'information society service', as interpreted by the CJEU, explored above in this Chapter. Its enactment could have been an opportunity to adapt the law to the factual business models that are developing in the digital sphere and properly determine the scope of application of the E-Commerce Directive. As lamented by many, in fact, the current factual application of the CJEU criterion, whether the intermediation service is indispensable for the provision of the subsequent service to which it relates, leads to different outcomes depending on the business models of the platforms.[94] The DSA does not fix the problem.

On a different matter, an idea of the DSA is also to make the process for the removal of content that is illegal or contrary to the provider's terms and conditions more effective, although this theme may open up the thorny issue of censorship and the questionable creation and powers of the figure of the so-called trusted flaggers. These aspects would require an additional book and are beyond the scope of this analysis. Nevertheless, they remain important issues to research and keep debating.[95]

A further profile concerns the delicate balancing of interests at stake that digital providers would be called upon to carry out. On this issue, although the legislator attempts to regulate every aspect, it is not unambiguously clarified whether the removal of illegal content must be preceded by a court order establishing the illegality

91. *Ibid.*
92. *See, also,* Cristina Poncibò, *AI Platforms: Safeguarding Consumer Rights in the EU*, in *The Cambridge Handbook of AI and Consumer Law: Comparative Perspectives*, 236-251 (Larry Di Matteo, Cristina Poncibò and Geraint Howells eds, Cambridge University Press 2024).
93. Christopher Busch and Vanessa Mak, *Putting the Digital Services Act in Context: Bridging the Gap Between EU Consumer Law and Platform Regulation*, 3 Journal of European Consumer and Market Law, 109-115 (2021) https://doi.org/10.2139/ssrn.3933675.
94. *Ibid.*
95. For initial literature on the topic, *see* Ioanna Tourkochoriti, *The Digital Services Act and the EU as the Global Regulator of the Internet*, 24 Chicago Journal of International Law, 129-147 (2023); Giulia Vasino, *Censura 'privata' e contrasto all'hate speech nell'era delle Internet Platforms*, 4 Federalismi.it, 130-159 (2023); Monika Szwarc, *EU Law and the Member States' Competence to Regulate the Operation of Collaborative Economy Platforms: Where Do We Stand after the Digital Services Act*, 35 European Business Law Review, 183-206 (2014) https://doi.org/10.54648/eulr 2024015.

in question. From an initial analysis of the DSA, the answer appears in the negative. The provider should be able to proceed with the direct adoption of restrictive measures without there being orders or other measures of an authority. Recital 54 DSA seems to implicitly support this interpretation. It specifies that if hosting service providers decide to remove information provided by a recipient of the service or disable access to it or otherwise restrict its visibility or monetisation because it constitutes illegal content or is incompatible with the general terms and conditions - e.g., following receipt of a notification or acting on its own initiative - they should inform the addressee of their decision and the reasons. If the decision was taken following the receipt of an alert, the hosting service providers should only disclose the identity of the persons or entities that submitted the alert to the recipient of the service, if such information is necessary to identify the illegality of the content, for instance in case of infringement of intellectual property rights.[96] On this aspect, therefore, the solution would comply with earlier jurisprudence of the CJEU based on the principle of proportionality, according to which a search engine may grant a deindexing request if the applicant succeeds in providing a likelihood of evidence of the manifest inaccuracy of the indexed news without the need for a prior court ruling.[97]

In sum, the implementation of the DSA and its coordination with the copious and articulated regulations that complement the regulation of digital markets will play a crucial role that will determine the final outcome of the type of consumer protection that the European legislator intends to tackle.

96. Recital 54 DSA.
97. Case C-460/20, *Google (Déréférencement d'un contenu prétendument inexact)*, ECLI:EU:C:2022:962.

CHAPTER 6

The Artificial Intelligence Act

6.1 INTRODUCTION TO AI

One of the most delicate aspects within the framework of the European digital strategy is undoubtedly the choice to regulate an innovative tool such as AI. As is well known, the EU has decided to follow this path, choosing a very different approach from other countries such as the United States of America (USA) and China.

AI is the ability of a machine to show human abilities such as reasoning, learning, planning and creativity, understanding their environment, relating to what they perceive, solving problems, and acting towards a specific goal. The computer receives data (already prepared or collected by sensors, like a video camera), processes it, and responds, thanks to incredible processing.

Under this process, AI can adapt its behaviour by analysing the effects of previous actions and working independently.

Generally speaking, there can be two different types of AI:

- Software: virtual assistants, image analysis software, search engines, facial and voice recognition systems.
- Embedded intelligence: robots, autonomous vehicles, drones, the IoT.

AI is becoming a fundamental element in many aspects of our lives, considering that it is the basis for the functioning of tools that are now daily:

- personal assistants who come to our rescue on smartphones and computers (e.g., *Alexa*);
- search engines (e.g., *Google* and *Safari*);
- machine translators (e.g., *Reverso, Google translate*);
- electric driving vehicles;
- IoT (e.g., refrigerators and robot vacuum cleaners);
- shopping and online advertising;

- intelligent agriculture;
- robots in factories;
- cybersecurity;
- etc.

Moreover, the focus on AI grew in 2022 after the launch of generative intelligence, which raised further questions about the benefits and risks associated with such a technology. The so-called Generative Artificial Intelligence[1] entailed a case of an unsupervised machine learning system that can generate autonomous and multimodal contents, including text, image, audio, video and eventually three dimensions (3D). It is increasingly clear that AI is destined to change profoundly every aspect of our lives, not only economic and legal but also political and ethical.

6.1.1 Benefits of AI

The EU believes that AI will bring great benefits from several different points of view.[2]

- Benefits for Citizens

AI could mean better healthcare, cars, and other safer transport systems and more cost-effective, durable, tailor-made products and services.

It can also facilitate access to information, education and training, making the place safer work and new jobs due to the growth of AI industries.

- Benefits for Businesses

AI could enable the development of a new generation of products and services, including in sectors where European companies are already well-positioned, such as the circular economy, agriculture, healthcare, fashion, and tourism. It can make sales more fluid and optimised, improve machinery maintenance, and increase both. It can foster a production that improves the quality of customer services and saves energy.

- Benefits for Public Services

AI applied to public services can reduce costs and offer new transport options for the public, education, energy, and waste management, as well as improve the sustainability of products, helping to achieve the objectives of the European Green Deal.

- Strengthening Democracy

Data-driven audits, the prevention of disinformation and cyber-attacks, and access to quality information can help strengthen democracy. They would also support diversity

1. Fiona Fui-Hoon Nah, Ruilin Zheng, Jinjyuan Cai, Keng Siau and Langtao Chen, *Generative AI and ChatGPT: Applications, Challenges, and AI-human Collaboration*, 25 Journal of Information Technology Case and Application Research, 277-304 (2023) https://doi.org/10.1080/15228053.2023.2233814.
2. *See* European Parliament, *Quali sono i rischi e i vantaggi dell'intelligenza artificiale?* (28 June 2023), available at https://www.europarl.europa.eu/pdfs/news/expert/2020/9/story/20200918STO87404/20200918STO87404_it.pdf.

and equal opportunities, for example, by reducing recruitment bias through analytical data.

- AI for Security

AI can be used in crime prevention and as an aid to criminal justice because it would require faster processing of large volumes of data, better assessment of the risks of prisoners escaping, and prediction and prevention of crime and terrorist attacks. Online platforms are already using AI to detect and respond to Illegal or inappropriate practices on the net. In the military field, AI could be used for defence and attacks in the case of cyber crimes or to attack key targets in the cyber-fight.

6.1.2 Risks of AI

However, besides these undeniable advantages, AI can also pose serious risks that must be considered.

- Risk of Underuse and Abuse

The growing use of AI systems also involves, at the same time, risks of abuse and underuse.

Failure to use AI to its full potential, for example, could lead to poor implementation of major programmes, such as the already mentioned European Green Deal, loss of competitive advantage over other regions of the world, economic stagnation and fewer opportunities for all. The underutilisation could have different causes, ranging from public and business mistrust to poor infrastructure, lack of entrepreneurial initiative, low investment, and fragmentation of digital markets because AI depends on data.

But abuse is also a problem. For example, it should not be used for problems that are unsuitable for explaining or solving complex social issues.

- Liability and AI

An important challenge is determining who is responsible for damages caused by a device or AI. For example, does the owner, manufacturer or programmer must pay for the damage in an accident involving a driving car?

If the producer was not liable, there might be insufficient incentive to provide a safe and efficient product. The public may have less confidence in technology. But at the same time, too strict standards could stifle innovation.

- Threats of AI to Fundamental Rights and Democracy[3]

The results produced by AI depend on how it is designed and what data is entered. This process may be affected intentionally or unintentionally. For example, some important aspects may not be programmed in the algorithm or may be programmed to reflect and

3. European Council, *Algorithms and Human Rights. Study on the Human Rights Dimensions of Automated Data Processing Techniques and Possible Regulatory Implications*, DGI(2017)12, available at https://rm.coe.int/algorithms-and-human-rights-en-rev/16807956b5.

perpetuate structural distortions or biases. Furthermore, using data and numbers to represent a complex reality makes the factual, precise and independent AI seem even when it is not. If not correctly programmed, AI could lead to decisions about job offers and the offer of loans, and criminal proceedings influenced by ethnicity, gender, and age. AI can also threaten data protection and the right to privacy. It can be used, for example, in devices for face recognition or online profiling. Furthermore, it can put together information about a person without awareness. The threat to democracy posed by AI passes through information. It has already been accused of creating 'bubbles'on the net, where the content is presented based on the content a person has interacted with in the past rather than creating an open environment for inclusive, multi-voice and accessible debate.

It can also create fake but highly realistic images, videos, and audio, known as 'deepfake', which can be used to scam, ruin reputations, and put confidence in decision-making processes. All these risks lead to the polarisation of public debate and the manipulation of elections.

AI could also threaten freedom of assembly and protest because somebody could use it to track and profile individuals linked to specific groups or opinions.

- The Effect of AI on Work

The use of AI could lead to the disappearance of many jobs. At the same time, there must be adequate training to ensure that the unemployed can access it, and there will be a long-term skilled workforce.

- Competition

The accumulation of information could also lead to a distortion of competition, mainly through how much advantage the parties with more information could gain and try to eliminate the competitors.

- The Safety Risks

AI applications in contact or integrated with the human body can be dangerous if poorly designed, misused or hacked. The use of unregulated AI in armaments could lead to a loss of control over destructive weapons.

- The Problems of Transparency

Inequalities in access to information could be exploited at the expense of users. For example, based on a person's online behaviour or other data used without his knowledge, a service provider can predict how much this person will pay for a service or political campaign and know what message to send.

Another transparency problem is that it may not be clear to the user whether they are interacting with a person or an AI system.

For this reason, it is not by chance that the approach chosen by the European regulator revolves around achieving an ethical use of AI; this is far from a simple purpose to be guaranteed, since the very definition of ethics related to a non-human entity has raised considerable debate in the doctrine.

6.2 THE ARTIFICIAL INTELLIGENCE ACT

The Regulation (EU) 2024/1689 (AI Act)[4] represents the EU's response to these complex issues. In particular, the AI Act represents an attempt to responsibly shape the development of AI technologies,[5] ensuring that innovation does not impact public safety, fairness, and ethical standards.[6]

This Act represents a fundamental part of the EU's digital strategy focused on achieving ethical standards, transparency, and accountability, demonstrating an opposite approach to other countries such as China.

The AI Act came into force on 1 August 2024 and will be fully implemented in the next two years, with some exceptions: bans will go into force after six months, the governance rules and requirements for general-purpose AI models will become applicable after twelve months, and the rules for AI systems - integrated into regulated products - will apply after thirty-six months. In addition, more than sixty secondary acts are expected to be adopted in the coming months to implement primary legislation fully. To facilitate the transition to the new regulatory framework, the European Commission launched the AI Pact. This voluntary initiative aims to support future implementation and calls on European AI developers not just to meet the basic obligations of the AI Act in advance.

6.2.1 The History of the AI Act

The discussion around regulating AI in the EU can be traced back to the early 2010s when AI and machine learning technologies began to rise to prominence due to their growing intervention in various sectors of human life.

Since 2014, the European Commission has begun to explore the implications of digital technologies, including AI. In this light, the Digital Agenda sets the foundation for future discussions about creating a framework for emerging technologies.[7] In 2018, the European Commission published a communication titled "Artificial Intelligence for Europe,"[8] which outlined the EU's vision to promote AI development in a human-centric way. This strategy highlighted the need for ethical guidelines, transparency, and accountability in AI systems, setting the stage for deeper regulatory discussions.

4. Regulation (EU) 2024/1689 of the European Parliament and of the Council of 13 June 2024 laying down harmonised rules on artificial intelligence and amending Regulations (EC) No. 300/2008, (EU) No. 167/2013, (EU) No. 168/2013, (EU) 2018/858, (EU) 2018/1139 and (EU) 2019/2144 and Directives 2014/90/EU, (EU) 2016/797 and (EU) 2020/1828 (Artificial Intelligence Act), OJ L, 2024/1689, 12.7.2024.
5. Patrik Mikalef, Kieran Conboy, Jenny Eriksson Lundström and Ales Popovič, *Thinking Responsibly about Responsible AI and 'the Dark Side' of AI*, 31 European Journal of Information Systems, 257-268 (2023) https://doi.org/10.1080/0960085x.2022.2026621.
6. Regarding the need of AI regulation, *see* Yuval Noah Harari, *Nexus: A Brief History of Information Networks from the Stone Age to AI* (Vintage Publishing 2024).
7. European Commission, Digital Agenda 2014-2017 (14 November 2014), available at https://digital-strategy.ec.europa.eu/en/library/digitale-agenda-2014-2017.
8. European Commission, Communication from the Commission to the European Parliament, the European Council, the Council, the European Economic and Social Committee and the Committee

In 2018, the European Commission took its first steps toward AI regulation, publishing the Ethics Guidelines for Trustworthy AI by the High-Level Expert Group on AI (AI HLEG),[9] laying out a series of key principles for AI development, including transparency, accountability, privacy and data protection, non-discrimination and fairness.

Two years later, in February 2020, the European Commission published the White Paper on Artificial Intelligence,[10] which provided a detailed analysis of AI's impact on the economy and society, proposing a strategy for fostering innovation in AI and a framework for managing risks. It identified the need for specific legal actions to mitigate risks associated with high-risk AI applications, especially in sensitive areas like healthcare, criminal justice, and autonomous systems.

The White Paper proposed principles which were introduced in the final text of the AI Act. In this document, the EU recognised the need for a regulatory framework concerning AI based upon the so-called risk-based approach, which entails that the different kinds of AI systems have to be classified into different levels of risks, from minimal to high, associated with progressively stringent regulation.

In particular, this approach could harmonise innovation and competition in the European market by protecting human rights, privacy, etc. This paper led to extensive consultations with stakeholders, including businesses, academics, and civil society groups, gathering feedback on how AI should be regulated.

In April 2021, following the White Paper's feedback and consultations, the European Commission presented the first proposal for the AI Act, which was based upon a series of principles such as the banning AI applications that pose an unacceptable risk to rights and freedoms (e.g., social scoring systems or real-time facial recognition in public spaces); promoting transparency, accountability, and trustworthiness; fostering collaboration and standardisation across Member States; and, the so-called four-tier risk classification system for AI systems, one of its most innovative features. In other words, applying the principle of proportionality, the EU proposed to classify AI systems according to a risk scale, prohibiting, as already mentioned, those which carried an excessive risk and then regulating them with progressively less restrictive measures as the level of risk decreases.

The proposal also focused on creating strong governance structures at the EU and national levels, ensuring compliance with the Act would be monitored and enforced effectively.

After the AI Act was proposed, it entered the legislative process, which involved intense debate among EU institutions, Member States, and stakeholders.[11]

---

of the Regions on Artificial Intelligence for Europe, 25 April 2018, in https://digital-strategy.ec.europa.eu/en/library/communication-artificial-intelligence-europe.

9. European Commission, Ethics Guidelines for Trustworthy AI (8 April 2019), available at https://digital-strategy.ec.europa.eu/en/library/ethics-guidelines-trustworthy-ai.

10. European Commission, White Paper on Artificial Intelligence: A European Approach to Excellence and Trust (19 February 2020), available at https://commission.europa.eu/publications/white-paper-artificial-intelligence-european-approach-excellence-and-trust_en.

11. To enter into the AI Act History details and follow the updates, *see* Future of Life Institute, *Historic Timeline*, available at https://artificialintelligenceact.eu/developments/.

The European Parliament played a central role in shaping the AI Act. The Parliament's Committee on Industry, Research and Energy (ITRE) and its Civil Liberties, Justice and Home Affairs Committee (LIBE), among others, were instrumental in examining the proposal. While members generally supported the Act's objectives, debates focused on key issues like the scope of high-risk AI, the regulation of biometric identification, and the balance between innovation and regulation. One of the key concerns was how to prevent over-regulation that might stifle innovation while ensuring that the AI Act could effectively address AI's potential risks.

The Council of the EU, representing the governments of EU Member States, also played a significant role in reviewing the proposal. Some countries, particularly those with strong technology sectors like Germany and France, advocated for stronger provisions to foster innovation, while others emphasised the need for robust ethical safeguards.

Numerous organisations and advocacy groups weighed in on the AI Act, raising concerns about the balance between regulation and market freedom and the impact on SMEs and the tech sector. Civil society groups emphasised the need for stronger protections for privacy and fundamental rights, while industry stakeholders often focused on reducing the regulatory burden for developers and start-ups.

6.2.2 The AI Act Structure

The AI Act is structured in 113 Articles and 13 Annexes. The articles are divided into 13 Chapters.

The first Chapter (Articles 1-4) of the AI Act contains general provisions regarding AI regulation. About the scope and purpose, Article 1 AI Act recalls the need to establish a legal framework to ensure people's and businesses' safety and fundamental rights when using AI systems while promoting AI innovation within the EU area. It introduces the four risk-based Classification of AI Systems: Unacceptable risk (AI systems banned due to serious risks); High-risk AI systems (subject to stringent regulatory requirements); Limited risk AI systems (subject to transparency obligations); Minimal risk AI systems (not subject to specific obligations).

The second Chapter is devoted to identifying the unacceptable model of AI (Article 5 AI Act).

The third Chapter lays down rules concerning High-Risk Systems and their classification (Articles 6-7 AI Act), providing specific obligations of conformity (Article 8 AI Act) and implementing risk management systems to ensure robustness, security, and accuracy (Article 9 AI Act); requesting adequate governance data (Article 10); duties of recording for traceability and documentation (Articles 11 & 12 AI Act); duties of transparency and information to deployers (Article 14 AI Act); obligations of human supervision (Article 15 AI Act). Section 3 focuses on providers, deployers, and other two parties' duties of the high-risk system (Articles 16-27 AI Act); section 4 regards the notifying authorities and notified bodies (Articles 28-39 AI Act). Section 5 specifies the rules on conformity assessment, certificates and registration (Articles 40-49 AI Act).

The fourth Chapter regards transparency and accountability duties for providers and deployers of certain AI systems (Article 50 AI Act).

The fifth Chapter refers to the general-purpose AI model, providing rules for their classification and procedures (Articles 51-52 AI Act) and specific duties for their providers (Articles 53-55 AI Act), including the adoption of good practice codes (Article 56 AI Act).

The sixth Chapter disciplines measures to support innovation, such as experimental spaces (Articles 57-59 AI Act) and experiments (Articles 60-61 AI Act), providing special rules for SMEs and start-ups (Article 62 AI Act).

The seventh Chapter refers to the governance and enforcement of AI procedures, introducing the European Artificial Intelligence Board (EAIB), which will oversee the implementation of the AI Act, issue guidelines, and facilitate coordination between national authorities (Articles 64-70 AI Act). The EAIB will also play a central role in resolving disputes among Member States.

The eighth Chapter introduces the EU database for high-risk systems listed in Annex III (Article 71 AI Act).

The ninth Chapter refers to the duties of post-market monitoring (Articles 72-94 AI Act).

The tenth Chapter contains rules regarding codes of conduct and guidelines (Articles 95-96 AI Act).

The eleventh Chapter disciplines the delegation of powers and committee procedures (Articles 97-98 AI Act).

The twelfth Chapter is concerned with sanctions (Articles 99-101 AI Act).

Finally, the thirteenth Chapter contains the final provisions, transitional arrangements, and how the AI Act interacts with other EU legislation, such as the GDPR[12] (Articles 102-113 GDPR).

The AI Act requires that the legislation on personal data processing applies, including the tasks and powers of the independent supervisory authorities and obligations of AI providers and deployers as controllers or processors under Union or national law on personal data protection, to the extent that AI systems' design, development or use involves processing personal data.

6.2.3 The Notion of AI Adopted by the AI Act

One of the foundational aspects of the Act is the definition of AI. In this sense, Article 3(1) AI Act defines an AI system as "a machine-based system that is designed to operate with varying levels of autonomy and that may exhibit adaptiveness after deployment, and that, for explicit or implicit objectives, infers, from the input it receives, how to generate outputs such as predictions, content, recommendations, or decisions that can influence physical or virtual environments."

12. Regulation (EU) 2016/679 of the European Parliament and of the Council of 27 April 2016 on the protection of natural persons with regard to the processing of personal data and on the free movement of such data, and repealing Directive 95/46/EC, OJ L 119, 4.5.2016, p. 1-88.

This notion can capture various systems and technologies capable of performing tasks typically requiring human intelligence while ensuring that the regulation remains flexible enough to adapt to technological advancements. For this reason, it can be considered a functional definition orientated to the principle of technological neutrality.

In this context, enter machine learning, including supervised, unsupervised, and reinforcement learning; logic- and knowledge-based approaches, including knowledge representation, inference, and expert systems; and statistical approaches,[13] search, and optimisation methods.

This broad categorisation ensures that the AI Act captures contemporary and emerging AI technologies, from basic machine learning models (MLM) to more complex AI systems built on knowledge representation and decision-making.

The AI Act also clarifies which systems are excluded from its scope. Article 2(3) AI Act excludes the AI systems used exclusively for military, defence or national security purposes, regardless of entity type; used by public authorities in a third country nor to international organisations; used solely for scientific research and development.

6.2.4 Objectives and Scope of the AI Act

The AI Act has various important objectives. First, it aims to foster innovation, encouraging the development of AI technologies within a regulatory framework that ensures a level playing field for businesses, researchers, and start-ups. This scope must safeguard human beings from this technology's risks, particularly regarding healthcare, transportation, and law enforcement. Moreover, the EU confirms its focus on fundamental rights protection, such as privacy, non-discrimination, and freedom, by regulating AI systems that could potentially infringe on these rights, promoting trust.

For this reason, the regulation tries to increase the AI systems' transparency and accountability, which is considered one of the key issues of a regulatory framework to promote trust.

Following the AI HLEG's suggestions, the AI Act is also oriented to other important principles, such as "Human intervention and supervision." This concept means that the systems must always be developed and used in light of human beings' advantages, respect human dignity and personal autonomy, and function so that humans can adequately control and supervise them. This principle is also known as "human in the loop," which implies the aim to realise an anthropocentric and affordable system. AI systems must be designed to fulfil tasks such as making decisions, providing recommendations, or generating predictions. The human-defined nature of these objectives highlights that AI systems are not autonomous in the sense of having their own "goals" but are designed to achieve outcomes defined by human operators or designers.

13. AI techniques that rely on statistical approaches, such as regression analysis, clustering, and optimisation, to model complex relationships in data. These methods are often used in AI systems for predictive analytics and decision support.

In particular, the outcomes can be formed by predictions, recommendations, and environmental interaction.

Another important request regards the AI system's 'technical robustness and safety', which entails developing and operating safely, protecting the system against illegal attack and manipulation, and compliance with the right of privacy and the duty of data governance while processing data to high standards of quality and integrity.

As mentioned, the so-called transparency is crucial in AI regulation. Also, in this case, it involves the developing and using phases that must allow adequate traceability and explicability. Transparency is often used as a synonym for explainability in literature.[14]

In other words, it can be said that 'transparency' implies making humans aware that they are communicating or interacting with an AI system and duly informing the implementers of the capabilities and limitations of such an AI system and the persons concerned about their rights.[15]

6.2.5 Area of Application

The AI Act encompasses all AI systems deployed within the EU or by entities established in the EU, regardless of whether they are based within or outside the region. Importantly, the AI Act also covers AI systems that impact individuals' safety and fundamental rights, even if non-EU actors use them. This global reach is essential to ensure the EU remains a regulatory leader in AI.

The act emphasises the subjects that must comply with its provisions, considered 'providers'. In this case, the term 'provider' refers to different subjects, such as developing bodies of AI systems, including organisations that develop AI systems for strictly internal use, which can be both a user and a provider at the same time.

The providers must ensure compliance with the standards, especially in high-risk system cases; instead, users are responsible for operating these AI systems within the AI Act's legal boundaries and according to the provider's specific instructions.

For this reason, the notion of 'provider' is one of the most essential concepts in understanding the AI act perimeter, as it takes responsibility for placing itself on the market or putting into service an AI system. From this point of view, according to Recital 83 AI ACT, the AI Act recognizes the precense of a complex value chain for AI systems; in other words, the act recognizes all the subjects usually involved in AI structures, to avoid legal uncertainty and enable compliance with the regulation.

---

14. With regard to this point, *see* the detailed analysis of Sabrina Goellner, Marina Tropmann-Frick and Bostjan Brumen, *Responsible Artificial Intelligence: A Structured Literature Review*, 3 cs.AI, no pages (2024), available at https://arxiv.org/abs/2403.06910.
15. Helen Nissenbaum, *Accountability in a Computerized Society*, 2 Science and engineering ethics, 25-42 (1996) https://doi.org/10.1007/bf02639315; more recently, *see also*, Feder Cooper, Emanuel Moss, Benjamin Laufer and Helen Nissenbaum, *Accountability in an Algorithmic Society: Relationality, Responsibility, and Robustness in Machine Learning*, ACM Conference on Fairness, Accountability, and Transparency, 864-876 (2022), available at https://dl.acm.org/doi/10.1145/3531146.3533150.

Consequently, it is essential to identify the role and the specific obligations of relevant operators along that value chain. Under this approach, the AI Act introduces a broad notion of provider that includes any "natural or legal person, public authority, agency or other body that develops an AI system or a general-purpose AI model or that has an AI system or a general-purpose AI model developed and places it on the market or puts the AI system into service under its own name or trademark, whether for payment or free of charge."[16]

Moreover, under certain conditions, any distributor,[17] importer,[18] deployer[19] or other third party should be considered a 'provider' and, therefore, assume all the relevant obligations.[20]

The regulation tries to consider many different hypotheses to take control of the responsibility, taking into account that many different subjects are involved (the so-called many hands problems),[21] which can interfere with AI execution.

At the same time, the regulation always requests a natural or legal person to be responsible for the AI action.

6.3 RISK-BASED CLASSIFICATION OF AI SYSTEMS

One of the most innovative features of the AI Act is its risk-based approach to regulation. In the opinion of EU governance, this principle should adapt the type and content of these rules to the intensity and extent of the risks that AI systems may generate, using the proportionality principle.

AI systems are classified into four categories based on the level of risk they pose:

Unacceptable Risk: AI systems that threaten public safety, health, or fundamental rights are banned outright. This includes AI systems for social scoring (e.g., systems that score individuals based on their behaviour) or real-time biometric identification in public spaces (unless strictly necessary for law enforcement).

High-Risk AI: These systems are subject to stringent regulatory requirements. High-risk AI applications include those used in critical sectors like healthcare (e.g., diagnostic AI), transportation (e.g., autonomous vehicles), and law enforcement (e.g., facial recognition for criminal investigations). These AI

16. Article 3(3) AI Act.
17. Under Article 3(7) AI Act, 'Distributor' means a natural or legal person in the supply chain, other than the provider or the importer, that makes an AI system available on the Union market.
18. Under Article 3(6) AI Act, 'Importer' means a natural or legal person located or established in the Union that places on the market an AI system that bears the name or trademark of a natural or legal person established in a third country.
19. Under Article 3(4) AI Act, 'Deployer' means a natural or legal person, public authority, agency or other body using an AI system under its authority except where the AI system is used in the course of personal non-professional activity.
20. Recital 84 AI Act.
21. Ibo van de Poel, Lambèr Royakkers and Sjoerd Zwart, *Moral Responsibility and the Problem of Many Hands* (Routledge 2018).

systems must comply with mandatory requirements for data quality, transparency, robustness, and human oversight.

Limited Risk AI: AI systems with lower risk, such as chatbots or recommendation systems, are subject to specific transparency obligations. For example, users must be informed when interacting with AI instead of humans. In this case, the regulation considers the risks associated with a lack of transparency in using AI, introducing obligations to ensure that humans are informed, when necessary, thereby promoting trust. For example, humans should know that they interact with a chatbot and that the AI-generated content is identifiable.

Minimal Risk AI: This category includes AI systems that pose little or no risk to individuals or society. These systems are not subject to regulatory requirements but may still be encouraged to adhere to best practices and guidelines.

6.3.1 Unacceptable AI Risk Systems: Banning Harmful Applications

The unacceptable risk category is one of the most powerful features of the AI Act, serving as a safeguard against deploying AI systems that could have a huge impact on society and involve AI applications that are deemed too dangerous or harmful to be permitted under any circumstances, as they pose clear and direct threats to safety, fundamental rights, or public order. For this reason, their use is banned.

Article 5 lists eight specific categories of AI applications considered unacceptable.

Letter a) refers to systems which use subliminal techniques that act without a person's knowledge or deliberately manipulative or misleading techniques with the purpose or effect of materially distorting the behaviour of a person or a group of people.

Meanwhile, letter b) refers to a recall system that exploits the human being's vulnerabilities - single or in a group - due to age, disability or a specific social or economic situation, with the aim or just the effect of altering its/their behaviour.

Letter c) states about one famous case: the so-called Social Scoring. As known, this notion refers to the assessment or classification of natural persons or groups of persons over a specified period of time based on their social behaviour or personal characteristics or personalities, inferred or expected, and the score is then used as a base for: (i) an injurious or unfavourable treatment without any connection with the context in which data were originally generated or collected; (ii) a prejudicial or unfavourable treatment unjustified or disproportionate.

One of the most famous examples of social scoring is undoubtedly what is being implemented in China, where the government has experimented with a system that tracks citizens' behaviour, rewarding those who comply with government expectations and penalising those who do not. This kind of AI system should not be considered in line with European principles and human rights.

Letter d) lists AI systems used to conduct risk assessments relating to natural persons to assess or predict the risk that a natural person will commit an offence solely based on profiling, without any connection with real and personal actions.

Letter e) bans a system that aims to create or expand facial recognition databases by non-targeted scraping of facial images from the internet or closed-circuit camera footage.

Letter f) avoids another harmful use of AI related to the inference of the emotions of humans in the workplace and educational institutions, except where the use of the AI system is intended to be put into operation or placed on the market for medical or safety reasons.

Letter g) prohibits another declension in using AI when it is aimed at biometric categorisation, that is, the individual classification of people to draw inferences or inferences about race, political opinions, trade union membership, religious or philosophical beliefs, sexual life or sexual orientation.

Finally, letter h) bans the use of remote biometric identification systems 'in real time' in publicly accessible areas for law enforcement purposes, unless it is intended to identify specific victims of abduction, trafficking in human beings or sexual exploitation of human beings, as well as the search for missing persons; prevention of a specific terrorist threat or attack; locating or identifying a person suspected of having committed a serious crime to conduct a criminal investigation.

The use of AI systems for Real-time Remote Biometric Identification (e.g., facial recognition) in public spaces for general surveillance purposes is also banned. This includes systems that continuously scan and identify people in real-time without their knowledge or consent, potentially violating privacy or data protection rights and leading to mass surveillance. For example, the Police cannot use facial recognition to track people's movements in public spaces without clear legal justifications or oversight.

6.3.2 Rationale Behind the Ban

The AI Act's unacceptable risk category reflects broader concerns about the ethical implications of AI technologies and the potential for abuse or harm. Several key reasons justify the blanket prohibition of certain AI systems, from the point of view of fundamental rights violations and lack of Transparency and accountability. The studies show that these AI systems frequently use the 'black box,'[22] making it substantially impossible for humans to understand and verify the decision-making process. This results in a dangerous absence of any human control.

From another point of view, the use of real-time biometric identification in public spaces for surveillance purposes poses a significant threat to individuals' privacy and freedom of movement, including no longer recognising any scope for the privacy of the individuals, in violation of the EU's GDPR. AI-powered facial recognition systems are increasingly being used for surveillance in cities worldwide. In some cases, authorities have used AI to track individuals across public spaces without consent, creating a 'big brother' effect.

22. Frank Pasquale, *The Black Box Society: The Secret Algorithms that Control Money and Information* (Harvard University Press 2015).

6.3.3 Enforcement of the Ban

The unacceptable risk category establishes a clear prohibition, but it could be critical to ensuring compliance. For this reason, the AI Act introduces several dispositions regarding the enforcement phase. For example, it is provided that each EU Member State has the duty to designate a national authority responsible for ensuring compliance with the AI Act, with the power to investigate, issue fines, and take legal action if unlawful AI systems are detected. The Act also introduces a new EAIB, with the duty to coordinate AI regulation at the EU level, provide guidance, address disputes between Member States, and monitor the implementation of the AI Act across Europe.

For any AI systems that violate the ban on unacceptable risk systems, severe penalties can be imposed, including financial fines and, in some cases, the seizure or destruction of the AI technology.

6.4 THE HIGH-RISK AI SYSTEM

In addition to the prohibited ones, the AI Act provides different categories of high-risk systems, which are not banned within the EU but are subject to strict rules.

From a general point of view, and by Article 6 AI Act, an AI system may be considered to be high risk if it is intended to be used as a safety component of a product or if the AI system itself is a product covered by the Union harmonisation legislation listed in Annex I and, at the same time, the product whose security component under a) is the AI system or the AI system itself as a product is subject to a third-party conformity assessment to place on the market or put into service of that product by the Union harmonisation legislation listed in Annex I.

In addition to the generic category just mentioned, the regulation provides for a second type of high-risk system listed in Annex III. The European Commission will also periodically update this list as new applications emerge.

This list can be summed up as follows:

(1) Biometrics, when and if this practice is allowed in the EU.
(2) Critical infrastructure: AI systems are intended to be used as security components in the management and operation of critical digital infrastructures, such as road traffic or water, gas, heating, or electricity supply.
(3) Vocational education and training, including the systems used for access, admission or staff assignment to different institutions; to assess learning outcomes; to assess the appropriate level of education that a person will receive or be able to access; to monitor and detect prohibited student behaviour during tests in the context or within vocational education and training institutions at all levels.
(4) Employment, worker management and access to self-employment.
(5) Access to and use of essential private services and essential public services and services, including IA systems intended to be used for the assessment of

creditworthiness and used for risk assessment and pricing about the case of life and health insurance of natural persons.

(6) Law enforcement, to the extent that relevant Union or national law allows its use.

(7) Migration, asylum, and management of border control should be done to the extent that relevant union or national law allows for its use.

(8) Administration of justice and democratic processes.

For this reason, it is very important to identify the cases that fall within this scope of application and which, as we will see, cover a variety of sectors, including financial ones.

Article 9 AI Act introduces specific rules regarding the Risk Management System, which must be designed, developed, and deployed with an integrated risk management system to identify, evaluate, and mitigate risks throughout the system's lifecycle. The risk management system must be continuously monitored and updated as new risks emerge or the system is updated or modified.

In this context, data governance plays a key role. Article 10 AI Act provides that High-risk systems must use high-quality datasets that are fit for purpose and minimise risks of bias, discrimination, and inaccuracy. For this reason, the AI Act provides details about this aspect.

For example, if used, the training AI models shall be developed based on training datasets, validation, and testing to ensure adequate quality criteria; moreover, they must be subject to governance and data management practices appropriate to the intended purpose of the high-risk IA system. These practices could regard the relevant design choices; the data collection processes, and the origin of the data, as well as the original purpose of the collection in the case of personal data; processing operations relevant to the preparation of data, such as annotation, labelling, cleaning, updating, enrichment and aggregation; the formulation of hypotheses; an assessment of the availability, quantity and adequacy of the required data sets; an examination to assess possible distortions which may affect the health and safety of persons; appropriate measures to identify, prevent and mitigate possible distortions; the identification of relevant data gaps or deficiencies which would affect compliance with this Regulation and how those gaps and deficiencies can be addressed.

The training, validation, and test data sets must be relevant, sufficiently representative, and, to the greatest possible extent, error-free and complete for the intended purpose. They also possess the appropriate statistical properties, where applicable. To the extent necessary for the intended purpose, they must consider the characteristics or elements of the specific geographical area and the contextual, behavioural, or functional within which the high-risk AI system is intended.

The AI Act also implies important technical documentation duties to demonstrate the regulatory compliance of each AI system.[23]

23. Article 11 AI Act.

In particular, the regulation requires that a record of the system's life cycle be kept and copy, ensuring traceability of the high-risk AI system operation appropriate to the system's intended purpose.[24]

High-risk AI systems must be designed and developed, ensuring that their operation is sufficiently transparent to enable the system's output to be interpreted by the deployers and used appropriately.[25]

Article 14 AI Act focuses on an important principle: the necessary human supervision. From this point of view, systems must be designed and developed, including appropriate human-machine interface tools, so that human beings can effectively always monitor them. This surveillance activity is essential to prevent or minimise health risks, the safety or fundamental rights that may arise when an AI system with a high risk is used following its intended purpose or under conditions of misuse which could reasonably be expected, in particular where such risks persist despite the application of other requirements set out in this Section.

After these general rules, the AI Act clearly identifies suppliers' obligations and AI high-risk system deployers and other parties. More in detail, it establishes a series of requirements that providers and users must meet to ensure the safety and trustworthiness of high-risk AI systems.

Considering the AI Act, the providers of high-risk AI systems shall:

- ensure that their high-risk AI systems are compliant with the requirements set out in section 2 AI Act;
- indicate on the high-risk AI system or, where that is not possible, on its packaging or its accompanying documentation, as applicable, their name, registered trade name or registered trademark, the address at which they can be contacted;
- have a quality management system which complies with Article 17 AI Act;
- keep the documentation referred to in Article 11 AI Act;
- when under their control, keep the logs automatically generated by their high-risk AI systems as referred to in Article 19 AI Act;
- ensure that the high-risk AI system undergoes the relevant conformity assessment procedure, as in Article 43 AI Act, before it is placed on the market or put into service;
- draw up an EU declaration of conformity by Article 47 AI Act;
- affix the EC marking to the high-risk AI system or, where that is not possible, on its packaging or its accompanying documentation to indicate conformity with the AI Act itself by Article 48 AI Act;
- comply with the registration obligations referred to in Article 12 AI Act;
- take the necessary corrective actions and provide information as required in Article 13 AI Act;

24. Article 12 AI Act.
25. Article 13 AI Act.

- upon a reasoned request of a national competent authority, demonstrate the conformity of the high-risk AI system with the requirements set out in section 2 AI Act;
- ensure the high-risk AI system complies with accessibility requirements following Directive (EU) 2016/2102[26] and Directive (EU) 2019/882.[27]

If a provider believes its own high-risk IA system does not comply with the Regulation, it must immediately introduce the necessary corrective measures to conform to such a device, withdraw, disable or recall it as appropriate, and then inform the distributors or the other subjects involved in the process.[28]

Article 21 AI Act also imposes that providers inform the competent authority in case of a request with all the necessary documentation.

Identifying a legal entity for each stage in which the provision or dissemination of a high-risk information system is involved also requires third-country suppliers to identify, using a written mandate, an authorised representative established in the Union,[29] the detailed requirements for importers[30] and distributors are also laid down.[31] As already underlined, any of these parties must be considered a 'supplier' subject to Article 16 AI Act whether it opposes its name or brand on a high-risk AI system already placed on the market or put into service, without prejudice to contractual arrangements providing for a different distribution of obligations in this respect; if it makes a substantial modification in such a way that it remains a high-risk AI system as defined in Article 6 AI Act; if it changes the intended purpose of an AI system, also a general purpose system, that has not been classified as high-risk and has already been placed on the market or put into service in such a way that the AI system concerned becomes a high-risk AI system following Article 6 AI Act.[32]

Before these systems are put on the market, an impact assessment of fundamental rights must be conducted.[33]

6.5 TRANSPARENCY REQUIREMENTS FOR CERTAIN KINDS OF AI MODELS

As anticipated, the fourth Chapter of the AI Act is devoted to the discipline of AI systems, which are not high-risk but still pose limited risks. The regulation imposes transparency duties on suppliers and developers concerning those intended to interact directly with natural persons.

26. Directive (EU) 2016/2102 of the European Parliament and of the Council of 26 October 2016 on the accessibility of the websites and mobile applications of public sector bodies, OJ L 327, 2.12.2016, p. 1-15.
27. Directive (EU) 2019/882 of the European Parliament and of the Council of 17 April 2019 on the accessibility requirements for products and services, OJ L 151, 7.6.2019, p. 70-115.
28. Article 20 AI Act.
29. Article 22 AI Act.
30. Article 23 AI Act.
31. Article 24 AI Act.
32. Article 25 AI Act.
33. Article 27 AI Act.

In this case, AI systems shall be designed and developed so that natural persons know they are not interacting with a human being, except for express exemption for general purposes. In addition, the creation of audio, image, video or synthetic text content must be accompanied by an indication of their origin.[34]

In particular, the deployers of an emotion recognition system or a biometric categorisation system inform the natural persons exposed to it about the functioning of the system and process personal data following the GDPR, Regulation (EU) 2018/1725 on the processing by Union institutions,[35] and Directive (EU) 2016/680 on the processing of data for the purposes of the prevention, investigation, detection or prosecution of crime,[36] as applicable, unless expressly authorised.

Systems that generate or manipulate images or audio or video content, i.e., 'deep fake', must make known this nature.

6.6 GENERAL-PURPOSE AND GENERATIVE AI MODELS

The AI Act also specifically addresses the hypothesis concerning the so-called models of AI generics, which can perform a multiplicity of different tasks. However, because of these characteristics, they can be particularly difficult to regulate and supervise.

In this category, we can also find the case of the so-called generative AI models (e.g., *ChatGPT 4*), which can generate text, images and other content based on developing and training models that require large amounts of data, subject to copyright regulation if necessary.

Therefore, the law introduces transparency requirements for all these types, aimed primarily at improving understanding and specific risk management requirements, including self-assessment and systemic risk mitigation, reporting major incidents, conducting test and model assessments, and cybersecurity requirements.

The European regulator has indeed considered it appropriate to introduce a specific methodology for classifying general-purpose AI models as general-purpose IA models with systemic risks, which results in a dedicated regulation. As a consequence, under Chapter V of the AI Act, the qualification of an AI general-purpose system with systemic risk requests high-impact capabilities assessed based on appropriate technical tools and methodologies, including indicators and benchmarks. Moreover, AI general-purpose system must be based on a Commission decision, ex officio or following a qualified panel report, it has an equivalent capacity or impact to those referred to in point a), considering the criteria set out in Annex XIII.

34. Article 50 AI Act.
35. Regulation (EU) 2018/1725 of the European Parliament and of the Council of 23 October 2018 on the protection of natural persons with regard to the processing of personal data by the Union institutions, bodies, offices and agencies and on the free movement of such data, and repealing Regulation (EC) No. 45/2001 and Decision No. 1247/2002/EC, OJ L 295, 21.11.2018, p. 39-98.
36. Directive (EU) 2016/680 of the European Parliament and of the Council of 27 April 2016 on the protection of natural persons with regard to the processing of personal data by competent authorities for the purposes of the prevention, investigation, detection or prosecution of criminal offences or the execution of criminal penalties and on the free movement of such data, and repealing Council Framework Decision 2008/977/JHA, OJ L 119, 4.5.2016, p. 89-131.

6.7 REGULATORY SANDBOXES

Also, for AI regulation, the EU considers it useful to push towards adopting regulatory sandboxes. The term generally refers to regulatory tools allowing businesses to test and experiment with new and innovative products, services, or businesses under a regulator's supervision for a limited period. They can have a double role: they foster business learning, i.e., the development and testing of innovations in a real-world environment, and they support regulatory learning, i.e., the formulation of experimental legal regimes to guide and support businesses in their innovation activities under the supervision of a regulatory authority. The approach aims to enable experimental innovation within a framework of controlled risks and supervision and improve regulators' understanding of new technologies.

Considering this approach, Chapter VI of the AI Act, regulating measures to support innovation, requests all Member States to establish at least one regulatory IA testing space at the national level, operational by 2 August 2026 (Article 57 AI Act). The EU's focus on small and medium-sized enterprises also emerges in the AI Act, where it is expected that particular consideration will be given to the interests of SMEs, including start-ups, providers or deployers of AI systems. To this end, the Regulation requires that appropriate initiatives be developed for these operators, including in terms of awareness and information communication, as well as providing them with priority access to regulatory testing spaces for AI; they meet the eligibility conditions and selection criteria.[37]

The obligation referred to in the first subparagraph may also be fulfilled by participating in an existing testing space, provided that such participation provides an equivalent level of national coverage for the participating Member States. Additional regulatory testing spaces for AI may also be established at the regional or local level or jointly with the competent authorities of other Member States.

After the test period, AI systems must be in real-life conditions outside of regulatory testing spaces for AI, which may be carried out by suppliers or potential suppliers of high-risk IA systems listed in Annex III, by this Article and the field test plan referred to in this Article, without prejudice to the prohibitions set out in Article 5 AI Act.

Using implementing acts, the European Commission shall specify in detail the elements of the field test plan.

6.8 THE EUROPEAN COUNCIL FOR AI, THE FORUM, THE INDEPENDENT SCIENTIFIC PANEL, AND AI DATABASE

Chapter VII of the AI Act regulates governance at the union level by providing the European Commission with the introduction of a new European Council for AI

37. Recital 143 AI Act.

composed of one representative per Member State; the European Data Protection Supervisor is also involved as an observer and the Office for DPOs.[38]

The AI Council has the important task of providing advice and assistance to the European Commission and the Member States to facilitate the consistent and effective application of this Regulation. To this end, the AI Council may, more in detail: contribute to the coordination between national competent authorities and relevant market surveillance authorities; collect and share knowledge, best practices and technical and regulatory practices among the Member States; provide advice on the implementation of the AI Act; contribute to the harmonisation of administrative practices in the Member States; at the request of the European Commission or on its own initiative, make written recommendations and opinions on any relevant issue relating to the implementation of this Regulation and its consistent and effective application, including the development and application of codes of conduct and codes of good practice and the European Commission's guidelines; on the assessment and review of Article 112 AI Act, including about major accident reporting under Article 73 AI Act, and the functioning of the EU database referred to in Article 71 AI Act, etc.[39]

Moreover, the AI Act, aware of the many interests involved, also provided a forum to give advice and technical expertise to the AI Council and the European Commission, ensuring a diverse and balanced representation that takes into account commercial and non-commercial interests (including SMEs again), industry, start-ups, SMEs, academia, civil society, including social partners, the Agency for Fundamental Rights, the European Union Agency for Cybersecurity (ENISA), the European Committee for Standardisation (CEN), the European Committee for Electrotechnical Standardisation (CENELEC), and the European Telecommunications Standards Institute (ETSI).[40]

Article 68 AI Act also provides for the establishment of an independent scientific panel to support the activities of implementing the regulation, composed of experts selected by the European Commission based on their knowledge and skills as well as scientific or technical expertise in the field of AI; independence from any provider of AI systems or general-purpose AI models; and ability to perform activities diligently, accurately and objectively. The expert group could also support, upon request and possible payment of compensation, individual Member States in implementing the regulation.

Another important forecast from the organisational point of view is that the European Commission will establish a database containing different kinds of data, listed in Annex VIII, concerning the information requested by Article 49(1) AI Act (such as the name, address and contact details of the supplier; the name, address and contact details of the authorised representative, where applicable; the commercial name of the AI system and any additional unambiguous references that allow identification and traceability; a description of the intended purpose of the AI system and the components

38. Article 65 AI Act.
39. Article 66 AI Act.
40. Article 67 AI Act.

and functions supported by that AI system; a concise basic description of the information used by the system (data, input) and its operational logic; etc.).[41]

6.9 POST-MARKET MONITORING, INFORMATION SHARING, AND SANCTIONS

The AI Act reserves Chapter IX of the AI Act to specific measures relating to monitoring and information-sharing activities that must occur after the AI model is placed on the market. In particular, suppliers must establish and document systems in proportion to the nature of AI technologies and their high-risk AI system risks, relative to their performance over the life cycle,[42] based on a monitoring plan.

Monitoring and control are reinforced in the case of general-purpose AI systems.[43] Confirming the importance of protecting fundamental rights, the AI Act provides that competent national public authorities or bodies are empowered to request any documentation created or maintained on high-risk systems in an accessible language and format where access is necessary to effectively perform their tasks.[44]

If a national authority considers that an AI system presents a risk, it shall assess its compliance with all the requirements and obligations of the regulation, with particular attention to the impact on vulnerable groups. In the event of risks to fundamental rights, the market surveillance authority shall also inform the competent national public authorities or bodies.[45]

The regulation, therefore, provides for a complex national procedure and, if necessary, a European safeguard phase to intervene if AI systems do not comply with the legislation. It also regulates the means of redress available to individuals.[46]

In case of violation of the regulatory rules, Chapter XII of the AI Act gives Member States the power to lay down rules on sanctions and other enforcement measures, which may also include warnings and non-pecuniary measures for operator infringements, considering the guidelines of the Commission. The principles of effectiveness, proportionality, and dissuasiveness should be applied when introducing such measures and considering the interests of SMEs, including start-ups, and their economic viability.[47]

6.10 CHALLENGES AND CRITICISMS

The AI Act is a bold and comprehensive attempt to regulate AI in a way that balances the potential of these technologies with the need to protect human rights, safety, and societal values. By focusing on a risk-based approach, the EU has set a high standard

41. Article 71 AI Act.
42. Article 72 AI Act.
43. Article 75 AI Act.
44. Article 77 AI Act.
45. Article 79 AI Act.
46. Chapter IX, section 4 AI Act.
47. Article 99 AI Act.

for the responsible development and use of AI systems. However, the success of the AI Act will depend on effective implementation, cooperation across borders, and the flexibility to adapt to rapidly evolving AI technologies. As AI continues to evolve, the AI Act will likely serve as both a model for other regions and a dynamic regulatory framework that will be updated to meet emerging challenges and opportunities in AI.

At the same time, several challenges and criticisms have been raised despite the AI Act's ambitious goals.

First, some critics argue that the AI Act's regulatory requirements, particularly for high-risk AI systems, may stifle innovation, especially for small businesses and start-ups that lack the resources to comply with complex regulations. On the other side, these stringent EU regulations could put European companies at a disadvantage compared to firms in jurisdictions with more lenient AI laws, particularly in the USA and China, which have different approaches to AI regulation.

Ensuring consistent enforcement across all EU Member States, each with its legal and administrative systems, will be challenging. Coordination between national authorities and the European AI Board will be critical to effective enforcement.

Finally, the AI Act does not solve one of the most difficult questions that such powerful technology requires: ensuring that human beings can use it fairly and ethically without being overwhelmed.[48]

48. Luciano Floridi, *The Ethics of Artificial Intelligence: Principles, Challenges, and Opportunities* (Oxford University Press 2023).

Part III Digital Identities and Consumer Protection

CHAPTER 7

The European Digital Identity

7.1 FROM PERSONAL TO DIGITAL (OR NUMERICAL) IDENTITY

Digitalisation has spread everywhere since Alan Turing felt that 'intelligent' machines would need instructions, given that they are in binary code. From this moment on, the digitalisation activity, in other words, the assignment of digital signage to the whole reality so that machines can understand its meaning, has become essential in every field.

This new world, however, also introduces new kinds of risk and, first, a dangerous simplification of reality itself reduced to mere numbers, with a consequent dehumanisation and simplification of information.[1]

Dehumanisation is a phenomenon that impacts the nature of human beings, becoming more and more mere numbers or codes.

From this point of view, according to Guido Alpa,[2] until now, the attribution of a number instead of a name was the exception (as, for example, a military or university serial number); from now on, instead, it will be the rule.

The need for simplification normally justifies replacing the name with the number and the service optimisation.

In other words, with the push of digitalisation, a new world is developing in which all reality is rewritten through the use of numbers and codes, the only ones that machines can read; the resulting simplification and marginalisation of all aspects which cannot be reduced to a mere numerical figure.

The human world is, therefore, gradually adapting to machines. The philosopher Luciano Floridi[3] has underlined this trend, describing the operation of robots that can

1. Guido Alpa, *L'identità digitale e la tutela della persona. Spunti di riflessione*, 33 Contratto e Impresa, 723-727 (2017).
2. *Ibid.*
3. Luciano Floridi, *The Fourth Revolution: How the Infosphere is Reshaping Human Reality* (Oxford University Press 2016).

cut the grass or the same machines with autonomous driving, which, however, need a suitable context (consider terrain without excessive slopes or the presence of road markings).

The emergence of a digital representation of the individuals using it has also produced other risks, such as the so-called identity theft, one of the most common cybercrimes, especially in financial matters, every time we purchase online. The birth of the 'digital person', understood as "a model of individual public personality based on data and maintained by transactions, intended to be used on behalf of the individual,"[4] has become increasingly widespread, as well as the risk that it will be stolen.

In this context, if in the past there was a close relationship between identity and privacy,[5] today, the right to privacy, or rather confidentiality, and the right to identity appear even more closely related to confidentiality.

As a response to the problem of the difficult coexistence between digital identity and privacy, some have begun to invoke the concept of the so-called self-essential sovereign identity,[6] considered a further step towards constructing a digital identity that puts the individual at the centre. From this point of view, it implies not only the possibility of using this type of identity in multiple contexts but also, above all, being able to entrust the owner of the identity with control and autonomy over the use of the same to ensure the protection of individual interests against any unlawful use that also results in financial damage or other types of loss.[7]

For this reason, it becomes essential to introduce appropriate protection and create a trust system around developing digital identity, even though introducing a common digital European identity system.

7.2 THE NOTION OF THE DIGITAL IDENTITY

As part of the European strategy to create a harmonious framework for digital regulation, attention is also paid to digital identity, which entails creating a new environment where the focus has shifted from the provision and use of rigid digital identities to the condition and reliance on specific attributes related to these. There is an increased demand for electronic identity solutions that can deliver these capabilities, providing efficiency gains and a high level of trust across the EU, both in the private and the public sector, relying on the need to identify and authenticate users with high assurance.

4. Roger Clarke, *The Digital Persona and Its Application to Data Surveillance*, 10 The Information Society, 77-92 (1994) https://doi.org/10.4324/9781315243566-10.
5. Alessandro Ortalda and Stefano Leucci, *Identità digitale e protezione dei dati personali: punti di incontro e rischi nelle discipline eIDAS e RGPD*, in *La internet governance e le sfide della trasformazione digitale*, 145-155 (Laura Abba, Adriana Lazzaroni and Marina Pietrangelo eds, 4 Rivista Italiana di Informatica e Diritto 2022).
6. Kim Cameron, *The Laws of Identity*, 1 ss. (May 2005), available at https://www.identityblog.com/stories/2005/05/13/TheLawsOfIdentity.pdf.
7. Christopher Allen, *The Path to Self-Sovereign Identity*, no pages (26 April 2016), available at https://www.lifewithalacrity.com/article/the-path-to-self-sovereign-identity/#fn:20.

As known, Article 6 of the Universal Declaration of Human Rights (UDHR) states that "every person has the right to be recognised as a person before the law"; in other words, it means that the legal personality is an element associated with our identity. In the physical world, this recognition begins now with registration in the civil registers. For this reason, the birth certificate is the basic prerequisite to obtaining an identity card, photograph, fingerprint, and fee.[8]

However, given the recent expansion and intensification of the digital life of European citizens, it was inevitable that real-traditional identification systems would have to be rethought and updated to take on a face that makes them usable online.

According to the EU, in the current context, it is now essential to introduce a common digital identity to create greater integration from a digital point of view. The current European context is characterised by excessive fragmentation due to different national solutions, further hindering the development of an integrated digital market. The introduction of such a tool could instead enable all EU citizens to identify themselves and provide authentication of their identity online and offline in a safe, reliable, easy-to-use, practical, accessible and harmonised way across the Union.

In 2023, the Joint European Declaration on Digital Rights and Principles for the Digital Decade[9] stresses every person's right to access technologies, digital products and services that are secure, data protection and privacy-sensitive from the design stage. This includes ensuring that all people living in the Union have an accessible, secure, and reliable digital identity, giving access to a wide range of online and offline services, and protecting against cybersecurity risks and cybercrime, as well as data breaches and identity theft or manipulation. The declaration also states that everyone has a right to protect their personal data. This right includes control over how data is used and with whom it is shared.

The EUDI Regulation will revolutionise digital identity in the EU by enabling the creation of a universal, trustworthy, and secure European digital identity wallet (EDIW).

8. UN General Assembly, Resolution 217A (III), Universal Declaration of Human Rights, A/RES/217(III) (10 December 1948). The UDHR is a milestone document in the history of human rights. Drafted by representatives with different legal and cultural backgrounds from all regions of the world, the Declaration was proclaimed by the United Nations General Assembly in Paris on 10 December 1948 (General Assembly resolution 217A) as a common standard of achievements for all peoples and all nations. It sets out, for the first time, fundamental human rights to be universally protected and it has been translated into over 500 languages. The UDHR is widely recognised as having inspired, and paved the way for, the adoption of more than seventy human rights treaties, applied today on a permanent basis at global and regional levels (all containing references to it in their preambles). *See* Universal Declaration of Human Rights, available at https://www.un.org/en/about-us/universal-declaration-of-human-rights. In the literature, *see* Julián Inza, *The European Digital Identity Wallet as Defined in the EIDAS 2 Regulation*, in *Governance and Control of Data and Digital Economy in the European Single Market*, 433-452 (Carmen Pastor Sempere ed., 71 Law, Governance and Technology Series, Springer 2025).
9. The Declaration on Digital Rights and Principles presents the EU's vision for digital transformation. This vision puts people at the centre, in line with EU values and fundamental rights. The Declaration provides a reference framework for citizens and guides the EU and Member States on our journey to digital transformation. The Declaration has been signed by the European Parliament, the Council and the Commission, available at https://digital-strategy.ec.europa.eu/en/library/european-declaration-digital-rights-and-principles.

7.3 FROM DIGITAL IDENTIFICATION TO DIGITAL WALLET

The new EU Regulation 2024/1183[10] (eIDAS 2) entered into force on the 20 of May 2024, amending the previous EU Digital Identity Framework Regulation (EU) 910/2014 (eIDAS) to establish the EUDI Framework.

In the framework provided by the previous eIDAS Regulation, EU Member States could decide to notify their citizens voluntarily, using national electronic identification schemes. In this case, the others were obliged to recognise after the mandatory provision in 2018. At the same time, Member States had no duty to introduce a national electronic identification system, and interoperability was achieved only by implementing an interoperability superstructure connecting the various identity systems, which was affected by technical problems and caused several discrepancies between countries and prevented the extension to private digital services.

In the discussion on adopting the eIDAS Regulation, the areas that have undoubtedly received the most attention are the aspects relating to privacy, data protection, and security. On the one hand, great attention has been paid to the tasks that the Supervisory Authorities of the Member States will have to carry out to monitor compliance with the act under the supervision of the European Data Protection Supervisor (EDPS) while promoting its application. On the other hand, it was considered that users need to become aware of this tool and the potential risks to their data protection and privacy.

The eIDAS Regulation faces these issues, improving the framework's efficiency for digital Identity and extending its benefits to the private sector.[11] In this new contest, Member States must offer citizens and businesses digital wallets to link their national digital identities with proof of other personal attributes like driving licences, diplomas, and bank accounts. These wallets may be issued by public authorities or recognised private entities to give Europeans full control over their data while accessing online services, eliminating unnecessary data sharing. Service providers legally obliged to identify their customers unequivocally will be obliged to accept the wallet for authentication.

From an operational point of view, the Wallet will allow citizens to manage a dashboard through their smartphone to control their data regarding circulation and verify its correct use. The Wallet will give access to a trusted service called "electronic attestation of attributes," the characteristics or qualities of the person (natural or legal) who uses the Wallet. Public or private entities may manage these attributes with prior authorisation.

10. Regulation (EU) 2024/1183 of the European Parliament and of the Council of 11 April 2024 amending Regulation (EU) No. 910/2014 as regards establishing the European Digital Identity Framework, OJ L, 2024/1183, 30.4.2024.
11. Linda Weigl, Alexandre Amard, Cristiano Codagnone and Gilbert Fridgen, *The EU's Digital Identity Policy: Tracing Policy Punctuations*, ICEGOV 22: Proceedings of the 15th International Conference on Theory and Practice of Electronic Governance, 74-81 (2022), available at https://dl.acm.org/doi/10.1145/3560107.3560121.

In addition to the portfolio, the new regulation introduces other digital trust services, including:

- Management of devices for the remote creation of qualified electronic signatures or qualified electronic seals.
- Electronic data storage.
- Electronic data recording.

7.4 THE MAIN BENEFITS OF THE EDIWS

According to the EU, digital Identification wallets can have several advantages and benefits:

- It helps users manage and control their own identities. In other words, citizens can choose which aspects of their identity and data they share with third parties, ensuring privacy and control over personal information.
- It has widespread usability because it is recognised across the EU, enabling citizens to access public and private digital services and making online interactions more seamless and efficient.
- It increases transparency and security, thanks to its open-source licence and features that guarantee against measures or illegal tracking.
- It is easily usable through a user-friendly interface, allowing individuals to manage their digital identities and access services by creating qualified eSignatures for non-professionals.
- It has smooth onboarding, allowing users to use their national eID scheme to register for the wallet.

Introducing this new instrument could also have advantages from the government's point of view:

- It can improve access to digital services and facilitate the process of identity verification.
- It can enhance fraud prevention, providing a secure and verifiable means of identity that permits the prevention of identity theft and related fraud.
- It can improve security.

About the providers of digital services, the introduction of a Digital ID Wallet could:

- improve security and privacy;
- reduce the cost of authentication;
- avoid relying on competing big platforms.

Finally, this kind of tool could also impact on the society's efficiency:

- Increasing online transactions, thanks to easier and more secure verification.
- Offering New business opportunities.

- Permitting a resource reallocation as a consequence of the new ID automated verification process.
- Pushing toward a greater adoption of online transactions, new business opportunities, and improved resource allocation can contribute to overall economic stability and growth.

7.5 THE EIDAS 2 REGULATION

Under the eIDAS 2 Regulation, the EUDI portfolios are designed to offer citizens a variety of functions, including a common management panel incorporated into the design, to ensure a higher level of transparency. A simple and user-friendly interface should allow easy and immediate access to all the data you want to share, track your transactions (based on time and date), and identify the counterparty, the personal data requested, and the shared data even if the transaction has not been successful.

All this in a way that guarantees confidentiality, including the so-called zero knowledge demonstration, thanks to the use of cryptographic techniques.[12]

From the point of view of its aims, Article 1 eIDAS 2 clarifies that the Regulation, to ensure the smooth functioning of the internal market and to provide an adequate level of security for electronic identification means and trust services used throughout the Union:

- lays down the conditions under which Member States shall recognise means of electronic identification of natural and legal persons, which are covered by a notified electronic identification scheme of another Member State and provide and recognise EUDI portfolios;
- lays down rules on trust services, in particular for electronic transactions;
- establishes a legal framework for electronic signatures, electronic seals, electronic time-stamping, electronic documents, e-certified delivery services, website authentication certificate services, electronic archiving, Electronic attribute certificates, electronic signature creation devices, electronic seal creation devices and electronic registers.

Both natural and legal persons are entitled to obtain a EUDI portfolio, which may be provided by:

- directly from a Member State;
- on behalf of a Member State;
- independently of a Member State, even if the latter recognises them.

Unless expressly and justifiably derogated, all source code of the software components of the EUDI portfolio application shall be open-source licensed.

12. Recitals 13 & 14 eIDAS 2 Regulation.

These portfolios allow the user to:

- request, obtain, select, combine, store, delete, share and present securely, under its control, personal identification data and, where appropriate, in combination with electronic attribute attestations, both online and offline, to access public and private services, while ensuring that selective disclosure of data is possible;
- generate and store pseudonyms in encrypted form;
- securely authenticate another person's EUDI portfolio and receive and share personal identification data and electronic attribute certificates securely between the two EUDI portfolios;
- sign by qualified electronic signatures or seal by qualified electronic seals;
- download, to the extent technically possible, user data, electronic attribute attestations and configurations;
- exercise your right to data portability.

The EUDI project is being carried out to promote individual freedom and rights. This is not only demonstrated by the fact that the use of EUDI portfolios is optional but also by the fact that there can be no restriction on access to public or private services due to its non-adoption.

In addition, the provider of the EUDI portfolio may not collect information relating to the use of the EUDI portfolio that is not necessary for the provision of the EUDI portfolio services, nor does it combine personal identification data or other personal data stored in the EDIW or related to its use with personal data from other services offered by that provider or from third party services which are not necessary for the EUDI portfolio services, unless the user has expressly requested it (Article 5 bis eIDAS 2 Regulation).

As already underlined, the rules on electronic identification are closely linked to the issue of personal data protection not only because many of the activities associated with the management and use of electronic identification means. Regimes may qualify as personal data processing within the meaning of the GDPR but also due to the explicit references to the GDPR contained in both the eIDAS 2 Regulation and its proposed amendment.

The user must be able to sign electronically in a qualified manner and always in a qualified manner be able to put electronic seals, that is to say, from a technical point of view, be able to download data and the electronic attestation of attributes and configurations, the possibility of data portability.

The EDIW also lays down detailed rules to protect the user on the movement of personal data, including electronic attestation of attributes and validity of the EDIW. In this case, the rules indicate what to do to manage the life cycle of the Portfolio from the point of view of regulatory regulation.

Each EDIW must be confirmed to several different requirements. First of all, it shall follow the rules on electronic identification schemes (Article 5 bis, paragraphs 4, 5 and 8 eIDAS 2 Regulation); the requirement for logical separation (Article 5, paragraph 14 eIDAS 2 Regulation); and, where applicable, the standards and technical specifications referred to in paragraph 24 of Article 5 bis eIDAS 2 Regulation. This conformity should be certified by conformity assessment bodies designated by the Member States, which should also consider aspects related to the European cybersecurity certification schemes.

To this end, Member States must establish national certification schemes subject to specific compliance rules with particular attention paid to aspects relating to cybersecurity[13] and submit their draft national certification schemes to the European Digital Identity Cooperation Group ('Cooperation Group'), which may also issue opinions and recommendations.

This body is set up by the European Commission to support and facilitate cooperation, and it is composed of representatives appointed by the Member States and representatives of the European Commission, which also chairs the new body.

The Cooperation Group carries out some important tasks, among which we may mention:

- exchange advice and cooperate with the European Commission on emerging strategic initiatives in the field of digital identity portfolios, electronic identification means and trust services;
- advise the European Commission, where appropriate, at an early stage in the preparation of draft delegated acts and implementing acts to be adopted under this Regulation;
- supporting the supervisory bodies in implementing the provisions of this Regulation by exchanging best practices and information on the implementation of the provisions of this Regulation; assessing developments in the areas of digital identity portfolios, electronic identification and trust services; organising joint meetings with relevant stakeholders across the Union to discuss the activities of the cooperation group and gather input on emerging policy challenges, etc.[14]

7.6 VIRTUAL WORDS, METAVERSE, AND THE ISSUE OF IDENTITY

With digitalisation, the study of 'identity' has acquired new relevance, which has been enhanced by the development of virtual worlds and augmented realities. These technologies can alter our perception of reality, influence our experiences, and change the way we interact with others.

The COVID-19 pandemic has accelerated the trend of purchasing goods and services online and using social media and virtual spaces, so the digital market and interest in virtual worlds have steadily increased. The global market for virtual worlds is projected to grow from EUR 27 billion in 2022 to over EUR 800 billion by 2030.[15]

---

13. Article 5 *quarter* eIDAS 2 Regulation.
14. Article 46 *sexies* eIDAS 2 Regulation.
15. On these data, *see* PricewaterhouseCoopers (PWC), *Virtual and Augmented Reality Could Deliver a £1.5 Trillion Boost to the Global Economy by 2030: PwC,* (2020), available at https://www.pwc.com/th/en/press-room/press-release/2020/press-release-29-01-20-en.html

Given the lack of centralised control, this situation has highlighted the need for even more attention and a legal definition and regulatory framework for access and identification in virtual worlds.[16]

Understanding how the eIDAS 2 Regulation differentiates between authentication and identification in the 'digital world' is essential to emphasise the differences from the 'physical dimension'[17] and the additional challenges arising in new environments.

Debates regarding the implications of digital identity in a single blended world – a combination of physical presence through avatars and virtual existence – are extensive and focus on two main aspects: the importance of 'digital recognizability' and the risks of data surveillance.[18] This aspect is relevant when considering virtual worlds such as the Metaverse.[19]

The Communication of the European Commission on Web 4.0[20] and virtual worlds defined virtual worlds as persistent, immersive environments based on technologies including 3D and extended reality (XR). These technologies make it possible to blend physical and digital worlds in real-time for various purposes, such as designing, creating simulations, collaborating, learning, socialising, carrying out transactions, or providing entertainment.[21]

The Council of the EU described Metaverse as "an immersive and constant virtual 3D world where people interact through an avatar to enjoy entertainment, make

---

and Bloomberg, *Metaverse May Be $800 Billion Market, Next Tech Platform* (1 December 2021), available at https://www.bloomberg.com/professional/insights/trading/metaverse-may-be-800-billion-market-next-tech-platform/.

16. Depending on the level of immersiveness (i.e., the quality or degree of being immersive), accessing the virtual worlds will require some headsets for virtual or augmented reality applications.
17. The eIDAS 2 Regulation introduces the definition of electronic identification and authentication (Article 3 eIDAS 2 Regulation).
18. *See* Keren Weitzberg, Margie Cheesman, Aaron Martin and Emrys Schoemaker, *Between Surveillance and Recognition: Rethinking Digital Identity in Aid*, 2 Big Data & Society, 1-7 (2021) https://doi.org/10.1177/20539517211006744, esp. 2; Silvia Masiero, *Digital Identity as Platform-Mediated Surveillance*, 10 Big Data & Society, 1-5 (2023) https://doi.org/10.1177/20539517221135176, esp. 2.
19. The word 'Metaverse' derives from the science fiction novel of Neil Stephenson, *Snow Crash*, (Penguin Books 1992).

    The origin of Metaverse is gaming, where multiple users participate in virtual online environments and communities and interact with characters in that world. Incremental development played a role in the evolution of previous virtual worlds, and the main difference is the user experience. *See* Shahper Richter and Alexander Richter, *What Is Novel about the Metaverse?*, 73 International Journal of Information Management, 1-11 (2023) https://doi.org/10.1016/j.ijinfomgt.2023.102684.
20. Web 4.0 is the expected fourth generation of the World Wide Web. Using advanced artificial and ambient intelligence, the IoT, trusted blockchain transactions, virtual worlds, and XR capabilities, digital and real objects and environments are fully integrated and communicate, enabling truly intuitive, immersive experiences that seamlessly blend the physical and digital worlds. *See* European Commission Communication, An EU initiative on Web 4.0 and virtual worlds: a head starts in the next technological transition, COM(2023) 442/final, 11 July 2023, p. 1.
21. *Ibid.*

purchases and carry out transactions, with crypto-assets or work without living the seat."[22]

The European Parliamentary Research Service underlines, "there is no uniform definition of 'virtual worlds' or 'metaverse(s)'. Both terms are still in use (in the singular and the plural), often interchangeably" and define Metaverse as "an immersive and constant virtual 3D world where people interact by means of an avatar to carry out a wide range of activities."[23]

The Metaverse is a 3D digital virtual space built on various blocks and technologies such as software, platforms, middleware, 5th generation of mobile communications (5G), high-performance computing (HPC), and clouds. In it, individuals from the physical world can interact with one another through avatars, which refer to users' virtual self-representation. The Metaverse alters how users present themselves and interact with others' avatars, facilitating exploration in virtual spaces. Users can choose which specific Metaverse to enter. While 'Metaverse' is a broad term, it refers to various distinct virtual dimensions.

5G technology has made Metaverse more accessible to consumers, thus increasing its socio-economic activities. According to the Organisation for Economic Co-operation and Development (OECD), the Metaverse promises an enhanced digital environment where individuals can work, play, connect, and collaborate. In that space, people will interact with each other with virtual objects and digitally rendered buildings, facilities, and landscapes. This new digital experience promises business opportunities across sectors and benefits across society.[24]

The European Commission has also adopted a strategy on Web 4.0 and virtual worlds to guide the next technological transition. This strategy ensures an open, secure, trustworthy, fair, and inclusive digital environment for EU citizens, businesses, and public administrations. Given that virtual worlds entail opportunities and risks to be addressed, the strategy, in line with the 2030 objectives of the Digital Decade Political Programme, identifies overcoming fragmentation and ensuring interoperability among virtual worlds as key priorities.[25]

---

22. Council of the European Union, General Secretariat, Metaverse: Virtual World, Real Challenges, (March 2022), available at https://www.consilium.europa.eu/media/54987/metaverse-paper-9-march-2022.pdf.
23. European Parliamentary Research Service (EPRS), Virtual Words (metaverses), no date, available at https://www.europarl.europa.eu/RegData/etudes/ATAG/2023/751408/EPRS_ATA(2023)751408_EN.pdf.
24. *See* Organisation for Economic Co-operation and Development (OECD), Privacy, Immersive Technologies and the Metaverse, (2022), available at https://www.businessatoecd.org/hubfs/Privacy%2C%20Immersive%20Technologies%20and%20the%20Metaverse%20Report.pdf.
25. Decision (EU) 2022/2481 of the European Parliament and of the Council of 14 December 2022 establishing the Digital Decade Policy Programme 2030, OJ L 323, 19.12.2022, p. 4-26. The European Commission has already launched the Virtual and Augmented Reality Industrial coalition, bringing together the industry and policymakers on 14 September 2022. The Virtual and Augmented Reality Industrial Coalition is a platform for structured dialogue between the European VR/AR ecosystem and policymakers. *See* European Commission, The Virtual and Augmented Reality Industrial Coalition, available at https://digital-strategy.ec.europa.eu/en/policies/virtual-and-augmented-reality-coalition. On these points, *see also* World Economic Forum, Interoperability in the Metaverse, Briefing Paper (January 2023), available at https://www3.weforum.org/docs/WEF_Interoperability_in_the_Metaverse.pdf; Fabiana Di Porto and

An important aspect is that these private Metaverses should be developed based on interoperable standards. This approach ensures that no single private entity will control access to the public square or dictate the terms and conditions. This question is crucial, especially when considering the competitive dynamics among large platforms addressed with the DMA (*see supra* – Chapter 4). If a platform has the power to control the formation and development of a Metaverse and impose its own rules, it can be a future gatekeeper. Furthermore, space risks become subject not only to public regulation but also to private regulation. Beyond the dominant market position, there are several related concerns, such as the execution of commercial transactions and the potential for collusive agreements between operators. The European Commissioner, Ms Margrethe Vestager, said, "in the gaming world, you already have people paying hundreds of thousands of dollars for 'skins and certain items that you can trade, and there are human traders that go in between the seller and the buyer."[26] Monitoring market practices will be much more challenging.

Former European Commissioner Breton emphasised that multiple Metaverses are being developed, and this new generation of digital platforms provides innovative ways for people to interact. The goal must be for individuals to feel as safe in virtual worlds as in real life.[27]

Indeed, the Metaverse and virtual worlds present challenges to fundamental rights and significant objectives of public interest in a democratic society. This includes issues related to children's rights, personal data protection and privacy, disinformation, cybersecurity, cybercrime, (gender-based) cyber violence, discrimination, exclusion, and hate speech.

7.7 AVATAR, DIGITAL IDENTITY, DATA PROTECTION AND PRIVACY

It is also helpful to remember the broader definition in a report from a few years ago, which can refer to logon and access control, digital signatures and non-repudiation, establishing legal identity, or using data to understand the consumer better.[28]

Daniel Foà, *Defining Virtual Worlds: Main Features and Regulatory Challenges,* Centre on Regulation in Europe (CERRE) (July 2023), available at https://cerre.eu/publications/defining-virtual-worlds-main-features-and-regulatory-challenges/.

26. *See* Politico, *Vestager: Metaverse Poses New Competition Challenges* (18 January 2022), available at https://www.politico.eu/article/metaverse-new-competition-challenges-margrethe-vestager/.
27. *See* European Commission, People, Technologies & Infrastructure: Europe's Plan to Thrive in the Metaverse I, Blog of Commissioner Thierry Breton (14 September 2022), available at https://ec.europa.eu/commission/presscorner/detail/es/STATEMENT_22_5525.
28. *See* Carly Nyst, Steve Pannifer, Edgar Whitley and Paul Makin, *Digital Identity: Issue Analysis* (2016), available at https://chyp.com/wp-content/uploads/2020/06/PRJ.1578-Digital-Identity-Issue-Analysis-Report-v1_6-1.pdf. Many definitions exist, for a summary *see* Margarita Robles-Carrillo, *Digital Identity: An Approach to Its Nature, Concept, and Functionalities*, 32 International Journal of Law and Information Technology, 1-21 (2024) https://doi.org/10.1093/ijlit/eaae019.

Digital identity is a crucial information system that typically supports identity verification, authentication, and authorisation to access the digital world and conduct commercial transactions and communications.

The European Declaration on Digital Rights and Principles for the Digital Decade[29] underlines that all people living in the Union are offered an accessible, secure, and trusted digital identity that enables access to a broad range of online and offline services and is protected against cybersecurity risks and cybercrime, including data breaches and identity theft or manipulation.

In the Metaverse, the user creates their digital actor, termed avatar, to be their identity in the virtual world.[30] In some cases, a Metaverse might allow one to make a persona that can be taken everywhere in the Metaverse with all its characteristics and belongings.[31] This will enable users to interact with one another, digital objects, and landscapes in real-time with three-dimensionality. With the development of virtual reality (VR) and AI, the Metaverse can be seen as a sophisticated space that facilitates human coexistence through their avatars.

These avatars serve as the interface through which users interact, communicate, and engage in economic activities within the Metaverse. There should always be a correspondence between the identity of the person using it and the avatar. However, this may not always be the case, not only due to the individual's desire to appear different from how they are in the real world but also due to possible identity theft cases.

OECD underlines that an avatar will serve as an identification document by which a user establishes who they are. Avatars will likely be custom-tailored to the individual, highly realistic, and able to resemble users' facial and physical features closely.[32] Avatars represent users and their ideal selves, significantly influencing choices. Although anti-cheating measures have gradually been adopted, they impact personalisation and user satisfaction.[33] The differences between the avatar and the actual person - especially regarding characteristics - highlight the importance of correct identification in these virtual environments.

Creating and customising multiple avatars enables users to express themselves freely, reflecting any facet of their digital personalities. These avatars can resemble realistic people or be completely fantastical, allowing individuals to present and behave differently from their real-world selves.

29. European Declaration on Digital Rights and Principles for the Digital Decade 2023/C 23/01, Official Journal of the European Union C23/1, 23 January 2023.
30. According to the International Organisation for Standardization (ISO), IT Security and Privacy: A Framework for Identity Management - Part 1: Terminology and Concepts, ISO/IEC 24760-1 (2019), identity is a collection of attributes associated with an entity.
31. *See* Europol, *Policing in the Metaverse: What Law Enforcement Needs to Know* (2022), available at https://www.europol.europa.eu/publications-events/publications/policing-in-metaverse-what-law-enforcement-needs-to-know.
32. OECD, *supra* n. 24.
33. The choice will also be affected by the different abilities an avatar can possess, many of which can themselves be chosen by the agent. On this point, *see* Edward Castranova, *Theory of the Avatar*, CESifo Working Paper No. 863, (February 2023), available at https://www.cesifo.org/en/publications/2003/working-paper/theory-avatar#: ~ :text = A%20human%20being%20experiences%20these,body%20in%20the%20virtual%20world.

The identification aspect is crucial for digital trust. Unlike the physical world, digital identity relies on cryptographic trust rather than personal trust. There is a risk that someone may impersonate another individual through their avatar to defraud other users and obtain their private information. In the case of avatars, such deceptions can be easier to execute, as a similar appearance or voice to a familiar person can lead to mistakes. This issue is particularly problematic because verifying the person's identity behind the avatar is complex and can be illusionary or fake.

Furthermore, unlike in the real world, actions recognised as illegal, *a priori*, or immoral can be perceived differently in the virtual world, where even rules to be respected are perceived differently.

An attacker can generate a fake avatar, which can deceive the user in many ways, from economic to financial fraud.[34] One approach to addressing such behaviors is blocking the avatar or imposing certain obligations. However, this may reignite the debate about legal personality that took place previously, which faced opposition from 193 states in 2021.[35]

Traditional authentication systems combine multiple factors of identities, such as cryptographic keys, biometric characteristics, and account passwords, to perform access authentication. In the Metaverse, however, entering an account and password is not user-friendly and requires authentication.

The avatar mediates our presence in the virtual world and allows us to receive and transmit sensory information. Its creation to make it capable of interacting requires a careful reconstruction of movements, posture, and even tone of voice if it is to be a digital twin of the person.

This environment provides a unique experience, allowing people to express emotions and engage without direct real-life interactions. AI will play a central role in creating avatars by enabling them to detect user emotions through interactions, vocal inflection, and facial expressions. This capability allows avatars to adjust their behaviour and dialogue to fit various environments and the user's emotional state. The resulting movements and perceptions can feel so realistic that, in some cases, adjustments were needed to prevent actions such as attacking other avatars or engaging in violent behaviors.

This also means that all experiences in virtual worlds can consider preferences and data derived from the avatar's behaviours. At the same time, however, similar considerations are derived from others, first connected to the correspondence between the avatar and the individual using it. Additionally, a wide range of data, including emotional data, is utilised in this context. These aspects contribute to a broader reflection on the difficulties of identifying the regulatory framework applicable to a

34. On the possible ways of carrying out similar actions and the possible success rates, *see* Zhenyong Zhang, Kedi Yang, Youliang Tian and Jianfeng Ma, *An Anti-disguise Authentication System Using the First Impression of Avatar in Metaverse*, 19 IEEE Transactions on Information Forensics and Security, 6393-6408 (2024) https://doi.org/10.1109/tifs.2024.3410527, available at https://ieeexplore.ieee.org/document/10551293.
35. *See* UNESCO, Recommendation on the ethics of artificial intelligence' SHS/BIO/PI/2021/1, https://unesdoc.unesco.org/ark:/48223/pf0000381137.

dimension like Metaverse.[36] The most complex issues arise when the avatar does not match the characteristics of its human owner.

Numerous legal issues relate to the specific virtual world and its services. In addition to IT security and data protection concerns – which can differ depending on the virtual environment – issues of responsibility, liability, and contractual rules are also significant. The DMA, DSA, Data Act, and the GDPR have addressed many aspects of data acquisition and exploitation.[37] If Metaverse platforms are viewed as hosting service providers, they must adhere to the contractual terms and conditions outlined in the DSA, especially regarding transparency obligations.

However, not all issues regarding Avatar and Metaverse have been resolved. To closely monitor market developments and their related implications, the European Commission identified the need for a structured approach for ongoing monitoring in the 2023 Communication.[38]

7.8 DEEPFAKE AND THE METAVERSE

Remembering deepfake[39] may also be helpful when considering Metaverse and the possible issues related to digital identity and authentication. Deepfakes involve the digital manipulation of audio or visual data and can be regarded as cybercrime. They enable individuals to assume false identities, often intending to spread misinformation and deceive viewers.[40] The development of AI has made the creation of deepfakes easier, making the Metaverse an "ideal place" for their use.

While deepfake does not originate in the Metaverse or virtual worlds, its implications for security and the ability to detect fakes are significant in this context. Additionally, deepfake represents one of the AI-driven practices that is particularly challenging to identify in the digital marketplace. For this reason, the AI Regulation addresses deepfakes in low-risk situations and establishes transparency requirements. The use of deepfakes to carry out malicious activities has highlighted the need for attention to similar situations in Metaverse, too. The ability to impersonate individuals by swapping faces or voices raises significant security concerns, increasing the risk of unauthorised access to services or secure locations.

36. *See* Ivan Osvaldo Epicoco, Marco Pierro and Fulvio Sarzana Di Sant'Ippolito, *Il diritto del metaverso: NFT, DeFi, GameFi e-privacy* (Giappichelli 2022).
37. European Commissioner Ms. Margarethe Vestager had stated that the European Commission does not want to add rules for the Metaverse. *See* Frank Mccarthy, *Internet: EU Commission and the Metaverse Digital Package – Digital* (2022), available at https://technewsinc.com/internet-eu-commission-and-the-metaverse-digital-package-digital/.
38. *See* European Commission Communication, *supra* n. 20.
39. Generative Adversarial Networks (GAN) are a technology with remarkable results because they create manipulations that are difficult to distinguish from original content. GANs are MLM in which two neural networks produce the most realistic result.
40. *See* Momina Masood, Marriam Nawaz, Khalid Mahmood Malik, Ali Javed and Aun Irtaza, *Deepfakes Generation and Detection: State-of-the-Art, Open Challenges, Countermeasures, and Way Forward*, 53 Applied Intelligence, 3974-4026 (2022) https://doi.org/10.1007/s10489-022-03766-z.

The breadth, variety, and difficulty of detecting deepfake make it not only difficult to detect but also to regulate.

Many methods have been suggested for preventing or quickly detecting Deepfakes, which are proposed to detect fake videos of people automatically.[41] These actions are based on analysing the detectable change in the eyebrows, the blinking rhythm of the eyes, and even any tiny colour variations. However, detection methods must evolve as deepfake technology advances to keep pace with increasingly sophisticated fake media. Moreover, these techniques are less effective in the Metaverse, where users interact through avatars rather than real faces.

Considering the Metaverse's unique characteristics, even educating recipients about potential deepfakes may be ineffective. Furthermore, in addition to the prevention, which is also complicated by the use of deepfake, which can be aimed at spreading false information and replacing identities to guide and make other subjects carry out actions, the identification of responsibilities also appears rather complex.[42] It is helpful to remember that deepfakes are also identified in the recently approved Regulation on AI among the limited-risk situations for which the contents should be labelled so that the contents or declarations result from deepfakes.

41. Felipe Romero-Moreno, *Deepfake Fraud Detection: Safeguarding Trust in Generative AI*, (2024), available at https://papers.ssrn.com/sol3/papers.cfm?abstract_id=5031627; Peter Broklyn, Axel Egon and Ralph Shad, *Deepfakes and Cybersecurity: Detection and Mitigation* (2024), available at https://papers.ssrn.com/sol3/papers.cfm?abstract_id=4904874; Sharv Sankpal, Junaid Kazi, Man Kadu, Avadhoot Jogade and Yuvraj Nikam, *Deepfake Detection* (2025), available at https://papers.ssrn.com/sol3/papers.cfm?abstract_id=5030191.
42. *See* Alberto Orlando, *La regolamentazione del deepfake in Europa, Stati Uniti e Cina*, Special Issue I/2024 – Media Laws, no page numbers (2025), available at https://www.medialaws.eu/rivista/la-regolamentazione-del-deepfake-in-europa-stati-uniti-e-cina/#_ftn2.

CHAPTER 8
The Protection of Digital Consumers

8.1 CONSUMERS IN DIGITAL MARKETS

The roadmap for realising the digital transformation of the EU by 2030 aims to achieve the objectives of the decade in the areas of digital skills, digital infrastructure and digitisation of businesses and public services. As products and services increasingly shift to the digital domain and private and digital lives become progressively intertwined, consumers will increasingly have to deal with this ever-evolving frontier - if not become dependent on it.[1]

In the rhetoric and narrative of the EU, digitalisation should empower consumers further, putting them at the centre of markets as arbiters. At the same time, addressing the needs of specific consumer groups, including certain aspects of consumer vulnerability, is one of the most critical objectives of the late policies. For instance, the needs of over-indebted, under-aged and disabled consumers are increasingly emphasised.[2]

As extensively explored in this book, the European legislator has been active in implementing a modernisation agenda that, to some extent, has taken consumer protection into account, with the creation of multiple regulatory initiatives aimed at aligning consumer needs with digitalisation. These include legislation covered in this book, such as the DMA,[3] the DSA,[4] the AI

1. European Commission, A Digital Single Market Strategy for Europe, (Communication) COM(2015) 0192 final; President of the European Commission Ursula von der Leyen, A Union that strives for more - My agenda for Europe. Political guidelines for the next European Commission 2019-2024 (16 July 2019).
2. Communication from the Commission to the European Parliament and the Council, New Consumer Agenda. Strengthening consumer resilience for sustainable recovery, COM/2020/696 final.
3. Regulation (EU) 2022/1925 of the European Parliament and of the Council of 14 September 2022 on contestable and fair markets in the digital sector and amending Directives (EU) 2019/1937 and (EU) 2020/1828 (Digital Markets Act), OJ L 265, 12.10.2022, p. 1-66.
4. Regulation (EU) 2022/2065 of the European Parliament and of the Council of 19 October 2022 on a Single Market for Digital Services and amending Directive 2000/31/EC (Digital Services Act), OJ L 277, 27.10.2022, p. 1-102.

Act,[5] the DGA,[6] and the Fair Access to and Fair Use of Data Act (Data Act)[7] – adding to regulations for the digital domain such as the Data Protection Regulation (GDPR)[8] and sector-specific regulations.[9]

New pieces of legislation have already been announced. Following a Digital Fairness Fitness Check, the newly established European Commission refers to the need to develop a Digital Fairness Act to tackle unethical techniques and commercial practices related to dark patterns, marketing by social media influencers, the addictive design of digital products and online profiling especially when consumer vulnerabilities are exploited for commercial purposes.[10]

According to the European Commission, existing EU consumer law is relevant and necessary in the Digital Single Market, but its objectives are only partially achieved. Consumers do not behave the same way online and offline. At the same time, traders have more effective means to influence consumers online. Consumer detriment remains very high.[11]

As it also emerged in the previous Chapters, the EU consumer legislation that forms the core of the framework of consumer protection is represented by the UCPD,[12] the UCTD,[13] and the CRD.[14]

---

5. Regulation (EU) 2024/1689 of the European Parliament and of the Council of 13 June 2024 laying down harmonised rules on artificial intelligence and amending Regulations (EC) No. 300/2008, (EU) No. 167/2013, (EU) No. 168/2013, (EU) 2018/858, (EU) 2018/1139 and (EU) 2019/2144 and Directives 2014/90/EU, (EU) 2016/797 and (EU) 2020/1828 (Artificial Intelligence Act), OJ L, 2024/1689, 12.7.2024.
6. Regulation (EU) 2022/868 of the European Parliament and of the Council of 30 May 2022 on European data governance and amending Regulation (EU) 2018/1724, OJ L 152, 3.6.2022, p. 1-44.
7. Regulation (EU) 2023/2854 of the European Parliament and of the Council of 13 December 2023 on harmonised rules on fair access to and use of data and amending Regulation (EU) 2017/2394 and Directive (EU) 2020/1828 (Data Act), OJ L, 2023/2854, 22.12.2023.
8. Regulation (EU) 2016/679 of the European Parliament and of the Council of 27 April 2016 on the protection of natural persons with regard to the processing of personal data and on the free movement of such data, and repealing Directive 95/46/EC (General Data Protection Regulation), OJ L 119, 4.5.2016, p. 1-88.
9. E.g., *see* Directive (EU) 2023/2225 of the European Parliament and of the Council of 18 October 2023 on credit agreements for consumers and repealing Directive 2008/48/EC, OJ L, 2023/2225, 30.10.2023; Directive (EU) 2015/2366 of the European Parliament and of the Council of 25 November 2015 on payment services in the internal market, amending Directives 2002/65/EC, 2009/110/EC and 2013/36/EU and Regulation (EU) No. 1093/2010, and repealing Directive 2007/64/EC, OJ L 337, 23.12.2015, p. 35-127, to name but a few.
10. Commission Staff Working Document, Fitness Check on EU consumer law on digital fairness, SWD(2024) 230 final.
11. *Ibid.*
12. Directive 2005/29/EC of the European Parliament and of the Council of 11 May 2005 concerning unfair business-to-consumer commercial practices in the internal market and amending Council Directive 84/450/EEC, Directives 97/7/EC, 98/27/EC and 2002/65/EC of the European Parliament and of the Council and Regulation (EC) No. 2006/2004 of the European Parliament and of the Council ('Unfair Commercial Practices Directive'), OJ L 149, 11.6.2005, p. 22-39.
13. Council Directive 93/13/EEC of 5 April 1993 on unfair terms in consumer contracts, OJ L 95, 21.4.1993, p. 29-34.
14. Directive 2011/83/EU of the European Parliament and of the Council of 25 October 2011 on consumer rights, amending Council Directive 93/13/EEC and Directive 1999/44/EC of the European Parliament and of the Council and repealing Council Directive 85/577/EEC and Directive 97/7/EC of the European Parliament and of the Council, OJ L 304, 22.11.2011, p. 64-88.

In short, the UCTD is a minimum harmonisation instrument which applies both offline and online.[15] It contains transparency requirements in contractual terms, and it aims to protect consumers against the use by traders of not individually negotiated contract terms which, contrary to the requirement of good faith, create a significant imbalance in the parties' rights and obligations to the detriment of the consumer. The UCTD provides that terms that are considered unfair are not binding on the consumer. Its Annex contains a non-exhaustive list of the most common types of terms that may be considered unfair, with the aim of guiding the national authorities and courts in their case-by-case assessments.

Instead, the UCPD is a maximum harmonisation instrument.[16] With few exceptions - it aims to protect consumers offline and online against unfair commercial practices and ensure better consumer information in the advertising, contractual and after-sale stages of transactions. The UCPD too contains an Annex with a blacklist of specific commercial practices which are always considered unfair. Except for the practices in the blacklist, it must be demonstrated that a commercial practice causes or is likely to cause an average or vulnerable consumer to take a transactional decision that they would not have taken otherwise.

Finally, the CRD is a maximum harmonisation measure which aims to provide specific protection concerning offline and online B2C contracts for goods and services.[17] The CRD provides for pre-contractual information requirements, it introduces a right of withdrawal from distance or off-premises contracts without giving reasons or incurring any costs, it sets out a number of other consumer rights such as those regarding the termination of contracts, and it prohibits charging fees for the use of the means of payment communications, or other hidden costs.

In principle, the UCPD, CRD and UCTD are technology-neutral measures, meaning that their rules apply to all types of traders, commercial practices, products and services, regardless of the underlying technology or business model being used.

Against this background of the acquis of EU consumer law, the main flaw of the new digital policies and strategies, alongside the resulting regulatory acts, is that they remain permeated with old concepts and paradigms that already struggle to protect consumers in the so-called analogue world. The question of who is the consumer and his/her image has been much debated and challenged, in particular from the behavioural sciences perspective. It remains to be seen the extent to which the consumer image under EU law has reached its limits, especially with the establishment of digital markets where consumers are subjected to sophisticated and opaque techniques capable of influencing or even manipulating their purchasing decisions.

To a certain extent, due to the asymmetry of information, the difference in bargaining power and the relative lack of transparency often inherent in private law

15. Minimum harmonisation means that Member States may lay down stricter consumer protection rules in their national legislation.
16. Contrary to minimum harmonisation, maximum harmonisation means that national law may not exceed the terms of the relevant EU legislation, unless the latter provides otherwise.
17. However, the CRD allows Member States in certain cases to impose additional rules as, for example, with respect to pre-contractual information requirements for on-premises contracts.

relationships between individual consumers and businesses, as well as the ever-present risk of falling victim to unfair commercial practices, all consumers can be considered a 'weak' or 'vulnerable' contractual party. This is especially true in the case of markets characterised by particularly complex transactions, where consumers are often ill-prepared to make sound decisions. Traditional examples are the financial markets and the markets for services of general interest, not only because of information asymmetries between the parties or a limited level of consumer education but also because of complexities or other factors inherent in the markets that push individuals towards choices that are inconsistent with their needs in the long run.[18]

The EU, while recognising the pitfalls of these problematic markets, seems largely unwilling to depart from its traditional and inflexible standard of consumer behaviour, based on the ideal of the so-called average consumer as a reasonably well-informed and attentive market agent, to whom it is sufficient to provide adequate information to rebalance the business relationship with firms.

The shortcomings of this traditional information paradigm become particularly evident in digital markets where the quantity and intricacy of available information, as well as the complexity of the architectures, products, services and underlying technologies, make it more difficult for the consumer to make informed decisions.

Mindful of these problems, this Chapter attempts to counter and reinterpret the fictional standard of the 'consumer' in the law (*fictio juris*) in light of recent possible jurisprudential prospects, especially when transposed to the sophistication of digital markets and their underlying technologies.

8.2 THE 'AVERAGE CONSUMER'

Historically, EU consumer law has developed in continuity with neoclassical economics, which starts from the premise that individuals seek to maximise the utility of consumption and are able to make optimal wise choices once they have all the relevant information about a product or service. The use of the traditional neoclassical economic model implies the understanding of the consumer as a *homo economicus*, i.e., an individual who acts in a manner that is always rational, capable of considering all available information, fully understanding and processing it, and able to weigh all the options available to him/her before arriving at a perfectly informed and logical decision. This view, in turn, implies that consumers are seen as active arbiters of markets, since the ability to optimise their choices would force markets to self-regulate.[19]

18. Peter Cartwright, *Understanding and Protecting Vulnerable Financial Consumers*, 38 Journal of Consumer Policy, 119-138 (2015) https://doi.org/10.1007/s10603-014-9278-9.
19. Hans Micklitz, Norbert Reich, Peter Rott and Klaus Tonner, *European Consumer Law* (Intersentia 2014); Geraint Howells and Stephen Weatherill, *Consumer Protection Law* (Ashgate 2005); Stephen Weatherill, *EU Consumer Law and Policy* (Edward Elgar 2013); Ian Ramsay, *Consumer Law and Policy* (Hart Publishing 2012); Paolo Siciliani, Christine Riefa and Harriet Gamper, *Consumer Theories of Harm, an Economic Approach to Consumer Law Enforcement and Policy Making* (Hart Publishing 2019).

Against this backdrop, consumer law has evolved on the premise that an imbalance exists in the market between consumers and businesses, where it is mainly information asymmetries that cause a substantial difference in the parties' bargaining power that can lead to significant market inefficiency (market failure). Therefore, faced with economic agents who are contractually weak and in a condition of intrinsic vulnerability, consumer law was conceived as a means of rebalancing and correcting the market, protecting the weak party in the relationship with businesses.[20]

The neoclassical economic narrative puts forward that the allocative efficiency of resources should be left to the market rather than to regulation,[21] even in those jurisdictions where consumer law is regarded in the context of a broader social focus, as it is the case, for example, in most EU Member States.[22]

Therefore, as well portrayed by Riefa and Gamper, EU consumer law has rapidly moved towards the use of information as a primary regulatory tool. More or less, from the very beginning, it was recognised that competition in markets can only work if consumers have all the information that they need to make efficient economic decisions. Consequently, the information remedies offered by regulation quickly became a widely adopted shortcut for market correction.[23]

This trend and regulatory technique have continued until these days. Indeed, it is worth noting how over time the EU's interpretation of the information paradigm has expanded and become increasingly pervasive, if not invasive. *See*, for example, how the consumer credit directive required creditors not only to provide consumers with comprehensive information but also to make it accessible in a standardised form.[24] The UCPD took a further step forward: its wording shows an attempt to reconcile the two objectives of internal market freedom and adequate consumer protection by moving from the minimum harmonisation approach of the previous directives to a maximum harmonisation approach. With this approach, European consumer law becomes capable of limiting the discretion of Member States to introduce social elements in the transposition of consumer protection rules while retaining the criticised element of consumer empowerment.[25]

The use of a high consumer standard seems aligned with the consideration that the EU consumer protection regime is generally governed by economic and not social

---

20. *Ibid.*
21. Katalin Cseres, *Competition Law and Consumer Protection* (Kluwer Law International 2005), esp. 178.
22. Jacobien Rutgers, *European Contract Law and the Welfare State* (Europa Law Publishing 2012); Irina Domurath, *Consumer Vulnerability and Welfare in Mortgage Contracts* (Hart Publishing 2017).
23. Christine Riefa and Harriet Gamper, *Economic Theory and Consumer Vulnerability: Exploring an Uneasy Relationship*, in *Vulnerable Consumers and the Law: Consumer Protection and Access to Justice*, 17-30 (Christine Riefa and Severine Saintier eds, Routledge 2020); Siciliani, Riefa and Gamper, *supra* n. 19, esp. 19.
24. Irina Domurath, *The Case for Vulnerability as the Normative Standard in European Consumer Credit and Mortgage Law: An Inquiry into the Paradigms of Consumer Law*, 2 Journal of European Consumer and Market Law, 124-137 (2018).
25. Norbert Reich, *Vulnerable Consumers in EU Law*, in *The Images of the Consumer in EU Law: Legislation, Free Movement and Competition Law*, 139-158 (Dorota Leczykiewicz and Stephen Weatherill, Hart Publishing 2018).

considerations. After all, as pointed out by Reich, consumer protection as a form of social protection is generally a matter for the national legislation of the Member States, not for the EU.[26]

The approach adopted by the European legislator - and in cascade by national legislators - has therefore been to oblige markets to provide as much information as possible, regardless of the efficiency of this instrument, in the belief that the 'rational and responsible' consumer would be able to correct market imbalances or failures.

In such a view, within the framework of EU law, information has been elevated from a 'method' to a 'right' and becomes, rightly or wrongly, the most fundamental specific right of the consumer.[27]

With the provision of information, the consumer is given the responsibility to pay attention, use the tools available to defend himself against market excesses and assess the suitability or otherwise of the offer to his/her needs.[28] Thus, the CJEU has established that consumers are endowed with high cognitive faculties capable of digesting the information provided to them and from there, it has developed the notion of the 'average consumer' as the benchmark. In interpreting the legal term 'consumer' as a natural person who (...) acts for purposes which are outside his or her trade or profession, the CJEU had to determine the extent of the protection to be afforded to anyone falling within the scope of the term. In line with previous cases where the question arose incidentally,[29] the Court constructed in the seminal *Gut Springenheide* its decision on the expectations of an 'average reasonably well-informed and reasonably observant and circumspect consumer'.[30]

The jurisprudence of the CJEU has continued to use the *Gut Springenheide* formula to interpret the behaviour of the average consumer, establishing a clear legal precedent[31]

26. *Ibid.*
27. In Case C-362/88, *GB- INNO- BM v. Confédération du Commerce* Luxembourgeois, ECLI:EU:C:1990:102, the CJEU has confirmed how information to consumers is 'king'. In the literature, *see* Jules Stuyck, *European Consumer Law after the Treaty of Amsterdam: Consumer Policy in or Beyond the Internal Market*, 37 Common Market Law Review, 367-400 (2000) https://doi.org/10.54648/260933.
28. Riefa and Gamper, *supra* n. 23.
29. *See*, for example, Case C-238/89, *Pall Corp. v. P.J. Dahlhausen & Co.*, ECLI:EU:C:1990:473; Case C-126/91, *Schutzverband gegen Unwesen in der Wirtschaft e.V. v. Yves Rocher GmbH*, ECLI:EU:C:1993:191; Case C-315/92, *Verband Sozialer Wettbewerb eV v. Clinique Laboratoires SNC e Estée Lauder Cosmetics GmbH*, ECLI:EU:C:1994:34; Case C-456/93, *Zentrale zur Bekämpfung unlauteren Wettbewerbs eV v. Privatkellerei Franz Wilhelm Langguth Erben GmbH & Co. KG*, EU:C:1995:206. Particularly interesting is Case C-470/93, *Verein gegen Unwesen in Handel und Gewerbe Köln eV v. Mars GmbH*, ECLI;EU:C:1995:224, as it marks the first explicit reference to the category of 'reasonably prudent consumers'.
30. Case C-210/96, *Gut Springenheide GmbH and Rudolf Tusky v. Oberkreisdirektor des Kreises Steinfurt - Amt für Lebensmittelüberwachung*, ECLI:EU:C:1998:369.
31. E.g., *see* Case C-342/97, *Lloyd Schuhfabrik Meyer & Co. GmbH v. Klijsen Handel BV*, ECLI:EU:C:1999:323; Case C-465/98, *Verein gegen Unwesen in Handel und Gewerbe Köln eV v. Adolf Darbo AG*, ECLI:EU:C:2000:184; Case C-239/02, *Douwe Egberts NV v. Westrom Pharma NV and Christophe Souranis, Carrying on Business under the Commerical Name of 'Etablissements FICS' and Douwe Egberts NV v. FICS-World BVBA*, ECLI:EU:C:2004:445. In the literature, *see* in particular Anna De Giuli, *Sul concetto di 'vulnerabilità' secondo la Corte di Giustizia UE*, 1 Diritto Penale e Uomo, 1-19 (2020); Cristina Poncibò, *Il consumatore medio*, Contratto Impresa Europa, 756-757 (2007); Rossella Incadorna and Cristina Poncibò, *The Average Consumer, the Unfair*

which has also been introduced into European consumer protection legislation with the UCPD.[32]

The assumption, therefore, becomes that the average consumer cannot be easily deceived, setting a high standard that emphasises empowerment, self-reliance and transfer of power to the active economic agent consumer (consumer empowerment).

Such a consumer standard has long been widely criticised by academics as unrealistically demanding, over-simplified and, more generally, as a legal fiction far removed from the actual behaviour of the individual consumer, both in terms of information and reasonableness.[33]

The idea of consumer empowerment as the 'holy grail' of the EU strategy, often combined with market deregulation policies, becomes difficult to accept when compared to the information overload, the increasing (sometimes artificial) complexity of markets and the overly (often artificially) complex ways in which essential information is provided. In such a market environment, consumers in reality often end up being disempowered, thus acting in a less informed and less circumspect manner, in stark contrast to the EU's own objectives.[34] A real consumer cannot always be expected to understand and/or be willing to thoroughly evaluate the amount of information available to him/her before making a consumption decision, nor can he be expected to make perfectly rational choices unclouded by emotions and social influences of various kinds.[35]

On the contrary, as it will be argued later, it is rational for consumers to be impulsive, passive or disengaged, a mechanism through which they become vulnerable or which amplifies existing vulnerabilities. This is a phenomenon that has been pointed out as particularly problematic in markets that are most essential for consumer welfare, including certain services of general interest such as energy and telecommunications, as well as the financial services sector, which are often accused of being characterised by unnecessary product complexity, lack of transparency within companies and lack of trust in companies themselves, poor or insufficient advice and/or

Commercial Practices Directive and the Cognitive Revolution, 30 Journal of Consumer Policy, 21-38 (2007) https://doi.org/10.1007/s10603-006-9027-9.

32. Article 2 UCPD explicitly refers to the economic behaviour of the 'average consumer' of a given product in the definition of 'unfair commercial practice'. It should also be noted that Recital 18 UCPD makes it clear that the directive "takes as its benchmark the average consumer, reasonably well-informed and reasonably observant and circumspect, taking into account social, cultural and linguistic factors, as interpreted by the Court of Justice."
33. E.g., *see*, without claiming completeness, the seminal writings of Geraint Howells, *The Potential and Limits of Consumer Empowerment by Information*, 32 Journal of law and Society, 349-370 (2005) https://doi.org/10.1111/j.1467-6478.2005.00328.x; Omri Ben Sahar and Carl Schneider, *More Than You Wanted to Know: The Failure of Mandated Disclosure* (Princeton University Press 2016); Hans Micklitz, *The Consumer: Marketised, Fragmentised, Constitutionalised*, in *The Images of the Consumer in EU Law: Legislation, Free Movement and Competition Law*, 21-42 (Dorota Leczykiewicz and Stephen Weatherill eds, Hart Publishing, 2018).
34. Cfr. BEUC, *EU Consumers' 2020 Vision* (2012), available at https://www.beuc.eu/publications/2012-00316-01-e.pdf.
35. Incadorna and Poncibò, *supra* n. 31.

hidden fees for intermediaries resulting in unsuitable product sales, or high costs and risks relative to investment returns.[36]

As will be seen below, the same applies to digital marketplaces that increasingly permeate contemporary society.

8.3 THE 'VULNERABLE CONSUMER'

The benchmark of the 'average' consumer can be used to examine the concepts of consumer further weakness or 'vulnerability'. This is because the notion of the 'vulnerable' consumer was developed to distinguish particular sub-populations less able from the so-called average ones.

The concept of vulnerability is a difficult one to untangle in legal theory as it borrows its conceptual frameworks from other disciplines in the humanities to address a broad range of problems. Its roots can be endogenous or exogenous, and it can be dynamic and change over time depending on heterogenous causes, making its measurement far from being universally accepted.[37] In consumer legal theory, it is also a challenging concept because it is not in line with the original economic objectives of the law first discussed above. In addition, the conceptual and legal difficulties stem from the codified stigmatisation of some consumers vis-à-vis others. Through this lens, vulnerable consumers are seen as inferior consumers, not as capable as their 'average' counterparts. Thus, the concept of 'vulnerability' is categorised as 'inferiority to the average', not least in the UCPD, where vulnerable consumers are presented as inferior to the average because of their mental or physical impairments, age or credulity.[38]

The concept of 'vulnerability' is in many ways related to the influence of behavioural economics, the discipline that incorporates the study of psychology into economic analysis to acknowledge the limitations consumers have in evaluating information and making rational choices. Conceding that consumers hardly make rational or logical decisions and that traders can exploit their behavioural biases to steer consumer behaviour to their own advantage, behavioural economics seeks to understand how such mechanisms develop and how biases can be overcome.[39]

---

36. Peter Cartwright, *Banks, Consumers and Regulation* (Hart Publishing, 2004); Cartwright, *supra* n. 18; Angus Johnston, *Seeking the EU 'Consumer' in Services of General Economic Interest*, in *The Images of the Consumer in EU Law: Legislation, Free Movement and Competition Law*, 93-138 (Dorota Leczykiewicz and Stephen Weatherill eds, Hart Publishing 2018); Hans Micklitz and Irina Domurath, *Consumer Debt and Social Exclusion in Europe* (Ashgate 2015); Hans Micklitz, *Access to, and Exclusion of, European Consumers from Financial Markets after the Global Financial Crisis*, in *International Responses to Issues of Credit and Over-Indebtedness in the Wake of the Crisis*, 47-75 (Teresa Wilson ed., Ashgate 2013).
37. Gianclaudio Malgieri and Niklas Jedrzej, *Vulnerable Data Subjects*, 37 Computer Law and Security Review, 1-16 (2020) https://doi.org/10.1016/j.clsr.2020.105415; Billie Turner II et al., *A Framework for Vulnerability Analysis Unsustainability Science*, 100 Proceedings of the National Academy of Sciences of the United States of America, 8074-8079 (2003) https://doi.org/10.1073/pnas.1231335100.
38. Cfr. Article 5(3) UCPD. In the literature, for all *see* Riefa and Gamper, *supra* n. 23; Siciliani, Riefa and Gamper, *supra* n. 19.
39. *See* Daniel Khaneman and Amos Tversky, *Prospect Theory: An Analysis of Decision under Risk*, 47 Econometrica, 263-292 (1979) https://doi.org/10.2307/1914185; Amos Tversky and Daniel

Scholarship has long gone beyond the assessment of strictly personal characteristics such as age, gender, geographic location, education and language to consider broadening socio-economic factors, observing how external elements can impact new or existing vulnerabilities.[40] Of particular interest here, Fineman has developed a theory of vulnerability that increasingly serves as a yardstick for the study of consumer law and policy. Fineman conceives of vulnerability as a universal and ubiquitous experience, which can emerge at any time due to individual circumstances or from what the author calls 'embeddedness', that is, an individual's relationship or integration with the institutions, society and culture that surround him/her. Fineman's approach focuses on the structure of society and takes a utilitarian view of equality. This model eliminates the need to categorise individuals and the stigmatisation of vulnerable consumers.[41]

At some point, EU policy appeared to show a degree of openness towards the latest behavioural theories and the recognition of vulnerable consumers in such a direction. The Report on Consumer Vulnerability in Key Markets of the EU proposed the adoption of a more comprehensive definition of a vulnerable consumer, emphasising how socio-demographic characteristics, behavioural characteristics, personal situation or market environment can have a decisive effect on consumption. Due to a combination of these factors, consumers are seen as more at risk of suffering negative market outcomes, have a limited capacity to maximise their own welfare, have difficulties in obtaining or assimilating information, are less able to choose or access suitable products, or are more susceptible to certain marketing practices.[42]

However, this modest glimmer is neither echoed in EU law nor cascades into the national law of the Member States, where the limited conceptualisation of consumer vulnerability remains.

It is worth mentioning, however, that although most CJEU case law continues to faithfully pursue the paradigm of information to the average consumer,[43] on rare

---

Khaneman, *Loss Aversion in Riskless Choice: A Reference Dependent Model*, 106 Quarterly Journal of Economics, 1039-1061 (1991) https://doi.org/10.2307/2937956; Amos Tversky and Daniel Khaneman, *Judgment under Uncertainty: Heuristics and Biases*, 185 Science, 1124-1131 (1974) https://doi.org/10.1126/science.185.4157.1124. The discipline has been further developed by Richard Thaler and Cass Sunstein, *Nudge: Improving Decisions about Health, Wealth, and Happiness* (Penguin 2008) who have brought aspects of behavioural economics, such as the nudge theory, into dominant legislative policies. Nudge theory argues that decision-making processes and behaviour can be influenced through indirect suggestions and reinforcements as effectively or more effectively than through the imposition of rules, laws or direct instructions.

40. Christine Riefa and Severine Saintier, *In Search of (Access to) Justice for Vulnerable Consumers*, in *Vulnerable Consumers and the Law: Consumer Protection and Access to Justice*, 1-16 (Christine Riefa and Severine Saintier eds, Routledge 2021).
41. Martha Fineman, *The Vulnerable Subject: Anchoring Equality in the Human Condition*, 20 Yale Journal of Law and Feminism, 1-23 (2008) https://doi.org/10.4324/9780203848531-26; Martha Fineman, *Vulnerability and Inevitable Inequality*, 4 Oslo Law Review, 133-149 (2017) https://doi.org/10.18261/issn.2387-3299-2017-03-02.
42. European Commission, Consumer Vulnerability Across Key Markets in the European Union (January 2016), available at https://op.europa.eu/en/publication-detail/-/publication/79b42553-de14-11e6-ad7c-01aa75ed71a1.
43. Lately, *see* Case C-139/22, *AM and PM v. mBank S.A.*, ECLI:EU:C:2023:692; Case C-265/22, *ZR e PI v. Banco Santander, SA.*, ECLI:EU:C:2023:578.

occasions, the Court itself has adopted a more protective approach.[44] This approach, however, has been very limited in scope, applicable only in specific contexts, remaining an exception to the general rule of interpreting the consumer as reasonably circumspect, applicable only in cases where the Court has examined national legislation providing additional protection to a narrow and specific group of consumers.[45]

However, with the most recent EU consumer protection legislation leaning towards a full harmonisation approach, it is doubtful whether national exceptions could lead to a similar result.

8.4 NEW MARKETS, OLD LAW

Proceeding with an examination of the digital markets, it should be noted from the outset that the perception of the consumer has not changed.

On the contrary, EU policies and regulations increasingly focus on consumer empowerment, reinforcing their role and aiming to provide them with more immediate ways of obtaining information, comparing products and sharing experiences, as well as having control over their own data.

Interestingly, the New Consumer Agenda reiterates that consumers are the weakest party in a transaction and need protection for their health, safety and economic interests. It is emphasised that some groups may be particularly vulnerable due to their social situation or particular characteristics (age, gender, health, digital literacy, numeracy or financial situation, lack of accessibility).[46] However, a quick overview of the regulations in place, or envisaged, by the European legislator shows a lack of deviation from the vision of the average consumer traditionally understood, yet reinforcing their empowerment in certain cases in aspiring to place consumers at the centre of the digital project and in full control of their data.[47]

44. The first and most significant of these decisions was the CJEU ruling in the Case C-382/87, *R. Buet e Educational Business Services (EBS) SARL v. Pubblico Ministero*, ECLI:EU:C:1989:198, where it held that a French regulation prohibiting the door-to-door sale of educational material did not constitute a disproportionate restriction on the provisions of the EU Treaty on the free movement of goods, since the potential purchaser usually belongs to a category of persons who, for one reason or another, are poorly educated and seek to make up for this deficiency, making them particularly vulnerable to sellers of educational material.
45. A small number of subsequent decisions present similar arguments. *See*, for example, Case C-441/04, *A-Punkt Schmuckhandel v. Claudia Schmidt*, ECLI:EU:C:2006:141.
46. New Consumer Agenda, *supra* n. 2.
47. *See*, for instance, the EU strategy on Open Finance, with the legislator's declared intention to put consumers at the centre of the project, giving them full control over their data, awareness of its use and protection from misuse. Cfr. Communication from the Commission to the European Parliament, the Council, the European Economic and Social Committee and the Committee of the Regions, A Digital Finance Strategy for the EU, COM/2020/591 final; Communication from the Commission to the European Parliament, the Council, the European Economic and Social Committee and the Committee of the Regions, A Retail Payments Strategy for the EU, COM/2020/592 final; European Commission, Targeted consultation on open finance framework and data sharing in the financial sector, available at https://finance.ec.europa.eu/regulation-and-supervision/consultations/finance-2022-open-finance_en.

All in all, the view of vulnerability remains anchored to personal factors, starting with the Data Protection Regulation (GDPR), which considers data pertaining to these categories as sensitive.[48]

More recently, the DSA - which, as seen in Chapter 5, focuses more on consumer protection - rather seeks to ensure confidence in the digital economy with a detailed section on online markets and rules that are considered complementary to the existing consumer protection acquis - in particular the Omnibus Directive - and lays down specific rules to increase the transparency of certain features offered by certain information society services.[49] However, in the DSA, situations of vulnerability do not emerge. On the rare occasions when this occurs, the conceptualisation of vulnerability remains in continuity with the past, focusing on gender, race or ethnic origin, religion, disability, age or sexual orientation as factors that make groups or persons vulnerable or disadvantaged when using digital services.

Likewise, the DMA, which to some extent is a consumer protection initiative, seeks to promote competition in digital markets by keeping large online platforms under control and imposing obligations to encourage free choice and portability. However, the Regulation does not mention any situations of vulnerability.[50]

Even the AI Act prohibits certain AI practices that have a significant potential to manipulate people through subliminal techniques beyond their consciousness or to exploit the vulnerabilities of specific vulnerable groups, such as children or persons with disabilities, in order to materially distort their behaviour in such a way as to cause them or another person psychological or physical harm, thus focusing on personal attributes. Other manipulative or exploitative practices towards adults that could be facilitated by AI systems could be covered by existing legislation on data protection, consumer protection and digital services, which ensures that individuals are adequately informed and have the opportunity to freely choose not to be subject to profiling or other practices that could influence their behaviour.[51] In detail, Article 5(1)(b) AI Act prohibits "the placing on the market, putting into service or use of an AI system that exploits any of the vulnerabilities of a specific group of persons due to their age, physical or mental disability, in order to materially distort the behaviour of a person pertaining to that group in a manner that causes or is likely to cause that person or another person physical or psychological harm."

As has already been pointed out by others, economic harm remains excluded from the scope of protection, leaving the possibility of the use of AI to take advantage of consumers in an economic context. To the extent that the definition of high-risk AI

48. Gianclaudio Malgieri, *Vulnerability and Data Protection Law* (Oxford University Press 2023).
49. Directive (EU) 2019/2161 of the European Parliament and of the Council of 27 November 2019 amending Council Directive 93/13/EEC and Directives 98/6/EC, 2005/29/EC and 2011/83/EU of the European Parliament and of the Council as regards the better enforcement and modernisation of Union consumer protection rules, OJ L 328, 18.12.2019, p. 7-28.
50. *See, also*, Christine Riefa, *Protecting Vulnerable Consumers in the Digital Single Market*, 33 European Business Law Review, 607-634 (2022) https://doi.org/10.54648/eulr2022028.
51. *Ibid. See also* European Commission, Explanatory Memorandum, Proposal for a Regulation of the European Parliament and of the Council Laying Down Harmonised Rules on Artificial Intelligence (Artificial Intelligence Act) and Amending Certain Union Legislative Acts, COM (2021) 206 final, para. 5.2.3.

in Article 7 AI Act allows the Commission to adopt delegated acts, it only considers vulnerability in a slightly broader way. Article 7(2)(f) AI Act considers the extent to which persons potentially harmed or adversely affected are in a vulnerable position vis-à-vis the user of an AI system, in particular, due to an imbalance of power, knowledge, economic or social circumstances or age. This is a broader notion of vulnerability, but it becomes applicable only if there is a high risk to health, safety or fundamental rights, hence limiting its applicability.[52]

Again, with a view to fostering innovation and competition, the EU recently passed a Regulation on fair access to and use of data (Data Act). It addresses the issue of data concentration in the market and aims to ensure fairness in the allocation of the value of data and to promote its access and use by creating a horizontal and cross-sectoral governance framework. To achieve this goal, the Data Act aims to ensure that a wider range of stakeholders have access to more data for innovative uses. Of relevance here is the isolated mention of consumer vulnerability and the subsequent uninterrupted view of the average consumer by the legislator. The Data Act aims to prevent digital operators from resorting to coercive, deceptive or manipulative means towards users, subverting or impairing their autonomy, decision-making or choices, including through the use of digital interfaces. In this context, they should not rely on so-called dark patterns, i.e., design techniques that mislead consumers into making decisions that have negative consequences for them. Recital 34 of the Data Act merely recognises that such manipulation techniques may be used to persuade users, particularly vulnerable consumers, to engage in undesirable behaviour, to trick them into making decisions in favour of data disclosure operations, or to unduly distort the decision-making process of service users, so as to subvert and impair their autonomy, decision-making and choice.

Turning to the examination of sectoral legislation, the review of the consumer credit directive barely refers to vulnerability, doing so in its explanatory memorandum. First, it acknowledges how the COVID-19 crisis and the ensuing confinement measures accelerated the digital transformation and also had a significant impact on the credit market and consumers, especially vulnerable ones, making many households financially more vulnerable.[53] Moreover, it limits its intervention to debt advice, information and some improvements in creditworthiness standards, although it may be considered that the broadening of its scope to a number of previously excluded loans and new forbearance measures should prove useful in assisting the most vulnerable consumers.[54] The text of the resulting Consumer Credit Directive 2023/2225 is limited to the statement in Recital 76, according to which "the applicable Union framework should give consumers the confidence that creditors and credit intermediaries take account of the interests of the consumer, including their possible vulnerability and difficulties in understanding the product, based on the information available to the creditor or the credit intermediary at the relevant time and on reasonable assumptions about risks to the consumer's situation over the term of the proposed credit agreement."

52. Riefa, *supra* n. 50.
53. Explanatory Memorandum, *supra* n. 51, at 1.
54. *Ibid.*, at 3.

As part of the priorities of the Digital Financial Strategy[55] – the Commission's policy to promote data-driven innovation in the financial sector – the EU aims to create a common financial data space through a number of more specific measures. Of relevance is the priority of creating greater sharing and access to data for reuse in the financial sector, thus paving the way for 'open finance'. Open Finance is intended to be a customer-centric initiative, the cornerstone of which is based on customer control of data. Among the possible legal issues to be analysed, it becomes essential to determine what is the legal condition for the processing of data, as well as the legal means for consumers to be empowered and maintain effective control, if these are the appropriate solutions for effective protection in the digital market.[56] Situations of vulnerability are mentioned only as they concern practices employed by data users to combine new and traditional customer data sources, which must be proportionate to ensure that they do not lead to financial exclusion risks for consumers. The legislative proposal considers in a Recital only practices that lead to a more sophisticated or comprehensive analysis of certain vulnerable segments of consumers, considering such groups as persons with a low income. The reason is that certain practices may increase the risk of unfair conditions or differential pricing practices like the charging of differential premiums. Accordingly, in fact, the potential for exclusion is increased in the provision of products and services that are priced according to the profile of a consumer, notably in credit scoring and the assessment of creditworthiness of natural persons as well for products and services related to the risk assessment and pricing of natural persons in the case of life and health insurance. Thus, given the risks, the use of data for these products and services should be subject to specific requirements to protect consumers and their fundamental rights.[57]

8.5 THE LATENT, DISPOSITIONAL, SYSTEMIC VULNERABILITY OF DIGITAL CONSUMERS

The academic literature has already been active in challenging the status quo and the established concepts of 'consumer' that are grounded in EU consumer law.

Rightly so, EU policy has been criticised for merely updating the existing consumer law acquis guidelines to ensure that consumers benefit from a level of protection and fairness online that is comparable to what they already benefit from offline.[58] This position has been recognised as "short-sighted as it assumes that offline markets work optimally for consumers."[59] Accordingly, for long, it was assumed that fairness would be achieved by relying on information as a remedy, placing expectations on the average consumer and shifting onto them the burden of responsibilities. As

55. A Digital Finance Strategy for the EU, *supra* n. 47.
56. On Open Finance, *see* Federico Ferretti and Peter Petkoff, *Open Finance and Consumer Protection: Uneasy Bedfellows*, 11 Law and Economics Yearly Review, 261-298 (2022).
57. Recital 18, Proposal for a Regulation of the European Parliament and of the Council on a framework for Financial Data Access and amending Regulations (EU) No. 1093/2010, (EU) No. 1094/2010, (EU) No. 1095/2010 and (EU) 2022/2554, COM(2023) 360 final.
58. New Consumer Agenda, *supra* n. 2.
59. Riefa, *supra* n. 50, 617.

the EU moves towards a digital single market, this approach would require radical changes in the concepts and methods used so far to protect consumers.[60]

The starting point is that digital markets are a conductor or breeding ground for a vulnerability that goes beyond the vulnerability based on inherent characteristics conceptualised until now. In principle, all consumers are affected – a feature often stated but seldom studied. The digital reality sharply contrasts with the fictional concept of the average consumer. Rationality is an aspirational state detached from experience. In digital markets, more than in traditional marketplaces, the average consumer encounters structural characteristics of markets where s/he can be expected to act in a manner further away from the idealised behaviour.

Technology itself is a driver of vulnerability, understood not in the fictional legal sense but as an ordinary state that is intrinsic, situational and relational to capture, rather than to limit, various types of vulnerabilities that create imbalances in market interactions. These may also be invisible vulnerabilities. For example, technological and market developments have made the average consumer increasingly dependent on data-driven services, and they find it difficult to make informed choices and understand the effects and consequences of data processing. Legal scholarship has developed the idea of digital vulnerability as a universal state of powerlessness present in the digital environment, where the key trait is in its contextual nature. As Fineman envisages, a growing recognition that external elements create, influence or reinforce vulnerabilities produces a phenomenon that can be identified as 'systemic vulnerability', i.e., a vulnerability created by the system itself, a vulnerability of the individual that derives from the way a system is designed – in other words, from its architecture.[61]

Sources of vulnerability can be identified not only in actual vulnerabilities (those that exist and have already materialised) but also in dispositional ones (those latent and not yet materialised). To begin with, digitalisation accelerates consumption. Another example includes the collection of data which may not harm consumers at the time or in every instant in which they are collected. But the collection of large amounts of data from diverse and unrelated sources, together with their fusion into a profile, may make consumers 'dispositionally' vulnerable. To prevent errors, abuse or unpredictable use, protection should therefore think about the future use of the data and not just the actual use.[62]

Expressions of latent vulnerabilities include the loss of control, the lack of understanding of the impact of technologies not only on the present or future economic sphere but also on the social sphere and deteriorating relationships, the diminishing of one's self, dependence, loss of critical sense and manipulation. From this angle, it may be said that vulnerabilities in the interactions with technologies emerge as a perverse by-product of their benefits. However, since the doctrine has gone even further turning towards the role of structures, vulnerability in the digital society resides also in the

60. Siciliani, Riefa and Gamper, *supra* n. 19.
61. Fineman, *supra* n. 41.
62. Natali Helberger et al., *EU Consumer Protection 2.0, Structured Asymmetries in Digital Consumer Markets* (Brussels, 2021); also in Natali Helberger et al., *Towards Digital Fairness*, 13 Journal of European Consumer and Market Law, 24-30 (2024).

architectures of digital choices in which consumers move on a daily basis, as they are designed to induce or create vulnerabilities. As argued by Helberger et al., such vulnerabilities - whether dispositional or contingent - would not be just an unfortunate by-product of digital markets but indeed the very product of digital markets. Thus, in digital practices, commercial configuration becomes only one part of a broader, systemic approach to influencing consumer behaviour.[63]

A feature of such a systemic vulnerability is that it leads to consumer disempowerment and disengagement, which leads to inertia. For example, digital consumers consent because they have to in order to benefit from the service, they accept lengthy and complex terms and conditions that they do not read (and even if they do so, they would struggle to understand and accept them anyway), they let the algorithm guide them and would not challenge it, they do not read data protection or cookies notices, the place a 'like' to something without knowing the effect on profiling; etc. In this regard, it has been colourfully stressed how 'disengaged' consumers find themselves in vulnerable situations not because of any particular cognitive deficiencies or socio-demographic characteristics but once more because the very structure of the markets in which they evolve leads to 'apathy through obfuscation',[64] numbness or simply routine. From this perspective, disengagement or inertia becomes the norm of the operation of the market. In such cases, it has been concluded that it becomes rational for consumers to disengage.[65]

To the extent that the views of these doctrines are accepted, the average digital consumer turns into a disengaged one - latently, dispositionally, or systemically vulnerable.

8.6 PROSPECTS FOR CONSUMER PROTECTION IN DIGITAL MARKETS

8.6.1 A Paradigm Shift in Regulation?

As extensively noted above, despite its well-documented limitations and numerous criticisms, information remains to this day the main legal instrument of consumer protection.

Here, it is reinforced the argument of that doctrine suggesting that, with the digital marketplaces, the information paradigm is becoming less and less appropriate and, in tandem with this, there is a need to re-evaluate the main notions of consumer law, starting with the legal concept of the 'average' consumer.

As seen above, the current doctrinal debates put forward the importance of not only cognitive limitations but also social constraints, habits, motivations, and architectures.

63. *Ibid.*
64. Siciliani, Riefa and Gamper, *supra* n. 19.
65. *Ibid.*

Accordingly, thus, the normative focus should shift from the definition of average or the identification of particular groups towards the concept of vulnerability established by Fineman and Helberg et al., which leads to the management of the sources of such dispositional vulnerabilities, with digital asymmetries and architectures as the primary sources. To this end, duties to provide essential information would remain important, but procedural fairness as a proxy for protection remains obsolete. This scholarship suggests that the provision of simple, intelligible and essential information should be integrated with the introduction of *ex ante* positive and substantive obligations. Conduct of business rules should be developed to ensure positive duties of fairness on the part of digital traders, who would be required to prove compliance with them. To the extent that the current regulatory wave in digital markets represented by the GDPR, DMA, DSA, Data Act, AI Act, etc., continues with a piecemeal approach that addresses various aspects of the new markets, it does not address digital or architectural asymmetries. Hence, there should be positive obligations on digital providers to operate in a fair manner *ex ante*, fostering digital operations in terms of fairness by design to reduce the causes of dispositional vulnerabilities.[66]

Malgieri and Pasquale argue that with the call for quality control measures prior to the deployment of new digital technologies, an *ex ante* approach could often mitigate and sometimes prevent altogether the harm they cause or contribute to the cause. For instance, a licensing system would be an important *ex ante* regulatory tool in various digital markets. Licensing agencies should require service providers to demonstrate that their digital technologies meet clear requirements for security, non-discrimination, accuracy, appropriateness and correctability before being deployed. Under this model of *ex ante* regulation, developers of new technologies would have the burden of proving that their use is not discriminatory, manipulative, unfair, inaccurate, or illegitimate,[67] even potentially. The scholars recognise that, unlike the regulations applicable to the digital domain to date, such a model is now somehow reflected in the AI Act as a first timid attempt at regulation towards an *ex ante* licensing regime in high-risk areas. This is done through the conformity assessment procedure that providers of high-risk AI systems must perform to demonstrate compliance with various design principles and guarantees, including data governance, integrity and human oversight.[68] However, such a regulatory framework should be strengthened through an extension of its scope and substantive content due to the limited scope of the authorisation model, the lack of transparency of the *ex ante* justification process, and the limited content of the AI Act justification.[69]

Such a call to reconsider consumer law across the various EU acts is justified by the fact that, without it, consumer harms would not only persist but would also risk worsening if consumer distrust in the markets were to assert itself, as well as becoming a limitation for healthy development of the digital economy. Rethinking law in terms of

66. *Ibid.*
67. Gianclaudio Malgieri and Frank Pasquale, *Licensing High-Risk Artificial Intelligence: Toward Ex ante Justification for a Disruptive Technology*, 52 Computer Law & Security Review, 1-18 (2024) https://doi.org/10.1016/j.clsr.2023.105899.
68. *See* Articles 9-15 AI Act.
69. Malgieri and Pasquale, *supra* n. 67.

ex ante obligations by default and architectural fairness by design would lead to ensuring that consumers can be treated fairly, justly or otherwise reasonably, reflecting their true behavioural nature. At the same time, it would empower digital traders by facilitating compliance, supervision and enforcement. Ultimately, fairness in digital markets should be systemic, architectural in nature and not something to be offered to consumers as a remedy after the harm has already occurred, especially if in mass.[70]

Arguably, these theories of *ex ante* regulation and fairness by design and by default are a remarkable intellectual exercise and desirable in principle. However, they underline an increment of the interference of public law in private law relationship, an area that has been witnessing a continuous erosion of contractual autonomy. To many, it could be hard to digest an additional layer of paternalism vis-à-vis freedom and autonomy, especially in new markets characterised by global competition where the EU is already lagging behind. An agreement in this direction would be particularly challenging to achieve at EU level, where political views of national States may not be so aligned.

At a more particular level, these theories appear too radical to find implementation. They are too far away from the reality of the current and upcoming legal infrastructure of consumer law and regulation of digital markets, which would require an improbable overturning of the entire EU legal architecture and economic underpinnings. If a criticism may be moved beyond their intellectual enlightenment, they appear too sweeping to be practicable and lack pragmatism. The EU has just enacted an important wave of norms in a different direction, with a degree of continuity with traditional consumer law, and more is already in the pipeline.

In addition, it is unclear how *ex ante* provisions would need to look like to tackle the multitude of practices and problems in diverse markets in continuous evolution. One should also be wary of non-secondary implications of undesirable standardisation effects and repercussions on restraints on competition and innovation. *Ex ante* regulation of digital markets and pre-emptive architectural design would also need to engage in a race against technology that – as known – the legislator will never match. Similarly, *ex ante* regulation and architectural fairness would require a system of supervision and enforcement that requires resources and skills that regulators simply do not – and most probably will never – have.

8.6.2 The Re-evaluation of the Notion of 'Consumer' under EU Law

Taking a more modest but practical line without disregarding the thoughtful findings of the recent literature, it is maintained that the law should rather recognise that in the dynamics of digital markets, the average consumer is vulnerable by default or, in other words, a second layer of latent/dispositional vulnerability represents the new standard of the 'average' consumer.

This implies that only certain notions of consumer law and the way they are conceived would need to change, not the entire normative paradigm.

70. Riefa, *supra* n. 50.

In this last regard, there is a modest prospect in sight with a request for a preliminary ruling to the CJEU by the Italian Council of State, asking whether the notion of the 'average consumer', understood as a normally informed and reasonably observant and circumspect consumer, should not be rather formulated with reference to the best science and experience of the most recent theories on 'bounded rationality', suggesting that all consumers have a basic level of vulnerability (an ordinary vulnerability).[71]

The concept of bounded rationality is still far from the evolutions of dispositional vulnerability studied above. In a simpler manner, it posits that, in general, individuals are limited in their capacity to assimilate complex information, and they do not engage with all of the information available to them.[72] These theories aim to show how people often act by reducing the necessary information with decisions that are unreasonable when compared to those that would be taken by a hypothetically attentive and circumspect subject. These findings impose a greater need for consumer protection in the cases, increasingly recurrent in modern market dynamics, of dangers of cognitive conditioning.[73]

Under this view, supported by the Advocate General of the EU, the 'average consumer' is not necessarily an individual who corresponds to the model of the *homo economicus* as the average consumer. Instead, since the concept of 'average consumer' is not a statistical test but depends on the evolution of the case law of the CJEU and needs to consider social, cultural and linguistic factors, it should be considered flexible enough to be perceived as an individual with bounded rationality.[74]

In short, under this prospect, in certain circumstances, the *homo economicus*, who is the average consumer, has bounded rationality.

If confirmed by the CJEU, the 'flexibility' introduced to the benchmark of the average consumer might in principle have enabled national courts to offer more protection in markets that are particularly complex. Such an interpretation could prima facie have represented a step forward in the protection of the digital consumer, especially if one considers that bounded rationality presupposes a degree of vulnerability.

71. Case C-646/22, *Request for a Preliminary Ruling from the Consiglio di Stato (Italy)*, lodged on 13 October 2022 – *Compass Banca SpA v. Autorità Garante della Concorrenza e del Mercato*, OJ C 24, 28-29.
72. For all, *see, e.g.*, Matthew Adler, *Bounded Rationality and Legal Scholarship*, University of Pennsylvania, Institute for Law & Economic Research Paper No. 08-03 (19 February 2008), available at SSRN: https: http://dx.doi.org/10.2139/ssrn.1095874 and the literature therein cited.
73. Herbert Simon, *Models of Man: Social and Rational- Mathematical Essays on Rational Human Behavior in a Social Setting* (Wiley & Sons 1957); Daniel Kahneman, *Maps of Bounded Rationality: Psychology for Behavioral Economics*, 93 The American Economic Review, 1449-1475 (2003) https://doi.org/10.1257/000282803322655392. However, note that Gerd Gigerenzer and Wolfgang Gaissmaier, *Heuristic Decision Making*, 62 Annual Review of Psychology, 451-482 (2011) https://doi.org/10.1146/annurev-psych-120709-145346 have critised the misuse of the term as economic rationality has mistakenly taken as the benchmark for human decision-making and thereby it is attached an overly pessimistic view of heuristics and human rationality to it.
74. Opinion of Mr Advocate General Emiliou in Case C–646/22, *Compass Banca SpA v. Autorità Garante della Concorrenza e del Mercato*, ECLI:EU:C:2024:367.

At the same time, it could be argued that this still would have been a limited prospect as digital vulnerability suggests the existence of that additional layer of vulnerability first studied above, where consumers are more than ordinarily vulnerable. Instead, there should be the recognition of that dispositional vulnerability put forward by the scholarship.

Instead, the CJEU ruled that:

> the concept of 'average consumer', within the meaning of that directive, must be defined by reference to a consumer who is reasonably well-informed and reasonably observant and circumspect. Such a definition does not, however, exclude the possibility that an individual's decision-making capacity may be impaired by constraints, such as cognitive biases.[75]

Hence, the ruling substantially reaffirms the traditional definition of the 'average consumer' as a fictive, rational actor. However, the CJEU acknowledges that consumer decisions are often influenced by contextual factors, including cognitive biases. These insights do not fundamentally alter the traditional image of the average consumer. However, the judgment recognises that cognitive biases can influence consumer behaviour, and it holds that national courts must consider such biases. In so deciding, the CJEU adds a not conclusive annotation to the notion of the 'average consumer'. As before, the average consumer is indeed "observant and circumspect" but only "reasonably," which allows a significant leeway and degree of flexibility. National Courts will have to assess, under the specific circumstances of a case, to what extent the practice in question could materially and demonstrably distort the behaviour of the consumer. In practice, they will have to balance the fictional idea of the average consumer with the reality of cognitive biases, ensuring that protections remain robust against sophisticated commercial business models and practices. The question moving forward is to what extent this balance between theory and practice is fit to adequately safeguard consumers in sophisticated markets such as digital ones.

Arguably, a more realistic consumer protection approach could have been achieved if the CJEU conceded straight away – if not on this occasion in others to come – that the bounded rationality of consumers is the new default position without any 'flexibility', at least in those highly specialised markets characterised by system complexity, such as the digital ones, where they are dispositionally vulnerable. This recognition should occur without having to clarify under which circumstances national courts could or should use empirical evidence on consumer decision-making in each situation. Therefore, the concept of 'flexibility' advanced by the Advocate General – to some extent confirmed by the CJEU – should require future correction by the CJEU, affirming instead the precise delimitation and acknowledgment of consumers' dispositional vulnerability in certain markets. Failing that, the prospect of bounded rationality posited by the Advocate General not only remains conceptually limited but would be problematic to be operationalised under the various and diverse commercial practices of different markets, offline and online. It would prove too intricate and

75. Case C-646/22, *Compass Banca SpA v. Autorità Garante della Concorrenza e del Mercato*, ECLI:EU:C:2024:957.

undesirable to think of a consumer law regime where national courts need to interpret the average consumer benchmark as 'flexible' within a discretion given to them by the CJEU.

In short, the judicial renewal of the notion of the average consumer, with a universalistic one affirming that s/he is dispositionally vulnerable and has bounded rationality, would be a more practicable implementation in the current consumer law regime with more tangible important implications in the protection of consumers in digital markets. Maintaining the fundamental architecture of consumer law, a redefinition of the average consumer could entail a scaling down in the importance of information provision and a 'fairer' unfairness test, which could grant a more realistic approach to protecting consumers in digital markets.

Concretely, such an approach would entail a pragmatic compromise that requires a reinterpretation of existing rules where protection is afforded regardless of consumers being duly informed.

Powerful legal instruments in the digital sphere could be the UCTD[76] and the UCPD.[77] Their context-dependent application in light of a novel interpretation of the average dispositionally vulnerable consumer (who has bounded rationality) could lead the judiciary to scrutinise the unilaterally imposed policies, terms and conditions, data processing operations, and execution of digital providers. Certain unfair commercial practices, such as those contrary to the requirements of that context-dependent professional diligence or that materially distort or are likely to materially distort the economic behaviour of the new average consumer, would be considered downright banned.[78] Hence, the manner in which products or services are presented to customers or data are used could play a key role in the assessment of whether a provider's commercial practice is 'unfair'.

Equally, unfair terms shall not be binding on the average dispositionally vulnerable consumer and the contract shall continue to bind the parties only to the extent that it is capable of continuing in existence without the unfair terms.[79] The manner in which products or services are presented to consumers by the trader could be considered capable of materially distorting their behaviour because they have bounded rationality and cannot process the information rationally. What was good for the old average consumer may no longer be good for the new one because s/he is not reasonably well-informed and attentive as a default position. To some extent, this is also what the AI Act provides for algorithms by prohibiting outright a number of AI practices (albeit, in this case, limited to physical or psychological harm or other detrimental treatments - *sic!*).[80]

The concept of 'average consumer' depends on the evolution of the case law of the CJEU, and the average consumer test is not a statistical one.[81] The UCPD and the UCTD already provide for substantial case law and examples where the judiciary has

76. Directive on unfair terms in consumer contracts, *supra* n. 13.
77. *Supra* n. 12.
78. Article 5 UCPD.
79. Article 6 UCTD.
80. Article 5 AI Act.
81. E.g., *see* Recital 18 UCPD.

been proactive in developing EU consumer law. The activist role of the CJEU in the control of unfair practices or unfair terms in context-dependent circumstances is not novel. Take the case law in the financial services market in the aftermath of the economic crisis, which erupted in 2008 and hit hard a large number of consumers. In Aziz[82] and the related cases, the CJEU provided a novel interpretation of the UCTD establishing a collective dimension far beyond individual litigation, and its remedies had a broader impact on market regulation.[83]

With all due differences and peculiarities, the CJEU may have a likely chance to take once again an activist role in the regulation of digital markets and the protection of consumers.

8.7 ADAPTING THE LEGAL BENCHMARKS OF AN 'AVERAGE CONSUMER'

In the policy narrative and intentions of the EU, consumers should be empowered further and be placed at the centre of digital markets as arbiters. Thus, it is not surprising that the resulting regulatory acts remain permeated with old concepts and paradigms of consumer law that have emerged over time under similar premises, notwithstanding the persistent criticisms of legal scholarship.

Even the European Commission has started to show awareness of the problem. The findings of the latest Fitness Check that it has conducted suggest that:

> the growing mismatch between the normative abstraction of the 'average consumer' and the realities of consumer behaviour in the digital environment undermines the effectiveness of EU consumer law. Consumers have limited comprehension about digital commercial practices, such as the functioning of the data collection ecosystem and algorithmic processes, coupled with their limited bargaining power and the constant exposure to information overload and dark patterns that target their behavioural biases. Consumers have adapted to this environment by paying less attention, agreeing to contract terms without reading them and accepting 'all cookies' against their own preference. Contrary to the premise underlying the average consumer standard, they are generally not in a position to bargain with the trader or to negotiate any terms.[84]

Nonetheless, despite such a recognition and the radical changes and unconventional features of digital markets, the EU legal framework currently being designed is not departing from its traditional and inflexible standard of consumer behaviour grounded on the ideal of the average consumer.

The EU now calls for a forthcoming Digital Fairness Act as a legislative follow-up "to tackle unethical techniques and commercial practices related to dark patterns,

82. Case C–415/11, *Mohamed Aziz v. Caixa d'Estalvis de Catalunya, Tarragona i Manresa (Catalunyacaixa)*, ECLI:EU:C:2013:164.
83. Hans Micklitz and Norbert Reich, *The Court and Sleeping Beauty: The Revival of the Unfair Contract Terms Directive (UCTD)*, 51 Common Market Law Review, 771-808 (2014) https://doi.org/10.54648/cola2014061.
84. Commission Staff Working Document, Fitness Check on EU consumer law on digital fairness, SWD(2024) 230 final, p. 46.

marketing by social media influencers, the addictive design of digital products and online profiling, especially when consumer vulnerabilities are exploited for commercial purposes."[85]

Yet, a leitmotiv of this book is the issue of over-regulation and the problems of coordination, inconsistency, and legal uncertainty of a regulatory patchwork.

The latest doctrinal debates point to a novel regulatory approach *ex ante* and the establishment of duties of digital and architectural fairness by design and by default. Rather than regulating by making a distinction between systems or between groups of consumers and their capacity, it would be more appropriate to focus on digital asymmetries. This would require the recognition of the concepts of dispositional and digital vulnerability cherished by Fineman and Helberger et al., respectively. These concepts describe a universal state of inability to defend oneself and unavoidable susceptibility to imbalances of economic power, in addition to the potential exploitation typical of increasing commercial automation, data governance and data processing relationships, and the architecture of the digital markets themselves.[86] Accordingly, it is put forward the desirability of a regulation that, recognising such vulnerability, would not focus on attempts to give it a definition but would turn to counter its sources *ex ante*, with obligations of fairness by design and by default. This would not only meet the need for fairness in protecting the weak party in the contractual synallagma at a particularly critical socio-economic moment in history but would also foster the confidence in the markets that is essential for their expansion.

This study considered that such an approach is a remarkable intellectual exercise and has merit, but it would hardly find consensus and falls short of pragmatism and attainability, thus leading to the status quo. It is currently not reflected in the EU legislative discussions and intervention addressing isolated matters of relevance to consumers, although with difficult coordination with the consumer law acquis.

Ever-growing paternalistic interferences of public law in the private law sphere of autonomy and contractual freedom may not be easily digested by many and would shove in the opposite direction of free markets and market economy of the EU.

Also, *ex ante* regulation and obligations of architectural fairness – no matter how problematic their design will be – may turn into a frustrating exercise when faced with ever-changing technologies and innovation in a globally competitive environment that sees the EU already lagging behind.

Instead, to support the legal discussion in protecting consumers in digital markets, it needs to consider the continuing relevance of the existing law, which can still be turned into a valuable asset. The legal reinterpretation of the concept of the 'average consumer' in terms of latent or dispositional vulnerability may be sufficient. Updating existing consumer benchmarks to reflect behavioural insights in markets characterised by novel systems should become the central issue in EU consumer law.

---

85. President of the European Commission Ursula Von der Leyen, *'Mission Letter' to Commissioner-designate for Democracy, Justice, Rule of Law* (Brussels, 17 September 2024), available at https://commission.europa.eu/document/download/907fd6b6-0474-47d7-99da-47007ca30d02_en?filename=Mission%20letter%20-%20McGRATH.pdf.
86. Helberg et al., *supra* n. 62.

To some extent, this need has finally reached the CJEU, and a decision is expected soon.

Although with a degree of scepticism, it longs here that the CJEU will have to be brave with a seminal decision recognising without degrees of flexibility the new standard of the average consumer as dispositionally vulnerable, bearing an ensuing bounded rationality to be applied in the framework of the current consumer law regime to be coordinated with the new wave of regulations of EU digital markets.

Bibliography

Aaron Perzanowski and Jason Schultz, *The End of Ownership. Personal Property in the Digital Economy* (MIT Press 2016).

Adam Moore, *Intangible Property: Privacy, Power, and Information Control*, 35 American Philosophical Quarterly, 365-378 (1998).

Alan Westin, *Privacy and Freedom* (Atheneum 1967).

Alberto De Franceschi and Michael Lehmann, *Data as Tradable Commodity and New Measures for their Protection*, 1 Italian Law Journal, 51-72 (2015).

Alberto Orlando, *La regolamentazione del deepfake in Europa, Stati Uniti e Cina*, Special Issue I/2024 – Media Laws, no page numbers (2025), available at https://www.medialaws.eu/rivista/la-regolamentazione-del-deepfake-in-europa-stati-uniti-e-cina/#_ftn2.

Alessandro Ortalda and Stefano Leucci, *Identità digitale e protezione dei dati personali: punti di incontro e rischi nelle discipline eIDAS e RGPD*, in *La internet governance e le sfide della trasformazione digitale*, 145-155 (Laura Abba, Adriana Lazzaroni and Marina Pietrangelo eds, 4 Rivista Italiana di Informatica e Diritto 2022).

Amos Tversky and Daniel Khaneman, *Judgment under Uncertainty: Heuristics and Biases*, 185 Science, 1124-1131 (1974).

Amos Tversky and Daniel Khaneman, *Loss Aversion in Riskless Choice: A Reference Dependent Model*, 106 Quarterly Journal of Economics, 1039-1061 (1991).

Andrea Lista, *EU Competition Law and the Financial Services Sector* (Informa Law 2013).

Andreas Wiebe, *Protection of Industrial Data: A New Property Right for the Digital Economy?*, 12 Journal of Intellectual Property Law & Practice, 62-71 (2017).

Angus Johnston, *Seeking the EU 'Consumer' in Services of General Economic Interest*, in *The Images of the Consumer in EU Law: Legislation, Free Movement and Competition Law*, 93-138 (Dorota Leczykiewicz and Stephen Weatherill eds, Hart Publishing 2018).

Anna De Giuli, *Sul concetto di 'vulnerabilità' secondo la Corte di Giustizia UE*, 1 Diritto Penale e Uomo, 1-19 (2020).

Anne Helmond, *The Platformization of the Web: Making Web Data Platform Ready*, 1 Social Media + Society, no pages (2015).

Annette Rouvroy and Yves Poullet, *The Right to Informational Self-Determination and the Value of Self-Development: Reassessing the Importance of Privacy for Democracy*, in *Reinventing Data Protection?*, 45-76 (Serge Gutwirth et al. eds, Springer 2009).

Antonio Capobianco, *Information Exchange under EC Competition Law*, 41 Common Market Law Review, 1247-1276 (2004).

Antti Aine, Tom Bjorkroth and Aki Koponen, *Horizontal Information Exchange and Innovation in the Platform Economy: A Need to Rethink?*, 15 European Competition Journal, 347-371 (2019).

Arno Lodder and Andrew Murray, *EU Regulation of E-Commerce: A Commentary* (Edward Elgar 2022).

Arno Lodder, *European Union E-Commerce Directive: Article by Article Comments (2017). Guide to European Union Law on E-Commerce, Update from 2016 (Published 2017) of the 2001 (Published 2002) Version, Published in EU Regulation of E-Commerce. A Commentary Elgar Commentaries series*, 15-58 (2017), available at SSRN: https://ssrn.com/abstract=1009945.

Article 29 Working Party, *Guidelines on the Right to Data Portability* (Adopted on 13 December 2016, last Revised and adopted on 5 April 2017).

Article 29 Working Party, *Opinion 4/2007 on the Concept of Personal Data* (20 June 2007).

Aysem Vanberg and Mehmet Unver, *The Right to Data Portability in the GDPR and EU Competition Law: Odd Couple or Dynamic Duo?*, 8 European Journal of Law and Technology, 1-22 (2017).

Barbara Engels, *Data Portability Amongst Online Platforms*, 5 Internet Policy Review, 1-17 (2016).

Barbara Evans, *Much Ado About Data Ownership*, 25 Harvard Journal of Law and Technology, 70-130 (2011).

Barbara Lazarotto, *The Right to Data Portability: A Holistic Analysis of GDPR, DMA and the Data Act*, 15 European Journal of Law and Technology, no pages (2024).

Barrington Moore, *Privacy: Studies in Social and Cultural History* (Routledge 1984).

Bart van der Sloot, *Editorial*, 3 European Data Protection Law Review, 351-357 (2021).

Bart van der Sloot, *Regulating Non-personal Data in the Age of Big Data*, in *Health Data Privacy under the GDPR*, 85-105 (Maria Tzanou ed., 2020).

Bernt Hugenholtz, *Implementing the European Database Directive*, in *Intellectual Property and Information Law. Essays in Honour of Herman Cohen Jehoram*, 183-199 (Jan Kabel and Gerard Mom eds, Kluwer law International 1998).

Bernt Hugenholtz, *Something Completely Different: Europe's Sui Generis Database Right Book*, in *The Internet and the Emerging Importance of New Forms of Intellectual Property*, 205-222 (Susy Frankel and Daniel Gervais eds, Wolters Kluwer 2016).

BEUC, *EU Consumers' 2020 Vision* (2012), available at https://www.beuc.eu/publications/2012-00316-01-e.pdf.

Billie Turner II et al., *A Framework for Vulnerability Analysis Unsustainability Science*, 100 Proceedings of the National Academy of Sciences of the United States of America, 8074-8079 (2003).

Bloomberg, *Metaverse May Be $800 Billion Market, Next Tech Platform* (1 December 2021), available at https://www.bloomberg.com/professional/insights/trading/metaverse-may-be-800-billion-market-next-tech-platform/.

Bram Duivenvoorde, *The Liability of Online Marketplaces under the Unfair Commercial Practices Directive, the E-commerce Directive and the Digital Services Act*, 2 Journal of European Consumer and Market Law, 43-52 (2022).

Carly Nyst, Steve Pannifer, Edgar Whitley and Paul Makin, *Digital Identity: Issue Analysis* (2016), available at https://chyp.com/wp-content/uploads/2020/06/PRJ.1578-Digital-Identity-Issue-Analysis-Report-v1_6-1.pdf.

Caroline Cauffman and Catalina Goanta, *A New Order: The Digital Services Act and Consumer Protection*, 12 European Journal of Risk Regulation, 758-774 (2021).

Chaim Zins, *Conceptual Approaches for Defining Data, Information, and Knowledge*, 58 Journal of the Association for Information Science and Technology, 479-493 (2007).

Chantal Mak, *Fundamental Rights in European Contract Law: A Comparison of the Impact of Fundamental Rights on Contractual Relationships in Germany, the Netherlands, Italy and England* (Kluwer Law International 2008).

Charles Fried, *An Anatomy of Values: Problems of Personal and Social Choice* (Harvard University Press 1970).

Christine Riefa and Harriet Gamper, *Economic Theory and Consumer Vulnerability: Exploring an Uneasy Relationship*, in *Vulnerable Consumers and the Law: Consumer Protection and Access to Justice*, 17-30 (Christine Riefa and Severine Saintier eds, Routledge 2020).

Christine Riefa and Severine Saintier, *In Search of (Access to) Justice for Vulnerable Consumers*, in *Vulnerable Consumers and the Law: Consumer Protection and Access to Justice*, 1-16 (Christine Riefa and Severine Saintier eds, Routledge 2021).

Christine Riefa, *Protecting Vulnerable Consumers in the Digital Single Market*, 33 European Business Law Review, 607-634 (2022).

Christopher Allen, *The Path to Self-Sovereign Identity*, no pages (26 April 2016), available at https://www.lifewithalacrity.com/article/the-path-to-self-sovererei gn-identity/#fn:20.

Christopher Busch and Vanessa Mak, *Putting the Digital Services Act in Context: Bridging the Gap Between EU Consumer Law and Platform Regulation*, 3 Journal of European Consumer and Market Law, 109-115 (2021).

Christopher Kuner et al., *When Two Worlds Collide: The Interface Between Competition Law and Data Protection*, 4 International Data Privacy Law, 247-248 (2014).

Colleen Cunningham, Florian Ederer and Song Ma, *Killer Acquisitions*, 129 Journal of Political Economy, 649-702 (2019).

Commission Staff Working Document Fitness Check on EU consumer law on digital fairness, SWD(2024) 230 final.

Commission Staff Working Document on the free flow of data and emerging issues of the European data economy Accompanying the document Communication Building a European data economy, SWD/2017/02 final.

Commission Staff Working Document, Guidance on sharing private sector data in the European data economy Accompanying the document Communication from the Commission to the European Parliament, the Council, the European economic and social Committee and the Committee of the Regions "Towards a common European data space," SWD(2018) 125 final.

Commission Staff Working Document, Fitness Check on EU consumer law on digital fairness, SWD(2024) 230 final.

Communication from the Commission to the European Parliament and the Council, New Consumer Agenda. Strengthening consumer resilience for sustainable recovery, COM/2020/696 final.

Communication from the Commission to the European Parliament, the Council, the European Economic and Social Committee and the Committee of the Regions, 'Towards a common European data space', COM/2018/232 final.

Communication from the Commission to the European Parliament, the Council, the European Economic and Social Committee and the Committee of the Regions, '2030 Digital Compass: the European way for the Digital Decade', COM(2021) 118 final.

Communication from the Commission to the European Parliament, the Council, the European Economic and Social Committee and the Committee of the Regions, A Digital Finance Strategy for the EU, COM/2020/591 final.

Communication from the Commission to the European Parliament, the Council, the European Economic and Social Committee and the Committee of the Regions, A Retail Payments Strategy for the EU, COM/2020/592 final.

Cosmo Graham, *EU and UK Competition Law* (Pearson Education 2013).

Council of Europe, *Declaration by Committee of Ministers on the Manipulative Capabilities of Algorithmic Processes*, Meeting of the Ministers' Deputies (February 2019), available at www.coe.int.

Council of Europe, *Explanatory Report to the Convention for the Protection of Individuals with regard to Automatic Processing of Personal Data* (Strasbourg, 28 January1981).

Council of the European Union, *General Secretariat, Metaverse: Virtual World, Real Challenges*, (March 2022), available at https://www.consilium.europa.eu/media/54987/metaverse-paper-9-march-2022.pdf.

Cristina Poncibò, *AI Platforms: Safeguarding Consumer Rights in the EU*, in *The Cambridge Handbook of AI and Consumer Law: Comparative Perspectives*, 236-251 (Larry Di Matteo, Cristina Poncibò and Geraint Howells eds, Cambridge University Press 2024).

Cristina Poncibò, *Il consumatore medio*, Contratto Impresa Europa, 756-757 (2007).

Daniel Gervais, *Exploring the Interfaces Between Big data and Intellectual Property Law*, 10 Journal of Intellectual Property, Information Technology and E-Commerce Law, 3-19 (2019).

Daniel Kahneman, *Maps of Bounded Rationality: Psychology for Behavioral Economics*, 93 The American Economic Review, 1449-1475 (2003).
Daniel Khaneman and Amos Tversky, *Prospect Theory: An Analysis of Decision under Risk*, 47 Econometrica, 263-292 (1979).
Daniel Rubinfeld and Michal Gal, *Access Barriers to Big Data*, 59 Arizona Law Review, 339-381 (2017).
David Banisar and Simon Davies, *Global Trends in Privacy Protection: An International Survey of Privacy, Data Protection, and Surveillance Laws and Developments*, 18 John Marshall Journal of Computer & Information Law, 1-111 (1999).
Dorothee Heisenberg, *Negotiating Privacy* (Lynne Rienner, 2005).
Duncan MacDonald, *Myths in the Privacy Debate*, in *The Future of Financial Privacy*, 54-75 (CEI Staff ed., Competitive Enterprise Institute 2000).
Edouard Bruc, *Data as an Essential Facility in European Law: How to Define the 'Target' Market and Divert the Data Pipeline?*, 15 European Competition Journal, 177-224 (2019).
Edward Bloustein, *Privacy as an Aspect of Human Dignity: An Answer to Dean Prosser*, 39 New York University Law Review, 962-1007 (1964).
Edward Castranova, *Theory of the Avatar*, CESifo Working Paper No. 863 (February 2023), available at https://www.cesifo.org/en/publications/2003/working-paper/theory-avatar#: ~ :text = A%20human%20being%20experiences%20these,body%20in%20the%20virtual%20world.
Ellen Frankel Paul, Fred Miller and Jeffrey Paul (eds), *The Right of Privacy* (Cambridge University Press 2000).
European Commission Communication, An EU Initiative on Web 4.0 and Virtual Worlds: A Head Starts in the Next Technological Transition, COM (2023) 442/ final.
European Commission, 'A Europe Fit for the Digital Age', available from https://ec.europa.eu/commission/priorities/digital-single-market_en.
European Commission, 'European Health Data Space', available at https://ec.europa.eu/health/ehealth/dataspace_en.
European Commission, A Digital Single Market Strategy for Europe, (Communication) COM (2015) 0192 final.
European Commission, A European Strategy for Data, (Communication) COM (2020) 66 final.
European Commission, Building a European Data Economy, (Communication) COM (2017) 9 final.
European Commission, Commission Communication, Amendments to the Communication from the Commission: Guidance on the Commission's Enforcement Priorities in Applying Article 82 of the EC Treaty to Abusive Exclusionary Conduct by Dominant Undertakings, 2023/C 116/01, OJ C116/1, 31th March 2023.
European Commission, Commission Notice on Cooperation within the Network of Competition Authorities, April 2004, OJ C 101, 27.4.2004, pp. 43-53.
European Commission, Communication from the Commission Amendments to the Communication from the Commission: Guidance on the Commission's

Enforcement Priorities in Applying Article 82 of the EC Treaty to Abusive Exclusionary Conduct by Dominant Undertakings (Text with EEA relevance) 2023/C 116/01, OJ C 116, 31.3.2023, pp. 1-5.

European Commission, Communication from the Commission Guidance on the Application of the Referral Mechanism Set Out in Article 22 of the Merger Regulation to Certain Categories of Cases 2021/C 113/01, OJ C 113, 31.3.2021.

European Commission, Communication from the Commission to the European Parliament, the European Council, the Council, the European Economic and Social Committee and the Committee of the Regions on Artificial Intelligence for Europe, 25 April 2018, in https://digital-strategy.ec.europa.eu/en/library/communication-artificial-intelligence-europe.

European Commission, Consumer Vulnerability Across Key Markets in the European Union (January 2016), available at https://op.europa.eu/en/publication-detail/-/publication/79b42553-de14-11e6-ad7c-01aa75ed71a1.

European Commission, 'Data Act Explained', available at https://digital-strategy.ec.europa.eu/en/factpages/data-act-explained.

European Commission, 'Digital Agenda 2014-2017' (14 November 2014), available at https://digital-strategy.ec.europa.eu/en/library/digitale-agenda-2014-2017.

European Commission, 'Ethics Guidelines for Trustworthy AI' (8 April 2019), available at https://digital-strategy.ec.europa.eu/en/library/ethics-guidelines-trustworthy-ai.

European Commission, Explanatory Memorandum to COM(2019)250: Guidance on the Regulation on a Framework for the Free Flow of Non-personal Data in the EU, COM(2019)250.

European Commission, Explanatory Memorandum, Proposal for a Regulation of the European Parliament and of the Council on Harmonised Rules on Fair Access to and Use of Data (Data Act), COM(2022) 68 final.

European Commission, Explanatory Memorandum, Proposal for a Regulation of the European Parliament and of the Council on a Single Market for Digital Services (Digital Services Act) and amending Directive 2000/31/EC, COM(2020) 825 final.

European Commission, Explanatory Memorandum, Proposal for a Regulation of the European Parliament and of the Council Laying Down Harmonised Rules on Artificial Intelligence (Artificial Intelligence Act) and Amending Certain Union Legislative Acts, COM(2021) 206 final.

European Commission, 'Impact Assessment Report and Support Studies Accompanying the Proposal for a Data Act', available from https://digital-strategy.ec.europa.eu/en/library/impact-assessment-report-and-support-studies-accompanying-proposal-data-act.

European Commission, Inception Impact Assessment, Digital Services Act Package: *Ex Ante* Regulatory Instrument for Large Online Platforms with Significant Network Effects Acting as Gatekeepers in the European Union's Internal Market (2020) 2877647, (June 2020).

European Commission, 'People, Technologies & Infrastructure: Europe's Plan to Thrive in the Metaverse I'. Blog of Commissioner Thierry Breton (14 September 2022),

available at https://ec.europa.eu/commission/presscorner/detail/es/STATEME NT_22_5525.
European Commission, 'Platform-to-Business Trading Practices', available at https://digital-strategy.ec.europa.eu/en/policies/platform-business-trading-practices.
European Commission, 'Recovery Plan for Europe', available at https://commission.europa.eu/strategy-and-policy/recovery-plan-europe_en.
European Commission, 'Shaping Europe's Digital Future' (2021), available at https://ec.europa.eu/info/strategy/priorities-2019-2024/europe-fit-digital-age/shaping-europe-digital-future_en.
European Commission, 'Smart Cities', available at https://commission.europa.eu/eu-regional-and-urban-development/topics/cities-and-urban-development/city-ini tiatives/smart-cities_en.
European Commission, 'Targeted Consultation on Open Finance Framework and Data Sharing in the Financial Sector', available at https://finance.ec.europa.eu/reg ulation-and-supervision/consultations/finance-2022-open-finance_en.
European Commission, 'The Virtual and Augmented Reality Industrial Coalition', available at https://digital-strategy.ec.europa.eu/en/policies/virtual-and-augm ented-reality-coalition.
European Commission, 'Towards a Thriving Data-Driven Economy', COM (2014) 442 final.
European Commission, 'White Paper on Artificial Intelligence: a European Approach to Excellence and Trust' (19 February 2020), available at https://commission.eur opa.eu/publications/white-paper-artificial-intelligence-european-approach-exce llence-and-trust_en.
European Consumer Summit 2022 held on 10 February 2022 under the French Presidency in cooperation with the European Commission, available at https://european-consumer-summit-2022.b2match.io/.
European Consumer Summit 2023 held on 28 March 2023 under the Swedish Presidency in cooperation with the European Commission, available at https://eism ea.ec.europa.eu/events/european-consumer-summit-2023-2023-03-28_en.
European Consumer Summit 2024 held on 18 April 2024 under the Belgian Presidency in cooperation with the European Commission, available at https://consumer-summit-2024.b2match.io/.
European Council, Algorithms and Human Rights. Study on the human rights dimensions of automated data processing techniques and possible regulatory implications, DGI(2017)12, available at https://rm.coe.int/algorithms-and-human-rig hts-en-rev/16807956b5.
European Data Protection Supervisor, Opinion 3/2020 on the European strategy for data (16 June 2020).
European Parliament, Digital Transformation. Briefing EU Policies: Delivering for Citizens, available at https://www.europarl.europa.eu/RegData/etudes/BRIE/2019/633171/EPRS_BRI(2019)633171_EN.pdf.
European Parliament, Quali sono i rischi e i vantaggi dell'intelligenza artificiale?, (28 June 2023), available at https://www.europarl.europa.eu/pdfs/news/expert/2020/9/story/20200918STO87404/20200918STO87404_it.pdf.

European Parliamentary Research Service (EPRS), Virtual words (metaverses), no date, available at https://www.europarl.europa.eu/RegData/etudes/ATAG/2023/751408/EPRS_ATA(2023)751408_EN.pdf.

Europol, Policing in the Metaverse: What Law Enforcement Needs to Know (2022), available at https://www.europol.europa.eu/publications-events/publications/policing-in-metaverse-what-law-enforcement-needs-to-know.

Fabiana Di Porto, Daniel Foà, *Defining Virtual Worlds: Main Features and Regulatory Challenges,* Centre on Regulation in Europe (CERRE) (July 2023), available at https://cerre.eu/publications/defining-virtual-worlds-main-features-and-regulatory-challenges/.

Feder Cooper, Emanuel Moss, Benjamin Laufer, Helen Nissenbaum, *Accountability in an Algorithmic Society: Relationality, Responsibility, and Robustness in Machine Learning,* ACM Conference on Fairness, Accountability, and Transparency, 864-76 (2022), available at https://dl.acm.org/doi/10.1145/3531146.3533150.

Federico Casolari, Carlotta Buttaboni, Luciano Floridi, *The EU Data Act in Context: A Legal Assessment,* 31 International Journal of Law and Information Technology, 399-412 (2023).

Federico Ferretti and Peter Petkoff, *Open Finance and Consumer Protection: Uneasy Bedfellows,* 11 Law and Economics Yearly Review, 261-298 (2022).

Federico Ferretti, *Competition, the Consumer Interest, and Data Protection* (Springer 2014).

Federico Ferretti, *Data Protection and the Legitimate Interest of Data Controllers: Much Ado About Nothing or the Winter of Rights?* 51 Common Market Law Review, 843-868 (2014).

Felipe Romero-Moreno, *Deepfake Fraud Detection: Safeguarding Trust in Generative AI* (2024), available at https://papers.ssrn.com/sol3/papers.cfm?abstract_id=5031627.

Ferdinand Schoeman (ed.), *Philosophical Dimensions of Privacy: An Anthology* (Cambridge University Press 1984).

Fiona Fui-Hoon Nah, Ruilin Zheng, Jinjyuan Cai, Keng Siau, Langtao Chen, *Generative AI and ChatGPT: Applications, Challenges, and AI-human Collaboration,* 25 Journal of Information Technology Case and Application Research, 277-304 (2023).

Florent Thouvenin and Aurelia Tamò-Larrieux, *Data Ownership and Data Access Rights,* in *Big Data and Global Trade Law,* 316-339 (Mira Burri ed., Cambridge University Press 2021).

Francesco Banterle, *Data Ownership in the Data Economy: a European Dilemma,* in *EU Internet Law in the Digital Era,* 199-225 (Tatiana-Eleni Synodinou et al. eds., Springer 2020).

Francesco Mezzanotte, *Access to Data: The Role of Consent and the Licensing Scheme,* in *Trading Data in the Digital Economy: Legal Concepts and Tools,* 159-187 (Sebastian Lohsse, Reiner Schulze and Dirk Staudenmayer eds, Nomos 2017).

Francisco Costa-Cabral and Orla Lynskey, *Family Ties: The Intersection Between Data Protection and Competition in EU Law,* 54 Common Market Law Review, 11-50 (2017).

Frank Mccarthy, *Internet: EU Commission and the Metaverse Digital Package – Digital* (2022), available at https://technewsinc.com/internet-eu-commission-and-the-metaverse-digital-package-digital/.

Frank Pasquale, *The Black Box Society: The Secret Algorithms that Control Money and Information* (Harvard Univ Press 2015).

Frits Hondius, *Emerging Data Protection in Europe* (North-Holland Publishing Company 1975).

Future of Life Institute, *Historic Timeline*, available at https://artificialintelligenceact.eu/developments/.

Gary Schober et al., *Transcript: Colloquium on Privacy & Security*, 50 Buffalo Law Review, 703-754 (2002).

Geoffrey Parker, Marshall van Alstyne and Sangeet Choudary, *Platform Revolution* (Norton 2017).

Geraint Howells, Stephen Weatherill, *Consumer Protection Law* (Ashgate 2005).

Geraint Howells, *The Potential and Limits of Consumer Empowerment by Information*, 32 Journal of law and Society, 349-370 (2005).

Gerd Gigerenzer and Wolfgang Gaissmaier, *Heuristic Decision Making*, 62 Annual Review of Psychology, 451-482 (2011).

Gianclaudio Malgieri and Frank Pasquale, *Licensing High-risk Artificial Intelligence: Toward Ex Ante Justification for a Disruptive Technology*, 52 Computer Law & Security Review, 1-18 (2024).

Gianclaudio Malgieri and Niklas Jedrzej, *Vulnerable Data Subjects*, 37 Computer Law and Security Review, 1-16 (2020).

Gianclaudio Malgieri, *Vulnerability and Data Protection Law* (Oxford University Press 2023).

Gintare Surblyte, *Data Mobility at the Intersection of Data, Trade Secret Protection and the Mobility of Employees in the Digital Economy*, 12 GRUR International, 1121-1129 (2016).

Giorgio Monti, *Abuse of Dominant Position: A Post-Intel Calm?*, 3 CPI Antitrust Chronicle (2019), available at https://www.competitionpolicyinternational.com/abuse-of-a-dominant-position-a-post-intel-calm/.

Giorgio Monti, *EC Competition Law* (Cambridge University Press 2012).

Giovanni Sartor, *Providers Liability. From the E-Commerce Directive to the Future: In-depth analysis for the IMCO Committee* (2017), available at https://www.europarl.europa.eu/RegData/etudes/IDAN/2017/614179/IPOL_IDA(2017)614179_EN.pdf.

Giulia Vasino, *Censura 'privata' e contrasto all'hate speech nell'era delle Internet Platforms*, 4 Federalismi.it, 130-159 (2023).

Giuseppe Colangelo and Maria Teresa Maggiolino, *Big Data as Misleading Facilities*, 13 European Competition Journal, 249-281 (2017).

Guido Alpa, *L'identità digitale e la tutela della persona. Spunti di riflessione*, 33 Contratto e Impresa, 723-727 (2017).

Hans Micklitz and Irina Domurath, *Consumer Debt and Social Exclusion in Europe* (Ashgate 2015).

Hans Micklitz and Norbert Reich, *The Court and Sleeping Beauty: The Revival of the Unfair Contract Terms Directive (UCTD)*, 51 Common Market Law Review, 771-808 (2014).

Hans Micklitz, *Access to, and Exclusion of, European Consumers from Financial Markets after the Global Financial Crisis*, in *International Responses to Issues of Credit and Over-indebtedness in the Wake of the Crisis*, 47-75 (Teresa Wilson ed., Ashgate 2013).

Hans Micklitz, Norbert Reich, Peter Rott, Klaus Tonner, *European Consumer Law* (Intersentia 2014).

Hans Micklitz, *The Consumer: Marketised, Fragmentised, Constitutionalised*, in *The Images of the Consumer in EU Law: Legislation, Free Movement and Competition Law*, 21-42 (Dorota Leczykiewicz and Stephen Weatherill eds., Hart Publishing, 2018).

Harold Demsetz, *Toward a Theory of Property Rights*, 57 The American Economic Review, 347-359 (1967).

Helen Nissenbaum, *Accountability in a Computerized Society*, 2 Science and engineering ethics, 25-42 (1996).

Herbert Simon, *Models of Man: Social and Rational- Mathematical Essays on Rational Human Behavior in a Social Setting* (Wiley & Sons 1957).

Herbert Zech, *Data as a Tradable Commodity* in *European Contract Law and the Digital Single Market*, 51-80 (Alberto De Franceschi ed., Intersentia 2017).

Ian Lloyd, *Information Technology Law* (Oxford University Press 2020), 27-38.

Ian Ramsay, *Consumer Law and Policy* (Hart Publishing 2012).

Ibo van de Poel, Lambèr Royakkers, Sjoerd Zwart, *Moral Responsibility and the Problem of Many Hands* (Routledge 2018).

Ikujiro Nonaka, *A Dynamic Theory of Organizational Knowledge Creation*, 5 Organization Science, 14-37 (1994).

Inge Graef and Francisco Costa-Cabral, *To regulate or not to regulate Big Tech*, 1 Concurrences, 24-29 (2020).

Inge Graef, *EU Competition Law, Data Protection and Online Platforms: Data as Essential Facility* (Kluwer 2016).

Inge Graef, *Market Definition and Market Power in Data: The Case of Online Platforms*, 38 World Competition, 473-505 (2015).

Inge Graef, Martin Husovec and Nadezhda Purtova, *Data Portability and Data Control: Lessons for an Emerging Concept in EU Law*, 19 German Law Journal, 1359-1398 (2018).

Inge Graef, Raphael Gellert, Nadezhda Purtova and Martin Husovec, *Feedback to the Commission's Proposal on a Framework for the Free Flow of Non-personal Data*, SRN Electronic Journal (January 2018), available at https://papers.ssrn.com/sol3/papers.cfm?abstract_id=3106791.

Inge Graef, *Rethinking the Essential Facilities Doctrine for the EU Digital Economy*, 53 Revue Juridique Thémis de l'Université de Montréal, 33-72 (2019).

Inge Graef, *The Opportunities and Limits of Data Portability for Stimulating Competition and Innovation*, 2 Competition Policy International – Antitrust Chronicle, 1-8 (2020).

International Organisation for Standardization (ISO), *IT Security and Privacy: A Framework for Identity Management – Part 1: Terminology and Concepts*, ISO/IEC 24760-1, (2019).

Ioanna Tourkochoriti, *The Digital Services Act and the EU as the Global Regulator of the Internet*, 24 Chicago Journal of International Law, 129-147 (2023).

Ioannis Lianos, *Competition Law for the Digital Era: A Complex Systems' Perspective* (30 August 2019), available at SSRN https://ssrn.com/abstract=3492730 or http://dx.doi.org/10.2139/ssrn3492730.

Ira Rubinstein, *Big Data: The End of Privacy or a New Beginning?*, 3 International Data Privacy Law, 74-87 (2013).

Irina Domurath, *Consumer Vulnerability and Welfare in Mortgage Contracts* (Hart Publishing 2017).

Irina Domurath, *The Case for Vulnerability as the Normative Standard in European Consumer Credit and Mortgage Law: An Inquiry into the Paradigms of Consumer Law*, 2 Journal of European Consumer and Market Law, 124-137 (2018).

Ivan Stepanov, *Introducing a Property Right Over Data in the EU: The Data Producer's Right – an Evaluation*, 34 International Review of Law, Computers & Technology, 65-86 (2020).

Jacobien Rutgers, *European Contract Law and the Welfare State* (Europa Law Publishing 2012).

Jacques Crémer, Yves-Alexandre De Montjoye, Heike Schweitzer, *Competition Policy in the Digital Era*, European Commission, Directorate-General for Competition Final Report, Publications Office (2019), available at https://op.europa.eu/en/publication-detail/-/publication/21dc175c-7b76-11e9-9f05-01aa75ed71a1/language-en.

James Gordley and Ugo Mattei, *Protecting Possession*, 44 The American Journal of Comparative Law, 293-334 (1996).

James Rachels, *Why Privacy Is Important*, 4 Philosophy and Public Affairs, 323-333 (1975).

Jaques Crémer, Yves-Alexandre de Montjoye and Heike Schweitzer, *Competition Policy for the Digital Era: Final Report* (European Commission 2019).

Jean Tirole, *Economics for the Common Good* (Princeton University Press 2017).

Jean-Sylvestre Bergé, Stephane Grumbach and Vincenzo Zeno-Zenchovic, *The 'Datasphere', Data Flows beyond Control, and the Challenges for Law and Governance*, 5 European Journal of Comparative Law, 144-178 (2018).

Jeffery Johnson, *Constitutional Privacy*, 13 Law and Philosophy, 161-193 (1994).

Jeffrey Rosen, *The Unwanted Gaze: The Destruction of Privacy in America* (Random House 2000).

Jerry Kang and Benedikt Bunter, *Privacy in Atlantis*, 18 Harvard Journal of Law and Technology, 229-267 (2004).

John Palfrey and Urs Gasser, *Interop: The Promise and Perils of Interconnected Systems* (Basic Books, 2012).

Josef Drexl, *Data Access and Control in the Era of Connected Devices* (Study on Behalf of the European Consumer Organisation BEUC, December 2018), available at https://www.beuc.eu/publications/beuc-x-2018-121_data_access_and_control_in_the_area_of_connected_devices.pdf.

Josef Drexl, *Legal Challenges of the Changing Role of Personal and Non-personal Data in the Data Economy*, Max Planck Institute for Innovation & Competition Research Paper No. 18-23 (2018), available at https://ssrn.com/abstract=3274519.

Joseph Drexl et al., *Data Ownership and Access to Data: Position Statement of the Max Planck Institute for Innovation and Competition of 16 August 2016 on the Current European Debate*, Max Planck Institute for Innovation & Competition Research Paper No. 16-10 (2016), available at https://papers.ssrn.com/sol3/papers.cfm?abstract_id=2833165.

Judith DeCew, *In Pursuit of Privacy: Law, Ethics, and the Rise of Technology* (Cornell University Press 1997).

Judith Thomson, *The Right to Privacy*, 4 Philosophy and Public Affairs, 295-314 (1975).

Jules Stuyck, *European Consumer Law after the Treaty of Amsterdam: Consumer Policy in or Beyond the Internal Market*, 37 Common Market Law Review, 367-400 (2000).

Julián Inza, *The European Digital Identity Wallet as Defined in the EIDAS 2 Regulation*, in *Governance and Control of Data and Digital Economy in the European Single Market*, 433-452 (Carmen Pastor Sempere eds, 71 Law, Governance and Technology Series, Springer 2025).

Juliane Kokott and Christoph Sobotta, *The Distinction Between Privacy and Data Protection in the Jurisprudence of the CJEU and the ECtHR*, 3 International Data Privacy Law, 222-228 (2013).

Julie Inness, *Privacy, Intimacy, and Isolation* (Oxford University Press 1992).

Katalin Cseres, *Competition Law and Consumer Protection* (Kluwer Law International 2005).

Keren Weitzberg, Margie Cheesman, Aaron Martin, Emrys Schoemaker, *Between Surveillance and Recognition: Rethinking Digital Identity in Aid*, 2 Big Data & Society, 1-7 (2021).

Kim Cameron, *The Laws of Identity*, no pages (May 2005), available at https://msdn.microsoft.com/en-us/library/ms996456.aspx.

Kristen Limarzi and Harry Phillips, *"Killer Acquisitions," Big Tech and Section Solution in Search of a Problem*, Antitrust Chronicle (26 May 2020), available at www.competitionpolicyinternational.com.

Lars Ilshammar, *When Computers Became Dangerous: The Swedish Computer Discourse of the 1960s*, 9 HUMAN IT, 7-37 (2007).

Lina Khan, *Amazon's Antitrust Paradox*, 126 The Yale Law Journal, 710-805 (2017).

Linda Weigl, Alexandre Amard, Cristiano Codagnone and Gilbert Fridgen, *The EU's Digital Identity Policy: Tracing Policy Punctuations*, ICEGOV 22: Proceedings of the 15th International Conference on Theory and Practice of Electronic Governance, 74-81 (2022), available at https://dl.acm.org/doi/10.1145/3560107.3560121.

Luciano Floridi, *The Ethics of Artificial Intelligence: Principles, Challenges, and Opportunities* (Oxford University Press 2023).

Luciano Floridi, *The Fourth Revolution: How the Infosphere Is Reshaping Human Reality* (Oxford University Press 2016).

Manuel Wörsdörfer, *Apple's Antitrust Paradox*, 20 European Competition Journal, 113-146 (2024).

Marc Bourreau and Alexandre de Streel, Alexandre, *Dgital Conglomerates and EU Competition Policy* (11 March 2019), available at SSRN https://ssrn.com/abstract=3350512 or http://dx.doi.org/10.2139/ssrn.3350512.

Margarita Robles-Carrillo, *Digital Identity: An Approach to Its Nature, Concept, and Functionalities*, 32 International Journal of Law and Information Technology, 1-21 (2024).

Margrethe Vestager, *Competition in the Digital Age* (European Internet Forum, 17 March 2021), available at https://ec.europa.eu/newsroom/comp/items/705929.

Mariarosaria Taddeo and Luciano Floridi (eds), *The Responsibilities of Online Service Providers* (Springer 2017).

Mark Lycett, *Datafication: Making Sense of (Big) Data in a Complex World*, 22 European Journal of Information Systems, 381-386 (2013).

Mark Patterson, *Antitrust Law in the New Economy* (Harvard University Press 2017).

Marko Milanovic, *Human Rights Treaties and Foreign Surveillance: Privacy in the Digital Age*, 56 Harvard International Law Journal, 81 (2015).

Martha Fineman, *The Vulnerable Subject: Anchoring Equality in the Human Condition*, 20 Yale Journal of Law and Feminism, 1-23 (2008).

Martha Fineman, *Vulnerability and Inevitable Inequality*, 4 Oslo Law Review, 133-149 (2017).

Matthew Adler, *Bounded Rationality and Legal Scholarship*, University of Pennsylvania, Institute for Law & Economic Research Paper No. 08-03 (19 February 2008), available at SSRN https: http://dx.doi.org/10.2139/ssrn.1095874.

Matthias Leistner and Lucie Antonie, *Attention, Here Comes the EU Data Act! A Critical In-depth Analysis of the Commission's 2022 Proposal*, 3 Journal of Intellectual Property, Information Technology and Electronic Commerce Law, 339-349 (2022).

Maureen Ohlhausen and Alexander Okuliar, *Competition, Consumer Protection, and the Right (Approach) to Privacy*, 80 Antitrust Law Journal, 121-156 (2015).

Maurice Stucke and Allen Grunes, *Big Data and Competition Policy* (Oxford University Press 2016).

Maurizio Borghi, Federico Ferretti and Stavroula Karapapa, *Online Data Processing Consent Under EU Law: A Theoretical Framework and Empirical Evidence from the UK*, 21 International Journal of Law and Information Technology, 109-153 (2013).

Max Boisot and Agustì Canals, *Data, Information and Knowledge: Have We Got It Right?*, 14 Journal of Evolutionary Economics, 43-67 (2004).

Michael Jacobides and Ioannis Lianos, *Ecosystems and Competition Law in Theory and Practice*, 30 Industrial and Corporate Change, 1199-1229 (2021).

Michael Jacobides, Carmelo Cennamo and Annabelle Gawer, *Towards a Theory of Ecosystems*, 39 Strategic Management Journal, 2255-2276 (2018).

Michael Kirby, *Transborder Data Flows and the 'Basic Rules' of Data Privacy*, 16 Stanford Journal of International Law, 27-66 (1980).
Michell Cini and Patryk Czulno, *Digital Single Market and the EU Competition Regime: An Explanation of Policy Change*, 44 Journal of European Integration, 41-57 (2022).
Momina Masood, Marriam Nawaz, Khalid Mahmood Malik, Ali Javed and Aun Irtaza, *Deepfakes Generation and Detection: State-of-the-art, Open Challenges, Countermeasures, and Way Forward*, 53 Applied Intelligence, 3974-4026 (2022).
Monika Szwarc, *EU Law and the Member States' Competence to Regulate the Operation of Collaborative Economy Platforms: Where Do We Stand after the Digital Services Act*, 35 European Business Law Review, 183-206 (2014).
Nadezhda Purtova, *Do Property Rights in Personal Data Make Sense after the Big Data Turn: Individual Control and Transparency*, 10 Journal of Law and Economic Regulation, 64-78 (2017).
Nadezhda Purtova, *The Illusion of Personal Data as No One's Property*, 7 Law, Innovation and Technology, 83-111 (2015).
Natali Helberger, Betül Kas, Hans-W. Micklitz, Monika Namysłowska, Laurens Naudts, Peter Rott, Marijn Sax and Michael Veale, *Towards Digital Fairness*, 13 Journal of European Consumer and Market Law, 24-30 (2024).
Natali Helberger, Orla Lynskey, Hans-W. Micklitz, Peter Rott and Marijn Sax a Joanna Strycharz, *EU Consumer Protection 2.0, Structured Asymmetries in Digital Consumer Markets* (Brussels, 2021).
Neha Mishra, *Regulatory Interoperability in the Digital Economy* (April 2024), available at https://papers.ssrn.com/sol3/papers.cfm?abstract_id=4990518.
Neil Stephenson, *Snow Crash* (Penguin Books 1992).
Nestor Duch-Brown, Bertin Martens and Frank Mueller-Langer, *The Economics of Ownership, Access and Trade in Digital Data*, JRC Digital Economy Working Paper 2017-01 (2017).
Niamh Dunne, *Competition Law and Economic Regulation, Making and Managing Markets* (Cambridge University Press 2015).
Nicolas Petit, *Big Tech and the Digital Economy: The Moligopoly Scenario* (Oxford University Press 2020).
Norbert Reich, *Vulnerable Consumers in EU Law*, in *The Images of the Consumer in EU Law: Legislation, Free Movement and Competition Law*, 139-158 (Dorota Leczykiewicz and Stephen Weatherill, Hart Publishing 2018).
OECD, *Handbook on Competition Policy in the Digital Age* (2022), available at www.oecd.org/daf/competition-policy-in-the-digital-age.
OECD, *Start-ups, Killer Acquisitions and Merger Control' Background Note*, DAF/COMP (2020)5, (May 2020), available at https://www.oecd.org/en/publications/start-ups-killer-acquisitions-and-merger-control_dac52a99-en.html.
Omri Ben Sahar and Carl Schneider, *More Than You Wanted to Know: The Failure of Mandated Disclosure* (Princeton University Press 2016).
Onntje Hinrichs, *Consumer Law and the Regulation of the Free Flow of Data: Upsetting the Balance of the European Data Protection Framework*, 13 Journal of European Consumer and Market Law, 78-86 (2024).

Organisation for Economic Co-operation and Development (OECD), *Privacy, Immersive Technologies and the Metaverse* (2022), available at https://www.businessatoecd.org/hubfs/Privacy%2C%20Immersive%20Technologies%20and%20the%20Metaverse%20Report.pdf.

Orla Lynskey, *Deconstructing Data Protection: The 'Added-Value' of A Right to Data Protection in the EU Legal Order*, 63 International and Comparative Law Quarterly, 569-597 (2014).

Paolo Siciliani, Christine Riefa, Harriet Gamper, *Consumer Theories of Harm, an Economic Approach to Consumer Law Enforcement and Policy Making* (Hart Publishing 2019).

Patrik Mikalef, Kieran Conboy, Jenny Eriksson Lundström, Ales Popovič, *Thinking Responsibly about Responsible AI and 'the Dark Side' of AI*, 31 European Journal of Information Systems, 257-268 (2023).

Paul Bierly, Eric Kessler and Edward Christensen, *Organisational Learning, Knowledge and Wisdom*, 13 Journal of Organisational Change Management, 595-618 (2000).

Paul De Hert and Serge Gutwirth, *Data Protection in the Case Law of Strasbourg and Luxembourg: Constitutionalization in Action*, in *Reinventing Data Protection?*, 3-44 (Serge Gutwirth et al. eds, Springer 2009).

Paul de Hert and Vagelis Papakostantinou, *The Council of Europe Data Protection Convention Reform: Analysis of the New Text and Critical Comment on Its Global Ambition*, 30 Computer Law & Security Review, 633-642 (2014).

Paul De Hert et al., *The Right to Data Portability in the GDPR: Towards User-Centric Interoperability of Digital Services*, 34 Computer Law and Security Review, 193-203 (2018).

Paul Du Plessis, *Borkowski's Textbook on Roman Law* (Oxford University Press 2020).

Peter Broklyn, Axel Egon and Ralph Shad, *Deepfakes and Cybersecurity: Detection and Mitigation*, (2024), available at https://papers.ssrn.com/sol3/papers.cfm?abstract_id=4904874.

Peter Cartwright, *Banks, Consumers and Regulation* (Hart Publishing, 2004).

Peter Cartwright, *Understanding and Protecting Vulnerable Financial Consumers*, 38 Journal of Consumer Policy, 119-138 (2015).

Peter Swire and Yianni Lagos, *Why the Right to Data Portability Likely Reduces Consumer Welfare: Antitrust and Privacy Critique*, 72 Maryland Law Review, 335-380 (2013).

Politico, *Vestager: Metaverse Poses New Competition Challenges* (18 January 2022), available at https://www.politico.eu/article/metaverse-new-competition-challenges-margrethe-vestager/.

President of the European Commission Ursula von der Leyen, *'Mission Letter' to Commissioner-designate for Democracy, Justice, Rule of Law* (Brussels, 17 September 2024), available at https://commission.europa.eu/document/download/907fd6b6-0474-47d7-99da-47007ca30d02_en?filename=Mission%20letter%20-%20McGRATH.pdf.

President of the European Commission Ursula von der Leyen, *A Union That Strives for More: My Agenda for Europe. Political Guidelines for the Next European Commission 2019-2024* (16 July 2019).

PricewaterhouseCoopers (PWC), *Virtual and Augmented Reality Could Deliver a £1.5 Trillion Boost to the Global Economy by 2030: PwC*, (2020), available at https://www.pwc.com/th/en/press-room/press-release/2020/press-release-29-01-20-en.html.

Priscilla Regan, *Legislating Privacy::Technology, Social Values, and Public Policy* (University of North Carolina Press 1995).

Priscilla Regan, *Privacy as a Common Good in the Digital World*, 5 Information, Communication and Society, 382-405 (2010).

Richard Hixson, *Privacy in a Public Society: Human Rights in Conflict* (Oxford University Press 1987).

Richard Posner, *The Economics of Justice* (Harvard University Press 1981).

Richard Thaler and Cass Sunstein, *Nudge: Improving Decisions about Health, Wealth, and Happiness* (Penguin 2008).

Richard Whish and David Bailey, *Competition Law* (Oxford University Press 2021).

Rob Kitchin, *The Data Revolution: Big Data, Open Data, Data Infrastructure and Their Consequences* (Sage 2014).

Robert Bork, *The Tempting of America: The Political Seduction of the Law* (Simon & Schuster 1990).

Robert Ellis Smith, *Ben Franklin's Web Site: Privacy and Curiosity from Plymouth Rock to the Internet* (Sheridan Books 2000).

Robert Gerstein, *Intimacy and privacy*, 89 Ethics, 76-81 (1978).

Robert Losee, *A Discipline Independent Definition of Information*, 48 American Society for Information Science, 254-269 (1997).

Robert O'Donoghue and Jorge Padilla, *The Law and Economics of Article 102 TFEU* (Hart Publishing 2013).

Rodrigo Fernandez, Reijer Hendrikse, Tobias Klinge and Ilke Adriaans, *The Financialisation of Big Tech* (SOMO 2020).

Roger Clarke, *The Digital Persona and Its Application to Data Surveillance*, 10 The Information Society, 77-92 (1994).

Roger Van den Bergh and Peter Camesasca, *European Competition Law and Economics: A Comparative Perspective* (London, Thomson Sweet and Maxwell 2006).

Roland Pennock and John Chapman (eds), *Privacy* (NOMOS XIII 1971).

Ron Adner, *Match Your Innovation Strategy to Your Innovation Ecosystem*, 84 Harvard Business Review, 98-107 (2006).

Ronaldo Vigo, *Complexity over Uncertainty in Generalized Representational Information Theory (GRIT): A Structure-Sensitive General Theory of Information*, 4 Information, 1-30 (2013).

Rosemary Jay and Angus Hamilton, *Data Protection: Law and Practice* (Thomson Sweet & Maxwell 2003).

Rossella Incadorna and Cristina Poncibò, *The Average Consumer, the Unfair Commercial Practices Directive and the Cognitive Revolution*, 30 Journal of Consumer Policy, 21-38 (2007).

Ruth Gavison, *Privacy and the Limits of the Law*, 89 Yale Law Journal, 421-471 (1980).

Sabrina Goellner, Marina Tropmann-Frick and Bostjan Brumen, *Responsible Artificial Intelligence: A Structured Literature Review,* 3 cs.AI, no pages (2024), available at https://arxiv.org/abs/2403.06910.

Samuel Warren and Louis Brandeis, *The Right to Privacy,* 4 Harvard Law Review, 193-220 (1890).

Shahper Richter and Alexander Richter, *What Is Novel About the Metaverse?,* 73 International Journal of Information Management, 1-11 (2023).

Sharv Sankpal, Junaid Kazi, Man Kadu, Avadhoot Jogade and Yuvraj Nikam, *Deepfake Detection,* (2025), available at https://papers.ssrn.com/sol3/papers.cfm?abstract_id=5030191.

Silvia Masiero, *Digital Identity as Platform-Mediated Surveillance,* 10 Big Data & Society, 1-5 (2023).

Simon Davis, *Re-engineering the Right to Privacy: How Privacy Has Been Transformed from a Right to a Commodity,* in *Technology and Privacy: The New Landscape,* 143-165 (Philip Agre and Marc Rotenberg eds., MIT Press 1997).

Sjef van Erp, *Ownership of Digital Assets and the Numerus Clausus of Legal Objects,* Maastricht European Private Law Institute Working Paper No. 2017 (2017), available at https://papers.ssrn.com/sol3/papers.cfm?abstract_id=3046402.

Spiros Simitis, *From the Market to the Polis: The EU Directive on the Protection of Personal Data,* 80 Iowa Law Review, 445-469 (1995).

Spiros Simitis, *Privacy: An Endless Debate?,* 98 California Law Review,1995-2005 (2010).

Stephen Weatherill, *EU Consumer Law and Policy* (Edward Elgar 2013).

Stig Stromholm, *Right of Privacy and Rights of the Personality* (Norstedt 1967).

Teresa Scassa, *Data Ownership,* CIGI Papers No. 187 (2018).

Thomas Margoni, Charlotte Ducuing and Luca Schirru, *Data Property, Data Governance and Common European Data Spaces,* Computerrecht: Tijdschrift voor Informatica, Telecommunicatie en Recht, no pages (2023), available at https://ssrn.com/abstract=4428364 and http://dx.doi.org/10.2139/ssrn.4428364.

Thomas Scanlon, *Thomson on Privacy,* 4 Philosophy and Public Affairs, 323-333 (1975).

Viktor Mayer-Schonberger and Kenneth Cukier, *Big Data: A Revolution That Will Transform How We Live, Work and Think* (John Murray 2013).

Viktor Mayer-Schonberger, *Generational Development of Data Protection in Europe,* in *Technology and Privacy: The New Landscape,* 219-241 (Philip Agre and Marc Rotenberg eds, MIT Press 1997).

Vincenzo Zeno-Zencovich, *Do 'Data Markets' Exist?,* 2 *Media Laws,* 22-38 (2019).

William Parent, *Privacy, Morality and the Law,* 12 Philosophy and Public Affairs, 269-288 (1983).

Wolfgang Kerber, *A New (Intellectual) Property Right for Non-Personal Data? An Economic Analysis,* 11 Gewerblicher Rechtsschutz und Urheberrecht, Internationaler Teil (GRUR Int), 989-999 (2016).

Wolfgang Kerber, *Governance of Data: Exclusive Property v. Access,* 47 IIC – International Review of Intellectual Property and Competition Law, 759-762 (2016).

World Economic Forum, *Interoperability in the Metaverse, Briefing Paper* (January 2023), available at https://www3.weforum.org/docs/WEF_Interoperability_in_the_Metaverse.pdf.

Yochai Benkler, *From Consumers to Users: Shifting the Deeper Structures of Regulation Toward Sustainable Commons and User Access*, 52 Federal Communications Law Journal, 561-579 (2000).

Yoram Barzel, *Economic Analysis of Property Rights* (Cambridge University Press 1997).

Yuval Noah Harari, *Nexus: A Brief History of Information Networks from the Stone Age to AI* (Vintage Publishing 2024).

Zhenyong Zhang, Kedi Yang, Youliang Tian and Jianfeng Ma, *An Anti-disguise Authentication System Using the First Impression of Avatar in Metaverse*, 19 IEEE Transactions on Information Forensics and Security, 6393-6408 (2024), available at https://ieeexplore.ieee.org/document/10551293.

Table of Cases

European Union

Case 172/80, *Zuchner v. Bayerisce Vereinsbamk AG*, ECLI:EU:C:1981:178, 70

Case AT.39740 *Google Search (Shopping)*, Commission Decision relating to proceedings under Article 102 of the Treaty on the Functioning of the European Union and Article 54 of the Agreement on the European Economic Area, C(2017) 4444 final, 57

Case AT.40411, *Google Search (AdSense)*, Commission Decision relating to a proceeding under Article 102 of the Treaty on the Functioning of the European Union (the Treaty) and Article 54 of the EEA Agreement, C(2019) 2173 final, 70

Case AT.40462, *Amazon Marketplace*, European Commission Decision of 17 July 2019, 116

Case AT.40703, *Amazon Buy Box*, European Commission Decision C(2022)9442 of 20 December 2022, 116

Case AT39740, *Google Search Shopping*, European Commission Decision C (2017) 4444 of 27 June 2017, 57, 115

Case C-101/01, *Criminal proceedings against Bodil Lindqvist*, ECLI:EU:C:2003:596, 26

Case C-108/09, *Ker-Optika bt v. ÀNTSZ Dél-dunántúli Regionális Intézete*, ECLI:EU:C: 2010:725, 128

Case C-112/00, *Eugen Schmidberger, Internationale Transporte und Planzüge v. Austria*, ECLI:EU:C:2003:333, 24

Case C-126/91, *Schutzverband gegen Unwesen in der Wirtschaft e.V. v. Yves Rocher GmbH*, ECLI:EU:C:1993:191, 190

Case C-131/12, *Google Spain SL and Google Inc v. Agencia Espanola de Protecciòn de Datos (AEPD) and Mario Costeja Gonzàlez*, ECLI:EU:C:2014:317, 31

Case C-139/22, *AM and PM v. mBank S.A.*, ECLI:EU:C:2023:692, 193

Case C-145/10, *Eva-Maria Painer v. Standard VerlagsGmbH and Others* ECLI:EU:C: 2011:798, 64

Case C–18/18, *Eva Glawischnig-Piesczek v. Facebook Ireland Limited*, ECLI:EU:C: 2019:821, 132

Case C-203/02, *The British Horseracing Board Ltd and Others v. William Hill Organization Ltd.*, ECLI:EU:C:2004:695, 66, 92
Case C-21/23, *Lindenapotheke – ND v. DR*, ECLI:EU:C:2024:846, 52, 80
Case C-210/96, *Gut Springenheide GmbH and Rudolf Tusky v. Oberkreisdirektor des Kreises Steinfurt - Amt für Lebensmittelüberwachung*, ECLI:EU:C:1998:369, 190
Case C-238/05, *Asnef-Equifax, Servicios de Información sobre Solvencia y Crédito, SL v. Asociación de Usuarios de Servicios Bancarios (Ausbanc)*, ECLI:EU:C:2006:734, 78
Case C-238/89, *Pall Corp. v. P.J. Dahlhausen & Co.*, ECLI:EU:C:1990:473, 190
Case C-239/02, *Douwe Egberts NV v. Westrom Pharma NV and Christophe Souranis, carrying on business under the commerical name of 'Etablissements FICS' and Douwe Egberts NV v. FICS-World BVBA*, ECLI:EU:C:2004:445, 190
Case C-252/21, *Meta Platforms Inc and Others v. Bundeskartellamt*, ECLI:EU:C:2023:537, 80
Case C-265/22, *ZR e PI v. Banco Santander, SA.*, ECLI:EU:C:2023:578, 193
Case C-275/06,*Productores de Música de España (Promusicae) v. Telefónica de España SAU*, ECLI:EU:C:2008:54, 25
Case C-291/13, *Sotiris Papasavvas v. O Fileleftheros Dimosia Etaireia Ltd and Others*, ECLI:EU:C:2014:2209, 128
Case C-311/18, *Data Protection Commissioner v. Facebook Ireland Limited and Maximillian Schrems*, ECLI:EU:C:2020:559, 3, 66
Case C-314/12, *UPC Telekabel Wien GmbH v. Constantin Film Verleih GmbH and Wega Filmproduktionsgesellschaft mbH*, EU:C:2014:192, 132
Case C-315/92, *Verband Sozialer Wettbewerb eV v. Clinique Laboratoires SNC e Estée Lauder Cosmetics GmbH*, ECLI:EU:C:1994:34, 190
Case C–324/09, *L'Oréal SA and Others v. eBay International AG and Others*, ECLI:EU:C:2011:474, 132
Case C-338/02, *Fixtures Marketing Ltd v. Svenska Spel AB.*, ECLI:EU:C:2004:696, 66, 92
Case C-342/97, *Lloyd Schuhfabrik Meyer & Co. GmbH v. Klijsen Handel BV*, ECLI:EU:C:1999:323, 190
Case C-360/10, *Belgische Vereniging van Auteurs, Componisten en Uitgevers CVBA (SABAM) v. Netlog NV*, ECLI:EU:C:2012:85, 26, 132
Case C-362/88, *GB- INNO- BM v. Confédération du Commerce* Luxembourgeois, ECLI:EU:C:1990:102, 190
Case C-382/87, *R. Buet e Educational Business Services (EBS) SARL v. Pubblico Ministero*, ECLI:EU:C:1989:198, 194
Case C-390/18, *Airbnb Irland UC*, ECLI:EU:C:2019:1112, 3, 127
Case C–415/11, *Mohamed Aziz v. Caixa d'Estalvis de Catalunya, Tarragona i Manresa (Catalunyacaixa)*, ECLI:EU:C:2013:164, 205
Case C-418/01, *IMS Health GmbH & Co. OHG v. NDC Health GmbH & Co. KG.*, ECLI:EU:C:2004:257, 75
Case C-434/15, *Asociación Profesional Elite Taxi v. Uber Systems Spain*, ECLI:EU:C:2017:981, 3, 127
Case C-434/16, *Peter Nowak v. Data Protection Commissioner*, ECLI:EU:C:2017:994, 63
Case C-441/04, *A-Punkt Schmuckhandel v. Claudia Schmidt*, ECLI:EU:C:2006:141, 194

Case C-444/02, *Fixtures Marketing Ltd v. Organismos prognostikon agonon podosfairou AE (OPAP)*, ECLI:EU:C:2004:697, 66
Case C-449/21, *Towercast SASU v. Autoritè de la cuncurrence, Ministre chargè de l'economie*, ECLI:EU:C:2023:207, 121
Case C-456/93, *Zentrale zur Bekämpfung unlauteren Wettbewerbs eV v. Privatkellerei Franz Wilhelm Langguth Erben GmbH & Co. KG*, EU:C:1995:206, 190
Case C-46/02, *Fixtures Marketing Ltd v. Oy Veikkaus Ab.*, ECLI:EU:C:2004:694, 66
Case C-460/20, *Google (Déréférencement d'un contenu prétendument inexact)*, ECLI:EU:C:2022:962, 143
Case C-465/98, *Verein gegen Unwesen in Handel und Gewerbe Köln eV v. Adolf Darbo AG*, ECLI:EU:C:2000:184, 190
Case C-470/93, *Verein gegen Unwesen in Handel und Gewerbe Köln eV v. Mars GmbH*, ECLI;EU:C:1995:224, 190
Case C-48/22 P, *Google and Alphabet v. Commission (Google Shopping)*, ECLI:EU:C:2024:726, 115
Case C-484/14, *Tobias Mc Fadden v. Sony Music Entertainment Germany GmbH*, ECLI:EU:C:2016:689, 128, 132
Case C-553/07, *College van burgemeester en wethouders van Rotterdam v. MEE Rijkeboer*, ECLI:EU:C:2009:293, 25
Case C-582/14, *Patrick Breyer v. Bundesrepublik Deutschland*, ECLI:EU:C:2016:779, 63
Case C-604/10, *Football Dataco Ltd and Others v. Yahoo! UK Ltd and Others* ECLI:EU:C:2012:115, 64
Case C-646/22, *Compass Banca SpA v. Autorità Garante della Concorrenza e del Mercato*, ECLI:EU:C:2024:957, 203
Case C-646/22, *Request for a preliminary ruling from the Consiglio di Stato (Italy)*, lodged on 13 October 2022 – *Compass Banca SpA v. Autorità Garante della Concorrenza e del Mercato*, OJ C 24, 28-29, 202
Case C-680/20, *Unilever Italia Mkt. Operations Srl/Autorità Garante della Concorrenza e del Mercato*, ECLI:EU:C:2023:33, 122
Case C-70/10, *Scarlet Extended SA v. Société belge des auteurs, compositeurs et éditeurs SCRL (SABAM)*, ECLI:EU:C:2011:771, 26, 132
Case C-73/07, *Tietosuojavaltuutettu v. Satakunnan Markkinaporssi Oy*, ECLI:EU:C:2008:727, 26
Case DMA.100203, *Apple – Operating systems – iOS – Article 6(7) – SP – Features for Connected Physical Devices*, European Commission Decision of 19 September 2024, 118
Case M.8788, *Apple – Shazam*, COM (2018)5784, European Commission Merger Procedure Decision of 6 September 2018, 120
Case No COMP/M.4854, *TomTom/TeleAtlas*, Commission decision declaring a concentration to be compatible with the common market and the EEA Agreement (14 May 2008), 78
Case No. COMP/M.4731, *Google/DoubleClick*, Commission decision declaring a concentration to be compatible with the common market and the functioning of the EEA Agreement (11 March 2008), 78
Case T-1077/23, *Bytedance v. European Commission*, ECLI:EU:T:2024:478, 114

Case T-201/04, *Microsoft Corp. v. Commission of the European Communities*, ECLI:EU:T:2007:289, 75

Case T-41/96, *Bayer AG v. Commission of the European Communities*, ECLI:EU:T:2000:242, 74

Case T-604/18, *Google and Alphabet v. Commission (Google Android)*, ECLI:EU:T:2022:541, 122

Case T-612/17 *Google LLC, formerly Google Inc. and Alphabet, Inc. v. European Commission*, ECLI:EU:T:2021:763, 70, 115

Joined Cases 6 and 7/73, *Istituto Chemioterapico Italiano S.p.A. and Commercial Solvents Corporation v. Commission of the European Communities*, ECLI:EU:C:1974:18, 74

Joined Cases C-236/08 to C-238/08, *Google France SARL and Google Inc. v. Louis Vuitton Malletier SA, Google France SARL v. Viaticum SA and Luteciel SARL, and Google France SARL v. Centre national de recherche en relations humaines (CNRRH) SARL and Others*, ECLI:EU:C:2010:159, 132

Joined Cases C-293/12 and C-594/12, *Digital Rights Ireland Ltd v. Minister for Communications, Marine and Natural Resources and Others and Kärntner Landesregierung and Others*, ECLI:EU:C:2014:238, 25

Joined Cases C-403/08 to C-429/08, *Football Association Premier League Ltd and Others v. QC Leisure and Others* and *Karen Murphy v. Media Protection Services Ltd, ECLI:* EU:C:2011:631, 64

Joined Cases C-465/00, C-138/01 and C-139/01, *Rechnungshof v. Österreichischer Rundfunk and Others and Christa Neukomm and Joseph Lauermann v. Österreichischer Rundfunk*, ECLI:EU:C:2003:294, 24

Joined Cases C-468/10 and C-469/10, *Asociación Nacional de Establecimientos Financieros de Crédito (ASNEF)* and *Federación de Comercio Electrónico y Marketing Directo (FECEMD) v. Administración del Estado*, ECLI:EU:C:2011:777, 35

Joined Cases C-92/09 and C-93/09, *Volker und Markus Schecke GbR and Hartmut Eifert v. Land Hessen*, ECLI:EU:C:2010:662, 25

Opinion of Mr Advocate General Emiliou in Case C–646/22, *Compass Banca SpA v. Autorità Garante della Concorrenza e del Mercato*, ECLI:EU:C:2024:367, 202

Opinion of Mr Advocate General Jacobs in Case C-7/97, *Oscar Bronner GmbH & Co. KG v. Mediaprint Zeitungs- und Zeitschriftenverlag GmbH & Co. KG, Mediaprint Zeitungsvertriebsgesellschaft mbH & Co. KG and Mediaprint Anzeigengesellschaft mbH & Co. KG.*, ECLI:EU:C:1998:264, 74

European Court of Human Rights

S and Marper v. United Kingdom (Applications 30562/04 and 30566/04) (2008) 48 EHRR 1169, [2009] Crim LR 355, [2008] All ER (D) 56 (Dec), 26

Other cases

German Constitutional Court Bundersverfassungsgericht, Judgment of 15 December1983, 1 BvR 209/83, BVerfGE 65, 15

Table of Legislation

Council of Europe

Council of Europe Committee of Ministers Resolution (73) 22 on the Protection of the Privacy of Individuals vis-à-vis Electronic Data Banks in the Private Sector (26 September 1973), 19

Council of Europe Committee of Ministers Resolution (74) 29 on the protection of the privacy of individuals vis-a-vis electronic data banks in the public sector (20 September 1974), 19

Council of Europe Convention of 28 January 1981 'for the protection of individuals with regard to automatic processing of personal data' ('Treaty 108'), 18, 19

Protocol amending the Convention for the Protection of Individuals with regard to Automatic Processing of Personal Data (CETS No. 223) or Treaty 223, 21

EU Legislation

Decisions

Decision (EU) 2022/2481 of the European Parliament and of the Council of 14 December 2022 establishing the Digital Decade Policy Programme 2030, OJ L 323, 19.12.2022, p. 4-26, 178

Directives

Council Directive 93/13/EEC of 5 April 1993 on unfair terms in consumer contracts, OJ L 95, 21.4.1993, p. 29-34, 10, 103, 186

Directive (EU) 2015/1535 of the European Parliament and of the Council of 9 September 2015 laying down a procedure for the provision of information in the field of technical regulations and of rules on Information Society services (codification), OJ L 241, 17/9/2015, p. 1-15, 127

Directive (EU) 2015/2366 of the European Parliament and of the Council of 25 November 2015 on payment services in the internal market, amending Directives 2002/65/EC, 2009/110/EC and 2013/36/EU and Regulation (EU) No. 1093/2010, and repealing Directive 2007/64/EC, OJ L 337, 23.12.2015, p. 35-127, 3, 91, 104–105, 186

Directive (EU) 2016/2102 of the European Parliament and of the Council of 26 October 2016 on the accessibility of the websites and mobile applications of public sector bodies, OJ L 327, 2.12.2016, p. 1-15, 161

Directive (EU) 2016/680 of the European Parliament and of the Council of 27 April 2016 on the protection of natural persons with regard to the processing of personal data by competent authorities for the purposes of the prevention, investigation, detection or prosecution of criminal offences or the execution of criminal penalties, and on the free movement of such data, and repealing Council Framework Decision 2008/977/JHA, OJ L 119, 4.5.2016, p. 89-131, 3, 16, 162

Directive (EU) 2016/681 of the European Parliament and of the Council of 27 April 2016 on the use of passenger name record (PNR) data for the prevention, detection, investigation and prosecution of terrorist offences and serious crime, OJ L 119, 4.5.2016, p. 132-149, 29

Directive (EU) 2016/943 of the European Parliament and of the Council of 8 June 2016 on the protection of undisclosed know-how and business information (trade secrets) against their unlawful acquisition, use and disclosure, OJ L 157, 15.6.2016, p. 1-18, 64

Directive (EU) 2019/1024 of the European Parliament and of the Council of 20 June 2019 on open data and the re-use of public sector information (recast), OJ L 172, 26.6.2019, p. 56-83, 3, 54, 104

Directive (EU) 2019/2161 of the European Parliament and of the Council of 27 November 2019 amending Council Directive 93/13/EEC and Directives 98/6/EC, 2005/29/EC and 2011/83/EU of the European Parliament and of the Council as regards the better enforcement and modernisation of Union consumer protection rules, OJ L 328, 18.12.2019, p. 7-28, 10, 141, 195

Directive (EU) 2019/882 of the European Parliament and of the Council of 17 April 2019 on the accessibility requirements for products and services, OJ L 151, 7.6.2019, p. 70-115, 161

Directive (EU) 2023/2225 of the European Parliament and of the Council of 18 October 2023 on credit agreements for consumers and repealing Directive 2008/48/EC, OJ L, 2023/2225, 30.10.2023, 186

Directive 2000/31/EC of the European Parliament and of the Council of 8 June 2000 on certain legal aspects of information society services, in particular electronic commerce, in the Internal Market ('Directive on electronic commerce'), OJ L 178, 17.7.2000, p. 1-16, 126

Directive 2005/29/EC of the European Parliament and of the Council of 11 May 2005 concerning unfair business-to-consumer commercial practices in the internal market and amending Council Directive 84/450/EEC, Directives 97/7/EC, 98/27/EC and 2002/65/EC of the European Parliament and of the Council and Regulation (EC) No. 2006/2004 of the European Parliament and of the Council ('Unfair Commercial Practices Directive'), OJ L 149, 11.6.2005, p. 22-39, 10, 103, 186

Directive 2006/24/EC of the European Parliament and of the Council of 15 March 2006 on the retention of data generated or processed in connection with the provision of publicly available electronic communications services or of public communications networks and amending Directive 2002/58/EC, OJ L 105, 13/4/2006, p. 54-63, 25
Directive 2011/83/EU of the European Parliament and of the Council of 25 October 2011 on consumer rights, amending Council Directive 93/13/EEC and Directive 1999/44/EC of the European Parliament and of the Council and repealing Council Directive 85/577/EEC and Directive 97/7/EC of the European Parliament and of the Council, OJ L 304, 22.11.2011, p. 64-88, 10, 103, 141, 186
Directive 95/46/EC of the European Parliament and of the Council of 24 October 1995 on the protection of individuals with regard to the processing of personal data and on the free movement of such data, OJ L 281, 23.11.1995, p. 31-50, 15
Directive 96/9/EC of the European Parliament and of the Council of 11 March 1996 on the legal protection of databases, OJ L 77, 27.3.1996, p. 20-28, 66, 92
Directive 98/34/EC as amended by Directive 98/48/EC laying down a procedure for the provision of information in the field of technical standards and regulations, OJ L 217, 5.8.1998, p. 18-26, 127

Proposals

Commission Proposal of 27 July 1990 for a Council Directive concerning the protection of individuals in relation to the processing of personal data (COM (90) 314 final), OJ No C277, 23
Proposal for a Directive on Protecting Personal Data Processed for the Purposes of Prevention, Detection, Investigation or Prosecution of Criminal Offences and Related Judicial Activities, COM/2012/010 final, 16
Proposal for a Regulation of the European Parliament and of the Council concerning the respect for private life and the protection of personal data in electronic communications and repealing Directive 2002/58/EC (Regulation on Privacy and Electronic Communications), COM/2017/010 final, 4
Proposal for a Regulation of the European Parliament and of the Council on horizontal cybersecurity requirements for products with digital elements and amending Regulation (EU) 2019/1020, COM/2022/454 final, 5
Proposal for a Regulation of the European Parliament and of the Council on the European Health Data Space, COM/2022/197 final, 5
Proposal for a Regulation of the European Parliament and of the Council on the Protection of Individuals with Regard to the Processing of Personal Data and on the Free Movement of Such Data (General Data Protection Regulation), COM/2012/011 final, 16
Proposal for a Regulation of the European Parliament and of the Council on a framework for Financial Data Access and amending Regulations (EU) No. 1093/2010, (EU) No. 1094/2010, (EU) No. 1095/2010 and (EU) 2022/2554, COM(2023) 360 final, 91, 197

Recommendations

Commission Recommendation of 29 July 1981 relating to the Council of Europe Convention for the protection of individuals with regard to automatic processing of personal data (81/679/EEC), EÜT L 246, 29.8.1981, p. 31–31, 21, 23

Recommendation for a Council Decision on the vote to be taken by Member States within the competent bodies of the Council of Europe, on behalf of the European Community, in favour of adopting the draft Recommendation on the protection of personal data collected and processed for insurance purposes, and of authorising the publication of its Explanatory Memorandum (SEC/2002/0280 final, 18 March 2002), 21

Regulations

Council Regulation (EC) No. 1/2003 of 16 December 2002 on the implementation of the rules on competition laid down in Articles 81 and 82 of the Treaty, OJ L 1, 4.1.2003, p. 1-25, 112

Council Regulation (EC) No. 139/2004 of 20 January 2004 on the control of concentrations between undertakings (the EC Merger Regulation), OJ L 24, 29.1.2004, p. 1-22, 120, 121

Regulation (EU) 2016/679 of the European Parliament and of the Council of 27 April 2016 on the protection of natural persons with regard to the processing of personal data and on the free movement of such data, and repealing Directive 95/46/EC, OJ L 119, 4.5.2016, p. 1-88, 3, 16, 54, 152, 186

Regulation (EU) 2018/1725 of the European Parliament and of the Council of 23 October 2018 on the protection of natural persons with regard to the processing of personal data by the Union institutions, bodies, offices and agencies and on the free movement of such data, and repealing Regulation (EC) No. 45/2001 and Decision No. 1247/2002/EC, OJ L 295, 21.11.2018, p. 39-98, 162

Regulation (EU) 2018/1807 of the European Parliament and of the Council of 14 November 2018 on a framework for the free flow of non-personal data in the European Union, OJ L 303, 28.11.2018, p. 59-68, 3, 54, 102

Regulation (EU) 2019/1150 of the European Parliament and of the Council of 20 June 2019 on promoting fairness and transparency for business users of online intermediation services, OJ L 186, 11.7.2019, p. 57-79, 104

Regulation (EU) 2019/881 of the European Parliament and of the Council of 17 April 2019 on ENISA (the European Union Agency for Cybersecurity) and on information and communications technology cybersecurity certification and repealing Regulation (EU) No. 526/2013 (Cybersecurity Act), OJ L 151, 7.6.2019, p. 15-69, 4, 54

Regulation (EU) 2021/241 of the European Parliament and of the Council of 12 February 2021 establishing the Recovery and Resilience Facility, OJ L 057 18.2.2021, p. 17, 2

Regulation (EU) 2022/1925 of the European Parliament and of the Council of 14 September 2022 on contestable and fair markets in the digital sector and amending Directives (EU) 2019/1937 and (EU) 2020/1828 (Digital Markets Act), OJ L 265, 12.10.2022, p. 1-66, 3, 54, 105, 109, 125, 185

Regulation (EU) 2022/2065 of the European Parliament and of the Council of 19 October 2022 on a Single Market for Digital Services and amending Directive 2000/31/EC (Digital Services Act), OJ L 277, 27.10.2022, p. 1-102, 4, 105, 125, 185

Regulation (EU) 2022/868 of the European Parliament and of the Council of 30 May 2022 on European data governance and amending Regulation (EU) 2018/1724 (Data Governance Act), OJ L 152, 3.6.2022, p. 1-44, 4, 56, 86, 186

Regulation (EU) 2023/2854 of the European Parliament and of the Council of 13 December 2023 on harmonised rules on fair access to and use of data and amending Regulation (EU) 2017/2394 and Directive (EU) 2020/1828 (Data Act), OJ L, 2023/2854, 22.12.2023, 4, 86, 186

Regulation (EU) 2023/814 of 14 April 2023 on detailed arrangements for the conduct of certain proceedings by the Commission pursuant to Regulation (EU) 2022/1925 of the European Parliament and of the Council, OJ L 102, 17.4.2023, p. 6-19, 109–110

Regulation (EU) 2024/1183 of the European Parliament and of the Council of 11 April 2024 amending Regulation (EU) No. 910/2014 as regards establishing the European Digital Identity Framework, OJ L, 2024/1183, 30.4.2024, 4, 172

Regulation (EU) 2024/1689 of the European Parliament and of the Council of 13 June 2024 laying down harmonised rules on artificial intelligence and amending Regulations (EC) No. 300/2008, (EU) No. 167/2013, (EU) No. 168/2013, (EU) 2018/858, (EU) 2018/1139 and (EU) 2019/2144 and Directives 2014/90/EU, (EU) 2016/797 and (EU) 2020/1828 (Artificial Intelligence Act), OJ L, 2024/1689, 12.7.2024, 4, 105, 149, 186

Regulation (EU) No. 910/2014 of the European Parliament and of the Council of 23 July 2014 on electronic identification and trust services for electronic transactions in the internal market and repealing Directive 1999/93/EC, OJ L 257, 28.8.2014, p. 73-114, 9

Other

European Commission Consolidated Jurisdictional Notice under Council Regulation (EC) No. 139/2004 on the control of concentrations between undertakings, 2008/C 95/01, OJ C 95, 16.4.2008, 121

European Declaration on Digital Rights and Principles for the Digital Decade 2023/C 23/01, Official Journal of the European Union C23/1, 23.1.2023, 180

National Legislations

Hessian Act of 7 October 1970 (Germany), 17

United Nations

UN General Assembly, Resolution 217A (III), Universal Declaration of Human Rights, A/RES/217(III) (10 December, 1948), 171

Index

Abuse, 17, 18, 30, 69, 70, 72, 73, 80, 81, 87, 92, 97, 121, 136, 147, 157, 198
Accuracy, 31, 39, 140, 151, 200
Advertisements, 136, 139
Advertising services, 111, 116, 117
Advocate General, 202, 203
AI database, 163–165
AI System, 155–161
Algorithm(s), 65, 82, 109, 110, 115, 117, 122, 126, 134, 136–138, 141, 147, 199, 204, 205
Anonymised data, 62, 102
Anti-competitive agreements, 71, 73
Anti-competitive practice(s), 9, 69, 70, 82
Artificial intelligence (AI), 4, 6, 145–166
Asymmetry of information, 187
Automated decision-making, 37, 38, 40–41
Avatar(s), 177–183
Average consumer, 188–192, 205–207
Bargaining power, 187, 189, 205
Behavioural economics, 192
Big data, 6, 63–69, 74, 75, 77, 79, 100, 102, 105, 136
Big Tech(s), 1, 6, 9, 54, 55
Binding corporate rules, 46–49
Biometrics, 151, 155, 157, 158, 162, 181
Bounded rationality, 202–204, 207
Business-to-business (B2B), 85, 86, 88, 91, 93, 94, 127
Business-to-Consumer (B2C), 85, 88, 91, 94, 103, 127, 187
Business-to-Government (B2G), 85, 86, 88, 96–97
Cartel(s), 70
Catching services, 129, 132
Certification, 41, 44–45, 47, 176
Charter of Fundamental Rights of the European Union, 16, 19, 24, 25, 134
Chicago School, 69
Child or children, 34, 39, 45, 137, 179, 195
Cloud computing services, 131
Cloud service providers, 131
Codes of conduct, 41, 44–45, 62, 138, 139, 152, 164
Commercial communications, 127–129, 136, 139
Competition law, 69–83
Complaints, 37, 38, 47–51, 97, 134–136
Complementors, 110, 122
Concerted practice(s), 71
Conduct of business rules, 200
Confidentiality, 17, 31, 64–65, 86, 87, 170, 174
Connected product, 87–93, 101
Consent, 31–35, 37, 39–41, 45, 48, 50, 76, 80–82, 100, 102, 157, 199
Consumer law acquis, 10, 103, 104, 106, 140, 142, 197, 206
Consumer empowerment, 101, 189, 191, 194

Consumer interest, 71, 79
Consumer law, 103–104
Consumer protection, 2, 5, 6, 10, 104, 125, 126, 129, 130, 140–143, 185, 186, 189–191, 194, 195, 199–205
Contestability, 82, 113, 118
Contractual imbalance(s), 87
Contractual necessity, 34, 100, 102
Contractual term(s), 87, 88, 94, 136, 182, 187
Control, 67–69, 118–121
Convention 108, 18–20, 23
Convention 108 +, 20–23
Cooperation Group, 176
Copyright, 26, 63–64, 66, 162
Council of Europe (CoE), 18–23, 122
Court of Justice of the EU (CJEU), 3, 24–26, 29, 31, 34, 39, 52, 66, 70, 71, 80, 81, 83, 114, 115, 121, 123, 127, 132, 142, 143, 190, 193, 202–205, 207
COVID-19, 1, 3, 87, 96, 176, 196
Credit, 122, 189, 196, 197
Cross-border processing, 28
Data access, 54, 55, 60, 62, 69, 73, 76, 78, 81, 91–94, 97, 100, 102, 104, 106
Data analytics, 8
Data breach(es), 43–45, 171, 180
Data Controller, 15, 17, 26, 30, 32–34, 38, 40, 50, 58, 61, 76, 99, 141
Data governance obligations, 41–43
Data Holder(s), 87, 89, 91–97, 99, 101, 103
Data management, 61, 159
Data market(s), 53–56, 62, 67, 69, 81, 87, 103
Data minimisation, 31, 41, 47, 61
Data portability, 8, 9, 37, 40, 61, 76–78, 102–103, 117, 175
Data processing service(s), 88, 93, 97–99
Data processor, 15
Data property, 59, 86
Data protection by default, 41, 45, 47
Data protection by design, 41, 45, 47
Data Protection Impact Assessments (DPIA), 42, 43
Data Protection Officer (DPO), 37, 42–44, 48, 164
Data Recipient(s), 89, 94, 96, 99
Data sharing, 8, 10, 33, 54, 83, 86–89, 91–94, 96–97, 99–101, 103, 104, 172
Data sovereignty, 53, 85
Data Subject, 36–41
Data transfer(s), 47, 48, 87, 89
Database rights, 65–67
Data-related right(s), 59–67
De facto control, 67–69, 73, 82
Deepfake(s), 148, 182–183
Dehumanisation, 169
Deployer, 9, 151, 152, 155, 160, 162, 163
Derived data, 91
Digital architectures, 126, 188, 198–201, 204, 206
Digital asymmetries, 200, 206
Digital Fairness Act, 5, 186, 205
Digital Financial Strategy, 197
Digital Identity, 9, 169–183
Digital Identity Wallet, 171, 173–175
Digital person, 170, 180
Digital Service Package, 111
Digital Services Coordinator(s), 135
Digital Single Market Strategy, 53
Discrimination, 7, 60, 159, 179
Disengaged consumers, 199
Dispositional vulnerability, 200–203, 206
Dispute resolution, 45, 135, 138
Distributor, 155, 161
Dominant position, 70, 72, 73, 80, 81, 111, 121
Due diligence, 125, 126, 130, 133–140
e-commerce or electronic commerce, 125–130
Embeddedness, 193
Erasure, 20, 27, 37–39, 76
Essential facility(ies), 69, 73–76, 82
European Consumer Summit(s), 5
European Convention for the Protection

of Human Rights and Fundamental Freedoms (ECHR), 18–19, 22, 26
European Council for Artificial Intelligence, 163–165
European Data Protection Board (EDPB), 49–50
European Data Space, 4, 8, 53, 55, 81, 85
European Data Strategy, 74, 85–88
European Declaration on Digital Rights and Principles for the Digital Decade, 171, 180
European Digital Identity Cooperation Group, 176
European Green Deal, 146, 147
Ex ante regulation, 81–83, 200, 206
Extended reality (XR), 177
Facial recognition, 150, 155, 157
Fair access, 115, 186, 196
Fairness by default, 201, 206
Fairness by design, 200, 201, 206
Financial Data Access (FIDA), 91
Financial services, 49, 91, 191, 205
Fines, 44, 140
Forum, 22, 163–165
Fundamental rights, 1, 6, 8, 9, 16, 19, 23–26, 28, 29, 34, 40, 51, 61, 67, 79, 80, 125, 126, 130, 134, 137, 147, 151, 153–157, 160, 161, 164, 165, 179, 196, 197
Gatekeeper(s) or gatekeeping, 68, 73, 82, 113–115
GDPR content, 28–30
GDPR derogations, 28–30
GDPR exclusions, 28–30
GDPR lawfulness, 30–36
GDPR principles, 30–36
GDPR structure, 28–30
General-purpose AI models, 149, 152, 155, 162, 164
German State of Hesse, 17
Harmful applications, 156–157
High-Risk AI System, 158–161
Homo economicus, 188, 202
Hosting services, 9, 129–135, 143, 182
Household activity, 29
Human supervision, 151, 160
Identity theft, 170, 171, 173, 180
Illegal content, 9, 132–138, 142, 143
Importer, 155, 161
Inaccuracy, 143, 159
Independent Scientific Panel, 163–165
Inferred data, 76
Information notice(s), 36–38, 141
Innovation, 2, 6–9, 14, 50, 53–55, 57, 64, 73, 74, 76, 81, 82, 85, 87, 93, 99, 105, 109, 111, 112, 122, 125, 135, 137, 147, 149–153, 163, 166, 196, 197, 201, 206
Integrity, 31, 60, 99, 154, 200
Intellectual property, 8, 63–67, 82, 85, 86, 91, 95, 143
Intermediary services or intermediary service providers, 126, 130–133, 140, 141
Intermediation services, 111, 127, 131, 142
Internal market, 9, 16, 23, 24, 62, 70–72, 88, 110, 113, 126–128, 130, 174, 189
Internet of Things (IoT), 88, 90, 91, 145
Interoperability, 9, 88, 89, 97–99, 113, 115–118, 172, 178
Interpersonal communication services, 111
Killer acquisitions, 118–121
Latent vulnerability, 198
Legal basis, 23, 35, 37, 47, 55, 80, 85, 88, 100–102, 134
Legal compliance, 34, 101
Legal fragmentation, 104–106
Legal overlaps, 7
Legal person(s), 27, 28, 89, 96, 102, 103, 126, 128, 130, 155, 171, 174, 181
Legal uncertainty, 7, 32, 105, 154, 206
Legitimate interest, 34–35, 37, 40, 42, 45, 49, 76, 95, 100–102
Liabilities, 47, 50–52, 64, 94, 95, 126,

127, 129, 130–133, 139, 141, 147, 182
Licensing, 200
Limited risk AI systems, 151, 156, 161, 183
Machine learning (ML), 68, 122, 136, 146, 149, 153
Main establishment, 28
Market failure(s), 67, 73, 104, 189
Market integration, 69, 70
Market power, 55, 69, 70, 72, 92, 109, 115, 118
Mere conduit services, 129, 131, 132
Merger control, 118–121
Metaverse, 176–179, 182–183
Minimal Risk AI System, 151, 156
Monopoly(ies), 6, 71, 73, 75, 103
More favorable treatment, 115, 117
Natural person(s), 16, 27, 28, 29, 30, 34, 40, 51, 58, 60, 62, 80, 85, 89, 94, 99, 102, 103, 129, 139, 156, 159, 161, 162, 190, 197
Nature of data, 55, 58, 59, 81
Network, 6, 9, 15, 29, 54, 65, 73, 74, 90, 90, 97, 110, 111, 113, 114, 118, 126, 131, 132, 135
New Consumer Agenda, 5, 194
Non-personal data, 61–63, 101–102
Notification, 43–45, 89, 113, 120, 121, 143
Online marketplace(s), 9, 131
Open Finance, 197
Operating systems, 111, 118
Out of Court dispute settlement, 127, 135
Paternalism, 201
Payment service(s), 122
Payment Services Directive 2 (PSD2), 3, 91
Personal activity, 29
Platform(s)1, 6, 9, 10, 54, 55, 68, 69, 73–76, 81, 82, 109–123, 125–127, 129–133, 135–139, 141, 142, 147, 173, 178, 179, 182, 195
Possession, 68
Prior authorisation, 128, 172
Privacy, 179–182
Private law, 49, 64, 187, 201, 206
Profiling, 37, 38, 40–42, 47, 60, 122, 136, 139, 148, 156, 186, 195, 199, 206
Proprietary rights, 6, 55, 67
Public interest, 20, 29, 31, 34–36, 39, 40, 48, 55, 76, 83, 87, 89, 96, 97, 179
Public law, 201, 206
Public sector, 8, 19, 54, 86–89, 96, 97, 170
Purpose limitation, 30, 32, 47
Rationality, 198, 202–204, 207
Real-time Remote Biometric Identification, 157
Recipient, 20, 27, 37–39, 89, 94, 96, 99, 127–140, 143, 183
Recommender system(s), 136, 137, 139
Rectification, 20, 37–39
Regulatory sandboxes, 163
Related service(s), 87, 89–93
Remedies, 20, 44, 46, 50–52, 65, 73, 94–96, 134, 142, 189, 197, 201, 205
Representative, 28, 30, 37, 159, 161, 164, 176
Res communis, 68
Restrictive measure(s), 134, 143, 150
Right of access, 25, 38
Right to be forgotten, 31, 39
Right to be left alone, 13
Right to data portability, 37, 40, 76, 102, 103, 117, 175
Rights of data subjects, 36–41, 45, 47, 52
Risk-based approach, 9, 150, 155, 165
Risks of bias, 159
search engines, 9, 31, 58, 111, 125, 126, 131, 136–138, 143, 145
Self-determination, 60
Self-essential sovereign identity, 170
Self-preference, 115–118
Sensitive data, 41, 42, 95, 100, 136

Services of General Economic Interest (SGEI), 79
Single Digital Market(s), 68
Single Market, 2, 8, 53
SMEs, 1, 6, 87, 88, 93, 94, 96, 135, 137, 151, 152, 163–165
Social media, 77, 92, 131, 176, 186, 206
Social networks, 9, 29, 111, 114, 126, 135
Social network services, 111
Social scoring, 150, 155, 156
Special categories of data, 20, 30, 100
Storage limitation, 31
Sui generis right, 66, 92, 93
Supervisory authority, 49–50
Supplier, 64, 71, 139, 160, 161, 163–165
Switching, 88, 89, 95, 97–98
Systemic vulnerability, 197–199
Technological neutrality, 153
Territorial scope, 30
Third countries, 18, 22, 37, 45–49, 88, 153, 161
Third Party(ies), 20, 27, 33, 34, 37, 40, 48, 65, 76, 77, 82, 86, 89, 90, 92, 93, 96, 98, 100–102, 115–118, 141, 155, 158, 173, 175
Trade between Member States, 71, 72, 120
Trade secret(s), 64–65, 95
Training datasets, 159
Transfer of personal data, 45–49, 66
Transparency, 9, 15, 30, 33, 36–37, 85, 94, 97, 101, 126, 148–154, 156, 157, 161–162, 173, 174, 182, 187, 191, 195, 200
Treaty of Lisbon, 15, 24
Trusted flaggers, 135, 142
Unacceptable risk, 150, 151, 155–157
Unfair competition, 52, 81, 110, 125
Unfair or unfairness, 10, 51, 52, 72, 73, 81, 82, 88, 94, 95, 110, 125, 126, 187, 188, 197, 200, 204, 205
Unfair practice, 205
Unfair trading, 72
User, 1, 6, 7, 9, 10, 13, 33, 62, 68, 69, 85, 87–93, 96–106, 109–111, 113, 116–123, 125–127, 129–131, 134, 142, 148, 154, 156, 160, 170, 172–175, 178, 180, 181, 183, 196, 197
Value chain, 56–59, 154, 155
Value chain of data, 56–59
Very Large Online Platforms (VLOPs), 9, 131, 133, 137–140
Very Large Search Engines (VLOSEs), 131, 133, 137–140
Video-sharing platform services, 111
Virtual assistants, 111, 118, 145
Virtual reality (VR), 180
Vital interest(s), 34, 35, 48, 76
Vulnerability, 197–199
Vulnerable consumer, 187, 192–194, 196, 204
Web browsers, 111
Zero knowledge demonstration, 174

EUROPEAN MONOGRAPH SERIES

1. Lammy Betten (ed.), *The Future of European Social Policy*, 1991 (ISBN 90-654-4585-4).
2. Annemarie Loman, Kamiel Mortelmans, Harry H.G. Post & Stewart Watson, *Culture and Common Law: Before and After Maastricht*, 1992 (ISBN 90-654-4638-9).
3. John A.E. Vervaele, *Fraud against the Community: The Need for European Fraud Legislation*, 1994 (ISBN 90-654-4634-6).
4. Philip Raworth, *The Legislative Process in the European Community*, 1993 (ISBN 90-654-4690-7).
5. Jules Stuyck, *Financial and Monetary Integration in the European Economic Community*, 1993 (ISBN 90-654-4718-0).
6. Jules Stuyck & A.J. Vossestein (eds), *State Entrepreneurship, National Monopolies and European Community Law*, 1993 (ISBN 90-654-4773-3).
7. Jules Stuyck & A. Looijestijn-Clearie (eds), *The European Economic Area EC-EFTA*, 1994 (ISBN 90-654-4815-2).
8. Rosita B. Bouterse, *Competition and Integration: What Goals Count?*, 1995 (ISBN 90-654-4816-0).
9. René Barents, *The Agricultural Law of the EU, 2nd Edition*, 2022 (ISBN 978-94-035-4411-3).
10. Nicholas Emiliou, *Principles of Proportionality in European Law: A Comparative Study*, 1996 (ISBN 90-411-0866-1).
11. Eivind Smith, *National Parliaments as Cornerstones of European Integration*, 1996 (ISBN 90-411-0898-X).
12. Jan H. Jans, *European Environmental Law*, 1996 (ISBN 90-411-0877-7).
13. Síofra O'Leary, *The Evolving Concept of Community Citizenship: From the Free Movement of Persons to Union Citizenship*, 1997 (ISBN 90-411-0878-5).
14. Laurence W. Gormley (ed.), *Current and Future Perspectives on EC Competition Law*, 1983 (ISBN 90-411-0691-X).
15. Simone White, *Protection of the Financial Interests of the European Communities: The Fight against Fraud and Corruption*, 1998 (ISBN 90-411-9647-1).
16. Morten P. Broberg, *Broberg on the European Commission's Jurisdiction to Scrutinise Mergers*, 4th Edition, 2013 (ISBN 978-90-411-3339-7).
17. Doris Hildebrand, *The Role of Economic Analysis in the EC Competition Rules: The European School*, 2nd Edition, 2002 (ISBN 90-411-1706-7).
18. Christof R.A. Swaak, *European Community Law and the Automobile Industry*, 1999 (ISBN 90-411-1140-9).

19. Dorthe Dahlgaard Dingel, *Public Procurement: A Harmonization of the National Judicial Review of the Application of European Community Law,* 1999 (ISBN 90-411-1161-1).
20. John A.E. Vervaele (ed.), *Compliance and Enforcement of European Community Law,* 1999 (ISBN 90-411-1151-4).
21. Martin Trybus, *European Defence Procurement Law: International and National Procurement Systems as Models for a Liberalized Defence Procurement Market in Europe,* 1999 (ISBN 90-411-1167-0).
22. Helen Staples, *The Legal Status of Third Country Nationals Resident in the European Union,* 1999 (ISBN 90-411-1277-4).
23. Damien Geradin (ed.), *The Liberalization of State Monopolies in the European Union and Beyond,* 1999 (ISBN 90-411-1264-2).
24. Katja Heede, *European Ombudsman: Redress and Control at Union Level,* 2000 (ISBN 90-411-1413-0).
25. Ulf Bernitz & Joakim Nergelius (eds), *General Principles of European Community Law,* 2000 (ISBN 90-411-1402-5).
26. Michaela Drahos, *Convergence of Competition Laws and Policies in the European Community,* 2002 (ISBN 90-411-1562-5).
27. Damien Geradin (ed.), *The Liberalization of Electricity and Natural Gas in the European Union,* 2001 (ISBN 90-411-1560-9).
28. Gisella Gori, *Towards an EU Right to Education,* 2001 (ISBN 90-411-1670-2).
29. Brendan P.G. Smith, *Constitution Building in the European Union,* 2001 (ISBN 90-411-1695-8).
30. Friedl Weiss & Frank Wooldridge, *Free Movement of Persons within the European Community,* 2nd Edition, 2007 (ISBN 978-90-411-2545-3).
31. Ingrid Boccardi, *Europe and Refugees: Towards an EU Asylum Policy,* 2002 (ISBN 90-411-1709-1).
32. John A.E. Vervaele & André Klip (eds), *European Cooperation Between Tax, Customs and Judicial Authorities,* 2001 (ISBN 90-411-1747-4).
33. Wouter P.J. Wils, *The Optimal Enforcement of EC Antitrust Law: Essays in Law and Economics,* 2002 (ISBN 90-411-1757-1).
34. Damien Geradin (ed.), *The Liberalization of Postal Services in the European Union,* 2002 (ISBN 90-411-1780-6).
35. Nick Bernard, *Multilevel Governance in the European Union,* 2002 (ISBN 90-411-1812-8).
36. Jill Wakefield, *Judicial Protection through the Use of Article 288(2) EC,* 2002 (ISBN 90-411-1823-3).
37. Sebastiaan Princen, *EU Regulation and Transatlantic Trade,* 2002 (ISBN 90-411-1871-3).
38. Amaryllis Verhoeven, *The European Union in Search of a Democratic and Constitutional Theory,* 2002 (ISBN 90-411-1872-1).
39. Paul L.C. Torremans, *Cross Border Insolvencies in EU, English and Belgian Law,* 2002 (ISBN 90-411-1888-8).

40. Malcolm Anderson & Joanna Apap (eds), *Police and Justice Cooperation and the New European Borders,* 2002 (ISBN 90-411-1893-4).
41. Christin M. Forstinger, *Takeover Law in EU and USA: A Comparative Analysis,* 2002 (ISBN 90-411-1919-1).
42. Antonio Bavasso, *Communications in EU Antitrust Law: Market Power and Public Interest,* 2003 (ISBN 90-411-1974-4).
43. Fiona G. Wishlade, *Regional State Aid and Competition Policy in the European Union,* 2003 (ISBN 90-411-1975-2).
44. Gareth Davies, *Nationality Discrimination in the European Internal Market,* 2003 (ISBN 90-411-1998-1).
45. René Barents, *The Autonomy of Community Law,* 2003 (ISBN 90-411-2251-6).
46. Gerhard Dannecker & Oswald Jansen (eds), *Competition Law Sanctioning in the European Union,* 2004 (ISBN 90-411-2100-5).
47. Nauta Dutilh (ed.), *Dealing with Dominance: The Experience of National Competition Authorities,* 2004 (ISBN 90-411-2211-7).
48. Stefaan van den Bogaert, *Practical Regulation of the Mobility of Sportsmen in the EU Post Bosman,* 2005 (ISBN 90-411-2327-X).
49. Katalin Judit Cseres, *Competition Law and Consumer Protection,* 2005 (ISBN 90-411-2380-6).
50. Philipp Kiiver, *The National Parliaments in the European Union: A Critical View on EU Constitution Building,* 2006 (ISBN 978-90-411-2452-4).
51. Alexander Turk, *The Concept of Legislation in European Community Law,* 2006 (ISBN 978-90-411-2472-2).
52. Dimitrios Sinaniotis, *The Interim Protection of Individuals before the European and National Courts,* 2006 (ISBN 978-90-411-2498-2).
53. M. Holoubek & D. Damjanovic, M. Traimer (eds), *Regulating Content: The European Regulatory Framework for the Media and Related Creative Sectors,* 2006 (ISBN 978-90-411-2597-2).
54. Anneli Albi & Jacques Ziller (eds), *The European Constitution and National Constitutions: Ratification and Beyond,* 2006 (ISBN 978-90-411-2524-8).
55. Gustavo E. Luengo, *Regulation of Subsidies and State Aids in WTO and EC Law: Conflicts in International Trade Law,* 2007 (ISBN 978-90-411-2547-7).
56. Eniko Horvath, *Mandating Identity: Citizenship, Kinship Laws and Plural Nationality in the European Union,* 2007 (ISBN 978-90-411-2662-7).
57. Rass Holdgaard, *External Relations Law of the European Community: Legal Reasoning and Legal Discourses,* 2007 (ISBN 978-90-411-2604-7).
58. Jill Wakefield, *The Right to Good Administration,* 2007 (ISBN 978-90-411-2697-9).
59. Dimitry Kochenov, *EU Enlargement and the Failure of Conditionality: Pre- accession Conditionality in the Fields of Democracy and the Rule of Law,* 2008 (ISBN 978-90-411-2696-2).
60. Despina Mavromati, *The Law of Payment Services in the EU: The EC Directive on Payment Services in the Internal Market,* 2008 (ISBN 978-90-411-2700-6).

61. Anne Meuwese, *Impact Assessment in EU Lawmaking*, 2008 (ISBN 978-90-411-2720-4).
62. Ulf Bernitz, Joakim Nergelius & Cecilia Cardner (eds), *General Principles of EC Law in a Process of Development*, 2008 (ISBN 978-90-411-2705-1).
63. Johan van de Gronden (ed.), *The EU and WTO Law on Services: Limits to the Realisation of General Interest Policies within the Services Markets?*, 2008 (ISBN 978-90-411-2809-6).
64. Alina Tryfonidou, *Reverse Discrimination in EC Law*, 2009 (ISBN 978-90-411-2751-8).
65. Mikael Berglund, *Cross-Border Enforcement of Claims in the EU: History Present Time and Future*, 2014 (ISBN 978-90-411-4564-2).
66. Theodore Konstadinides, *Division of Powers in European Union Law: The Delimitation of Internal Competence between the EU and the Member States*, 2009 (ISBN 978-90-411-2615-3).
67. Mattias Derlén, *Multilingual Interpretation of European Union Law*, 2009 (ISBN 978-90-411-2853-9).
68. René Barents, *Directory of EU Case Law on the Preliminary Ruling Procedure*, 2009 (ISBN 978-90-411-3150-8).
69. Yan Luo, *Anti-dumping in the WTO, the EU and China: The Rise of Legalization in the Trade Regime and Its Consequences*, 2010 (ISBN 978-90-411-3207-9).
70. Patrick Birkinshaw & Mike Varney (eds), *The European Union Legal Order after Lisbon*, 2010 (ISBN 978-90-411-3152-2).
71. Thomas Gr. Papadopoulos, *EU Law and Harmonization of Takeovers in the Internal Market*, 2010 (ISBN 978-90-411-3340-3).
72. Bas van Bockel, *The* Ne Bis In Idem *Principle in EU Law*, 2010 (ISBN 978-90-411-3156-0).
73. Veljko Milutinović, *The 'Right to Damages' under EU Competition Law: From* Courage v. Crehan *to the White Paper and Beyond*, 2010 (ISBN 978-90-411-3235-2).
74. Amandine Garde, *EU Law and Obesity Prevention*, 2010 (ISBN 978-90-411-2706-8).
75. Leonard Besselink, Frans Pennings & Sacha Prechal (eds), *The Eclipse of the Legality Principle in the European Union*, 2011 (ISBN 978-90-411-3262-8).
76. Sacha Garben, *EU Higher Education Law: The Bologna Process and Harmonization by Stealth*, 2011 (ISBN 978-90-411-3365-6).
77. Dimitry Kochenov (ed.), *EU Law of the Overseas: Outermost Regions, Associated Overseas Countries and Territories, Territories Sui Generis*, 2011 (ISBN 978-90-411-3445-5).
78. Pablo Ibáñez Colomo, *European Communications Law and Technological Convergence: Deregulation, Re-regulation and Regulatory Convergence in Television and Telecommunications*, 2012 (ISBN 978-90-411-3829-3).
79. Elise Muir, *EU Regulation of Access to Labour Markets: A Case Study of EU Constraints on Member State Competences*, 2012 (ISBN 978-90-411-3823-1).
80. Tim Corthaut, *EU Ordre Public*, 2012 (ISBN 978-90-411-3232-1).

81. Oana Ştefan, *Soft Law in Court: Competition Law, State Aid and the Court of Justice of the European Union*, 2013 (ISBN 978-90-411-3997-9).
82. Francesco Rossi dal Pozzo, *Citizenship Rights and Freedom of Movement in the European Union*, 2013 (ISBN 978-90-411-4660-1).
83. Jens Hartig Danielsen, *EU Agricultural Law*, 2013 (ISBN 978-90-411-3280-2).
84. Ulf Bernitz, Xavier Groussot & Felix Schulyok (eds), *General Principles of EU Law and European Private Law*, 2013 (ISBN 978-90-411-4683-0).
85. Michelle Everson, Cosimo Monda & Ellen Vos (eds), *European Agencies in between Institutions and Member States*, 2014 (ISBN 978-90-411-2843-0).
86. Stefan Leible & Matthias Lehmann (eds), *European Contract Law and German Law*, 2014 (ISBN 978-90-411-2588-0).
87. Piero Leanza & Ondrej Pridal, *The Right to a Fair Trial: Article 6 of the European Convention on Human Rights*, 2014 (ISBN 978-90-411-4855-1).
88. Patrick J. Birkinshaw, *European Public Law: The Achievement and the Brexit Challenge*, 3rd Edition, 2020 (ISBN 978-90-411-9751-1).
89. George Cumming, *Expert Evidence Deficiencies in the Judgments of the Courts of the European Union and the European Court of Human Rights*, 2014 (ISBN 978-90-411-4123-1).
90. Vesna Rijavec, Tomaž Keresteš & Tjaša Ivanc (eds), *Simplification of Debt Collection in the EU*, 2014 (ISBN 978-90-411-4854-4).
91. Nina Półtorak, *European Union Rights in National Courts*, 2015 (ISBN 978-90-411-5863-5).
92. Kyriaki-Korina Raptopoulou, *EU Law and Healthcare Services: Normative Approaches to Public Health Systems*, 2015 (ISBN 978-90-411-5013-4).
93. Torsten Frank Koschinka & Piero Leanza, *Preliminary Injunctions: Germany, England/Wales, Italy and France*, 2015 (ISBN 978-90-411-5833-8).
94. Vesna Rijavec, Tomaž Keresteš & Tjaša Ivanc (eds), *Dimensions of Evidence in European Civil Procedure*, 2016 (ISBN 978-90-411-6662-3).
95. Stefan Leible (ed.), *General Principles of European Private International Law*, 2016 (ISBN 978-90-411-5955-7).
96. Patrick J. Birkinshaw & Andrea Biondi (eds), *Britain Alone!: The Implications and Consequences of United Kingdom Exit from the EU*, 2016 (ISBN 978-90-411-5832-1).
97. René Barents, *Remedies and Procedures before the EU Courts*, 2nd Edition, 2020 (ISBN 978-94-035-1140-5).
98. Luca Prete, *Infringement Proceedings in EU Law*, 2017 (ISBN 978-90-411-6900-6).
99. Robert van den Hoven van Genderen, *Privacy Limitation Clauses: Trojan Horses under the Disguise of Democracy*, 2017 (ISBN 978-90-411-8599-0).
100. Mariusz Krzysztofek, *Post-Reform Personal Data Protection in the European Union: General Data Protection Regulation (EU) 2016/679*, 2017 (ISBN 978-90-411-6237-3).
101. Gianni Lo Schiavo, *The Role of Financial Stability in EU Law and Policy*, 2017 (ISBN 978-90-411-8230-2).

102. Emmanuel Guinchard & Marie-Pierre Granger (eds), *The New EU Judiciary: An Analysis of Current Judicial Reforms*, 2017 (ISBN 978-90-411-6834-4).
103. Kirsten Henckel, *Cross-Border Transfers of Undertakings: A European Perspective*, 2017 (ISBN 978-90-411-9227-1).
104. Vesna Rijavec, Wendy Kennett, Tomaž Keresteš & Tjaša Ivanc, *Remedies Concerning Enforcement of Foreign Judgements: Brussels I Recast*, 2018 (ISBN 978-90-411-9416-9).
105. Albert Sanchez-Graells & Constant De Koninck, *Shaping EU Public Procurement Law: A Critical Analysis of the CJEU Case Law 2015–2017*, 2018 (ISBN 978-94-035-0160-4).
106. Andrea Biondi, Patrick J. Birkinshaw & Maria Kendrick, *Brexit: The Legal Implications*, 2019 (ISBN 978-90-411-9540-1).
107. Mariusz Krzysztofek, *GDPR: General Data Protection Regulation (EU) 2016/679: Post-Reform Personal Data Protection in the European Union*, 2019 (ISBN 978-94-035-0594-7).
108. Giovanni Bassani, *The Legal Framework Applicable to the Single Supervisory Mechanism: Tapestry or Patchwork?*, 2019 (ISBN 978-94-035-0872-6).
109. Piotr Staszczyk, *A Legal Analysis of NGOs and European Civil Society*, 2019 (ISBN 978-94-035-1251-8).
110. Patrizio Messina, *Finance for SMEs: European Regulation and Capital Markets Union – Focus on Securitization and Alternative Finance Tools*, 2019 (ISBN 978-94-035-0161-1).
111. Jacques H.J. Bourgeois (ed.), *EU Framework for Foreign Direct Investment Control*, 2020 (ISBN 978-94-035-1883-1).
112. Ulf Bernitz, Xavier Groussot, Jaan Paju & Sybe de Vries (eds), *General Principles of EU Law and the EU Digital Order*, 2020 (ISBN 978-94-035-1165-8).
113. Aleksandra Drożdż, *Protection of Natural Persons with Regard to Automated Individual Decision-Making in the GDPR*, 2020 (ISBN 978-94-035-2045-2).
114. Mariusz Krzysztofek, *GDPR: Personal Data Protection in the European Union*, 2021 (ISBN 978-94-035-3270-7).
115. Katarzyna Gromek-Broc (ed.), *Public Law in a Troubled Era: A Tribute to Professor Patrick Birkinshaw*, 2023 (ISBN 978-94-035-3576-0).
116. Guido Alpa, *Solidarity: A Normative Principle*, 2023 (ISBN 978-94-035-3596-8).
117. Frederik Behre, *Fixing the Euro Within the National Constitutional Guardrails: A Comparative Assessment of the National Constitutional Space for EU (Fiscal) Integration*, 2023 (ISBN 978-94-035-3586-9).
118. Berdien B.E. van der Donk, *Digital Bouncers: A European Roadmap to Navigate Access Rights and Moderation Issues on Social Media Platforms*, 2024 (ISBN 978-94-035-2858-8).
119. Natalia Charalampidou, *The Financial and Other Sanctions of the European Union*, 2025 (ISBN 978-94-035-4357-4).
120. Federico Ferretti, Allegra Canepa & Francesca Mattassoglio, *EU Digital Markets Law*, 2025 (ISBN 978-94-035-0888-7).

www.ingramcontent.com/pod-product-compliance
Ingram Content Group UK Ltd.
Pitfield, Milton Keynes, MK11 3LW, UK
UKHW020800290926
15470UKWH00003B/872

9 789403 508887